Romance Fiction

Genreflecting Advisory Series

Diana Tixier Herald, Series Editor

Genreflecting: A Guide to Reading Interests in Genre Fiction, 4th Edition. By Diana Tixier Herald.

Teen Genreflecting. By Diana Tixier Herald.

Romance Fiction: A Guide to the Genre. By Kristin Ramsdell.

Fluent in Fantasy: A Guide to Reading Interests. By Diana Tixier Herald.

Now Read This: A Guide to Mainstream Fiction, 1978-1998. By Nancy Pearl. With assistance from Martha Knappe and Chris Higashi.

Hooked on Horror: A Guide to Reading Interests in Horror Fiction. By Anthony J. Fonseca and June Michele Pulliam.

Junior Genreflecting: A Guide to Good Reads and Series Fiction for Children. By Bridget Dealy Volz, Lynda Blackburn Welborn, and Cheryl Perkins Scheer.

Romance Fiction

A Guide to the Genre

Kristin Ramsdell
California State University, Hayward

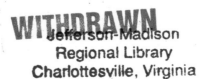

1999
Libraries Unlimited, Inc.
Englewood, Colorado

Illustrations that are from NoveList (of the CARL Corporation)
are used with permission.

Libraries Unlimited, Inc.
P.O. Box 6633
Englewood, CO 80155-6633
1-800-237-6124
www.lu.com

Library of Congress Cataloging-in-Publication Data

Ramsdell, Kristin, 1940-
    Romance fiction : a guide to the genre / Kristin Ramsdell.
    xvi, 435 p. 19x26 cm. -- (Genreflecting advisory series)
    Includes bibliographical references and index.
    ISBN 1-56308-335-3
    1. Love stories--Bibliography. 2. Love stories--History and
criticism. 3. Books and reading--United States. I. Title. II. Series.
Z1231.L68R37 1999
[PN3448.L67]
016.80883'85--dc21   99-10207
                                      CIP

Contents

Acknowledgments

Many people contributed in many different ways, knowingly or unknowingly, to both versions of this book. I am particularly indebted to the staff members of my local libraries, especially the Alabama County Public Library System, the Palo Alto Public Library, and the San Francisco Public Library (especially the Eureka Valley-Harvey Milk Branch) for their endurance as I rummaged through their fiction sections; to my long-suffering colleagues and family for their patience and support; to my editors for their incredible forbearance; to Lynn Coddington, Shelley Mosley, Johanna Tuñon, Joyce Saricks, Florence Mitchell, and Bill Stanton for their suggestions and comments; to Deborah Cloninger, Barbara Johnson, Stephanie Wells, June Gerlach, Jennifer Stringer, Celeste Steward, and Linda Zimmerman for contributing formally and informally to the bibliography sections; to Lynn LaFleur, head of Interlibrary Loan at California State University, Hayward, for obvious reasons; to the Romance Writers of America (especially the San Francisco Area Chapter) and the Romance Novelists Association for generously answering my varied and sundry requests; to *Library Journal* and Harlequin Enterprises Ltd. for graciously allowing me to reprint various materials; and, in particular, to the late Betty Rosenberg, without whose suggestions and advice the first edition of this book would never have been written and to Mary K. Chelton, without whose "gentle encouragement" this second edition would still be waiting until I had more time.

In spite of the input I have had from various sources, an effort like this is a highly subjective undertaking; and it is entirely possible that through ignorance, error, or chance, a favorite author or work has been omitted or miscategorized. I would appreciate comments from readers on the authors and their works and also the definitions of the various subgenres. Comments are helpful, particularly if a revision of this work should be required. Comments should be directed to me at kramsdell@csuhayward.edu.

We are grateful to NoveList for their permission to use images from their program throughout the Genreflecting Advisory Series. NoveList is the electronic readers advisory resource from CARL Corporation that provides subject and genre access to thousands of fiction titles for readers of all ages, and contains numerous annotations from the Genreflecting Advisory series. For more information about NoveList, contact (888) 439-2275, or visit http://www.carl.org/novelist. ©1998 CARL Corporation.

Preface to the Second Edition

Since the publication of *Happily Ever After: A Guide to Reading Interests in Romance Fiction* in 1987, the romance genre has changed tremendously. Not only have the numbers of books and writers increased dramatically, with romance fiction now accounting for more than 50 percent of all mass-market fiction sales, but the genre has also become increasingly diverse, including within its ranks a number of alternative reality subgenres (time travel, fantasy, futuristic, paranormal, etc.), ethnic romance, and novels verging on mainstream women's fiction, as well as the more familiar varieties. Characters, settings, plot patterns, sensuality levels, themes, and relationship portrayals are also evolving. In addition, interest in the genre from the academic community, particularly among women's studies and popular culture scholars, is growing rapidly—and the relevant literature is beginning to compound. In short, the romance genre of the 1980s is not the romance genre of the 1990s, and it was clear that if *Happily Ever After* were to remain relevant and useful, it definitely needed to be revised.

Romance Fiction: A Guide to the Genre is, essentially, the second edition of *Happily Ever After: A Guide to Reading Interests in Romance Fiction*, retaining the basic structure and organization of the original but expanding and updating it in a number of areas. Four new chapters have been added—two to meet the demands of the changing romance genre itself ("Ethnic and Multicultural Romance" and "Alternative Reality Romance"), one specifically to address the professional needs of librarians ("Building the Collection"), and one to allow more complete coverage of a distinct subgenre ("Regency Period Romance," which was originally included within "Historical Romance"). One chapter, "Young Adult Romance," was deleted because that subject is diverse enough to merit a separate guide of its own; however, a brief reading list of Young Adult romances has been added to this book as an appendix.

All original genre chapters have been revised. Where necessary, definitions, appeal, and readers' advisory sections have been redone, histories have been updated to include the most recent decade, and bibliographies have been revised to include recent authors and titles. In addition, two chapters ("Contemporary Romance" and "Historical Romance") have been extensively reorganized and expanded to reflect recent changes within the genre. This overall expansion has meant that, for space limitations, a number of author and title entries included in the first edition have either been omitted or condensed. In addition, selected annotations, especially for earlier works, have been deleted. Readers should consult *Happily Ever After* or other appropriate sources for older information.

Two sections, "Plantation Romance" and "Medical Romance," have been deleted—again, a result of the changing genre. The original chapters discussing the Introduction to Romance Fiction have been reworked: The history section has been updated to include the newer genres and the events of the past decade, and the appeal and readers' advisory sections have been revised and expanded to incorporate newer trends and concerns. The chapters concerning Research Aids have been updated and revised as necessary; in particular, the chapter "History and Criticism" has been greatly expanded because of increased scholarship in the field.

Introduction

"Lady Peabury was in the morning room reading a novel; early training gave a guilty spice to this recreation, for she had been brought up to believe that to read a novel before luncheon was one of the gravest sins it was possible for a gentlewoman to commit."
Evelyn Waugh

"Romance has Arrived!"
Jayne Ann Krentz

"Never apologize for your reading tastes."
Betty Rosenberg

PURPOSE AND SCOPE

This guide attempts to organize the existing literature of romance fiction in such a way that it will define the outlines of the genre and provide a useful resource for those interested in it, including those searching for reading material. Although its primary focus is librarians, especially those who are involved in readers' advisory service and may not be familiar with romance literature, it may be of interest to romance readers and writers as well. Also, while it is not intended as a comprehensive research guide, it does contain a fair amount of research information and, therefore, may also be useful to researchers and students of popular culture or women's studies.

The focus of this book is on the romance literature itself, especially that currently available to American readers. The titles listed, except for some prototypes or early examples, are listed either in *Books in Print* or *British Books in Print*, or they can be found in some of the larger libraries (as indicated in OCLC). Most are readily available in local public libraries. Except when of historical interest, titles not written in English are excluded, although English translations of some foreign works are included. Individual short stories are also excluded. Both male and female authors are represented. However, because it is available elsewhere and because this guide takes a genre approach, biographical information relating to authors is not included. Sources for this information are included in chapter 15, "Author Biography and Bibliography."

ORGANIZATION

Although this guide includes a definition of romance, a brief general history of the genre, and sections on appeal, readers' advisory, and research and reference sources, its basic arrangement is by subgenre. Each subgenre has its own chapter, and each chapter includes sections devoted to the definition of the subgenre, reasons for its appeal, specific hints for readers' advisory service, a brief history of the development of the particular subgenre, and pertinent bibliographies. The entries within the bibliographies are arranged alphabetically by author. An author/title and a subject index are also included at the end of the book.

BIBLIOGRAPHIES

The bibliographies form the major part of this guide and are selective in both authors and titles included.

Authors Included

The authors included were selected because they are writers of typical or classic examples in a particular subgenre, are exceptionally prolific or popular or both, are important from a historical point of view, or are in some way unique to romance fiction. In addition, those included are currently available to the American public, either because they are still in print, have been recently reprinted, or are still generally available in public library collections. As a rule, new writers are not included because there has been insufficient time to assess their contributions to the genre. Also, unless they are exceptionally prolific and enduring, or write in other capacities, mass market paperback series authors are not included separately. (The series themselves, however, are discussed.) Authors of single titles in either paperback or hardcover format are included.

Titles Included

Except for rare instances, only the authors' romance works are listed. In general, a writer's works are selectively listed, and only in unusual circumstances are an author's entire list of titles included. However, because several publications that list bibliographies for a number of romance writers already exist—see chapter 15, "Author Biography and Bibliography"—this should not present a problem. The books included were selected because they typical, unusual, particularly good, interesting, or important examples of the genre. Occasionally, a book is included because it is the only, or one of the only, readily available book by the author. This is often the case with older writers or writers of genres that have gone out of fashion.

Years Covered

Although there is some emphasis on recent books, especially those written since the publication of *Happily Ever After: A Guide to Reading Interests in Romance Fiction* (Libraries Unlimited, 1987), both classic and contemporary romances (dating from 1740 to the present) are included and no effort has been made specifically to omit works from a particular time period.

Entries and Annotations

Original publication information (publisher and date) is provided for each title. If the work was first published elsewhere and later in the United States, the American publication information is also given. In addition, if a work was published at some time under a different title, this fact is usually mentioned. (Publication under different titles occasionally happens if an older book is being reprinted, or if the same book is being released in both England and the United States. Interestingly, the same titles don't always appeal to both audiences—even though the stories do.) Imprint information in parentheses is usually British. Although the original publication date is always listed for the older and prototype novels, current publishing information is also provided when useful.

Because this book arranges romance fiction primarily by type, not all entries are annotated. In cases where a major writer has a rather short list and all titles are important (e.g., Mary Stewart), all entries are annotated. In other instances, especially if an author has a long list of relevant titles, entries are annotated selectively because they are more important, more typical of the category, more interesting, or available. Prototypes and classic works receive the most detailed coverage. Other works will be annotated in less depth, and some will receive only brief comments. Except in rare cases, no annotation provides a synopsis of the story, reveals the ending, or provides information that would otherwise spoil the story for the reader. Quotes appearing in the annotations are from publishers' promotional material, book jackets, book reviews, or occasionally, the book itself.

Cross-Indexing

Authors who write romance fiction under various names are linked by notes with their names when appropriate, e.g., Gwendoline Butler (also writes as Jennie Melville). In addition, *see also* references are given for authors who write in various subgenres, e.g., *see also* Historical Romance bibliography. Writers' entries are also linked through the Author/Title Index.

SUGGESTIONS FOR USE

Although the arrangement of this guide is fairly straightforward and its use will be intuitive to many, not all readers will be using this book for the same purposes and, as a result, will not be accessing the information in the same ways. For example, students and scholars may be looking for academic materials as well as examples of the genre; librarians and booksellers may be looking for genre overviews and authors and titles to recommend; writers may be looking for information about and important books and authors in particular subgenres; and readers may simply be looking for good books to read. The following suggestions may be helpful:

1. When looking for a specific title or author, consult the Author/Title Index in the back of the book to find out whether the author or title is included and, if it is, where the information is located—e.g., *Divine Evil* by Nora Roberts is found on page 96 in the Romantic Suspense section of the Romantic Mysteries chapter.

2. When looking for authors or titles in a particular subgenre, use the Contents at the beginning of the book or the Subject Index to find the bibliography for that particular subgenre—e.g., the bibliography for Regencies begins on page 193.

3. When looking for general information on a particular subgenre (history, definition, etc.), use the Contents, but when looking for more specific bits of information, the Subject Index at the back of the book may be more helpful—e.g., references to "The Season" or the *ton* will be found in the Subject Index but not in Contents.

4. When looking for scholarly materials and reference sources about the genre and its authors, consult the appropriate chapters in the Research Aids section of the guide.

5. When looking for books similar to known authors or titles, locate the writer's entry(ies) and consider others in the bibliography that sound interesting. When looking for books similar to known authors or titles, locate the entries for that author or title and consider other books in the same subgenre. If the book is an award winner or covers a specific subject that appeals to the reader, check the Subject Index. Finally, lists of selected romance writers by style, plot pattern, or theme appear in Appendix Two, p. 379.

Part 1

Introduction to Romance Fiction

Chapter 1

Definition and Brief History of Romance Fiction

"Romance has been elegantly defined as
the offspring of fiction and love."
Benjamin Disraeli

"Not all love stories are romances.
Some are simply novels about love."
Janice A. Radway

Romance, as a part of the human experience, has existed from the first time a pair of lovers gazed at each other with love-blinded eyes and saw the world around them not as it was but as they wanted it to be. The world has never been the same since. Romance, as a literary form, has been around a somewhat shorter amount of time, and while its impact can't compare with that of the "real thing," the first heroine who ever agonized over the intentions of her beloved similarly ensured that the world of fiction would never again be quite the same. From the chilling tales of Ann Radcliffe and the witty novels of Jane Austen to the wide variety of types available today, romances have been written and published by the thousands and read by the millions. Maligned by their critics and adored by their readers, romances have definitely had an effect upon the literary world. But what, exactly, is this flourishing genre? Just what is a romance?

DEFINITION

In the strictest literary sense, of course, "all popular fiction is romantic."[1] It portrays the world as it ought to be, not as it is, and is, therefore, unrealistic—or romantic. However, when today's readers refer to a romance, it is not usually fiction-in-general that they have in mind. On the contrary, the term "romance," as it is used today, has a much more specific meaning and refers to a particular kind of fiction—the love story. *Webster's Ninth New Collegiate Dictionary* makes this distinction clear by giving one of the meanings of romance as "a love story [and/or] a class of such literature." Disraeli agreed when he proclaimed that romance is a combination of love and fiction. In the simplest sense, of course, this definition is true. Romances *are* love stories, and they do apply a fictional treatment to the subject of love. But there is more to it than that. Not just any love story will do. Certain criteria must be met before a love story can qualify as a proper romance, at least by today's standards.

To begin with, there is the matter of *focus*. In a romance the central (and occasionally the only) focus of the plot is the love relationship between the two main characters. Of course, there are usually other complications and problems, such as mysteries to be solved, career goals or social successes to be achieved, and daring escapes to be made. But these are always secondary to the love interest (from the reader's point of view, not necessarily from the character's), although they are often instrumental in seeing that the love interest succeeds.

On the other hand, the primary plotline of a non-romance, even though it may contain a well-defined love story, revolves around something else entirely. Consider, for example, the myriad adventure stories, most of which contain a definite love interest. Although the love relationship is important and certainly adds to the story, the main emphasis is on the successful solution of the mystery or the outwitting of the villain by the hero or heroine. Compare the romantic suspense novels of Mary Stewart to the international espionage tales of Ian Fleming. Romantic relationships figure prominently in both authors' works. But in Stewart's novels, the romance drives the plot; in Fleming's works, it is merely peripheral. Of course, not all books lend themselves to such obvious analysis, and some are downright obscure. But, as a general rule, unless it is the resolution of romantic entanglements that ultimately sustains the reader's interest in the story, the book is probably not a romance.

But it is not only subject matter and focus that determine a romance; a romance must also attempt to engage the reader's feelings. To put it simply, a romance must have a quality—whether through character development, plot structure, point of view, or style—that allows, almost demands, a certain emotional involvement on the part of the reader. In other words, a book cannot simply describe a love relationship; it must allow the reader to participate in it. As Janice Radway states, "To qualify as a romance, the story must chronicle not merely the events of a courtship but *what it feels like* to the *object* of one."[2] Some books, of course, do this better than others, and how successfully it is done is a matter of opinion to individual readers. Nevertheless, unless a book manages to connect with the reader's romantic emotions—even to a limited extent—the book will probably not be perceived as a romance; it will simply be a novel about love.

Another criterion for romance fiction is the *Satisfactory Ending*. Usually, but not always, this is the traditional happy one, with the two protagonists forming some kind of committed relationship (usually marriage) by the book's conclusion. Other refinements, of course, may be added (e.g., no rape, no hero-against-heroine violence, honorable characters, monogamous relationships, heroines who "win"). But these are all extras, and while they may make the story better, they can't make it a true romance if qualifying aspects of focus and emotional involvement aren't already there.

Obviously, it is possible to define a romance quite narrowly—and many people do; however, because of the wide variance in public reading tastes and my desire to include as many of them as is reasonably possible, I have chosen to use a more all-encompassing definition. Therefore, for the purposes of this guide, a romance is defined as a love story in which the central focus is on the development and satisfactory resolution of the love relationship between the two main characters, written in such a way as to provide the reader with some degree of vicarious emotional participation in the courtship process.

A BRIEF HISTORY OF THE ROMANCE NOVEL

Early Influences

Love stories have existed since the earliest times, as any quick glance through the Bible (e.g., Ruth and Boaz, David and Bathsheba, Sampson and Delilah) or a volume of early Greek myths will affirm. Stories of love and adventure (and usually war) were also popular throughout the Middle Ages, and it is from these epic tales of derring-do that our current term "romance" derives. Although the learned language of the period was still Latin, the people more commonly spoke in the derivative vernacular languages that were developing (those languages that would eventually become today's romance languages, such as French, Spanish, and Italian). As a result, the popular literature of the period (e.g., *Guy of Warwick, Fairie Queen*) was also being written in or translated into these languages and, subsequently, these works themselves became known as romances.

Eventually, the term came to include not only the language, but the subjects and the qualities of the literature itself. Thus, a romance came to be identified as a popular tale that centered around a theme of adventure and love. These romances of Medieval times, however, are not the popular romances of today, and except for the name and the fact that love is a component in both, they bear little relation to each other.

Other romantic stories and poems can be found throughout history, and for a brief, interesting attempt to trace the history of the romance from the fourth century A.D., consult Annette Townend's "Historical Overview" section in *Words of Love: A Complete Guide to Romance Fiction* (New York: Garland, 1984) by Eileen Fallon.

Beginnings

Although bits and pieces of earlier love stories might have had an effect on the current romance genre, it is generally held that the direct antecedent of today's romances is the 1740 epistolary novel by Samuel Richardson titled *Pamela: or Virtue Rewarded*. This extremely popular novel in which a young servant girl resists repeated attempts on her virtue by "Mr. B—" and, as a result, ends up marrying him, was followed by Richardson's *Clarissa Harlowe* (1747) in which the heroine does not resist temptation and, therefore, in keeping with the fascinating logic of the time, dies. These stories spawned a host of imitations that were popular on both sides of the Atlantic until the end of the century. One of the most important of these was Susanna Haswell Rowson's classic seduction novel, *Charlotte Temple: A Tale of Truth*, first published in England in 1791 and in America in 1794, and considered by most to be America's first popular romance novel.

At the same time that *Pamela* and her sister novels were enjoying favor, a new variety of romance, the Gothic, was being born. When in 1764 Horace Walpole produced his macabre Gothic tale of the supernatural, *The Castle of Otranto*, primarily for the amusement of his female relatives, he had little idea what he was starting. Although some writers, such as Monk Lewis, adhered to and expanded upon Walpole's true terror Gothic, in the hands of Anne Radcliffe, it mellowed into the less gruesome, more romantic, and always rationally explained, sentimental Gothic. By the end of the century, Radcliffe's *The Mysteries of Udolpho* (1794) and its successors, complete with threatened heroines and mysterious settings, had become the favorite "forbidden" reading material of young women in both England and America. These stories remained popular well into the Regency period (1811-1820), and even Jane Austen, whose works written during this decade would inspire the later Regency-type novels, acknowledged the Gothics in *Northanger Abbey,* a parody of the subgenre. (Incidentally, in today's Regencies, if the heroine is found reading a novel or other "unimproving" book, it often is one by "Mrs. Radcliffe.") It is also this same Gothic thread that was picked up by the Brontës, most notably in *Wuthering Heights* and *Jane Eyre,* in the mid-1800s, almost a century after the Gothic's first appearance.

The Nineteenth Century

Although the sentimental Gothic continued to be popular well into the nineteenth century, a new form, the Historical Romance, was beginning to spark the reading public's imagination. With the anonymous publication of *Waverly* in 1814, Sir Walter Scott ignited a movement that, while it would periodically be submerged in favor of what was currently popular, was never to completely die out. Scott was avidly read in both England and the United States, but following the War of 1812, Americans began to favor novels with American settings. When James Fenimore Cooper produced *The Spy* (a romantic adventure of the American Revolution) in 1821, he was hailed enthusiastically as "The American Scott." The Historical Romance attracted numerous new practitioners, and for the next several decades it enjoyed widespread popularity.

About the same time, a group of women writers who would eventually become known as the Domestic Sentimentalists began to make their presence felt. Picking up the threads of both the earlier sentimental romance and the sentimental Gothic, these writers produced a wide variety of romances, some of which tended toward the Gothic, complete with adventure, suspense, and danger, and others which were of a more domestic and conventionally romantic bent. Many of these novels also used historical settings, and some incorporated religious themes. The unifying factor in these works was one common to all romances: they dealt with the relationships between men and women.[3] From about the 1820s on, the influence of the Domestic Sentimentalists increased until their works completely dominated the market in the 1850s. Among the more popular Domestic Sentimentalists were Catharine Maria Sedgwick, E.D.E.N. Southworth, Elizabeth Wetherell (Susan Warner), Mary Jane Holmes, Caroline Lee Hentz, Susanna Maria Cummins, and Augusta Jane Evans Wilson. Once referred to by a frustrated Nathaniel Hawthorne as "a d—d mob of scribbling women," these novelists maintained their popularity until well after the Civil War.

Although a number of the novels written during the "Golden Age of the Sentimental Domestic Romance" had religious or inspirational aspects, during and just after the Civil War, (perhaps somewhat predictably) novels that emphasized these principles were particularly popular. Augusta Jane Evans' *St. Elmo* (1867) and *The Gates Ajar* (1868) by Elizabeth Stuart Phelps are two especially popular examples of this type.

The decades that followed were host to a wide variety of romance types. The sentimental domestic continued to be widely read, but it was augmented by the highly popular weekly story papers and dime novel series. Of the many writers of the serialized story paper romances, Laura Jean Libbey was one of the most popular. Her works were published from the mid-1880s to the 1920s, and she remains one of the best remembered today. Bertha M. Clay, another popular name of the period, produced a dime novel series of Gothic romances. Interestingly, Clay was not an individual at all but a group of writers who wrote under the Bertha M. Clay pseudonym. (This idea of different writers writing under the same name surfaced again in the next century when the Stratemeyer Syndicate began publication of series such as Nancy Drew and the Hardy Boys.) Unfortunately, because of the ephemeral nature of their physical formats (cheap paper, poor quality bindings), many of these works were not preserved, and, as a result, much of the literature from this period has been lost forever.

Following the American Centennial of 1876, there was a renewed interest in Historical Romances, particularly those set in America, and until the first decade of the new century, the Historical Romance in its myriad variations enjoyed great popularity. Religious novels with historical settings, such as Lew Wallace's *Ben Hur* (1880) or Henryk Sienkiewicz' *Quo Vadis?* (1896); novels with mythical settings, such as Anthony Hope's *The Prisoner of Zenda* (1894); and novels with historical American settings, such as Mary Johnston's *To Have and To Hold* (1900) and Helen Hunt Jackson's classic *Ramona* (1884), are just a few of the many variations on this type.

The Twentieth Century

Although the Historical Romance was by far the most popular type of romance written at the end of the nineteenth century, other varieties continued to be written. It was during the last part of the nineteenth century that Grace Livingston Hill began to produce her still-popular contemporary, domestically oriented, inspirational novels. The Contemporary Romance, with and without inspirational overtones, continued into the new century and in later decades achieved new importance in the hands of such popular practitioners as Kathleen Norris, Faith Baldwin, and Emilie Loring, along with Grace Livingston Hill. During the first part of this century, two other authors were also producing Contemporary Romances that today are considered the forerunners of the contemporary Young Adult (YA) Romance. Lucy Maud Montgomery's Anne of Green Gables series (first one in 1908) and Emily series (first one in 1923), along with Jean Webster's *Daddy-Long-Legs* (1912) were some of the first books to address teenage concerns related to growing up and falling in love. Although they were originally intended for the adult market, they are now read primarily by young adults and are considered well within the YA Romance subgenre.

During this same time period, the earliest prototypes of the Saga subgenre were also being written. *A Man of Property*, the first volume in John Galsworthy's The Forsyte Saga, appeared in 1906, and by the 1920s and 1930s, with the start of Mazo De la Roche's Jalna series, Hugh Walpole's Herries series, and G. B. Stern's Matriarch series, the popularity of the Saga was guaranteed.

The 1920s saw a revival of interest in the Historical Romance with the advent of books such as Rafael Sabatini's *Scaramouche* (1921) and *Captain Blood* (1922). However, the real resurgence of interest in the Historical did not take place until the 1930s and 1940s when, to escape the realties of both the Great Depression and World War II, readers began to demand stories set in a more romantic and pleasant past. This was the time of *Anthony Adverse* (1933) by Hervey Allen (a rollicking romp through the Napoleonic era), *Gone With the Wind* (1936) by Margaret Mitchell (a sweeping view of the Civil War South through the eyes of a willful, beautiful, and not particularly "good" heroine), and *Forever Amber* (1944) by Kathleen Winsor (a slightly scandalous story of an English country girl who became the mistress to a king but could never forget the man who first loved her). A host of others soon joined the ranks, and it is during this period that writers such as Samuel Shellabarger, Frank Yerby, and Anya Seton either began their careers or achieved their greatest popularity.

Not surprisingly, there was also a new interest in romances with religious or inspirational themes during this time period, and works like Lloyd C. Douglas's *Magnificent Obsession* (1932) and *The Robe* (1942) were particularly popular.

This period also witnessed the birth of the modern prototype of the Gothic Romance, *Rebecca,* by Daphne Du Maurier, published in 1938. Although its roots are well established in the earlier works of the Brontës and even Ann Radcliffe, it is Du Maurier's classic that solidified the mold and established the pattern for the modern Gothic that would dominate the romance fiction market during the 1960s.

The decade of the 1950s is not particularly easy to define in terms of romance fiction. It was a time of relative quiet, and although romances with historical settings were still popular, the emphasis was primarily on the traditional contemporary vein. The Canadian firm Harlequin had just begun to publish reprints of the British Mills and Boon light romances; the inspirational and traditional romances of Faith Baldwin, Grace Livingston Hill, and others were widely read; and the adolescent market, yet to be officially crowned "Young Adult" by the publishing industry in the 1960s, was largely composed of light high school or early career romances written by popular authors such as Betty Cavanna and Rosamund Du Jardin. *The Price of Salt* (1952), a contemporary classic of lesbian literature by Claire Morgan, was acclaimed with some enthusiasm.

The 1960s—The Gothic Touch

With the advent of the 1960s, the atmosphere changed. Suddenly, brooding castles on windswept cliffs; distraught, threatened, but exceedingly curious, heroines; and dark, saturnine heroes with hooded eyes and sardonic expressions were everywhere. Books with covers displaying gloomy castles, glowing candles, and diaphanously clad, fleeing heroines lined the book racks; and readers haunted the libraries and book stores, impatiently awaiting the next Victoria Holt, Barbara Michaels, or Phyllis Whitney title. The catalyst, of course, was the publication of Victoria Holt's classic, contemporary Gothic, *Mistress of Mellyn*, in 1960. Apparently ready for some mystery and excitement, the romance reading public made this book an instant success, and the demand for more of the same type soared. The demand was not limited to the Gothic, however; readers were also devouring novels of Romantic Suspense with equal relish. Publishers reprinted suitable titles from their backlists and actively sought new writers. Older writers of Romantic Suspense and Gothic novels suddenly became popular, and the careers of many new authors were launched. Phyllis Whitney, Mary Stewart, Susan Howatch, Dorothy Eden, Barbara Michaels, and Victoria Holt are only a few of the writers who contributed in this field. In addition, the Regencies of Georgette Heyer were attracting a growing readership.

It was also during this decade that the term "young adult" was devised by the publishing industry as a sales device "to make it more convenient to market books to those who bring books and adolescent children together."[4] The term stuck, and today Young Adult Romance is a recognized subdivision of Romance.

During the late 1960s, two events resulted in a popularity surge of two rather different types of romance literature, the Gay Romance and the Saga. The police raid on the Stonewall gay bar in 1969 launched the modern gay movement (which brought with it the publishing of gay and lesbian fiction, including romance), and the serialization of Galsworthy's The Forsyte Saga for television revived interest in the Saga.

The 1970s—The Hot Historical Explosion

Both the Saga and the Gay Romance gained in importance during the next decade, but they were not alone. The decade of the 1970s saw the beginning of a romance boom. With the introduction of the Sensual Historical in 1972 (*The Flame and the Flower* by Kathleen Woodiwiss) and the Sweet/Savage Historical in 1974 (*Sweet Savage Love* by Rosemary Rogers) the romance market exploded and Historicals were suddenly fashionable after a relative absence from the market of more than 20 years. These new Historicals, however, were not the innocent Historicals of the past. Flamboyant, adventuresome, and, above all, passionate and sexy, these highly romantic stories reached out to the new, contemporary reader—and sold beyond all expectations.

The spillover from this popularity also affected other types of Historicals. The Historical Novel and the Romantic Historical, both of which usually treated history quite seriously and often more sedately than the newer varieties, gained in readership, and even the more innocent varieties of Period Romance were widely read. As was mentioned earlier, the Saga (which was usually historical) also increased in popularity during this decade, due in part to the establishment of Book Creations, Inc. by Lyle Kenyon Engel. This company literally created Saga series, first developing the ideas and then contracting with writers to realize them. Engel died in 1986; however, many of these series, such as Wagons West and The Colonization of America/White Indian, continued.

The Historicals weren't the only game in town during the 1970s; light, innocent, category (usually contemporary) romances were popular as well. The field was dominated by Harlequin, but by the beginning of the 1980s it had been joined by a number of other publishers, including Dell and Pocket.

The 1980s—The Romance Boom

The 1980s saw the romance movement expand and change directions, somewhat. Although Historicals were still published and read, interest was shifting away from them and toward Contemporary Romances—particularly those of the Category or Series variety. But the Category Romances themselves were changing. To be sure, the original innocent Harlequins and Silhouettes were still being published, but a number of new series were joining them. These new lines, reflecting the changing lifestyles and sexual mores of society, featured more aggressive and independent heroines and were much more sensual in nature; and soon series with names like Ecstasy, Desire, Rapture, Loveswept, and Temptation were appearing in the paperback racks. (Silhouette's Desire and Harlequin's Temptation are two of these early series that survive as of this writing; Bantam's Loveswept series was discontinued at the end of 1998.)

At the same time, other series, generally those of the innocent variety, were disappearing from the racks. One new series, Bantam's Circle of Love, a sweet, innocent series, was obsolete before it was even released, largely because of the rapidly changing tastes in romance fiction.[5] And this was not an isolated incident. Sensual series proliferated and the market exploded—and eventually, after a somewhat bloody battle, Silhouette and Harlequin merged and today are part of the same company.

But society's more contemporary attitudes were not reflected exclusively in the Category Romances. Single title romances were also becoming more realistic in their approaches, and although the traditional romances of the more innocent variety were still read (and written by some), many of the new stories featured independent, career-minded heroines; high-powered settings; and more casual, but not necessarily promiscuous, attitudes toward sex. In addition, several trends that foreshadowed the phenomenon of "genreblending" so prevalent during the 1990s were established within the Contemporary Romance of the 1980s. One was the growing tendency of the "sexy novel of the rich and famous [to fall] into a genre pattern"[6] eventually becoming the fast-paced, steamy novel of the Glitz and Glamour variety. Another was the increased blurring of the lines between Contemporary Romance, women's fiction, and the mainstream novel.

There was also activity in other romance areas during this decade. In 1980 Vincent Virga published *Gaywick*, a classic gay costume Gothic, and by the mid-1980s a small but growing number of gay and lesbian romances began to appear. Interest also increased in other genre varieties—e.g., mysteries, science fiction, fantasy—all with a gay orientation. Sagas, particularly those with American settings, continued to be extremely popular, attracting new readers and writers, some of whom were already well known as writers of other romance subgenres. By the end of the decade, interest in Historicals was again on the rise, especially those with American settings—particularly those set in the American West. The Gothic, considered by many long dead, became a bit sexier and once more began to attract attention, as did Romantic Suspense. Regencies were holding their own, but the Inspirational, although it had profited earlier from the generally conservative and traditional atmosphere of the 1980s, was in decline. In addition, a number of romance authors were heading into mainstream or nongenre fiction.

But adult romance fiction wasn't the only arena of innovation during the 1980s. In 1980, noting the popularity of its light, innocent romances sold through its school book clubs, Scholastic launched the Wildfire Romance series, and in doing so, changed the way books were marketed to young adults for the foreseeable future. Prior to this time, publishers had concentrated on reaching young adults indirectly through schools and libraries; now they tried selling to them directly, with spectacular results. The series approach was as popular with YAs as it was with adults, and the young adult romance consumers soon added appreciably to the growing romance boom. By the mid-1980s, the YA romance market had grown to include original romance series, reprint series lines, and a variety of thematic and soap opera lines. Eventually, however, the market faltered, and although YA Romance continued to be written and read during the late 1980s, sales declined and remained low throughout much of the 1990s. Recently, however, there are signs of renewed interest, at least on the part of the publishers, and a variety of series focusing on everything from Sci-Fi Romance to contemporary humor and separately targeting the younger and older YA markets are beginning to appear. Their appeal, of course, remains to be seen. Nevertheless, publishers are optimistic, convinced that despite societal and lifestyle changes "one thing remains constant for teenagers: the allure of first romance."[7]

But the publishing industry is anything but static, and just as a correction comes in the stock market after a meteoric rise, a "shake down" came in the romance industry in the mid-1980s. Heavy competition, particularly in the Categories, resulted in cutbacks and the demise of a number of contemporary lines, and only Harlequin, Silhouette, and Bantam emerged relatively unscathed. This process was painful; however, given the earlier growth in the romance field, this fallout was not unexpected, and by the end of the decade, the genre was healthier, more sophisticated, and definitely on the upswing as it headed into the 1990s.

The 1990s—A Decade of Diversity and Change

Characterized by diversity, growth, and change, the decade of the 1990s has been good to the romance genre. The period began on an upbeat note and, except for the expected volatility and a few unexpected industry moves, continues in much the same vein. Interest is strong, sales are increasing, and the genre continues to display its amazing ability to provide something for everyone.

From a literary point of view, the genre has become more diverse and inclusive, expanding to incorporate not only the traditional romance subgenres, but several new ones as well. Two of the more important of these are the Ethnic or Multicultural Romance, which features protagonists from various cultures and ethnic backgrounds, and the eclectic Alternative Reality Romance, which covers a wide range of love stories with paranormal, supernatural, fantasy, or science fiction themes. In addition, the phenomenon of "genreblending," the migration of various elements across fiction genre boundaries—or across subgenres within genres—has become one of the major trends of the decade. The results of cross-genre mergers are apparent everywhere, especially in many of the Alternative Reality Romance subgenres, Romantic Suspense, and more recently, Women's Romantic Fiction. The intra-genre blends are less flamboyant but no less innovative, as anyone who has read a vampire Regency or a psychic Futuristic romance knows. A side effect of this blending is that romance is becoming harder and harder to categorize, causing problems for both marketers and librarians.

Although Historicals still account for approximately one-fourth of the titles published each year, the market has softened a bit, and Contemporaries, while always the market dominator responsible for more than 50 percent of the titles released each year, have been busy adding to their market share. At least one publisher of Historicals has branched out into the Contemporary single title market with great success. In addition, during this decade Gothics as a separate subgenre briefly peaked and then plummeted almost out of existence, the Regency ranks have solidified (although Regency historicals grew in popularity), and Romantic Suspense has expanded. The Ethnic Romance mentioned earlier has gained in popularity and diversity, and the Inspirational Romance, after losing readership earlier, is on the upswing. The 1990s have also seen the rise of the anthology, and while collections of Christmas novellas have been by far the favorite, other themes and holidays are also well represented. Linked books (especially trilogies) and limited series have also been popular.

Although the standard romance themes were still the norm, several innovative (or recycled) trends attracted a significant amount of attention, and by the mid-1990s, stories featuring wounded or imperfect heroes (and sometimes heroines), bad-boy heroes, older heroes and heroines, reunions and rekindled love, or serious social issues were commonplace. In addition, the Alternative Reality subgenre had made its mark, and the romances during this period were filled with angels, ghosts, vampires, reincarnated people, and time traveling characters. Humor in romance became increasingly important; a number of publishers either produced new romantic comedy lines or actively solicited funny manuscripts. Many romances, especially those highlighting social issues, exhibited a new intensity, and several publishers and writers pushed their attention toward erotica. In addition, various writers were pushing the romance envelope to the limit—crossing genre and subgenre boundaries, introducing elements traditionally excluded from the Romance, and producing books with definite mainstream or women's fiction elements. At the same time, in two not necessarily related trends, more romance writers were published in hardcover, and the overall quality of romance writing improved.

The publishing houses of the genre also underwent a few changes. Cutbacks, startups, and regroupings have all been part of the 1990s, and while numerous lines were discontinued and at least one romance publisher folded during the decade (Meteor/Kismet 1990–1994), several smaller and less traditional companies set up shop (e.g., Odyssey Books, Lionhearted, Red Sage, Starlog). In addition, established publishers, responding to reader demand, have produced new, more focused lines (e.g., Pinnacle's Arabesque, Harlequin's Love and Laughter, Jove's Homespun, Silhouette's Shadows) or formed new partnerships (e.g., One World's Indigo Love Stories—a collaboration of Ballantine Books and Genesis Press).

Formats also have changed, and although neither audio nor video versions have come close to replacing the printed romance—nor are they likely to do so in the near future—the 1990s saw increased experimentation with romance offerings in several new media. Building on early efforts begun during the 1980s and early 1990s (primarily on the part of smaller companies), the trend gradually gained wider acceptance, as evidenced in 1995 when Harlequin published unabridged audiotape versions of four romances by best-selling writers.

Romance also took to the television airways during this decade—with varying degrees of success—as several romances were made into television movies. Cable television has also become important to the genre, as Harlequin joined forces with the Romantic Classics channel in 1997 to sponsor a series of romance author roundtable discussions on "Romantically Speaking—Harlequin Goes Primetime" and then linked up with Alliance Communications to produce television movies for The Movie Channel. The first aired on Valentine's Day in 1998, and the program continued on a monthly basis throughout the year.[8]

Other format changes of the 1990s have included more romances being published in hardcover, including Ballantine's innovative paperback-size hardcover in 1997, as well as fledgling attempts at publishing romances in computerized formats or online. In addition, as the result of discussions held during the Public Library Association's Cluster Workshops in 1995, Harlequin also began providing romances in various language translations to American markets.

Another interesting phenomenon during the 1990s has been the increase in authors' involvement in promoting their books. Romance writers are savvy when it comes to marketing their own books, and with the growth of the Internet (and the fact that many romance writers and readers are active participants), marketing has taken on a new dimension. Most publishers and many writers have home pages on the Net (complete with excerpts of works in progress, chat groups, and other reader-relevant offerings), and with more and more people going online, the potential is astounding. (URLs for selected publishers' Web sites are listed in chapter 17—Miscellaneous Romance Reference Sources.)

Other, more negative, things that began to affect the genre by the middle of the decade were the shrinking midlist and a consolidation of the distribution system.[9] Faced with a consolidation of the market and bottom-line concerns, publishers began to focus more attention and money on their best-selling authors and those they had newly acquired with high expectations of stardom, to the neglect of their solid, dependable, but not necessarily upward-bound, midlist writers. They also began to reprint and promote the backlist titles of popular writers, leaving less shelf space for the midlist romances.

During this same time, there was massive consolidation in the mass market distribution system, squeezing the independent distributors almost out of existence (an 89 percent reduction by some accounts) and resulting, once again, in fewer outlets, less shelf space, and lower sell-throughs for romance titles.[10] As of this writing, the midlist crunch is still on. Publishing history, however, predicts that, like other previous shakeouts or "corrections," this one will be short-lived and will eventually result in a healthier and better environment for the genre. Of course, whether history repeats itself remains to be seen.

THE ROMANCE GENRE COMES OF AGE

As the romance boom blossomed, a number of organizations, publications, and adjunct groups developed to serve it. Best known, perhaps, is the Romance Writers of America, an organization established in 1979 to support writers of romances and champion the cause of romance readers and writers in general. Over the years, it has evolved from a small group of founding writers who were focused primarily on perfecting their craft and nurturing fledgling writers into a sophisticated and influential organization capable of fighting for its members' rights and for the romance genre as a whole. Currently, RWA has more than 8,200 members and is the largest genre fiction organization in existence. (For more information on RWA, see chapter 18—Societies and Organizations.)

In addition, over the years a number of romance-related periodicals have sprung up. Some of the more important are *Romantic Times*, a periodical that provides reviews, biographical sketches, industry news, and other information for the romance reader; *Affaire de Coeur*, a similar publication but not as comprehensive as RT; *Rendezvous*, one of the more critical review-only publications; *Heartland Critiques*, a newsletter that focuses only on reviews; and *The Gothic Journal*, a specialized publication that features reviews of Gothics and Romantic Suspense. Also of note are *Boy Meets Girl: A Weekly Review of Romance Authors, Agents, Publishers, and Fiction*, a specialized and pricey romance industry newsletter that was influential during the early 1980s but folded in 1986, and *Romance Forever*, a promising magazine still in its infancy. Most of these publications are blatantly uncritical of romance and need to be regarded in that light; nevertheless, they are widely read and do provide useful information about the romance industry and most current releases. By their very existence, they have contributed to the success of the romance market, simply by promoting the validity of the genre as a whole. (See chapter 16—Periodicals and Review Sources—for more information.)

The 1990s have also seen increased interest in the romance genre in diverse areas, including universities, libraries, and on the Internet. The academic community was forced to take notice when *Dangerous Men and Adventurous Women: Romance Writers on the Appeal of the Romance*, edited by Jayne Ann Krentz, was published by the University of Pennsylvania Press in 1992. It subsequently became one of the press's bestsellers, was reissued as a mass market paperback in 1996, and received the American Popular Culture Association's Susan Brownmiller Award. Other indications of increased scholarly interest are the Internet presence of AIR: Academics in Libraries, a listserv for scholars interested in the romance; an increase in the number of theses, dissertations, books, and articles analyzing the romance genre; and a number of professional conferences on the topic of romance fiction (e.g., "A Passionate Journey: Writing into the New Millennium" at Penn State in 1996, and a similar conference, "ReReading the Romance" at Bowling Green State University in June 1997).

There has also been an increased interest in the romance within the library community. In recent years, romance fiction has been the subject of professional workshops; programs at both PLA, ALA, and a number of state and regional library associations; and at least one pre-conference workshop. In addition, in 1994 *Library Journal* became the first mainstream publication to produce a romance review column on a regular basis; it now appears quarterly. *Publishers Weekly* is attempting to give romances fairer review treatment. There has also been increased collaboration between RWA and the library world. For example, RWA has had a booth at recent ALA conferences, librarians have presented programs at recent RWA conferences, and since 1995 librarians have been honored by RWA's Librarian of the Year award, presented at their annual conference.

Finally, the decade of the 1990s has also been the decade of the Internet, and strange though it may seem to some, many romance readers and writers are completely at home in cyberspace. A number of listservs cater to these groups [e.g., RRA-L (Romance Readers Anonymous); rw-l (romance writers); AIR (Academics in Romance); and the various romance groups on the commercial services such as GEnie, Prodigy, CompuServe, or AOL] and the number of participants is on the upswing. The Web currently has much to offer the romance fan—reviews; lists; authors' and publishers' home pages; direct book ordering; direct contacts with readers, writers, and publishers; etc.—and in the light of rapidly changing technology, the growing computer literacy of the country, and the flexibility of the romance genre, it seems safe to say that there will only be more in the years to come.

Despite the recent midlist and distribution crunch, the romance market continues to hold its own. Most romance types are still available and selling well, and although the favorites of the moment seem to be Contemporaries and Romantic Suspense—some of which display mainstream tendencies—reading tastes change so rapidly that it is difficult to say exactly what will be popular in the future. But whether it is by returning to the obsolete seduction novels, remaining with the status quo, or leaping ahead to some as yet unknown romance type, it is certain that the romance with its incredible flexibility will survive in some form. After all, the romance, like love, has been around a long time, and it is, indeed, a most enduring genre.

NOTES

1. Kay J. Mussell, "Romantic Fiction," in *Handbook of American Popular Culture,* ed. M. Thomas Inge (Westport, CT: Greenwood, 1980), 317.

2. Janice A. Radway, *Reading the Romance: Women, Patriarchy, and Popular Literature* (Chapel Hill, NC: University of North Carolina Press, 1984), 64.

3. Kay Mussell, *Women's Gothic and Romantic Fiction: A Reference Guide* (Westport, CT: Greenwood, 1981), 7.

4. Dorothy Briley, "Publishing for the Young Adult Market," in *Librarians and Young Adults: Media, Services, and Librarianship*, ed. JoAnn V. Rogers (Littleton, CO: Libraries Unlimited, 1979), 5-6.

5. Daisy Maryles, "Love Springs Eternal," *Publishers Weekly* (January 14, 1983): 56.

6. Diana Tixier Herald, *Genreflecting: A Guide to Reading Interests in Genre Fiction*, 4th ed. (Englewood, CO: Libraries Unlimited, 1995), 168.

7. Heather Vogel Frederick, "The Future Looks Bright for Teen Romance," *Publishers Weekly* (November 10, 1997): 47.

8. Lucinda Dyer and Robert Dahlin, "Birds Do It, Bees Do It; These Days Players on the Net Do It," *Publishers Weekly* (November 10, 1997): 46.

9. Theresa Meyers, "Publish or Perish: Dissecting the Midlist Crisis—Part One," *RWR: Romance Writers' Report* 17 (January 1997): 12.

10. Ibid., 13.

Chapter 2

The Appeal of Romance Fiction

"These books [romances] offer a vast reassurance
that the world will come out right."
Gaye Tuchman, Sociologist

"We must select the illusion which appeals to our temperament,
and embrace it with passion, if we want to be happy."
Cyril Connolly

"People choose to read certain stories because they enjoy them."
John Cawelti

"Romances are fun."
Sandra Brown

The current popularity of the romance novel is undeniable. Bookstores overflow with them, library shelves abound with them, and it is a rare bestseller list that doesn't include romance titles on a regular basis. Persistent and pervasive, romance novels are everywhere.

In one sense, this is not a particularly new phenomenon. As mentioned in chapter 1, love stories have been popular from the earliest times, and ever since Pamela first fainted her way to wedded bliss, readers have demanded a steady supply of romance fantasies, varying with the current vogue (e.g., seduction, Gothic, sentimental, romantic suspense).

In another sense, however, this current fascination with the romance is almost unprecedented. Never before have so many writers produced so many love stories for so many people—and never before have they been marketed so aggressively by publishers, acknowledged so proudly by writers, or read so openly by fans. Indeed, the romance has arrived[1] and the figures for the genre are staggering. Recent statistics indicate that romances account for 55 percent of the mass fiction market and generate $1 billion in yearly sales. More than 182 million romances were sold in 1996 alone.[2]

Organizations and publications specifically aimed at readers and writers of romance fiction are varied and thriving, romances are finding their way into films and their authors are appearing on television.[3] Major mainstream review sources such as *Library Journal*, as well as several national newspapers, have finally begun to critically review romances on a regular basis (see sections on organizations and periodicals in this guide). In addition, the romance genre is at last receiving serious consideration by a growing number of scholars from within the academic community (see chapter 14, "History and Criticism").

Obviously, romances are popular, and the lure of the love story is a given. But who are the romance readers, and just what is it that makes the romance genre so appealing to so many people?

According to one groundbreaking survey of 600 romance readers conducted by Carol Thurston, they are a cross section of "the general population in age, education, and martial and socioeconomic status."[4] She found that half the readers have attended college, most watch less television than the national average, 40 percent work full-time outside the home, and 40 percent are in the financial middle class. Subsequent studies have generally confirmed her findings, and the latest data as reported by the Romance Writers of America[5] and various magazines including *Forbes* list the average romance reader as 39 years old, with a 45 percent chance of being college educated, a 50 percent chance of working outside the home, and a family income of $40,000.[6] Obviously, the average romance reader is not the undereducated, uninformed, frustrated housewife of recent mythology. Romances apparently appeal to a broad range of readers, but why?

The appeal of the romance is straightforward, yet multifaceted, and the current definitive source on the subject is *Dangerous Men and Adventurous Women: Romance Writers on the Appeal of the Romance* (Philadelphia: University of Pennsylvania Press, 1992), edited by Jayne Ann Krentz. This wide-ranging anthology is a groundbreaking effort and should be mandatory reading for anyone seriously interested in the topic. It is tempting simply to refer people to this collection and consider the subject covered; however, that would not serve the purpose of those who want something more succinct. The discussion that follows is intended to be neither theoretical nor complete; it is merely an attempt to meet the needs of the reader who wants a few basic reasons for the appeal of the romance.

The genre romance novel appeals both generally and specifically. Its general appeal is that of all genre fiction—an escape fantasy that is predictable, enjoyable, and safe. Romance's specific appeal is more complex. It attracts readers for diverse reasons that include emotional involvement, female empowerment, the promotion of moral values, the celebration of life, the ultimate triumph of love, and a sense of unflagging optimism.

THE GENERAL APPEAL OF THE ROMANCE

The fundamental general appeal of the romance novel, like that of all genre fiction, is to our basic human desire and need for escape—from the routine and anxiety of everyday life into a fantasy where things are new, different, or exciting, and where everything will usually turn out "right." (Rarely do romances end with the protagonists separating; however, when this does happen, it usually is the "right" ending.) The term "escape" can be defined in various ways, but whether identified as "relaxation," "time for myself," "wish fulfillment," "enjoyment," "refreshment," or "fun," it all comes down to the same thing—the desire to leave reality behind and experience an alternative, if only for a brief time. So basic is this aspect to the reading of romances that a study by Janice Radway reports that a full 75 percent of the readers in her sample stated that they read romances primarily to escape.[7]

Escape is not used here as a negative concept. It is a part of everyday life and comes in forms that are acceptable (e.g., vacations, sports, reading, games, crafts, hobbies) and those that are not (e.g., drugs, alcohol, suicide, and certain types of mental illness). As Constance Casey satirically comments in her review of Radway's book, "Better . . . curled up by the hearth with *The Flame and The Flower* than popping Librium or downing vodka at midday."[8] Incidentally, reading as a means of escape is not limited to the female, romance-reading population. Adventure stories serve the same purpose for many male readers, and both sexes enjoy the escape attributes of mysteries, science fiction, and fantasy.

Romances are also generally appealing because they are predictable. Although fiction genres, especially the romance, are often criticized because they follow a type of pattern and adhere to certain conventions, it is this very predictability that is so attractive to most genre readers, including romance readers. They *know* that everything is going to work out right in the end. They may not know how, why, when, where, or even who, but readers do know that by the time the last page is turned, all mysteries will be solved, all criminals brought to justice, all desperadoes dealt with, all new or alien worlds tamed, and all couples appropriately aligned. This predictable, satisfactory resolution to the story is the promise of the genre writer to his or her reader, and the writer who breaks it ends up with a confused and disappointed audience.

Finally, romances appeal simply because they are enjoyable. John Cawelti said it about all the genres in general, and Sandra Brown said it about the romance in particular (see quotes at the beginning of chapter 2). People read them because they like them; people read them because they are fun. No better reason is needed.

THE SPECIFIC APPEAL OF THE ROMANCE

Although romances are read and enjoyed for all of the generic reasons mentioned above, they are also read for elements that are specific to the romance genre itself.

One of the primary attractions of the romance is that it is emotionally engaging. Romances are books about relationships, and they appeal directly to readers' feelings and emotions. They are compelling, and they make the reader care about the characters and what happens to them. Interestingly, this emotional appeal is also one of the reasons that romance is so highly criticized. One can only wonder why it is assumed by some that if a book makes you feel, it cannot also make you think or that thinking and logic are inherently preferable to intuition and feeling.

Another important, and perhaps most controversial, of the attractions of romance is the theme of female empowerment. Contrary to popular misconceptions, romances are not about submissive heroines who give up everything for the hero. In fact, they are not about women giving up at all. They are stories of women who win, who get what they want, and who tame the hero in the process. As Krentz says, "With courage, intelligence, and gentleness she brings the most dangerous creature on earth, the human male, to his knees. More than that, she forces him to acknowledge her power as a woman."[9] This aspect of the romance makes the genre one of the most subversive genres of all literatures, because in affirming the empowerment of women, romances invert the traditional patriarchal, male-dominated order and allow women to be "heroes" in their own right.[10]

Even though it is not always acknowledged openly, romances also appeal because they are sensual, sexual fantasies for women. Written primarily by women for women, these novels describe relationships, romance, and sex in ways with which women can identify; and while this is rarely the primary reason a woman reads a romance or enjoys a particular author, it is a factor that needs to be recognized.

Romances are also appealing because they promote the importance of moral values. Strong interpersonal relationships, family, fidelity, caring, and similar themes are all well represented within the genre, and in a time when literature rarely advocates such ideas and often dismisses or denigrates them, romances have an obvious appeal.

Closely linked to this moral advocacy is the fact that romances are increasingly dealing with serious social issues such as spousal or child abuse, alcoholism, racism, and mental and physical illness. While this aspect might not seem to be appealing on the surface, it speaks to the needs of many readers as it allows them not only to confront real-life problems through fiction, but also to envision healthy, hopeful, and successful solutions to them.

Finally, one of the most basic reasons for the enduring appeal of the romance is simply that it is the most optimistic and hopeful of all the fiction genres. It celebrates life and love with abandon and reaffirms one of the most basic of all fantasies, the triumph of true love against all odds. Of course, women know that real-life endings are not always happy, but that doesn't stop them from wanting everyone to live "happily ever after." The genre romance allows readers to temporarily suspend reality and enjoy the fantasy without jeopardizing their lives in the real world. After all, most romance readers are firmly rooted in reality, and while they enjoy building their dream fantasies, they are generally wise enough not to try to live in them.

Obviously, romances attract readers for many reasons, but whatever the reason, romance readers know exactly what they are reading and why. Although they may read both Faulkner and Mitchell, or Shakespeare and Plaidy, few would confuse the two or think that they serve the same purpose or accomplish the same goals.

Predictable, empowering, optimistic, and just plain fun, romances have something for everyone. Perhaps this is the greatest reason of all for the genre's broad popularity and enduring appeal.

NOTES

1. Jayne Ann Krentz, speech at the Public Library Association Conference, Portland, Oregon, March 27-30, 1996.

2. Olivia M. Hall, president, Romance Writers of America to Terry Lay, president, Lee Company, letter, October 6, 1997. http://www.rwanational.com/lee-jeans.html (Accessed October 27, 1997).

3. "Romance Authors Hit Prime Time TV: Romance Classics Channel Airs Harlequin Talk Show." http://www.rwanational.com/harlequinTV.html (Accessed October 27, 1997).

4. Carol Thurston, "The Liberation of Pulp Romances," *Psychology Today* (April 1983): 14.

5. Romance Writiers of America. http://www.rwanational.com/infosta.html (Accessed October 27, 1997).

6. Dana Wechsler Linden and Matt Rees, "I'm Hungry. But Not for Food," *Forbes* (July 6, 1992): 70+.

7. Janice Radway, *Reading the Romance: Women, Patriarchy, and Popular Literature* (Chapel Hill, NC: University of North Carolina Press, 1984), 60-61.

8. Constance Casey, "The Great Escape: Better a Romance Novel Than a Swig of Vodka," *San Jose Mercury News,* Arts and Books Section (February 10, 1985).

9. Jayne Ann Krentz, ed., *Dangerous Men and Adventurous Women: Romance Writers on the Appeal of the Romance* (Philadelphia, PA: University of Pennsylvania Press, 1992), 5.

10. See various essays in Jayne Ann Krentz, ed., *Dangerous Men and Adventurous Women: Romance Writers on the Appeal of the Romance* (Philadelphia, PA: University of Pennsylvania Press, 1992), for a more complete discussion of this idea.

Chapter 3

Advising the Reader

    Readers' advisory service is essentially the process of putting the reader in touch with a book that he or she will enjoy reading. Romance readers' advisory service connects the romance reader with the proper romantic story. Unfortunately, such a reference service is not so simple to accomplish as it might seem, especially when it comes to romances. In the first place, reading tastes in fiction, particularly in the area of romance, are highly subjective, and a good deal of interaction is necessary to determine what the reader actually wants. Second, the variation in romances, both in subgenre and in the handling of such particulars as sex, is extremely wide. Therefore, a good working knowledge of the literature is necessary. Third, effective advisory service takes time, an almost nonexistent commodity in most libraries today.

    Despite these difficulties, it is still possible to provide good readers' advisory service for romance readers. The ideal situation is to have a staff librarian who is an avid reader and connoisseur of all types of romances, who has annotated every romance he or she has read, maintains an extensive card file on them, and who has enough time to spend talking in depth with readers who need advice. Since this is all rather unlikely, alternative measures are necessary.

    First, the two cardinal rules of readers' advisory service, know your literature and know your reader, cannot be ignored. Without them there is no service. Some suggestions for achieving both and putting them together in a practical way, specifically for the romance genre, is the subject of the rest of this section. For an excellent discussion of readers' advisory service in general, consult the following:

Saricks, Joyce G., and Brown, Nancy. *Readers' Advisory Service in the Public Library*. 2nd Ed. Chicago: American Library Association, 1997.

Although not specifically focused on the romance genre, this updated volume should be required reading for anyone who intends to provide readers' advisory service in the genre. It is one of the best and most practical sources on the topic of readers' advisory services available. Chapters include: "A History and Introduction," "Reference Sources," "Articulating a Book's Appeal," "The Readers' Advisory Interview," "The Background Readers' Advisors Need in Popular Fiction," "Promotion," and "Training."

KNOW THE LITERATURE

Even though it is impossible to read everything, librarians responsible for providing readers' advisory service for romance fiction should at least be conversant with the various subgenres and should have read several good, typical examples within each. (Actually, this is a necessary requirement for speaking the romance "language" when you seek help in other places.) See the book *Readers' Advisory Service in the Public Library* mentioned above for hints on developing a reading plan.

Once familiar with the genre, you can then obtain help from a variety of outside sources. Begin by querying the library staff. Depending upon the size of your library and system, you may find one or more romance readers. These people can be gold mines of information, providing recommendations on authors and books, keeping you apprised of new entries in the field, and alerting you to other important trends and developments.

Library patrons who read romances are other good sources of information. Readers are usually more than happy to discuss their favorite books and writers, and once you have established yourself as a "romance-reader-friendly librarian," you may find yourself pleasantly inundated with readers who will love keeping you romantically informed.

In addition, colleagues in other libraries are wonderful resources. Many are successfully dealing with large romance-reading clienteles already and may have answers to many of your questions. Also, some of the online groups, especially RRA-L (see page 348), include a number of librarians and can provide good recommendations for specific titles and other romance fiction matters.

Don't neglect local bookstores, especially ones with large romance collections and buyers who understand the genre; they can be excellent sources of current genre information.

Finally, reviews, bibliographies, and reading lists are all good sources of romance fiction information for the librarian and for the reader, as well. Reading lists are particularly useful, and some libraries, library systems, and library schools produce lists of romance fiction, often arranged by subgenre, that they would be willing to share. Ask around; personal contacts can prove to be a valuable tool when seeking information of this sort.

Note: Because of the role reviews play in the collection development process, romance reviews and their sources are discussed in chapter 4, "Building the Collection." Bibliographies are discussed in chapter 15, "Author Biography and Bibliography." For a breakdown of the various series and lines currently available, consult the chart titled "The Pattern for Romance" on pages 30–31 of this chapter.

KNOW THE READER

In addition to knowing the literature, it is also necessary to know the readers and understand what types of romances they want to read. This is best accomplished by talking with them one-to-one; and while it is time consuming, this is the most effective way of determining what a reader really wants. But you don't have to do this all by yourself; other people can help. For example, if there is a romance fan on the staff, consider consulting or putting the reader in touch with this person.

In addition, because readers enjoy discussing books and authors with other readers, introducing romance-reading patrons to each other may indirectly provide them with readers' advisory service. In fact, you might want to consider something more formal, such as a romance readers interest group. This group, in turn, might want to contribute to the general effort by producing bibliographies or maintaining a card file or computerized bibliographies for other readers to consult. Personal contact and interest is very important to the success of readers' advisory service, and as both publishers and librarians know, a personal word-of-mouth recommendation is probably the most effective form of advertising.

Finally, in addition to knowing what individual readers prefer to read, it is helpful for you to have an idea of the types of romances the library community reads as a whole. Does the community seem to prefer Regencies or sexy Historicals? Do they zero in on the contemporary paperbacks, or do they go for hardcover? If the romances in your collection are catalogued and your circulation system is automated, all of this information should be fairly easy to obtain. (This is a major argument for cataloging romances, by the way.) If not, you can still get a good idea by checking with those who work at the circulation desk and those who shelve books. Most of these people will have a fairly accurate idea of what is popular because they watch the books circulate, checking them out and in and putting them away.

CONNECTING THE READER AND THE ROMANCE

Although many readers discuss their reading habits and preferences with the library staff, an even larger number do not. This does not, however, mean they don't need help. They often need it more than those who ask, and it is important to provide some sort of advisory service for these "silent readers." However, because they do not ask for it, help and advice should be offered in a way that they can take advantage of on their own. Fortunately, there are several reference sources that can help. In addition to the groundbreaking classic *Genreflecting* (discussed in chapter 14), the following sources might be of particular interest:

> *What Do I Read Next? A Reader's Guide to Current Genre Fiction*. Detroit, MI: Gale Research, 1990-
>
> Edited by Neil Barron, Wayne Barton, Kristin Ramsdell, and Steven A. Stilwell, this index produced annually since 1990 provides access to more than 1,300 titles published during the previous year in the Mystery, Romance, Western, Fantasy, Horror and Science Fiction genres. Entries provide bibliographic, character, time, and setting information, a brief plot synopsis, lists of reviews

and other works by the author, and a list of other titles the reader might like. Entries are arranged alphabetically by author by genre section. Each section is prefaced by an overview for the year, and eight indexes are included—series, time period, geographic, genre, character name, character description, author, and title. Although this is not a romance-specific resource, it does have a discrete romance section, and the fact that it also includes other genres that have stories with a strong romance emphasis, is a definite plus. A version including all editions is available on CD-ROM and online on the Internet, and a single retrospective volume of the romance entries entitled *What Romance Do I Read Next? A Reader's Guide to Recent Romance Fiction* was published in 1997.

NoveList. Denver, CO: CARL Corporation, 1994-

Using materials from several sources, most notably Minnesota's Hennepin County Public Library, and several classic genre bibliographies, this interactive database contains entries for all the major fiction genres, including romance, and allows readers to connect quickly to a wide variety of titles through different access points. The subject headings are especially useful and impressive. Similar to the electronic version of *What Do I Read Next?*, this source also provides links to other books the reader might enjoy.

Bontly, Susan W., and Sheridan, Carol J. *Enchanted Journeys Beyond the Imagination: An Annotated Bibliography of Fantasy, Futuristic, Supernatural, and Time Travel Romances.* 3 vols. Beavercreek, OH: Blue Diamond Publications, 1996-1997. Index.

Providing access to information on more than 1,100 alternative reality romances, this handy bibliography (in two volumes—1 and 2 are combined) is arranged by type of romance, then further divided by subtype, if applicable; within each section, works are listed alphabetically by author. Each entry includes bibliographic information, a very brief annotation, and the author's pseudonym(s), if applicable. Various appendixes and separate author and title indexes complete the volumes, and a separate master index for authors and titles aids access. This easy-to-use resource is useful as readers' advisory tools and for collection development information (even though many of the titles are already out of print). Coverage extends from the middle of this century, but most titles included were published in the 1980s and 1990s.

In addition to using the commercial sources available, there are a number of other methods for providing a reader with information and connecting him or her to the appropriate book. One simple and extremely effective way to accomplish this task is to place copies of reviews or dustcover blurbs inside the books. This provides the browser with pertinent information directly at the point of need so he or she can make a better informed decision then and there. After all, only rarely will a reader go to the trouble of looking up a review of a book that is basically going to be read for pleasure.

Another way to provide this sort of passive readers' advisory service is to set up displays featuring various types of romance fiction. Rather than displaying romance fiction in general, focus on one particular type (e.g., Sagas, Romantic Historicals, Basic Contemporaries, Regencies). In the first place, it is easier. In the second, it is less misleading to the public since there is a big difference between, for example, Victoria Holt's Gothics and Susan Johnson's erotic historical adventures.

A variation on the fiction display idea is to integrate both relevant non-fiction materials and romances within the display. For example, if the display features Medieval Historicals, include some books on castles; the history of the period; social, costume, and food customs; contemporary art and artists (tapestries, stained glass, etc.); travel guides to the area; or any other relevant materials that might interest the reader. The same idea works by including contemporary romances with displays featuring travel or "place" information, biographies, or materials about particular industries, businesses, or careers.

Readers can also be reached through bibliographic bookmarks or flyers providing genre-specific lists of authors and titles. These lists can be plain or annotated, but a well-annotated bibliography is by far a more helpful tool than a simple listing of authors and titles.

Another way to provide information to romance readers is to maintain files or binders of book reviews or annotations and have them available for public perusal. These can be arranged either by subgenre and cross-indexed according to author, title, and topic or by author and cross-indexed according to subgenre, title, and topic. Whatever the method, good cross-indexing is a necessity. The physical format for this resource can vary; however, it should be something that can be easily updated and added to. Both card files and binders work. (Some prefer binders because they can be browsed like a book.) However, if the library has the facilities (computer, appropriate software, scanner, etc.) and the staff time, a computer-based file, searchable by a variety of topics (genre, author, words in title, time period, place, etc.) is another option. Some libraries even have readers review books and make their reviews available for public use. (This is a job that might appeal to a romance reader's interest group.)

Readers can also be reached en masse by such means as a library romance review column published in the local paper, a romance review segment on a local radio or television program, or booktalk sessions centering on various romance subgenres. While these methods provide good advice to readers, they are also excellent promotional opportunities for the library, the collection, and the genre, and in the hands of an enthusiastic staff or readers' group, could yield rewarding and exciting results. Local author panels, Regency or Victorian teas, and genre workshops are only a few of the activities that have been used successfully in libraries across the country, and the possibilities are endless. Many romance writers are willing to participate in library programs or present workshops on the genre; and your local chapter of the Romance Writers of America and RWA's Library Liaison are excellent resources. Contact RWA headquarters in Houston (see page 346) for current names and numbers.

SELECTED ISSUES

Although many of the issues surrounding romance fiction are purely theoretical or philosophical and are the subject of scholarly debate, several also have practical implications, particularly for the library and the readers' advisory staff. One that often comes up in discussions about romance readers' advisory service is the way in which violence and sex are handled in today's romances. Because these aspects vary so widely and because what is acceptable to one reader may not be acceptable to another, providing guidance for readers in this area is usually helpful. (The account of the irate patron who slammed *Sweet Savage Love* down on the reference desk exclaiming, "This isn't at all like Barbara Cartland!" is legendary.)

The category or series romances are the easiest to deal with in this respect because the sensuality levels, as well as other characteristics of the various lines, are clearly specified. A short list describing the various series and posted near the collection is a help to readers and fairly easy to do. (Note: Most of the series publishing houses will send tip sheets upon request. See chapter 21, "Publishers" for addresses and pages 63-65 for examples.)

Non-category or single title romances, however, present a different problem. Although most single titles are fairly sensual, the treatment and levels of explicitness vary widely—as do plot patterns, the handling of violence and social issues, and most other elements—and unless one knows the styles of particular writers, it is not always easy to determine how sexually graphic a book really is. However, since many writers often handle sexuality in a similar manner from book to book, lists of authors arranged by sensuality level and either posted or placed in binders near the romance collection can be helpful. The books could also be labeled symbolically with hearts, flowers, rising steam, fireworks, etc. However, this demands intimate knowledge of the book's contents by the "labeler" and is labor intensive.

Perhaps the most important issue related to advising the romance reader is one that is key to good readers' advisory service in general—librarian attitude. Closely linked to censorship, which is addressed in chapter 4 on "Building the Collection," this issue has been the subject of several articles, including Mary K. Chelton's groundbreaking "Unrestricted Body Parts and Predictable Bliss: The Audience Appeal of Formula Romances" (*Library Journal*, July 1991, 44-49) and, more recently, "Exploring the World of Romance Novels" by Cathie Linz, Ann Bouricius, and Carole Byrnes (*Public Libraries*, May/June 1995, 144-151) and "The Librarian as Effete Snob: Why Romance?" by Shelley Mosley, John Charles, and Julie Havir, (*Wilson Library Bulletin*, May 1995, 24–25+). The fact that this last article received the Romance Writers of America's 1995 Veritas Award for the best article positively representing the romance genre indicates the importance of the issue and pervasiveness of the problem.

The "problem," of course, is the condescending attitude toward romance fiction on the part of some librarians and the effect of this attitude on the readers. Disparagement of the popular fiction genres in general and romance in particular is a time-honored tradition in many library circles, and although science fiction and mysteries have gained an aura of acceptability over the years, it is still considered permissible, even a professional duty by some, to denigrate the romance. The historical roots of this practice are many and deep, and the current attitude is, in part, a holdover from the time when all fiction was considered suspect and beneath the regard of any person of intelligence. Add to that the vaguely puritanical idea that anything enjoyable is bad, the elitist view that anything popular is substandard, and the perceived superiority of logic and reason over emotion. Overlay it all with a bit of the hopeless pessimism of existentialism, and it's easy to see how attitudes toward romance—optimistic, highly popular, feeling-based, and relationship-oriented—have ended up where they have. It's also easy to see how librarians, teachers, and others charged with the educational and cultural enlightenment of society developed their bias. Nevertheless, tradition is no reason to continue bad practice, and as appealing and noble as it may seem to set one's self up as an arbiter of good taste by criticizing the reading preferences of the masses, it is a luxury in which no librarian can indulge and remain true to the service ethic of the profession. Our job as librarians is to help readers find the books they want, not the books we think they should have. Whether we realize it or not, our attitude toward both the reader and the literature makes a difference.

Although all three articles mentioned above should be required reading for anyone responsible for romance readers' advisory service, "The Librarian as Effete Snob: Why Romance?"—short, direct, succinct, and practical—is the place to start.

Finally, here are a few things to think about:

- You don't have to like romance to advise readers (although it helps); however, you do have to know and understand it and be able to represent it fairly. If you truly dislike the genre and can't keep your feelings from showing, you'd be better off not advising readers about romance. Stick to a genre you like, and let someone else take care of romance advising.

- Not all romances are equal; there are good romances and there are those that are not-so-good. It is all right to distinguish among them and make recommendations to readers based on quality. It is not productive, however, to criticize a romance for being a romance, e.g, for having a happy ending, a focus on the relationship between the two protagonists, or a belief in the power of love. That would be the same as criticizing a mystery for solving the crime.

- Romance fiction, like all genre fiction, is generally read for pleasure and relaxation; it is a recreational activity (much the same as going to the movies, listening to music, working a puzzle, or watching football) and should be viewed as one. Reading a romance novel is as legitimate a recreational choice as any other.

- Your attitude is important and will affect readers more than you realize. While it is hard to believe that any librarian would deliberately discourage anyone from reading or make them feel that their choice of material was less than acceptable, a thoughtless remark, a raised eyebrow, or a dismissive gesture can have the same effect.

Effective readers' advisory service, then, is based on three things: knowing the literature, knowing the reader, and putting them in contact with each other. How this is most effectively accomplished is up to the individual librarian and is largely dependent upon the library, its staff, and its clientele. But whatever the situation, a librarian who reads, who cares, and who makes the effort will be amply rewarded in terms of satisfied readers.

The Pattern for Romance

Series/Lines	General Setting						Sexual Scale			Special Focus or Style							
(by number of words)	Anywhere/ Contemporary	North American Contemporary	Undesignated Past	Regency England, usually 1811-1820	Prior to 1900, often 1100-1910	Future	Innocent/ Sweet	Sensual (Subtle to Steamy)	Explicit	Romantic Suspense	Gothic	Regency	Multicultural	Inspirational	Time Travel	Fantasy/ Paranormal	Futuristic/ Science Fiction
Avalon Romance		●					●										
Avalon Career Romance		●					●										
Avalon Mystery Romance		●					●			●							
Avon Regency				●			●					●					
Bantam Loveswept	●							●									
Barbour Heartsong	●													●			
Fawcett Crest Regency				●								●					
Harlequin Love and Laughter	●							●									
Harlequin Presents	●							●									
Harlequin Romance	●						●										
Harlequin Temptation		●							●								
Odyssey Books	●							●					●				
Signet Regency				●			●					●					
Silhouette Desire	●								●								
Silhouette Romance	●						●										
Silhouette Yours Truly	●							●									
Harlequin American		●						●									
Harlequin Intrigue	●							●		●							
Indigo Love Stories (Genesis)					●								●				
Silhouette Intimate Moments	●							●									
Silhouette Shadows	●						●	●									
Silhouette Special Edition	●						●	●									
Steeple Hill Love Inspired	●						●							●			

Fewer Than 60,000 Words

60,000 to 85,000 Words

The Pattern for Romance

Series/Lines (by number of words)	General Setting — Anywhere (Contemporary)	North American Contemporary	Undesignated Past	Regency England usually 1811-1820	Prior to 1900, Often 1100-1910	Future	Sexual Scale — Innocent/Sweet	Sensual (Subtle to Steamy)	Explicit	Special Focus or Style — Romantic Suspense	Gothic	Regency	Multicultural	Inspirational	Time Travel	Fantasy/Paranormal	Futuristic/Science Fiction
Avon	●							●									
Harlequin Historical			●					●									
Harlequin Mira	●							●									
Harlequin SuperRomance	●							●									
Jove Haunting Hearts	●				●			●							●	●	
Jove Time Passages	●				●			●							●		
Leisure			● ●					●								●	
Love Spell			●			●		●					●			●	●
Pinnacle Arabesque	● ●							●					●				
Pocket Books	●		● ● ●					●									
Topaz Romance	●		●					●									
Zebra Lovegram	●							●									
Zebra Regency				●			●					●					

More Than 85,000 Words

Additional publishers/imprints of interest

Ballantine
Bantam
Berkley
Bethany (Inspirational)
Dell
Diamond
Fawcett
Harper
Island
Ivy
Jove
Lionhearted
Kensington
Naiad (lesbian)
Onyx
Palisades (Inspirational)
Pocket
Putnam
Red Sage (Erotica)
Scarlet
Severn House (primarily reprints)
Signet
St. Martin
Tyndale House (Inspirational)
Warner

The information provided above is not necessarily all-inclusive and is subject to rapid change.

Original grid created by Mary K. Chelton [In "Unrestricted Body Parts and Predictable Bliss: the Audience Appeal of Formula Romances." Library Journal 116 (July 1991): 44-49.]
Revised by Kristin Ramsdell 3/95, 3/96, 9/96, 1/98

Chapter 4

Building the Collection

Ideally, romance fiction collections should be handled in the same way as any other fiction collection—thoughtfully acquired, carefully catalogued, appropriately processed, attractively shelved, and systematically maintained. In practice, this is rarely the case. Romances tend to be haphazardly acquired (often through gifts), minimally catalogued and processed (if at all), randomly tossed onto revolving paperback racks, and weeded without thought of replacement when they fall apart. In some libraries, this is how all genre paperbacks are handled, and staffing limitations may preclude any other options. However, in other libraries, only romance is singled out for this "specialized" treatment, while mysteries and science fiction paperbacks receive the same attention as hardcover fiction. It goes without saying that all the genres should be handled in the same manner; not to do so instantly raises the issues of discrimination, sexism, and censorship—sins of which most librarians do not want to be guilty. It should be equally obvious that to provide the best service to romance readers, a useful, viable collection, appropriately developed and maintained, is essential.

Building a needs-based, reader-centered romance collection is not especially difficult, but it does take desire, commitment, creativity, and, upon occasion, a sense of adventure and a willingness to take risks. Like providing good readers' advisory service, good collection development is worth the effort, and the library that takes the time to do it well will be amply rewarded in terms of satisfied readers. The comments that follow are suggestions for achieving this goal.

COLLECTION BUILDING

Selection and Acquisition

Selection is key to the quality of any fiction collection, and it is doubly important to the popular genre collections. However, as alluded to above, it is often ignored or, at best, given only minimal attention. Perhaps this is not surprising given the time constraints on librarians and the tendency to view the genres as trivial literature. This situation is unfortunate because building any popular fiction collection is not simple and creating a good romance collection is definitely more time consuming than it would seem. In the first place, the sheer volume of new titles alone—currently more than 150 each month—makes it difficult to choose intelligently, and it goes without saying that these numbers effectively preclude purchasing everything in all but the most comprehensive of collections (but not impossible in some of the less prolific subgenres). In addition, even though romances are rapidly increasing their hardcover presence, most are still published in paperback, a format that remains subject to substandard treatment in a number of libraries and by some review sources. Finally, as with advisors of readers, selectors who understand and appreciate the romance genre are crucial, and equally hard to come by. Note: Since the functions of choosing a book for the collection and recommending one to a reader have much in common and require a similar expertise, many of the issues relevant to collection development have already been discussed in chapter 3, "Advising the Reader," and are not repeated here.

This being said, how do you select books for a romance collection? In addition to reading romances yourself, becoming familiar with the genre, and enlisting the aid of knowledgeable readers, colleagues in other libraries, and staff members (all ideas discussed in chapter 3), consider the following:

If you oversee the selection process, but do not actively select materials

1.   Choose someone who likes, appreciates, and understands the genre to select romances or, failing that, a person who, at the very least, doesn't actively dislike the genre and is willing to learn about it;

2.   Provide the selector with appropriate review materials, including print and online resources;

3.   Consider relaxing the traditional "no purchase without a favorable review" requirement for the genre because most romances are not reviewed in traditional library sources and reliable reviews are still difficult to find. Rely, instead, on the judgment of your selector;

4.   Provide the selector with adequate time to do the job properly;

5.   Give the selector the necessary authority to do the job properly. If you are also a romance reader, you may want to make suggestions, but the ultimate decisions should belong to the selector;

6.   Provide a separate and adequate budget for romance materials, including individual purchases, series subscriptions, review sources, online costs, and miscellaneous book processing expenses; and

7. If you really want to endear yourself to the selector, provide time and funding for the selector to attend a conference or workshop related to the genre.

If you are responsible for selecting romances

1. Become familiar yourself with the romance genre and its various sub-genres by

    • reading books and articles about the genre. (Reading this book is a good first step);
    • reading some titles in each subgenre;
    • taking a look at "The Pattern for Romance" at the end of chapter 3; and
    • developing a network of people who like and understand the genre. (Consider subscribing to RRA-L or joining some other list or chat group.)

2. Become familiar yourself with the romance-reading tastes of your library's clientele by

    • checking circulation statistics if your romances are catalogued, or talking to those who staff the circulation desk if they aren't;
    • talking with readers; and
    • observing the romance collection and how it is used.

3. Become familiar with the romance-reading habits of the community surrounding your library and learn what is popular by

    • checking the paperback racks in local supermarkets and drug stores;
    • checking local newspapers for lists of local bestsellers; and
    • developing a relationship with the romance selector at your local book store.

4. Once reader preferences have been established, consider carrying a variety of romance types and titles within these types, monitoring them closely to see what is popular and what isn't. Also consider trying a few good "out of scope" titles periodically to see if tastes have changed, then adjust your selection accordingly.

5. Carry paperbacks as well as hardcovers and series romance lines as well as single titles. (The vast majority of romances are still published in paperback, and about half of those are series lines.) If you don't carry the full range, your collection will be missing some of the best of the genre.

6. Regularly consult appropriate review materials, including both print and online resources. (See section on reviews below.) Because romances have a very short shelf life (series, for example, are often available for only four to six weeks and are rarely backlisted), keeping up with the literature is important.

7. Develop a plan for systematic acquisition of romances, including budgeting for both hardcover and paperback purchases and regular subscriptions to selected romance series.

Reviews

While romance fiction is still rarely reviewed in many major review sources (e.g., *New York Times Book Review*, *Kirkus Reviews*), several important publications have begun to pay more attention to the genre. For example, *Library Journal* has a quarterly column devoted exclusively to romance reviews, *USA Today* is reviewing romances more often, *Publishers Weekly* is making an attempt to use people who understand the genre as romance reviewers and *Booklist* is beginning to include some romances in its reviews. In addition, several newspapers around the country have added romance review columns on a regular basis. (Check your local paper, and if it doesn't include romance reviews, ask the review editor to consider it.) However, despite these advances, the majority of romance reviews still appear in genre-specific review sources, some of which are mentioned in chapter 16 "Periodicals and Review Sources," of this guide (e.g., *Romantic Times*, *Affaire de Coeur*, *Rendezvous*, *The Romance Reader*). While many of these sources are overly positive, they do review a large percentage of the titles published each month and are helpful in determining not only what is available but also what trends are developing for the future. For these reasons alone, they are well worth the price of a subscription.

Selected Issues

One major concern for romance selectors is the issue of gifts and donations. Ideally, romances, both hardcover and paperback, should be purchased as part of a regular collection development plan, complete with budget allocation, systematic purchasing plan, regular buying trips, and monthly series subscriptions. But this is not always the case. In many libraries, gifts and donations make up much of the collection, and in some libraries, the romance collection is acquired exclusively in this way. On the surface this cheap and easy method of acquisition may sound appealing; nevertheless, allowing your collection to be determined by readers' cast-offs has little to recommend it. This is especially true of the romance genre, because romance readers are notorious for retaining their favorites, or "keepers," and discarding the ones they don't like, thereby ensuring a library collection filled with losers. However, this is not to say that gifts don't have a place in the romance collection. They do—but as a supplement to, not a substitute for, the regularly selected purchases.

Another issue that often plagues romance selection and acquisition is the relatively short shelf life of many of the titles. Series are notorious for this, often available for a mere month and then disappearing forever. Single title paperback romances fare a little better, but older titles can still be hard to find, especially if they sold better than expected and the publisher was unprepared to make additional print runs. What this means is that titles need to be chosen and purchased quickly—even before reviews are available—or they often can't be gotten at all. In the case of series, the best solution is to have ongoing subscriptions. This also alleviates the problem of going to the vendor or bookstore each month to pick up the newest series titles, only to find that others were there ahead of you and the books that you wanted are gone. Hardcover romances are available for a much longer period of time and can be treated in the same way as general fiction.

A related issue is that of format. The vast majority of romances (more than 97 percent in 1996) are still published only in paperback,[1] and despite an improvement in the quality of paperback bindings, a bias against the format still exists. Because paperbacks are seen as cheap and substandard (despite the high prices attached to many trade paperbacks and the fact that some librarians swear that they last at least as long as some hardcovers), a bias also exists against the content of paperbacks. Paperbacks are still viewed by many librarians as cheap and trivial and are treated accordingly. The effect of this on the romance genre is unfortunate. It is, however, a problem that can be remedied by an enlightened selector.

Another potential format issue that is emerging concerns romance on tape, both video and audio. So far this trend is not a big problem for most libraries, simply because currently, few romances are available in this form. Nevertheless, the trend is moving in this direction, and romances in non-print formats of all kinds may well become an issue in a few years. It is something to be aware of and to consider in planning for the future.

Finally, there is the issue of censorship—not the overt kind in which people march into the library and demand that a certain book be taken off the shelves, but a less obvious censorship—that of selection. By its very nature, all selection is a form of censorship. Each day librarians choose which materials will be in their collections and which won't, in effect "censoring" those that are excluded. Of course, choices must be made. No library can collect everything, and it is understandable that librarians want only the best and most appropriate materials in the collection. However, "the best" is a highly subjective concept, and the individual taste and attitude of the selecting librarian can have an enormous impact on the collection, inadvertently skewing it to reflect the librarian's personal bias rather than patron demand. Most would agree that this is indefensible both professionally and fiscally. (See the related discussion of librarian attitude in chapter 3, "Advising the Reader.") Mosley, Charles, and Havir assert that "As librarians, our job is not to judge cultural relativity, but to provide a service relative to our culture."[2] And that service includes providing a collection that reflects the informational needs and reading interests of the library's clientele. If those needs and interests include romance fiction, it should be provided.

Obviously, no responsible librarian deliberately makes selections solely on the basis of personal choice, and no conscientious librarian purposely excludes materials requested or needed by the clientele. Nevertheless, there are still libraries that, regardless of user demand, do not collect subjects, formats, or genres that they consider to be "substandard," and that often includes romance fiction. No library wants to be accused of prejudicial behavior. After all, freedom of information is an integral part of the professional code. However, when a library gives a genre short shrift, despite strong consumer demand, it skirts the edge of censorship. If a library elects to exclude or treat as inferior only the romance genre, one largely written and read by women, it opens itself up to accusations of sexism.

COLLECTION CONTROL AND DISPLAY

Cataloging

Although more libraries are beginning to fully catalog their paperback romances (hardcovers are routinely cataloged in most cases), the vast majority still do not, opting instead to place romances into their collections with minimal, if any, cataloging. Cost, convenience, time, value and perception are all factors in this decision, and the circumstances and reasons vary from library to library. Nevertheless, despite the fact that many libraries have legitimate reasons for not cataloging paperback romances, there are a number of equally compelling reasons for doing so. In "Exploring the World of Romance Novels" (*Public Libraries*, May/June 1995, 144-151), Cathie Linz, Ann Bouricius, and Carole Byrnes provide an excellent discussion of the subject and list several logical, well-thought-out reasons for cataloging romances. Each is important; however, two stand out as especially critical—first, improved access to the collection (and with it improved circulation), and second, the positive implications for collection development and management.

Access to a collection is key to its usability, and without proper cataloging, neither reader nor librarian will know what materials are on hand. Even if romances are not fully cataloged, their mere presence in the catalog, accessible for searching by author and title (and series and subject, if possible), is a tremendous service to readers. More and more often, romance readers are requesting books by author and title, and while they may browse the shelves looking for interesting titles, if they are looking for a particular book, without its being cataloged, they won't know if the library owns it, and they will find it only by luck. In addition, a side benefit of cataloging romances is an increase in circulation statistics, locally as well as through interlibrary loan.

Cataloging romances also makes selection and collection maintenance easier and more accurate. Many circulation systems have features that allow statistics to be gathered and reported in a variety of ways. Knowing which titles, and types of romance circulate best is invaluable to the selector when it comes to determining what to purchase, replace, or weed out in the collection. These statistics are also useful when it comes to budget allocation, and may even surprise some skeptics into re-evaluating their opinion of the importance of the genre.

Processing, Displaying, and Shelving

How romances are processed, displayed, and shelved depends upon the individual practices of each library or system and that library's specific physical arrangement. Nevertheless, there are a few common basics for libraries to consider.

- Treat all genres alike. If Mysteries and Science Fiction are shelved, processed, or promoted in some unique way, then Romance, Westerns, and other genres should receive the same treatment.
- Consider separate genre sections, including a separate romance section. Fiction readers typically read by genre, and they appreciate having their particular specialties separated out. Romance readers are no exception. This separation allows readers to browse in a location where books that interest them are concentrated, allowing serendipity full reign. Also, consider shelving books in alphabetical order by author or by series. As mentioned earlier, most readers choose books either by author or by series.

Using this information to create a user-friendly shelving arrangement benefits both users and librarians.

- Consider special processing. Placing some kind of identifying label on romances (and other genre fiction) often is helpful to readers. These labels can consist of anything from a simple genre tag to more sophisticated indications of sensuality, and violence levels, or other characteristics that are important to a particular group of readers.

- Consider special promotions or advertising. In *Readers' Advisory Service in the Public Library*, Saricks and Brown provide an excellent discussion of various ways to promote genre fiction.[3] The segments on exhibits, bookmarks, and book lists are especially important for those interested in promoting romance. For example, the idea of a Good Books You May Have Missed display is excellent and could easily be transformed into a Good Romances You May Have Missed exhibit.

4

COLLECTION MAINTENANCE

The counterpart to selection, deselection—or weeding the collection—is an often neglected part of the romance collection development process. The reason is that weeding is usually done by attrition and not by design (i.e., when the book falls apart, it is discarded). The problem with this method is that popular books circulate, disintegrate, and are weeded out while unpopular books remain pristine and on the shelves. The obvious solution to this problem is to replace books that circulate and eventually remove those that don't. Unfortunately, because romance titles often go out of print within a month or two (especially the series romances), replacing them is difficult. Suggestions for replacing popular books include:

- Contact the publisher or your vendor and try to reorder. At the very least, it will send the message that there is a continuing demand for particular books.

- Check with large-print publishers. Often popular authors (including romance writers) are available from them.

- Check with used book stores. This is not the best solution, but at times it is the only way to replenish the collection and meet reader demands.

- Keep a list of popular authors and titles you are looking for. That way if they ever come back into print, you will know which ones to order. This is especially important now because publishers are beginning to see the value of keeping popular authors' backlists in print, and some titles you are looking for might be available in the future.

- Prevent the problem in the first place by buying multiple copies of popular writers while they are still available.

As mentioned above, weeding based on circulation (if it circulates, keep it; if it sits on the shelf, toss it) is common; it is also practical and logical because it is specific to your particular clientele. The hard part is getting rid of books that aren't read. Nevertheless, a useful, viable collection is not filled with dead wood, and the books that don't circulate must be removed. Circulation statistics should help you determine which books should be weeded.

BASIC RESOURCES

Basic collection development information is relatively easy to come by and is provided by several professional books on the topic. An LC subject search under Acquisitions or Collection Development should yield several choices; and while a number of these tend toward the theoretical or may be more comprehensive than necessary, they are a place to begin. However, information specific to romance fiction collection development is a little less prevalent, and most of the information available is in the form of articles rather than books. Johanna Tuñon's "A Fine Romance: How to Select Romances For Your Collection" (*Wilson Library Bulletin,* May 1995, 31-34) is definitely worth reading, and selected sections of "Exploring the World of Romance Novels" by Cathie Linz, Ann Bouricius, and Carole Byrnes (*Public Libraries*, May/June 1995, 144-151) and Mary K. Chelton's "Unrestricted Body Parts and Predictable Bliss: The Audience Appeal of Formula Romances" (*Library Journal*, July 1991, 44-49) will provide useful information on this, as well as other topics. You may also wish to consult the Sample Core Collection in Appendix 1 of this book.

NOTES

1. Shirley Hailstock, "Romstat: 1996 Romance Statistics," *Romance Writers' Report* 17 (June 1997): 12-15.

2. Shelley Mosley, John Charles, and Julie Havir, "The Librarian as Effete Snob: Why Romance?" *Wilson Library Bulletin* (May 1995): 24–25+.

3. Joyce G. Saricks and Nancy Brown, *Readers' Advisory Service in the Public Library,* 2nd ed. (Chicago: American Library Association, 1997), 106-127.

Part 2

The Literature

Chapter 5

Contemporary Romance

"The life of every woman is a romance!"
Mme. de Genlis

DEFINITION

The largest and possibly the most inclusive of all romance subgenres, the Contemporary Romance, is what most people have in mind when they refer to the generic romance novel. Essentially love stories with contemporary settings, these novels usually focus on the attempts of a woman to find success and happiness both professionally and romantically. Usually by the end of the book, she has attained both. A committed, permanent, monogamous relationship, one that usually includes marriage and often a family, is still the ultimate goal for this type of romance. However, many recent heroines, in line with current social trends, do not retire to hearth and home but continue in their careers, not only after marriage, but after childbirth as well. Novels written prior to 1970 do not feature this trend, and the heroine of those written during the early part of this century is typically not employed. Rather, these early heroines are likely doing volunteer work, helping their families at home, or pursuing some other properly genteel pastime.

It is worth noting that the term "contemporary," as it is used in this book, is not merely a synonym for "modern day." Although by far the majority of contemporary romances read today are both contemporary and modern-day, many novels of this classification written well before World War II are still in print. These novels, while now exhibiting a historical flavor, were actually written as contemporary love stories and had as their purpose the telling of modern-day love relationships, relevant to the times. Many works by prototypical authors such as Grace Livingston Hill and Faith Baldwin are examples of this. Eventually these works (if they remain in print) will be classified largely as Historicals as are the works by earlier writers of Contemporary Romances such as Jane Austen and Samuel Richardson.

43

It is interesting to consider that the Contemporary Romances of today that survive may well become the Historicals of the future. Of course, romances written as Historicals and romances that endure to become historical are actually two different types, varying both in purpose and the amount of background information supplied to the reader. Most Contemporaries will not survive to become Historicals. They will merely become dated and irrelevant and will eventually go out of print. Only those with exceptionally well-drawn, believable characters involved in basic human conflicts have even a chance for survival.

The settings used in Contemporary Romances are diverse and can vary widely. Some typical settings include small town domestic, social, or local business situations; urban business, artistic, or community organizational settings (both upscale and inner city); and romantic foreign or domestic vacation or job situations (e.g., Western cattle ranch, mountain or coastal retreat, cruise ship, ski resort, Mediterranean or Caribbean Island).

The plots are also varied, dependent to a large extent upon the physical settings and occupations of the main characters; however, the basic boy-meets-girl, boy-misunderstands-and-therefore-loses-girl, boy-gets-girl structure (or its reverse) tends to remain more or less the same. In a typical plot, the heroine (either young and innocent or, more recently, older, independent, and a bit more experienced—but always attractive "in her own way") sets off to seek her fortune. She soon encounters the hero (traditionally, but not always, handsome, self-assured—even arrogant—and successful or rich), to whom she takes an instant dislike; however, she is usually "strangely attracted" to him and can't understand why. Through a convenient set of circumstances, they are thrown together (e.g., they share a common goal or interest, they must work together, they are staying in the same resort, they are stranded together in the same jungle). Eventually, they fall in love. Inevitably, conflicts arise, and the lovers spend a large portion of the book trying to work things out. The conflict can be external (e.g., other people or situations keep the protagonists apart) or internal (e.g., the feelings, values, and past histories of the hero and heroine cause problems), and misunderstandings, both real and imagined, play a large part in keeping the pair at odds. However, by the end of the story, all differences are resolved, the hero and heroine reconcile, and their happy future is generally assured. Although the main plot in all romances is the love story line dealing with the protagonists, subplots of various kinds appear in many of the longer romance works. These subplots are rarely as well developed as is the main story line, but they do add interest and depth to the story as a whole.

While this basic romance plot pattern is a constant (just as the pattern for the Mystery genre will always revolve around the sleuth, the crime, and the solution), the past few years have seen major developments in the way in which it is applied. Situations and issues that were once seen as either taboo or too serious for romance (e.g., alcoholism, abuse, illness, homosexuality, prostitution, and impotence) are now not uncommon, and characters who were considered unacceptable for the genre (e.g., the ex-convict hero or the unwed mother heroine) are appearing. This trend toward more contemporary relevance, as well as more complex plotting and realistic characters, may be one reason that the lines between Romance and more mainstream Women's Fiction are beginning to blur. The boundaries between the two are increasingly fluid and, while this makes it more difficult to neatly categorize the genres, it also indicates a maturing of the genre and is not at all a bad thing.

Characters in Contemporaries are as varied as the settings and the plots. Nevertheless, most protagonists have several characteristics in common, whatever the romance style. Key among these are self-motivation, resilience, honesty, and above all, a highly developed sense of honor. The protagonists' actions may be suspect, but they are always performed for the "right" reasons—reasons that usually are selfless and have to do with helping or saving others (e.g., the hero kills his father because he was molesting his sister, the heroine lies about her job qualifications so she can support her younger siblings). Approval of these characters is critical for reader identification, and while they have imperfections, they must be able to generate enough respect and admiration (along with likability, if possible) for the reader to care.

In addition, the Contemporary heroine often displays a high degree of independence, intelligence, initiative, and determination, relying more on herself to solve her problems than on the hero. Usually, the more daring heroines are found in the more sensual romances, and the less adventuresome women appear in romances of the Innocent (or Sweet) variety; however, this is not a hard and fast rule, and there are numerous exceptions. Heroines are also no longer necessarily pure and virginal. Changing societal patterns have paved the way for an older, more sexually experienced heroine—often one who has been widowed or divorced, but more recently, one who has simply had an earlier serious relationship that didn't work out (usually through no fault of her own). Of course, the innocent heroine still exists and is, in fact, practically mandatory in most traditional Regencies and Inspirationals and in the Innocent category lines. However, in recent years, the trend in both publishing and in reader demand has been toward heroines of the more modern variety.

Like heroines, heroes in Contemporaries come in all shapes and sizes. Often they are strong, take-charge men, handsome, and possibly wealthy, who have already achieved success in their business or professional fields. Recently, however, another breed of hero, one with a softer, more sensitive side, has begun to emerge, and the classic, dominant, alpha-male type is no longer the only hero choice available. Although "pure" heroes of both types exist, there has been a trend toward the blending of these characteristics, and in reality, the most successful heroes combine elements of both. However, whatever their type, heroes typically appear to be aloof, mysterious, and unwilling to become emotionally involved with anyone. Nevertheless, they are attracted to the heroine "in spite of themselves," and eventually they must come to terms with the reasons for their feelings. (Typically, they have been hurt by a woman at some time in the past and assume that "women are all alike." Of course, the insightful, perceptive, caring heroine changes all that.)

Finally, in keeping with the recent changes in issues and topics dealt with in today's romances, a new type of protagonist has surfaced—the wounded hero or heroine. These characters have suffered severely in the past and need the healing touch of love to become whole. These characters have not suffered a mere jilting or similar romantic heartbreak; their problems are usually much deeper and darker. Physical, sexual, or emotional abuse; mental illness; the murder of one's family; the total destruction of a way of life; the ravages of war; or something equally devastating is often at their core.

Supporting characters also appear in these stories, and in the longer romances they are often described in a fair amount of detail. (The best friend, the other woman, the other man, and the villain are examples of typical supporting characters.) Nevertheless, in these stories the emphasis is still on the hero and heroine, and rarely are the supporting characters developed more than is necessary to provide background for the main story line. The longer and more complex the story, the more subplots there are and the greater the chance for more thorough development of the minor characters. However, in most cases, these secondary characters are not as fully delineated as the protagonists.

Wide-ranging and occasionally murky, the Contemporary Romance subgenre essentially consists of two broad, primary groups—the Basic Contemporary Romance and the Category Romance. These are supplemented by several other separate, but closely related and often overlapping, fiction types (e.g., Soap Opera and, for lack of a better term, Women's Romantic Fiction, each of which can further be blended or broken down into a number of diverse subsets, which include such categories as Glitz and Glamour, Contemporary Americana, and Medical Romance).

Basic Contemporary Romance

The most enduring and encompassing of all the Contemporary Romance subgenres, the Basic Contemporary Romance, is simply a non-formula love story with a contemporary setting. This subset includes within it most contemporary romances that are not subsumed within the other contemporary groups, and most are single title romances, an industry term used to distinguish them from the various category romances and indicate the way in which they are published. Unbound by certain restraints inherent in the other types, especially the Category Romance, the Basic Contemporary Romance uses a wide variety of characters and settings, occasionally employing plot patterns that are both unconventional and unpredictable.

The way in which sex is handled also varies greatly in these stories, ranging from the innocent to the erotic, and there are even some contemporary romances that display sweet/savage characteristics (e.g., certain titles by Rosemary Rogers). As might be expected, older novels, especially those written prior to the 1970s, are generally of the more innocent variety, while many of those written within the past few decades can contain much more sexually explicit material. Recently, there has been an increasing interest in erotica that runs across all romance subgenres, including some of the category lines, and publishers focusing on erotic romance have begun to emerge (e.g., Red Sage Publishing, which specializes in "sensuous, bold, spicy, untamed, hot, and sometimes politically incorrect" romances, both contemporary and historical). These more sensual contributions to the subgenre enjoyed a surge in popularity during the mid 1980s, and the entire Basic Contemporary Romance subgenre is currently attracting a fair amount of attention. This category is exemplified by the works of writers such as Nora Roberts, Barbara Freethy, Susan Elizabeth Phillips, and Janet Dailey. However, popularity is not limited to just the current materials within the subgenre. Many best-selling authors of past decades are either still in print or have been reprinted and are still read occasionally by today's romance readers. Among these authors are Grace Livingston Hill, Faith Baldwin, and Elizabeth Cadell.

Category Romance

The Category Romance, typified by the series romance lines published by Harlequin and Silhouette, is essentially a love story written to a particular pattern. These patterns are determined by each publisher and are series-specific. Most series follow a variation of the boy-meets-girl, boy-loses-girl, boy-gets-girl plot pattern, with the specific requirements of each series being spelled out in a tip sheet available from the publisher. A tip sheet includes such guidelines as the overall focus of the line, the degree of sensuality allowed, and the acceptable word length. (An example of a tip sheet is included in the section on Category Romance.) While in recent years a number of category authors such as Nora Roberts, Barbara Samuel, and Barbara McMahon have become known in their own right and are sought out by readers, most series are still marketed on the basis of their series appeal, regardless of author.

An increased degree of flexibility is creeping into these lines, and if some of the titles were published individually, they would be classified in the Basic Contemporary Romance subgroup. But despite such variations in style, the books within a specific series basically follow the same guidelines; the readers know, more or less, just what they are getting before they buy (or check out) the book.

Category Romances can be divided into three basic types—the Innocent (or Sweet), the Sensual, and the Young Adult (YA). The Innocent Category Romance, the most chaste of the categories, is exemplified by a warm emotional tone; engaging, charismatic characters; no explicit sex; and a fixed length of 50,000–60,000 words. The original Harlequin and Silhouette lines are series of this type. The Sensual Category Romance—typified by series such as Silhouette Desire, Harlequin American Romance, and Bantam Loveswept—comes in several lengths (the shorter ones are similar in length to the Innocents, the longer ones can contain up to 85,000 words); features a wide selection of themes, characters, and treatments; and is much more sensual, containing varying amounts of explicit sex, depending upon the line. The Young Adult Category Romance is shorter in length, but similar in type to the Innocent Category. Its characters are younger—usually in high school or, occasionally, college—and most of them weave typical adolescent problems into the romance plotline. (The Young Adult romance is outside the scope of this book and is mentioned here only to indicate the range of the Category Romance.)

5

Although most Category Romances are individual stories, there has been a recent move to include trilogies and other short series involving the same characters, theme, or place. Stories focusing on the romances of family members, especially sisters or brothers, are especially popular. A longer vehicle, and one that has proved to be quite popular, is the limited series. Such series consist of 12 books, one released each month and written by different authors. They are usually linked by setting and include some kind of running thread, often a mystery, that is eventually resolved in the final volume of the series. Crystal Creek and Montana Mavericks are examples.

Soap Opera

While not totally within the Romance genre, the Soap Opera, with links to the family Saga and closely related to the popular radio and television serials of the same name, is a complex, introspective type of romantic fiction that concentrates on the sins and sufferings of an individual, a family, or even a whole community. Although not actually adult versions of the "problem novel" (popular among young adults during the 1970s), these often slow-paced melodramas certainly contain their share of difficulties and are rife with divorce, unrequited love, illegitimacy, self-sacrifice, revenge, scandal, mental and physical illness, retribution, and misery and anguish in general. Understandably, the characters in Soap Operas spend a lot of time thinking about their problems and discussing them among themselves. It is this interaction among the characters and their various reactions to events and situations that serve as the action of the plot, and rarely do Soap Operas employ the rescue, chase, or deeds-of-great-valor scenes popular in other romance types. Because of their concentration on the vicissitudes of life, Soap Operas do not necessarily have happy endings (at least not for all the characters). Nevertheless, the reader is usually left with some feeling of hope for the future.

The family is another important element in this type of romance, and family loyalty and pride are often critical elements in the story line. In addition, the Soap Opera often features a central character (usually older, influential, and often powerful) around whom all the other characters' lives revolve. While this "tent-pole" character is usually not the protagonist, his or her decisions and opinions do have an important effect on the lives of the other characters, and without this individual, the complicated plotline of the Soap would completely disintegrate.

Because the line that divides the Soap Opera from some of the longer contemporary types of romance and other fiction is often blurred, many writers have produced books that seem to have a foot in more than one genre. Helen Van Slyke, Fern Michaels, Cynthia Freeman, and Danielle Steel are examples of writers who have written books that occasionally stray across the soapy border. Recently, the Soap Opera's appeal as a written form has declined, and while it is still quite popular in its television format, few pure books of this kind are currently being produced, although some of its sudsy elements are beginning to show up in other types of contemporary romance and fiction. However, there is still a readership for these books, and many are still either in print or are available in library collections.

Medical Romance

Essentially a Soap Opera with a medical setting, the Medical Romance, like its parent Soap Opera, is in decline. Once quite popular, especially in England where there is still some interest, these stories derived much of their drama and tension from the highly-charged atmosphere of a hospital setting. Focusing primarily on the personal and professional lives of the doctors, nurses, and other medical staff, these stories led their characters through a series of disasters, critical illnesses, drug overdoses, epidemics, delicate and dangerous surgeries, and a host of everyday emergency situations that provided ample opportunity for a wide variety of plotlines, both simple and complex, complete with conflict, passion, and romance. A more innocent version of this type is the Nurse Romance, similar to a contemporary category romance with a hospital setting. For a more complete discussion of the Medical Romance, refer to the first version of this book, *Happily Ever After* (Littleton CO: Libraries Unlimited, 1987).

Women's Romantic Fiction

Another group not totally within the confines of the Romance genre is Women's Romantic Fiction. Straddling the line between the larger Women's Fiction genre and Romance, these stories are generally longer, multi-layered books that feature a strong heroine, often with goals other than love and marriage, and yet contain an important romance element. Any number of plot patterns, characters, and locales are used, and while settings are most often contemporary, they can also be historical or Saga-like, spanning a number of years. In addition, writing style, tone, use of humor, and other technical aspects vary widely. In fact, this category is so flexible that it might simply be considered "Women's Fiction with a satisfactory romantic ending." Obviously, this is a most inclusive subgenre, and its boundaries are blurry, evolving, and subjective. In fact, works of this type often are classified by publishers as "Fiction," and both readers and writers may disagree over the correct designation for a particular title. Genreblending (the current trend whereby elements from one fiction genre or subgenre migrate into another) is apparently alive and well in this area, too. Writers who have written stories of this type are Sandra Bregman and Barbara Delinsky. A flashy, fast-paced, jet-set version of this type is often called Glitz and Glamour and is written by such luminaries as Jackie Collins, Judith Krantz, and Danielle Steel.

Contemporary Americana Romance

Another type of Romance that is becoming more important is the Contemporary Americana Romance. Its counterpart, the Period Americana Romance, is probably better known; nevertheless, a number of Contemporary Romances of all types have this particular emphasis and should be considered firmly within the broader Americana classification. Often set in the small town or rural American Midwest, these stories focus on the everyday lives of ordinary people and their "ordinary" problems (no foreign intrigue or Hollywood hype here). A number of limited series (e.g., Harlequin's Tyler series) are of this type.

As might be expected, there is a certain amount of crossover readership among the Contemporary Romance types. Those who enjoy the Sensual Category Contemporaries may also like Basic Contemporaries or Women's Romantic Fiction, readers of the older Medical Romances may also find Soap Operas appealing, and readers of Innocent Categories may find some early Basic Contemporaries interesting. In addition to crossover within the contemporary grouping, there is also some degree of crossover reading between the Contemporary and other romance subgenres. For example, because of their similarities, Soap Operas and Sagas may appeal to the same people, just as some of the Innocent Categories or early Basic Contemporaries may appeal to readers of Inspirational Romance or Traditional Regencies. Also, as might be expected, readers who enjoy longer, more complex Contemporary Romances or Women's Romantic Fiction may also enjoy reading Women's Fiction or literary fiction in general. Interestingly, there is less reader crossover between Contemporary and Historical Romances than one might expect. Readers, it seems, have definite preferences in this regard—they like either the present or the past, but usually not both, and while there are always those exceptional readers who enjoy all time periods, most choose to spend their reading time in one period.

APPEAL

The specific appeal of the Contemporary Romance is to our basic desire to see the present as we wish it were, not as it is. Just as some readers want to vicariously experience the novelty and excitement of the past without its attendant inconveniences, others want to experience a new, romantically enhanced present without the mundane details of real, everyday life. Most of us occasionally indulge in playing the game of "What if . . ." (e.g., What if I were an artist in New York? What if I were a cruise director? What if I were rich? What if I were vacationing in Europe and . . .?). A Contemporary Romance allows us to experience one author's version of the answer. The infinite variety of questions and answers accounts for this diversity within the subgenre.

Within the Contemporary subgenre, each type has its own particular appeal. The Category Romance offers consistency; the readers basically know what they are going to get before they open the book. On the other hand, the Basic Contemporary Romance provides more variety and, occasionally, the unexpected. The Soap Opera appeals to those who prefer a little scandal and anguish with their romance. Women's Romantic Fiction attracts those who enjoy a romance painted on a broader canvas with a slightly different brush. However, the overall appeal of the Contemporary Romance is a brief escape into a romantic version of the present.

ADVISING THE READER

While general readers' advisory information is provided in chapter 3, below are several points to consider specifically when advising Contemporary Romance readers.

- Consider suggesting other Contemporary subtypes in addition to the one the reader is currently reading. Innocent Categories might appeal to readers of some of the less racy Basic Contemporaries, those who like Women's Romantic Fiction might also enjoy Soap Operas or more complex Basic Contemporaries, and Glitz and Glamour fans might also enjoy Soap Operas or Women's Romantic Fiction.

- Readers who enjoy older Contemporary Romances, such as those by Grace Livingston Hill and Emilie Loring, may also like Inspirational Romances, and vice versa.

- Readers who like Soap Operas might also enjoy Sagas, and readers who enjoy Women's Fiction may like Women's Romantic Fiction as well. In addition, some readers of Innocent Category Romances may also enjoy Traditional Regencies or some of the less sexually explicit Historicals.

- Determine what kind of Contemporary Romance the reader prefers —innocent, sensual, erotic, complex, short, predictable, funny, dark, filled with social issues, etc. Keep in mind that lines and writers vary greatly—the original Harlequins are quite different from the more recent Silhouette Desires, and Jennifer Crusie is not Sharon Sala. If the reader prefers Innocent Categories, don't recommend *Peyton Place*. Likewise, don't suggest a short category romance to someone who wants a complex, intricately plotted story; try Women's Romantic Fiction or Basic Contemporaries instead. As always, common sense and a good knowledge of authors and types are your best allies in making successful recommendations.

- For the reader who is new to the Contemporary subgenre, recommend standard works by major authors in the field (e.g., Nora Roberts, Barbara Samuel, Sharon Elizabeth Phillips, Naomi Horton, Barbara Freethy, and Anne Stuart) and then branch out to others. That way, if the reader doesn't care for the book, it will be a judgment of the subgenre itself rather than the quality of the writing.

BRIEF HISTORY

When Samuel Richardson's epistolary tale *Pamela: or Virtue Rewarded* was published in England in 1740, it launched what was generally considered to be a new form of literature—the novel. It is interesting that this "first novel" was also a Contemporary Romance. To be sure, *Pamela*, as well as Richardson's other sentimental romances, had its roots in the past, especially in some of the long, fantastically exaggerated romances by earlier women writers such as Delarivière Manley, Aphra Behn, Madeleine de Scudéry, and Eliza Haywood, as well as in the introspective religious works of the previous century. However, it was the combination of the outward dramatic action with the inner emotional turmoil and reflection that made the novel something new and appealing.[1] In addition, the facts that the story's situation (young, impoverished girl goes to work in wealthy home, only to be pursued with dishonorable intent by the son of the family) was a familiar one to many members of the working class and that the heroine was spunky, determined, and non-aristocratic gave it an intense appeal for the newly rising, newly literate middle class. The book achieved tremendous popularity on both sides of the Atlantic, and although imported copies were available, Benjamin Franklin published it in the United States in 1744, only four years after it had first appeared in England.[2]

 5

The success of *Pamela* gave rise to a number of imitations, many of them copying not only the basic plot but the letter/diary format as well. Until the end of the century when the sentimental Gothics of Ann Radcliffe began to find favor with the reading public, the contemporary sentimental novel, or romance, reigned supreme. Among the most popular in the United States were *Charlotte Temple: A Tale of Truth* (1791) by Susanna Haswell Rowson and *The Coquette* (1797) by Mrs. Hannah Foster. Often considered the first American popular romantic novel (even though it was first published in England by a woman who moved to America soon after), *Charlotte Temple* (published in America in 1794) was a classic novel of seduction in which the heroine was seduced, impregnated, abandoned, and then left to die. Given the social mores of the time, Charlotte naturally had to pay for the sin of allowing herself to be seduced! Set in the United States and reputed to be based on fact (there is even a gravestone in New York with the name Charlotte Temple on it), this novel had immediate appeal for American readers; in all, more than 200 editions of *Charlotte* have been produced. Popular through the first few years of the nineteenth century, seduction stories shared the spotlight with the sentimental Gothics. Eventually, however, they gave way to a new wave of interest in Historical Romances that peaked in the 1820s, and today the seduction story is remembered largely as a curiosity of the late eighteenth and early nineteenth centuries.

About the same time, the influence of a group of women writers, the domestic sentimentalists, was beginning to be felt. For the next few decades, their works grew in popularity, and by the 1850s, much to the dismay and mystification of more serious contemporary writers such as Nathaniel Hawthorne and Herman Melville, these writers completely dominated the romantic fiction market. Although many of these authors used historical settings or Gothic conventions, particularly during the 1820s, most of these novels were Contemporary Romances, intent on depicting the domestic here-and-now and the ways in which various women dealt with it.

Truly novels of the times, these domestic romances reflected the prevailing wisdom that while men might excel in worldly and business affairs, women are stronger in the moral, cultural, and domestic realms. Therefore, women had the duty to "improve" people (often the men in their lives), promote the cultural aspects of life, and see to the smooth running of the home and domestic tranquility in general. Although the woman was definitely the ruling force within her domestic sphere, her place and influence was firmly within the home, and there was little for her to look forward to outside of marriage, home, and family. This attitude is reflected in most of these stories by the fact that the heroine, although she almost always overcomes numerous obstacles independently and becomes quite self-sufficient, is usually happily married by the end of the book.

Although a great number of women wrote contemporary domestic romances during this period, especially popular and prolific were E.D.E.N. Southworth, Mary Jane Holmes, Caroline Lee Hentz, and Elizabeth Oakes Smith. Some of the more popular books of this period are *The Lamplighter* (1854) by Susanna Maria Cummins, *Ruth Hall* (1855) by Fanny Fern (Sara Payson Willis), and *The Wide, Wide World* (1850) by Elizabeth Wetherell (Susan Warner).

Not surprisingly, domestic romances by English women writers were also popular in America during this period. One of the best known is *The Heir of Redclyffe* (1853) by Charlotte M. Yonge. Considered by some to be the book to which the beginnings of popular romantic fiction can be traced, according to Rachel Anderson this book differs from the "'didactic' novels of the times . . . [in] its combination of the important message [religious, in this case] with the author's own emotional involvement with her hero, her heroine, her theme, and her readers."[3] It is this increased emotional involvement that Anderson feels makes this the forerunner of today's romance novels. It also is interesting to note that *The Heir of Redclyffe* makes the point that love solves all problems, an underlying tenet of most romances today.

Following the Civil War, the works of the Domestic Sentimentalists continued to be popular, although romances of other types and in other formats were beginning to appear. Especially popular were the weekly story papers, which published serialized romance novels by many, now largely unremembered, writers. One of the most prolific and popular of these authors was Laura Jean Libbey. All of her more than 80 "working girl" novels, published from the mid-1880s to the mid-1920s, center around the plights of poor, virtuous girls forced to fend for themselves in the "wicked city." Eventually they are rescued from danger and drudgery by financially secure, upstanding heroes who whisk them off to futures of domestic wedded bliss. Unfortunately, although many of her serialized romances were reprinted in paperback as complete novels, few of Libbey's novels were hardbound. Her works are now dated and primarily of interest to students of popular culture, but a large number of them are listed in OCLC and are found in libraries scattered throughout the country.

Toward the end of the nineteenth century, Historical Romances became increasingly popular, and works by writers such as Mary Johnston and Amelia E. Barr were in vogue. Interest in Contemporary Romances, however, did not die out, and after the turn of the century, writers such as Grace Livingston Hill, Emilie Loring, Faith Baldwin, and Kathleen Norris continued the contemporary, domestic tradition.

Although the twentieth century has witnessed the rise in popularity of a number of romance types (e.g., the Historicals of the 1930s and 1940s, the Gothics of the 1960s, the Sensual Historical and Sweet/Savage romances of the 1970s), Contemporary Romances have never lost their appeal for vast number of readers. Throughout the century, no matter what the current literary rage, Contemporary Romances have maintained a quiet, yet devoted audience.

With the decline of the erotic Historicals in the late 1970s, Contemporary Romances became increasingly popular with the public in general. By the early 1980s, they were a dominant form. Exceptionally popular were Contemporary Category Romances, or stories written to conform to preset guidelines. Although romances of this type had been around for a number of years (Harlequin began publishing romances in 1949), it wasn't until the late 1970s that the market really exploded. Publishers, anxious to profit from the new surge of interest in romances, hurriedly launched new romance lines, and during the first few years of the 1980s, most major paperback publishers were trying either to break into the romance field or to increase their existing business within it. The market burgeoned with new romance series.

But many of these new romances were not the Innocent Category fare of earlier years. To be sure, romances of the Innocent variety were still available and were supported by a loyal readership, but public taste was changing. The earlier success of the more sensual Historicals had shown that readers wanted a little more spice in their romances, and writers and publishers were more than happy to oblige. Many of these new series not only included more explicit sex scenes but also often featured independent, older heroines with definite career goals beyond the more traditional ones of marriage and family. These romances were simply reflecting our changing society. With the median age of the population rising, more women entering the workforce at career levels, and sexual mores changing, these romances were merely attempting to do what Contemporary Romance novels have always done—romanticize the realities of everyday life.

5

Eventually, the excesses of the early 1980s resulted in a shakedown within the industry, and as Contemporaries came off their sales highs, competition was fierce, lines were cut back or discontinued, and consolidation became a growing trend with publishers. However, Contemporaries have rarely been unpopular for long, and despite a renewed interest in Sagas and Historicals, especially those with American settings, Contemporaries of all types continued to hold their own. Many even appeared on various bestseller lists.

Despite a few ups and downs, including the unfortunate demise of a promising new publishing house, Meteor, the Contemporary Romance continues to thrive into the 1990s, changing as necessary to meet the needs of an increasingly diverse and demanding readership. Change is rampant. New lines have been established, houses that never published Contemporaries before are testing the waters (e.g. Avon), a wide variety of relevant and sometimes controversial subjects are being addressed in the stories, and a number of established Contemporary writers are breaking with tradition and producing romances that cross boundaries to link genres in new and different ways. Currently, Contemporary Romance accounts for more than 50 percent of the titles published each year, and the trend shows no signs of diminishing. Considering this, and given the historical longevity of the type (*Pamela*, after all, was a contemporary romance!), it is safe to assume that the Contemporary Romance genre is here to stay. It may wax and wane in popularity with the current trends, but because it deals with the here and now, it will continue to appeal to the many readers who prefer their romances portrayed in present times.

BASIC CONTEMPORARY ROMANCE

The most inclusive of all contemporary romance types, the Basic Contemporary Romance, is essentially a non-category romance with a contemporary setting. Thirty years ago it would have simply been called a love story; today, however, because of the plethora of romances and their many variations, it is now considered a distinct, although somewhat encompassing, type.

Because of its all-inclusive character, the Basic Contemporary incorporates a wide variety of settings, plots, and characters. For example, the settings for Basic Contemporaries can vary from small town to big city, from the United States to all parts of the world, and from dingy tenement to posh estate; situations range from suburban domesticity to the high-powered business world. Plot patterns also can differ tremendously, from the young-girl-in-search-of-a-suitable-husband to the single-minded-career-woman-who-finds-love-by-accident. In general, although these are all basically love stories, because they do not adhere to a preset pattern, the plots of Basic Contemporaries can take unexpected twists and turns, and the endings are often unpredictable. The degree of sensuality in these novels can also vary greatly. However, in general, novels written since the 1970s are likely to be more sensual than those written earlier. Characters, too, come in many shapes and flavors. Heroines may be innocent or experienced, beautiful or plain, aggressive or retiring. They all, however, tend to have "character," determination, common sense, and a sense of humor. Likewise, heroes can be reserved or outgoing, sophisticated or less than perfectly polished, handsome or charmingly homely. They are, however, most often successful, strong, purposeful, and honorable.

Early Basic Contemporary Romance Writers

Over the years, many writers have contributed to the development of the Basic Contemporary Romance subgenre. Several authors of early and prototypical works are listed below.

Ayres, Ruby M.

A prolific British writer of more than 150 romances, Ayres produced light, admittedly escapist novels from the 1910s until her death in the mid-1950s. Exhibiting a popular and timeless quality, her works were often reissued decades later (with exceptionally few changes) as "new" books. Currently, several of her books are still in print in the United States; however, large American public libraries should have copies of some of her more popular works.

Baldwin, Faith

Producing close to 90 novels in a 50-year span (the first published in 1921, the last in 1977, the year before she died), Baldwin specialized in solid, almost old-fashioned romances filled with an assortment of well-rounded, likable, and unusually believable characters. Her stories, too, while not always realistic, are warm, comfortable, and full of hope and good humor. In addition, many of her books contain inspirational elements and could be classified within that category. At least 40 of her books are still in print. Following are some typical examples.

> **Woman on Her Way.** *Rinehart, 1945.* The story of Meg Lewis and her difficult journey from innocent girl to mature, successful woman set during the first part of the twentieth century.

The Whole Armor. *Rinehart, 1951.* The story of young Pastor Paul Marshall, one year in his ministry, and Connie, the woman who loves him. This is very much in the inspirational vein.

Blaze of Sunlight. *Rinehart, 1959.* A widow comes to terms with her intense, exclusive devotion to her late husband and discovers how this has affected her family, her community, and herself. One of Baldwin's best and most substantial novels.

Time and the Hour. *Holt, Rinehart & Winston, 1974.* A gentle, warm love story of newly divorced Stacy Armitage and troubled Lee Osborne set in the town of Little Oxford. Baldwin has set previous stories in this town, and many of the characters from these works appear in this one.

Bloom, Ursula

Writing under a number of pseudonyms, Bloom produced more than 500 novels. As diverse as she was prolific, Bloom wrote romances of the contemporary, historical, and hospital varieties (all under separate names) as well as many nonfiction works including cookbooks, articles, plays, newspaper columns, and biographies. Her stories exhibit integrity and honesty, and they occasionally include inspirational or religious elements. Currently, only a few of her books are in print in the United States; however, large American public libraries should have copies of her more popular works. Typical examples include:

The Great Beginning. *Hutchinson, 1924.* Betrayed by her mother into a disastrous marriage, a young girl finally finds happiness and love. Bloom's first novel.

Wonder Cruise. *Dutton, 1934.* Hutchinson, 1933. Spinster heroine defies her autocratic brother and goes on a cruise.

Laughter in Cheyne Walk. *Lippincott, 1937.* Collins, 1936. Lucy is the only one in her family who isn't the "greatest" at something. Feeling rejected, she searches elsewhere for fulfillment and finds love.

Our Dearest Emma. *London: Museum Press, 1949.* Published in the United States as **The Magnificent Courtesan.** *McBride, 1950.* First in a series of biographical novels of several famous women, this tells the story of the infamous Lady Hamilton.

Price Above Rubies. *Hutchinson, 1965.* One of Bloom's family biographies, this one is about her mother.

Dell, Ethel M.

One of the most popular writers of the first half of this century, Dell produced exciting, daring novels of adventure and romance, replete with "hot kisses" and passionate embraces. Although her themes are often somewhat religious in nature (e.g., featuring a virginal heroine who faces some sort of inner spiritual difficulty or is on a spiritual quest), they are actually too sensual and unorthodox to fall within the Inspirational subgenre. Of this author, the *Book Review Digest* says "Miss Dell writes a good story. She has emotional strength and the faculty of contriving dramatic situations." Currently, approximately ten of her books are in print. They include:

The Way of an Eagle. *Putnam, 1911.* A spoiled young woman changes her ways and charms the hero.

The Knave of Diamonds. *Putnam, 1913.* A black sheep hero is redeemed by love.

Bars of Iron. *Putnam, 1916.* Secrets devastate a marriage.

The Hundredth Chance. *Putnam, 1917.* The story of social class and financial differences.

Hill, Grace Livingston

An extremely popular and prolific writer, Hill produced Basic Contemporary Romances for more than 50 years. However, because most of her romances emphasize the spiritual and religious aspects of the situations, she is more properly considered a writer of Inspirationals and is, therefore, discussed in the Inspirational Romance section of this guide (see chapter 12).

Norris, Kathleen

A writer of popular American novels for more than 40 years, Norris produced works that often deal with "real" or "ordinary" people and their struggles to achieve happiness. The family is an important element in her stories, as is money and its corrupting power, and many of her works combine these two themes dramatically. Currently, several of her works are in print, and others are available in public libraries. Selected examples of her work include:

Certain People of Importance. *Doubleday, 1922.* The Crabtree family is followed from 1849 and their arrival in San Francisco until the last of the nineteenth century. They rise to become a powerful northern California family, the Flaggs.

The American Flaggs. *Doubleday, 1936.* Published in England as **The Flagg Family.** *Murray, 1936.* The story of the Flaggs continues into the next generation.

Shadow Marriage. *Doubleday, 1952.* Married to one man and in love with another, Georgia struggles in a stifling marriage to a shallow, cruel man. A traditional, but soapy, romance.

Through a Glass Darkly. *Doubleday, 1957.* Published in England as **Cherry.** *Murray, 1958.* A strange, mystical story of love, faith, and the righting of an old wrong.

As mentioned earlier, one important current trend in romance fiction is in the direction of Contemporary Romance, including the Basic Contemporary type, and many writers continue to produce titles in this vein.

The following authors are known for their Basic Contemporary Romances, although they may also write and be noted for works in other subgenres. Only their Basic Contemporaries are listed below. Any of their other romance works included in this book are discussed in the appropriate chapters.

Selected Basic Contemporary Romance Bibliography

Becnel, Rexanne

Christmas Journey. *Dell, 1992.* A couple rekindles their relationship and sorts out family difficulties during the holidays in upstate New York.

The Christmas Wish. *Dell, 1993.* A sensitive story of the opposition to a mother who wants to reclaim the daughter she gave up 16 years earlier.

Blake, Jennifer (Patricia Maxwell)

Blake is a veteran, well-respected writer of both contemporary and historical romance. Many of her contemporary romances have an element of mystery or suspense. Her settings are primarily southern, and the ambience is steamy. *(See also Period Romance bibliography.)*

Love and Smoke. *Ballantine Books, 1989.* A widowed, wealthy heroine is determined to settle some old scores and come to terms with her feelings for her stepson.

Joy and Anger. *Fawcett Columbine, 1991.* Passion flares between the film director heroine and the bayou expert hero in this steamy story of sabotage and greed.

Shameless. *Fawcett Columbine, 1994.* The hero returns to his hometown and becomes involved with the one woman he could never forget.

Tigress. *Fawcett Gold Medal, 1996.*

Kane. *Mira Books, 1998.* First in a series set in Turn-Coupe, Louisiana.

Bretton, Barbara

One and Only. *Berkley, 1994.* A dispossessed princess finds happiness with a businessman. A dash of politics and intrigue add to this story.

Maybe This Time. *Berkley, 1995.* A television superstar and a reporter find love as they travel cross-country in a bizarre turn of events.

Brown, Sandra

A noted writer of Period and Contemporary romance and Romantic Suspense, her stories are sensual and lively and often focus on the wealthy and successful. *(See also Romantic Suspense bibliography.)*

Texas Trilogy

Texas! Lucky. *Doubleday, 1990.*

Texas! Chase. *Doubleday, 1991.*

Texas! Sage. *Doubleday, 1991.*

Cadell, Elizabeth

A British writer of traditional, middle-class romances that exhibit a sense of humor, a large dash of realism, and an occasional bit of mystery, Cadell has written more than 50 novels. Many of these are still in print or are available at many public libraries. They include:

The Cuckoo in Spring. *William Morrow, 1954.*

Honey for Tea. *William Morrow, 1962.* Hodder & Stoughton, 1961. One of her best.

Out of the Rain. *Hodder and Stoughton, 1987.* Her last.

Cameron, Stella

(See also Period Romance bibliography.)

Breathless. *Avon Books, 1994.* Danger and mystery stalk a writer and the wealthy owner of an island called Hell in this sensual story with an exotic setting.

True Bliss. *Zebra, 1996.* Former lovers are reunited but are on opposite sides of a political issue.

The Best Revenge. *Zebra, 1998.* Incest and abuse set the scene for this story of deception and revenge

Dailey, Janet

One of the most prolific and well-known romance novelists and the first American to write for Harlequin (*No Quarter Asked.* Mills & Boon, 1974. Harlequin, 1976), Dailey has written more than 90 Contemporary Romances of varying types. Her style is fast-paced and captivating, and she is at her best in her longer novels when she can spend more time on character development. Some of her books cross over into the Glitz and Glamour and Soap Opera subgenres, and her later efforts incorporate some conventions of the mainstream novel, often including mystery and suspense elements. Unfortunately, in 1997 Dailey admitted to plagiarizing sections from romances by another popular writer, Nora Roberts, and including them in her own books. This admission shocked the romance world and effectively put an end to Dailey's career. In addition, the respected Janet Dailey Award for the romance that best dealt with a serious social issue was not given in 1998. All litigation was concluded in 1998 with the proceeds donated to literacy efforts. Several recent works are listed below. *(See also Ethnic and Multicultural Romance Bibliographies.)*

Silver Wings, Santiago Blue. *Poseidon, 1984.*

Heiress. *Little, Brown, 1987.*

Rivals. *Little, Brown, 1989.*

Masquerade. *Little, Brown, 1990.* Someone is out to murder the heroine, but she has lost her memory and can't remember who it is. Mystery and suspense in a Mardi Gras setting.

Tangled Vines. *Little, Brown, 1992.* A reporter finds love and more in California's Napa Valley.

Notorious. *HarperCollins, 1996.* Nevada ranch setting.

Illusions. *HarperCollins, 1997.* Security expert must protect rock star from a deranged killer in a Colorado ski resort setting.

Eagle, Kathleen

Many of Eagle's books deal with Native American issues. *(See also Multicultural Romance bibliography.)*

The Last True Cowboy. *Avon Books, 1988.* Wyoming, wild horses, and troubled teenagers combine in a story of unexpected love.

Freethy, Barbara

Freethy's contemporary romances often have a dash of the paranormal. *(See Alternative Reality Romance bibliography.)*

Gaskin, Catherine

Most of Gaskin's works are either contemporary romances with Gothic overtones or are pure period romances. The one listed below is unusual and one of her best. *(See also Romantic Suspense and Gothic bibliographies.)*

Corporation Wife. *Doubleday, 1960.*

Krentz, Jayne Ann

Krentz is a popular writer in several romance subgenres, and she currently writes under the pseudonyms of Amanda Quick (Period Romance) and Jayne Castle (Futuristic Romance). Her single title contemporary romances combine elements of both the Basic Contemporary Romance and Romantic Suspense subgenres. Her style is lively, with flashes of humor. Her heroines are intelligent, successful, determined, often take-charge types who aren't about to take a back seat to anyone. Her heroes are also successful, determined, used to having their own way, and are both intrigued and irritated by the heroine. Her contemporary romances are usually set in the Seattle area. They include:

The Golden Chance. *Pocket Books, 1990.*

Silver Linings. *Pocket Books, 1991.*

Sweet Fortune. *Pocket Books, 1991.*

Perfect Partners. *Pocket Books, 1992.*

Family Man. *Pocket Books, 1993.*

Wildest Hearts. *Pocket Books, 1993.*

Grand Passion. *Pocket Books, 1994.*

Trust Me. *Pocket Books, 1995.*

Absolutely, Positively. *Pocket Books, 1996.*

Deep Waters. *Pocket Books, 1996.*

Sharp Edges. *Pocket Books, 1998.*

Loring, Emilie

Although Loring's 50-plus novels are mixtures of romance, suspense, intrigue, patriotic nationalism, moralism, and upon occasion, inspiration, they are essentially contemporary love stories. Often containing commentary on political and social events of the period in which they were written (filtered through Loring's conservative perspective), most are now quite dated, although they still can be interesting reading. *(See also Inspirational Romance bibliography.)*

Lowell, Elizabeth

Lowell writes in a variety of romance subgenres. She also writes novels under her own name, Ann Maxwell, and as A. E. Maxwell in conjunction with Evan Lowell Maxwell. Most of her contemporary romances have been written for the category series lines. Recently, several of her more popular books, such as those listed below, have been reprinted as single titles. *(See also Alternative Reality and Western Romance bibliographies.)*

Lover in the Rough. *Silhouette, 1984.* Avon Books, 1994.

A Woman Without Lies. *Silhouette, 1984.* Avon Books, 1995.

McCaffrey, Anne

Stitch in Snow. *Brandywyne Books, 1984.* Writer Dana Jane Lovell never thought she'd find love in an airport in the middle of a snowstorm—but she did.

The Lady. *Ultramarine, 1987.* A delightful mix of Ireland, horses, and romance.

5

McNaught, Judith

McNaught also writes well-received Period Romance. *(See also Period Romance bibliography.)*

Tender Triumph. *Harlequin, 1983.*

Double Standards. *Harlequin, 1984.*

Paradise. *Pocket Books, 1991.* A business partnership between two supposedly ex-spouses has romantic results.

Perfect. *Simon & Schuster, 1993.* Adult illiteracy is a theme.

Remember When. *Pocket Books, 1996.* A year-long marriage of convenience turns into one that is surprisingly real in this story featuring an elegant magazine publisher heroine and a wealthy hero.

Marshall, Alexandra

The Brass Bed. *Doubleday, 1986.*

Something Borrowed. *Houghton Mifflin, 1997.*

Maxwell, Evan

All the Winters That Have Been. *HarperCollins, 1995.* A naturalist writer returns to the Pacific Northwest and is reunited with the woman he has loved for 20 years. Mid-twentieth-century setting.

Phillips, Susan Elizabeth

Phillips is a popular writer of lively, fast-paced, humorous contemporary romances. Her titles include:

Fancy Pants. *Pocket Books, 1989.* Spoiled, rich British socialite ends up broke in America and is ultimately rescued by the golf pro hero, who has little patience for her brattiness.

Hot Shot. *Pocket Books, 1991.* Love, ambition, and computers.

Honey Moon. *Pocket Books, 1993.*

It Had To Be You. *Avon Books, 1994.* Heroine inherits a football team with interesting results. A Rita Award winner.

Heaven, Texas. *Avon Books, 1995.* More football players.

Kiss an Angel. *Avon Books, 1996.*

No Body's Baby But Mine. *Avon Books, 1997.* A physics scholar chooses a football star to be the father of her baby and gets more than she intended or wanted. A double Rita Award winner.

Dream a Little Dream. *Avon Books, 1998.*

Roberts, Nora

Award-winning, best-selling Roberts is one of the genre's luminaries; she writes contemporary series, single title romances, and Romantic Suspense. She has written more than 100 romances, many of which are among the best in the genre. Her works are fast paced and well written. They feature engaging, believable characters and are skillfully plotted. She also writes Futuristic detective stories with a strong romance element as J. D. Robb. She is a member of the RWA Hall of Fame. *(See also Romantic Suspense and Futuristic Romance bibliographies.)* Many of her recent non-suspense romances have been written as trilogies, including:

Concannon Trilogy (Irish Trilogy)

Three sisters find love—and each other—in an Irish setting.

Born in Fire. *Jove, 1994.*

 Born in Ice. *Jove, 1995.*

Born in Shame. *Jove, 1996.*

Dream Trilogy

Three women raised almost as sisters find love and happiness.

Daring to Dream. *Jove, 1996.*

Holding the Dream. *Jove, 1996.*

Finding the Dream. *Jove, 1997.*

Quinn Brothers Trilogy

Sea Swept. *Jove, 1998.*

Rising Tides. *(Forthcoming)*

Ross, JoAnn

A Woman's Heart. *Mira Books, 1998.* An Irish setting with a bit of Hollywood thrown in.

Seidel, Kathleen Gilles

Seidel's well-written, often complex romances feature well-developed characters whose actions derive from their backgrounds. Although Seidel sometimes uses Hollywood or show business settings, they are not as superficial as some others of this type.

Maybe This Time. *Pocket Books, 1990.*

More Than You Dreamed. *Pocket Books, 1991.*

Till the Stars Fall. *Onyx, 1994.*

 Again. *Onyx, 1994.* A Rita Award winner.

Spencer, LaVyrle

(See Contemporary Americana and Period Americana bibliographies.)

Stevenson, D. E.

A British writer of close to 50 novels, Stevenson excels in traditional English romances that are, in reality, novels of manners and character. She is probably best known for her Mrs. Tim series.

Mrs. Tim Series

The continuing story of the wife of an English officer, set during World War II and after, told with warmth and a delightful sense of humor.

Villars, Elizabeth (Ellen Feldman)

Adam's Daughters. *Doubleday, 1984.*

CONTEMPORARY CATEGORY ROMANCE

Contemporary Category Romances are basically stories written to conform to a specific pattern that has been established by the publisher. Usually produced in series format, these romances tend to follow the classic boy-meets-girl, boy-loses-girl, boy-gets-girl pattern, varying within the proscribed guidelines of the individual series. However, while the plot patterns are similar and the guidelines must be observed, these books are not carbon copies of one another. They vary more than one might expect, even within the specific lines. Settings, style, characterization, dialogue, and quality of writing are all variables in the hands of the writer, and the differences occasionally are startling. For example, a Harlequin American Romance by Anne Stuart is not at all the same as one by Barbara Bretton, and a Silhouette Desire by Naomi Horton is quite different from one by Cathie Linz.

Each series has a particular emphasis (e.g., mystery/intrigue, humor, adventure), and this, as well as the length of the story and the way in which sex is handled, varies among lines. Series can be either short (60,000 words or fewer) or long (60,000 to 85,000 words). The shorter books focus primarily on the hero and heroine, and longer books often include additional subplots and peripheral characters.

A book can also be either Innocent (Sweet) or Sensual. While the Innocent variety almost always includes a virginal (or at least not terribly experienced) heroine and concludes with a passionate kiss and a promise of marriage, the Sensuals vary from lines that contain very little explicit sexual description (but lots of passionate imagery) to those that border on the erotic. As alluded to earlier, the individual books within a series are not identical; nevertheless, the parameters are adhered to, and once the reader has found an acceptable series, he or she should be assured of getting something similar when it comes to length, theme, and level of sensuality in each succeeding volume of the series.

In many instances, "tip sheets" detailing the particulars of the individual series are available to authors. In recent years publishers have become somewhat less proscriptive in these guidelines, opting for a more general approach and allowing the writer more latitude than in earlier years when the specifics were spelled out in some detail. For an example of one of these older tip sheet versions, see the predecessor to this book, *Happily Ever After* (Littleton, Colorado: Libraries Unlimited, 1987), 44-45. An example of a current tip sheet follows on pages 63 and 64.

· SABRINA · PRETTY WOMAN · SLEEPLESS IN SEATTLE · NIGHT SHIFT · TOOTSIE ·

HARLEQUIN'S LOVE AND LAUGHTER™

From Gable and Lombard, to Hepburn and Tracy, to Jamie and Paul Buchman in "Mad About You," we adore romantic comedies and the heroes and heroines in them. In fact, love and laughter are such a natural combination that we've decided to create a new series featuring just that—love and laughter. The lighter side of love.

Your story must be a contemporary romance of 50,000 to 55,000 words and it must be humorous. Whether your book is a screwball comedy, whether it contains slapstick, whether a cast of secondary characters maintains a running commentary of one-liners, how you tell your love and laughter story is up to you. We, the editors, just like the readers, want to laugh, be entertained and sigh over the love story.

Let us repeat romance and humor—other than that there are no limitations. A high degree of sexual tension should be present in the story, and while love scenes are encouraged, they are not a requirement.

Please submit queries, partials or complete manuscripts with synopses to:

LOVE AND LAUGHTER COORDINATOR:
Malle Vallik,
Associate Senior Editor
Love and Laughter
Harlequin Books
225 Duncan Mill Road
Don Mills, Ontario M3B 3K9
CANADA

SILHOUETTE CONTACT:
Marcia Adirim,
Editor
Silhouette Books
300 East 42nd Street, Sixth Floor
New York, 10017
U.S.A.

· HOW TO MARRY A MILLIONAIRE · ONLY YOU · PILLOW TALK · FUNNY FACE ·

GENTLEMEN PREFER BLONDES · HEAVEN CAN WAIT · SOME LIKE IT HOT · SAY ANYTHING · MOONSTRUCK

FOUL PLAY · IT HAPPENED ONE NIGHT · TEACHER'S PET · WHAT'S UP, DOC? · ROXANNE · WORKING GIRL

5

Isabel Swift—Editorial Director

SILHOUETTE ROMANCE™
53,000-58,000 words
Senior Editor: Melissa Senate

Silhouette Romance requires talented authors able to portray modern relationships in the context of romantic love. Although the hero and heroine don't actually make love unless married, sexual tension is a vitally important element. Writers are encouraged to try new twists and creative approaches to this winning formula. Our ultimate goal is to give readers a romance with heightened emotional impact—books that make them laugh or cry, books that touch their hearts.

SILHOUETTE DESIRE®
55,000-60,000 words
Senior Editor: Lucia Macro

Sensual, believable, compelling, these books are written for today's woman. Innocent or experienced, the heroine is someone we identify with; the hero irresistible. The conflict should be an emotional one, springing naturally from the unique characters you've chosen. The focus is on the developing relationship, set in a believable plot. The characters don't have to be married to make love, but lovemaking is never taken lightly. Secondary characters and subplots must blend with the core story. Innovative new directions in storytelling and fresh approaches to classic romantic plots are welcome.

SILHOUETTE SPECIAL EDITION®
75,000-80,000 words
Senior Editor: Tara Gavin

Sophisticated, substantial, and packed with emotion, Special Edition demands writers eager to probe characters deeply, to explore issues that heighten the drama of living and loving, to create compelling romantic plots. Whether the sensuality is sizzling or subtle, whether the plot is wildly innovative or satisfyingly traditional, the novel's emotional vividness, its depth and dimension, should clearly label it a very special contemporary romance. Subplots are welcome, but must further or parallel the developing romantic relationship in a meaningful way.

SILHOUETTE INTIMATE MOMENTS®
80,000-85,000 words
Senior Editor & Editorial Coordinator: Leslie Wainger

Believable characters swept into a world of larger-than-life romance, such is the magic of Silhouette Intimate Moments. These books offer you the freedom to combine the universally appealing elements of a category romance with the flash and excitement of mainstream fiction. Adventure, suspense, melodrama, glamour—let your imagination be your guide as you blend old and new to create a novel with emotional depth and tantalizing complexity, a novel that explores new directions in romantic fiction, a novel that is quintessentially Intimate Moments.

Over for submission guidelines
© 1992 Silhouette Books

300 EAST 42ND STREET, SIXTH FLOOR, NEW YORK, NEW YORK 10017/TEL (212) 682 6080/FAX (212) 682 4539

The early 1980s saw an explosion in the Contemporary Category Romance market, and series proliferated. However, that trend quickly changed in the middle of the decade, and today the only major publishers still producing Contemporary Category Romance are Harlequin and Silhouette. Unfortunately, Bantam's Loveswept line closed at the end of 1998. (Pinnacle's Arabesque line is discussed in chapter 13, "Ethnic/Multicultural Romance," and Steeple Hill's Love Inspired (Harlequin) line is discussed in chapter 12, "Inspirational Romance.") Although for space reasons individual titles have not been annotated and included, a list of representative authors for specific series is included in the Sample Core Collection in appendix 1. A selection of series currently being published or readily found in most libraries is listed below.

Selected Category Romance Series

Bantam Loveswept

A short, sensual contemporary line that features "humor, believability, and surprises."

Harlequin American Romance

This series features upbeat, fun, mid-length, sensual contemporary romances with lively dialogue and an "anything's possible" ambience. The heroines are sassy, and the heroes are adventurous in this series of American-set stories.

Harlequin Intrigue

This series of mid-length, somewhat sensual contemporary romances combines love stories with elements of intrigue, suspense, and the unexpected.

Harlequin Love and Laughter

A short, sexy, funny series that features "the lighter side of love."

Harlequin Presents

A series of short, sensual romances that feature realistic, contemporary issues and lively, independent heroines.

Harlequin Romance

The original series, featuring short, innocent, heartwarming romances with engaging heroines and heroes guaranteed to "fulfill every woman's dreams."

Harlequin Superromance

In Harlequin's longest series, these sophisticated, contemporary romances feature multidimensional characters, fairly complex story lines, and a high degree of sensuality.

Harlequin Temptation

"Harlequin's boldest, most sensuous series." A fast-paced series of romances that feature a variety of contemporary problems all solved within an atmosphere of romantic fantasy.

Silhouette Desire

Short, sensual contemporary romances that feature modern heroines, irresistible heroes, and plots with believable emotional conflict.

Silhouette Intimate Moments

Longer, sensual, larger-than-life romances that combine strong love stories with melodrama, adventure, suspense, and glamour with the "flash and excitement of mainstream fiction."

Silhouette Romance

Much like the original Harlequin series, these short, innocent contemporary romances feature relationships that touch readers' hearts and involve them emotionally.

Silhouette Special Editions

Longer, sensual contemporary romances that make use of high emotional tension, well-rounded characters, contemporary issues, and believable situations.

Silhouette Yours Truly

A "line of short, sassy contemporary romance novels about unexpectedly meeting, dating . . . and marrying Mr. Right" in which the characters meet through some form of written communication.

SOAP OPERA

Soap Operas are essentially complex, introspective, often many-peopled stories that center around the difficulties of a particular individual, family, or town. A love story usually figures prominently in the plot, but there are also a number of other sufficiently anguishing aspects that serve to engage the reader's interest. Suffering, affliction, illness, sin, revenge, and retribution permeate the plots, and happy endings are not a foregone conclusion.

The form for this particular subgenre was establish last century by Ellen Price Wood's *East Lynne* (1861) and was continued by several others including the legendary *Stella Dallas* (1923) by Olive Higgins Prouty. Both of these extremely popular novels were adapted for the stage, and *East Lynne* was one of the most popular plays in the United States during the first part of this century. *Stella Dallas* has been made into a film and served as the basis for a radio serial (soap opera) that endured for more than 15 years. Modern readers, however, are probably more familiar with the more recent soap opera prototypes, *Peyton Place* (1956) by Grace Metalious and *Love Story* (1970) by Erich Segal. Both of these have been translated into films, and *Peyton Place* was even the inspiration for a television soap opera serial during the 1970s. Although the pattern for this particular subgenre was established much earlier, its name derives directly from the radio and television serials, many of which were sponsored by soap companies.

Currently, the Soap Opera as a separate romance subgenre is less common than it once was; nevertheless, romances of this type are still being written, and some of the older ones are still read. In addition, genreblending is also affecting the Soaps, and as has happened with both the Gothic and Plantation Romances, many of the subgenre's characteristic elements have been quietly slipping into a variety of romance subtypes. Today it is not uncommon to find a fair degree of sudsy angst in romances in a number of other categories, including Women's Romantic Fiction, Glitz and Glamour, Basic Contemporary Romance, and the Saga. All this makes for increasingly fuzzy boundaries between the Soap Opera and the other subgenres, and many writers and books can legitimately be categorized within several. In addition, books are rarely given the Soap Opera label (even when they qualify), and even though some of the subgenre's classic credits include books by best-selling writers such as Danielle Steel and the late Helen Van Slyke, books of this type currently are listed within the other subgenres.

Soap Opera Prototypes

The prototypes listed below are dated but still interesting.

Finley, Martha

Elsie Dinsmore series (1868-1905)

Prouty, Olive Higgins

Prouty wrote a number of popular sentimental romances. Two of her best remembered novels are listed below.

> **Stella Dallas.** *Houghton Mifflin, 1923.* The classic story of the disastrous marriage of Stephen and Stella Dallas and the "ultimate sacrifice" Stella makes for their daughter, Laurel. Filled with anguish, retribution, and suffering, *Stella Dallas* describes how Stella's lower-class habits and flirtations repel her more cultured husband and force him to leave her. Eventually realizing that Stephen can give Laurel a better life, Stella releases him to marry again. She then marries a man she despises to ensure that Laurel will leave and go to her father.

> **Now, Voyager.** *Houghton Mifflin, 1941.* Recovering from a serious psychological illness, spinster Charlotte Vale takes a cruise, has an affair with a married man, learns much about herself, and gains an independence she's never had. This sentimental story contains aspects of the Ugly Duckling plot pattern and takes a sympathetic view of psychological illness. One of five books about the wealthy Boston Vales.

Wood, Ellen Price

> **East Lynne.** *Rutgers, 1984.* Bentley, 1861. One of the most popular novels of the nineteenth century, *East Lynne* early established the pattern for the modern-day novel of pain and suffering. By combining elements of both the sentimental romance and sensational romance, "the novel renders a compelling analysis of the great social and moral issues of the day—class and money, feminine oppression, crime, guilt and sin—and venerates all of the traditional middle-class virtues." The Rutgers edition is essentially a study edition, intended primarily for use by students of Victorian culture and literature.

The following more recent examples of the soap opera subgenre are still read.

Metalious, Grace

> **Peyton Place.** *Messner, 1956.* The passionately scandalous doings of the inhabitants of a small New England town complete with infidelity, illegitimacy, pregnancy, incest, lust, and murder. This became both a movie and the basis for a television series.

Segal, Erich

Love Story. *HarperCollins, 1970.* A "Romeo and Juliet" story in which rich Oliver and poor Jenny fall in love and marry despite parental objections. After many struggles and just when it looks as though everything will turn out right, tragedy strikes and Jenny develops a fatal illness.

Selected Soap Opera Bibliography

The following authors are usually included within other subgenres. However, the several examples listed below exhibit enough soap opera characteristics to be considered part of the tradition.

Amiel, Joseph

Birthright. *Atheneum, 1985.*

Hawks. *Putnam, 1979.*

Cowie, Vera

The Rich and the Mighty. *Doubleday, 1985.*

Games. *Doubleday, 1986.*

Feldman, Ellen (also Elizabeth Villars)

Conjugal Rights. *William Morrow, 1986.*

Freeman, Cynthia

Many of her saga-like stories focus on family and self-discovery.

Come Pour the Wind. *Arbor House, 1980.* A story of self-discovery, pain, joy, and acceptance as Janet struggles with the choices and changes in her life.

Illusions of Love. *Putnam, 1985.*

Seasons of the Heart. *Putnam, 1986.* Suffering, anguish, and self-sacrifice are the order of the day.

The Last Princess. *Putnam, 1988.*

Goudge, Eileen

Garden of Lies. *Viking, 1989.* Two women raised apart are forced to come to terms with their surprising relationship.

Thorns of Truth. *Viking, 1998.* This sequel to *Garden of Lies* reveals even more secrets and lies.

Harris, Ruth

The Rich and the Beautiful. *Simon & Schuster, 1978.*

A Self-Made Woman. *Macmillan, 1983.*

Husbands and Lovers. *Macmillan, 1985.* Tangled relationships, sexual dependencies, and the general Manhattan frenzy combine in this glitzy, somewhat soapy novel.

Houston, James D.

Love Life. *Alfred A. Knopf, 1985.*

Jaffe, Rona

Jaffe is a master of the small-group-of-women-recounting-past-problems-and-dealing-with-the-equally-problematic-present type of story. Her stories are fast-paced, melodramatic, and very popular.

Class Reunion. *Delacorte Press, 1979.* One of her best known.

After the Reunion. *Delacorte Press, 1985.* Now in their late 40s, four classmates from Radcliffe meet again. Sequel to *Class Reunion*.

The Cousins. *Donald I. Fine, 1995.* Dark family secrets surface in this liberally-peopled, soapy saga.

Five Women. *Donald I. Fine, 1997.*

Michaels, Fern (Roberta Anderson and Mary Kuczkir; after 1989, Kuczkir only)

Michaels' romantic Sagas have enough angst and suffering to place them well within the Soap Opera subgenre.

Texas Rich. *Ballantine Books, 1985.* A soapy *Dallas*-like Saga of four generations of the Colemans.

Texas Heat. *Ballantine Books, 1986.* Sequel to *Texas Rich*.

Texas Fury. *Ballantine Books, 1989.* Another Coleman story.

Texas Sunrise. *Ballantine Books, 1993.* More Colemans.

Vegas Rich. *Kensington, 1996.* More generation-spanning suds, Vegas-style.

Vegas Heat. *Kensington, 1997.* Sequel to *Vegas Rich*.

Vegas Sunrise. *Kensington, 1997.*

Steel, Danielle

Most of Steel's novels exhibit numerous soap opera tendencies, and many are on the borderline between Women's Romantic Fiction (often of the Glitz and Glamour variety) and the Soap Opera. Note: Except for some of her earlier works, most of Steel's stories are not considered true romances by most romance readers. *(See also Women's Romantic Fiction bibliography.)*

Season of Passion. *Dell, 1979.*

Now and Forever. *Dell, 1978.*

Fine Things. *Delacorte Press, 1983.*

Heartbeat. *Bantam Books, 1991.* A supermarket meeting spells happiness for the wounded, rejected hero and the successful, but unsatisfied, heroine.

Accident. *Delacorte Press, 1994.* With the help of sympathetic hero, heroine copes with her husband's infidelity and a serious car accident that leaves her daughter brain damaged.

The Long Road Home. *Delacorte Press, 1998.* A truly soapy saga filled with child abuse, an affair between a would-be nun and a priest, suicide, passion, and, eventually, true love.

Thayer, Nancy

Bodies and Souls. *Doubleday, 1983.*

An Act of Love. *St. Martin's Press, 1997.*

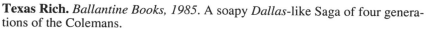

Van Slyke, Helen

Van Slyke's stories are on the borderline between the Basic Romance and the Soap Opera—good, strong love stories with lots of pain and suffering. *(See Women's Romantic Fiction bibliography.)*

The Mixed Blessing. *Doubleday, 1975.*

Always Is Not Forever. *Doubleday, 1977.*

Sisters and Strangers. *Doubleday, 1978.*

WOMEN'S ROMANTIC FICTION

Essentially a blend between the Basic Contemporary Romance (or occasionally Period Romance) and mainstream Women's Fiction, Women's Romantic Fiction has become increasingly popular in recent years. While these stories have strong romance plotlines, they also have definite mainstream tendencies and, like much of traditional Women's Fiction, are complex, multifaceted stories in which the growth or triumph of the heroine is more important than the development or success of the romantic relationship. Ideally, of course, both occur. Many books of this type span a number of years and have much in common with some sagas. *(See also the Saga bibliography.)* Not unexpectedly, the boundaries of this evolving romance type are fairly fluid and are definitely open to discussion.

Selected Women's Romantic Fiction Bibliography

The works and writers listed below are merely a sampling of those who may fall within this designation.

Alexander, Kate

Most of Alexander's works are set during the first part of the twentieth century and feature strong, resourceful women who usually find love and success despite obstacles. Well-developed characters and realistic situations are hallmarks of Alexander's works.

Fields of Battle. *St. Martin's Press, 1981.*

Friends and Enemies. *St. Martin's Press, 1982.*

Bright Tomorrows. *Macdonald, 1985.*

Great Possessions. *Macdonald, 1989.*

The House of Hope. *Century, 1992.*

Allen, Charlotte Vale

Strong, resourceful, but often ill-used, heroines who take charge of their own destinies, usually finding fulfillment and love, are central to most of Allen's novels. Her stories often span a number of years and have saga-like tendencies. Note: In 1998 she released her first mystery, *Mood Indigo: A Novel*, under the imprint of her own publishing company, Island Nation Press.

Hidden Meanings. *Warner Books, 1976.*

Meet Me in Time. *Warner Books, 1978.*

Intimate Friends. *E. P. Dutton, 1983.*

Pieces of Dreams. *Berkley, 1985.*

Illusions. *Atheneum, 1987.*

Leftover Dreams. *Doubleday, 1992.* Maggie, her mother, and her daughters struggle to find happiness in this story that spans two decades. A saga of the Toronto working class.

Dreaming in Color. *Doubleday, 1993.* Escaping an abusive husband, Bobby and her young daughter find refuge with an aging stroke victim and her writer daughter with eventual happy results for all.

Claudia's Shadow. *Mira Books, 1996.* Rowena's attempts to learn the truth behind her troubled sister's untimely death lead her into a morass of old memories and dark family secrets.

Battle, Lois

War Brides. *St. Martin's Press, 1982.*

The Past Is Another Country. *Fawcett, 1992.* Three school friends help and support each other as they fight for love and happiness in contemporary Australia.

Storyville. *Viking, 1993.* A child and political feminist ideals hold the keys to the relationship between two women from diverse backgrounds in turn-of-the-century New Orleans.

Binchy, Maeve

Binchy is a popular writer of longish novels, often set in rural Ireland and focusing on friends, family, and relationships. Her novels often span a number of years and include a fair amount of pain and suffering, as well as joy. She is noted for her appealing characters, especially her strong, capable heroines, and her storytelling abilities.

Light a Penny Candle. *Viking, 1983.* Century, 1982.

Echoes. *Viking. 1986.* Century, 1985.

Firefly Summer. *Delacorte Press, 1988.* Century, 1987.

Circle of Friends. *Delacorte Press, 1991.* Century, 1990. Three women confront betrayal and discover the real meaning of friendship.

The Copper Beech. *Delacorte Press, 1992.* Focuses on the lives and loves of the people of the small Irish village of Shancarrig.

The Glass Lake. *Delacorte Press, 1995.* A woman's desertion of her family (and subsequent "drowning") has far-reaching results for all involved.

Evening Class. *Delacorte Press, 1996.* A class in Italian links a diverse group of working-class Dubliners in this typical Binchy tale, complete with an abundance of interesting characters, various trials and tribulations, and the expected happy endings.

Cookson, Catherine

Both prolific and popular, Cookson produces compelling works that are generally filled with memorable characters, realistic settings and situations, and plots that often focus on relevant social issues—particularly class differences. She was one of the first popular writers to focus on working-class characters and their situations. Her works often span decades and can be historical, contemporary, or both. *(See Saga and Period Romance bibliographies.)*

Delinsky, Barbara

A former writer of series romances, Delinsky produces well-crafted novels that feature well-developed characters and often focus on the psychological aspects of the situation.

Facets. *Piatkus, 1991.* Love and revenge.

The Passions of Chelsea Kane. *Piatkus, 1992.* A woman searches for her heritage.

A Woman Betrayed. *Piatkus, 1992.* A strong heroine survives her husband's disappearance and betrayal.

More Than Friends. *HarperCollins, 1993.* Infidelity has disastrous effects on a long-standing friendship.

Suddenly. *HarperCollins, 1993.*

Three Wishes. *Simon & Schuster, 1997.* A near death experience by the heroine and the vague memory of being granted three wishes before dying has far-reaching results for the protagonists.

Coast Road. *Simon & Schuster, 1998.* A tragic automobile accident near Big Sur, California, brings the hero back into the lives of his daughters, his former wife, and his ex-wife's best friend.

Ellis, Julie

Rich Is Best. *Arbor House, 1985.*

Loyalties. *William Morrow, 1990.*

Hannah, Kristin

Hannah writes both Contemporary and Period Romance, much of which contains Alternative Reality or Americana elements. *(See also Alternative Reality and Period Americana Romance bibliographies.)*

Home Again. *Fawcett, 1996.* A profligate actor returns home in need of a heart transplant and discovers a daughter he never knew he had and a love he had never forgotten. Contains some paranormal elements and a mesmerizing heroic priest.

Pilcher, Rosamunde

Noted for their excellent characterizations, beautiful descriptions. and meticulous detail, Pilcher's novels are essentially of two types. Her earlier ones are very much in the romance tradition; however, with the publication of *The Shell Seekers* in 1987 her works take on mainstream characteristics and become increasingly complex in plotting, character development, and relationships.

Sleeping Tiger. *St. Martin's Press, 1967.*

The End of Summer. *St. Martin's Press, 1975.* Collins, 1971.

The Day of the Storm. *St. Martin's Press, 1975.*

Under Gemini. *St. Martin's Press, 1976.*

Voices in Summer. *St. Martin's Press, 1984.*

Wild Mountain Thyme. *St. Martin's Press, 1978.*

The Shell Seekers. *St. Martin's Press, 1987.* A woman comes to terms with her life and mortality in this family-based novel. This novel brought Pilcher international attention.

September. *St. Martin's Press, 1990.* A spin-off of *The Shell Seekers.*

Coming Home. *St. Martin's Press, 1995.*

Plain, Belva

(See also Saga bibliography.)

Blessings. *Delacorte Press, 1994.*

Secrecy. *Delacorte Press, 1997.*

Spindler, Erica

Red. *Mira Books, 1995.* An abuse/rape victim leaves the South, heads for Hollywood, and becomes a successful model.

Forbidden Fruit. *Mira Books, 1996.* A New Orleans prostitute seeks a better life for her daughter, who in turn almost destroys the life of her own daughter with her obsessions.

Fortune. *Mira Books, 1997.*

Steel, Danielle

Most of Steel's novels concern the wealthy, privileged, and powerful "beautiful people." They are often on the borderline between Women's Romantic Fiction (often of the Glitz and Glamour variety) and the Soap Opera. Depending upon one's point of view, they can easily be classified under several romance subtypes. Strong heroines are besieged with numerous problems and often face difficult, life-changing choices. Their happiness is not guaranteed. Note: Except for some of her earlier works, most of Steel's stories are not considered true romances by most romance readers. *(See also Soap Opera and Glitz and Glamour bibliographies.)* Her works include:

Summer's End. *Dell, 1979.*

The Ring. *Delacorte Press, 1980.*

Palomino. *Dell, 1981.*

Crossings. *Delacorte Press, 1982.*

Changes. *Delacorte Press, 1983.*

Full Circle. *Delacorte Press, 1984.*

Wanderlust. *Delacorte Press, 1986.*

Star. *Delacorte Press, 1989.*

No Greater Love. *Delacorte Press, 1991.* Heroine sacrifices her future to raise her siblings after their parents die in the Titanic disaster.

Mixed Blessings. *Delacorte Press, 1992.* Infertility is a primary topic. Considered one of Steel's best.

Stone, Katherine

Stone's books often have enough glitz and glamour to be categorized in that particular subgenre. *(See also Ethnic and Multicultural Romance bibliography.)*

Imagine Love. *Fawcett Columbine, 1996.* A blind music teacher and a famous singer rekindle their love amid a bit of international glitz and very real danger.

Illusions. *Kensington, 1994.* Twins, deception, and murder.

Happy Endings. *Kensington, 1996.* Two couples find happiness in this rather glitzy story of the rich and famous.

Bed of Roses. *Warner Books, 1998.* An actress and a wealthy vintner reconcile after the heroine is brutally attacked.

Thomas, Rosie

A number of Thomas's stories contain Glitz and Glamour elements.

Follies. *Piatkus, 1983.* Fawcett Gold Medal, 1984.

Sunrise. *Piatkus, 1984.* Fawcett Gold Medal, 1984. Named Romantic Novel of the Year by the Romantic Novelists' Association, 1985.

The White Dove. *Viking, 1986.*

Strangers. *Collins, 1986.* Simon & Schuster, 1987.

Bad Girls, Good Women. *Bantam Books, 1989.* Joseph, 1988.

A Woman of Our Times. *Bantam Books, 1990.*

Other People's Marriages. *Joseph, 1993.*

Trollope, Joanna

Trollope's highly readable novels are usually set in rural or small-town England, involve several families, and often focus on troubled marriages. *(See also Twentieth-Century Historical Novel bibliography.)*

The Rector's Wife. *Bloomsbury, 1991.* Disillusioned, unhappy, and tired of scrimping, a country rector's wife takes matters into her own hands and finds fulfillment.

A Spanish Lover. *Bloomsbury, 1993.* A middle-aged English spinster moves to Spain and takes a lover, with unexpected consequences for all concerned.

The Best of Friends. *Viking, 1998.* The breakup of a marriage has far-reaching effects on the lives of everyone involved. Friendship, loss, and the many variations of love.

Van Slyke, Helen

One of the most popular American writers of traditional romances, Van Slyke tells stories of strong women who experience contemporary problems and come out on top. Van Slyke often referred to her works as "soap operas between covers," and inasmuch as they include all kinds of trials and tribulations, they can be considered to fall within the genre. However, they all aren't anguish-filled or gloomy enough to rate that designation in this guide.

A Necessary Woman. *Doubleday, 1979.*

No Love Lost. *Lippincott & Crowell, 1980.*

Public Smiles, Private Tears. *Harper & Row, 1982.*

Glitz and Glamour Romance and Selected Bibliography

Flashy, filled with larger-than-life characters, and occasionally a bit soapy, these stories have mainstream tendencies and usually focus on the romantic, glitzy lives of the "rich and famous." As Betty Rosenberg observes, "The sexy novel of the rich and famous is falling into a genre pattern . . . the 'bestseller formula of charmed lives, repressed passion, and fantasies come true.'"[4] Hollywood, New York, Las Vegas, and other glamorous, high-profile settings are common in these stories, as are rags-to-riches or Cinderella-type themes.

Bailey, Hilary

All the Days of My Life. *Fawcett Gold Medal, 1984.*

Beauman, Sally

Destiny. *Bantam Books, 1988.*

Booth, Pat

Glitzy, steamy books about the romances of the rich set in their titles' cities.

Palm Beach. *Crown, 1985.*

Beverly Hills. *Crown, 1989.*

Malibu. *Crown, 1990.*

Miami. *Ballantine Books, 1992.*

Marry Me. *Little, Brown, 1996.* Set in Santa Fe, this story is less sexy, but no less interesting, than some of Booth's others.

Bradford, Barbara Taylor

Many of Bradford's novels are filled with the glitter of the life of the rich and famous and the greed, ambition, betrayal, and love that accompany it.

Voice of the Heart. *Doubleday, 1983.*

Act of Will. *Doubleday, 1988.*

The Women in His Life. *Random House, 1990.* Hero ponders his life and the women he loved in this story that sweeps from the beginnings of Nazism to the fall of the Berlin Wall.

Remember. *HarperCollins, 1992.* A television reporter puts her life back together after the death of her fiancé and then learns he may not be dead after all.

Angel. *HarperCollins, 1993.*

Everything to Gain. *HarperCollins, 1994.* The heroine struggles to put her life back together after the tragic murder of her husband and children.

Dangerous to Know. *Harper Collins, 1995.* When a charming millionaire is murdered, his ex-wife (and reporter) determines to discover the truth.

Her Own Rules. *HarperCollins, 1996.* The emotionally troubled heroine heads for England in search of her past.

A Secret Affair. *HarperCollins, 1996.*

Power of a Woman. *HarperCollins, 1997.* The heroine is forced to deal with dark secrets when tragedy strikes.

Brayfield, Celia

Pearls. *William Morrow, 1987.* Two wealthy, talented sisters search for the mysterious person who left them each a pink pearl.

Briskin, Jacqueline

Briskin writes fast-paced, rags-to-riches stories filled with larger-than-life characters who struggle and succeed against incredible odds. *(See also Saga bibliography.)*

Everything and More. *Putnam, 1983.*

Too Much Too Soon. *Putnam, 1985.*

Dreams Are Not Enough. *Putnam, 1987.* Spanning the decades of the 1960s to the 1980s, this is the passionate story of one family's desire for success and the one woman around whom it all revolves, beautiful, talented Alyssia Del Mar.

Collins, Jackie

Collins is a master at producing compelling novels of this type. Her situations and characters are larger than life, and her knowledge of the lifestyles of the super-rich comes through with exaggerated accuracy.

Chances. *Warner Books, 1981.* First of the Lucky Santangelo series.

Hollywood Wives. *Simon & Schuster, 1983.*

Lucky. *Simon & Schuster, 1985.* Next in the Santangelo series.

Hollywood Husbands. *Simon & Schuster, 1986.*

Lady Boss. *Simon & Schuster, 1990.* Third in the Santangelo series.

American Star: A Love Story. *Simon & Schuster, 1993.* High school sweethearts are separated, achieve success, suffer a bit, and eventually find each other again.

Hollywood Kids. *Simon & Schuster, 1994.*

Vendetta: Lucky's Revenge. *Regan, 1997.* More mob action and Hollywood glamour in the fourth in the Santangelo series.

Thrill. *Simon & Schuster, 1998.* Actress Lara falls in love with the enigmatic actor Joey in this glitzy, sexy, fast-paced story of life in Hollywood's fast lane.

Conran, Shirley

Lace. *Pocket Books, 1982.* A celebrity sets out to discover which of three women is the mother who gave her away as a baby.

Lace II. *Pocket Books, 1985.*

Savages. *Simon & Schuster, 1987.*

Crimson. *Simon & Schuster, 1992.* The wealthy O'Dare women (writer grandmother and three granddaughters) manage to save their fortune from a slimy, but handsome and charming, lawyer in this fast-paced, glitzy story.

Coscarelli, Kate

Fame and Fortune. *St. Martin's Press, 1984.*

Perfect Order. *New American Library, 1985.*

Living Color. *New American Library, 1987.*

Pretty Women. *New American Library, 1989.* A reunion of military wives provides the solution to an old mystery.

Leading Lady. *St. Martin's Press, 1991.* Child of a famous celebrity survives abuse to find happiness.

Heir Apparent. *St. Martin's Press, 1993.*

Dailey, Janet

Some of Dailey's single title contemporary romances focus on the world of the rich and famous. *(See also Contemporary Romance and Saga bibliographies.)*

The Glory Game. *Pocket Books, 1985.*

Aspen Gold. *Little, Brown, 1990.*

Harvey, Kathryn (Barbara Wood)

Butterfly. *Villard, 1988.*

Stars. *Villard, 1992.*

Emerald. *Bantam Books, 1994.*

Krantz, Judith

Hollywood glitz and glamour by one of the writers who started it all.

Scruples. *Crown, 1978.*

Princess Daisy. *Crown, 1980.*

I'll Take Manhattan. *Crown, 1986.*

Till We Meet Again. *Crown, 1988.*

Dazzle. *Crown, 1990.*

Scruples Two. *Crown, 1992.*

Mann, Catherine

Tinsel Town: A Novel. *Simon & Schuster, 1985.*

Michael, Judith (Judith Barnard and Michael Fain)

Deceptions. *Pocket Books, 1982.*

Possessions. *Pocket Books, 1984.*

Private Affairs. *Pocket Books, 1986.*

Sleeping Beauty. *Poseidon Press, 1991.* Incest, sexual abuse, and politics combine in this fast-paced novel of the rich and famous.

Phillips, Susan Elizabeth

Glitter Baby. *Dell, 1987.*

Reed, Rex

Personal Effects. *Arbor House, 1986.*

Sheldon, Sidney

Sheldon's stories often feature beautiful, mistreated heroines, who succeed in exacting appropriate retribution.

If Tomorrow Comes. *William Morrow, 1985.*

Windmills of the Gods. *William Morrow, 1987.*

Steel, Danielle

(See also Soap Opera bibliographies.)

Passion's Promise. *Dell, 1976.*

Secrets. *Delacorte Press, 1985.*

Daddy. *Delacorte Press, 1989.*

Susann, Jacqueline

Valley of the Dolls. *Geis, 1966.* A classic example of the type.

The Love Machine. *Simon & Schuster, 1969.*

Once Is Not Enough. *William Morrow, 1973.*

SELECTED CONTEMPORARY AMERICANA ROMANCE BIBLIOGRAPHY

Americana elements can be found in many Contemporary Romances and are especially prevalent in some of the category lines (e.g., Silhouette Romance, Harlequin Romance. Avalon Books, a publisher of hardcover, short, sweet contemporary romances, often features a number of romances that would fall within this category. The writers and works listed below are merely a few examples of the many that exist.

Bulock, Lynn

Roses for Caroline. *Avalon, 1989.*

The Promise of Summer. *Avalon, 1990.* Follows *Roses for Caroline.*

Kimberlin, Annie

Kimberlin is a writer of small-town Ohio romances, complete with an abundance of charming animals.

Stray Hearts. *Leisure, 1997.* A veterinarian and a school principal are brought together by an injured dog.

Lonely Hearts. *Leisure, 1997.* A postman and a rubber stamp artist unexpectedly find love.

Macomber, Debbie

Macomber is a well-known writer of Contemporary Series Romances, most often of the sweet and innocent variety. She has also written a series of books that features angels. Her stories are warm, tender, and family focused.

Morning Comes Softly. *HarperPaperbacks, 1993.* Rancher Travis Thompson advertises for a wife to help him care for his late brother's three children and ends up falling in love with the spinster librarian who answers his ad.

Someday Soon. *HarperPaperbacks, 1995.* A young widow and a mercenary adventurer fight their mutual attraction, and eventually lose.

Mrs. Miracle. *HarperPaperbacks, 1996.* The rather miraculous housekeeper Mrs. Miracle helps the bereaved father of twins cope, and find love.

This Matter of Marriage. *Mira, 1997.* Two friends and neighbors have their romantic sites set on other people, even though they would be perfect for each other. Eventually, they wake up to the truth.

Pace, Miriam

Warm Creature Comforts. *Avalon, 1991.* A veterinarian and a zoo keeper fight to save a local zoo in California's central valley.

Parrish, Laura

Love's Quiet Corner. *Avalon, 1989.* A store owner and a developer clash in a small-town setting.

Spencer, LaVyrle

Spencer is a noted writer of Period Americana and Contemporary Americana romances.

Forsaking All Others. *Berkley, 1982.* After one heartbreaking betrayal by a gorgeous model, can photographer Allison Scott ever trust another man?

A Promise to Cherish. *Berkley, 1983.* Lee struggles to succeed in a man's world of construction estimates and to overcome her heartbreak of losing her two young sons.

The Hellion. *Harlequin, 1984.* Berkley, 1989. Rachel and Tommy Lee are thrown together after living in separate worlds after a heartbreaking separation in high school. Can romance with an elegant, worldly woman and a wild, free-wheeling roué really work?

Sweet Memories. *Harlequin, 1984.* Theresa makes a momentous decision by herself. Will it jeopardize her new love with Brian?

Separate Beds. *Berkley, 1985.* Published in London by *Macdonald, 1988.* A marriage of convenience threatens to become more when love arrives on the scene.

Spring Fancy. *Harlequin, 1986.* Winn had her life and world well organized. Even her wedding plans ran smoothly until Joseph appeared in her life. Was this real love, or just a fleeting passion?

A Heart Speaks (includes *A Promise To Cherish* and *Forsaking All Others*). *Berkley, 1986.*

Bittersweet. *Putnam, 1990.* High school sweethearts long ago, Maggie and Eric are thrown together in northern Wisconsin when Maggie returns there after her husband's sudden death.

Bygones. *Putnam, 1992.* After a bitter divorce six years earlier, Bess and Michael are forced to work together for the wedding of their daughter, Lisa, who is nursing a hope of their reconciliation.

Family Blessings. *Putnam, 1993.* The difficulties of a romance between an older woman and younger man are legion when Lee Reston finds herself attracted to her son Greg's best friend, following Greg's untimely death.

Home Song. *Putnam, 1995.* Tom Gardner watches his stable, comfortable life unravel as his wife, son, and daughter are all forced to deal with the consequences of his youthful fling.

Small Town Girl. *Putnam, 1997.* Country music star Tess "Mac" McPhail reluctantly returns home to help care for her mother. She encounters indifference and resentment from her family and friends and is ignored by Kenny, the "boy-next-door," now grown to local prominence.

NOTES

1. Martin C. Battestin, ed., "British Novelists, 1660-1800," in *Dictionary of Literary Biography* 39 (Detroit: Gale, 1985), 379.

2. James D. Hart, *The Popular Book: A History of America's Literary Taste* (Westport, CT: Greenwood Press, 1950), 52.

3. Rachel Anderson, *The Purple Heart Throbs: An Entertaining Survey of the Subliterature of Love* (London: Hodder & Stoughton, 1974), 25.

4. Betty Rosenberg, *Reading Interests in Genre Fiction*, 2nd ed. (Littleton, CO: Libraries Unlimited, 1986), 138.

Chapter 6

Romantic Mysteries

"Mystery magnifies danger [in Romance] as the fog the sun."
Charles Caleb Colton (1925)

"It is the dim haze of mystery that adds enchantment to pursuit."
Antoine Rivarol

DEFINITION

Romantic Mysteries, as their designation indicates, are combinations of mystery-adventure and romance. These stories usually employ two distinct plot-lines—one romance, one mystery. The two plotlines may begin separately but are eventually linked in some way, most often through the heroine. As the story progresses, the story lines increasingly overlap and intertwine, ultimately arriving at the successful, nearly simultaneous, conclusion of both.

Because of its dual story line, there is often a certain amount of difficulty in identifying the genre to which a book belongs—is it a romance or is it a mystery? The general rule is: If the emphasis is on the romance, the story is a Romantic Mystery; if the emphasis is on the mystery, the story is Mystery-Suspense. This is, however, a much simpler rule to say than to apply because many authors seem to have a foot in each camp. For example, the spy thrillers of Helen MacInnes often have a female protagonist and a strong romance story line; they also have a hard-core espionage plotline. Similarly, Mary Stewart produces suspense stories with equally strong mystery and romance plotlines. There is, however, a difference between the two. Stewart always uses the mystery to enhance the romance story line. In MacInnes's work, the romance is generally secondary to the espionage aspects. Although both authors are read by mystery and romance fans alike, MacInnes' works are usually considered in the spy/espionage subgenre, while Stewart's are classed as Romantic Mysteries. It is worth noting, incidentally, that such crossover in readership is not uncommon. Readers of Romantic Mysteries often read Mystery-Suspense stories as long as there is a strong love interest in the story, just as mystery fans read Romantic Mysteries that contain effective suspense story lines. Gothic and romantic suspense novels are included in the bibliography of Allen J. Hubin's *Crime Fiction, 1749-1980*, (Garland, 1984). *Twentieth Century Crime and Mystery Writers* (St. Martin's Press, 1985) also lists a number of romantic suspense and Gothic writers, including Victoria Holt, Mary Stewart, and Phyllis Whitney.

Included within the Romantic Mystery subgenre are two distinct, yet closely related types, the novel of Romantic Suspense and the Gothic Romance. Although the specific conventions, story lines, and geographical and historical settings can vary widely, the common denominator of both types is the threatened, vulnerable—although seldom helpless—heroine. Thrown, either by choice or chance, into a mysterious, puzzling, or frightening situation, she seeks to unravel the mystery, thereby placing herself in danger. At the same time, she becomes romantically involved with the hero. Complications ensue, tensions mount, and at some point the heroine usually finds herself at the mercy of the villain and often in fear for her life. Nevertheless, by the story's end, the mystery is properly solved and the hero and heroine are safe in each other's arms.

In general, the difference between the two subtypes is one of setting, convention, and tone, rather than basic plot. Novels of Romantic Suspense are usually given a contemporary setting (hence today's common designation, Contemporary Romantic Suspense); Gothics are usually, but certainly not always, set in the past, often during the Victorian period. In the novel of Romantic Suspense, the heroine may travel to far-flung, exotic places; in the Gothic, she usually travels to an isolated mansion, castle, or estate—and stays there. While ensconced in the castle, the Gothic heroine may witness mysterious, unexplained events, sometimes of a supernatural nature. The heroine of Romantic Suspense rarely experiences anything that cannot be explained rationally. In addition, the pacing and style of the Romantic Suspense novel is usually lively, upbeat, and direct, whereas that of the Gothic is often measured and more circumspect.

The characters also vary between the types. Hero and villain characters are common to both, but their typical personal characteristics may differ greatly. The sardonic, brooding hero of the classic Gothic is hardly the engaging, competent hero of the Romantic Suspense. However, while in the Romantic Suspense novel, the heroine may interact with a large number of people, including colleagues, fellow travelers, locals, and even criminal types, in the Gothic she relates almost exclusively to a small, intimate group of assorted family members and servants and, of course, to the house itself—which in the Gothic assumes the role of a major character. An obvious corollary of this is that in the novel of Romantic Suspense, the heroine is most often threatened by strangers (although the villain may eventually turn out to be someone she knows and even likes, as in Mary Stewart's *Wildfire at Midnight*). In the Gothic, her greatest danger comes from someone close to her. The atmosphere of the novel of Romantic Suspense is open, active, expansive, and dangerous; that of the Gothic is closed, secretive, and ingrown, but equally dangerous.

Obviously, all Romantic Mysteries do not divide themselves so easily along these rather arbitrary lines, and elements from one type have long been found in the other. In fact, recently the lines between the Romantic Suspense and the Gothic, as well as those between the Romantic Mystery, and the larger Mystery/Thriller genre, have become increasingly blurred. With the growing tendency toward genreblending and the increasing number of romance writers crossing over into the popular Mystery genre, as well as the gradual demise of the Gothic as a specific romance subgenre and the dispersal of many of its elements into other subgenres (especially the Paranormal), it is becoming more and more difficult to relegate some of these books to a specific category. For example, Kay Hooper's *Amanda* is labeled Romantic Suspense but falls within the definition of a contemporary Gothic. Fortunately, this is not always a problem because many readers do not consciously distinguish between types, reading Romantic Suspense, Gothics, and mainstream mysteries with strong romance plotlines with equal enjoyment. Nevertheless, defining the subgenre is becoming an increasingly subjective task, and when it comes right down to it, there is only way to be certain what category a particular book is in—read it and decide for yourself.

One word of warning—by either accident or design books of this type are often mislabeled. Romantic Suspense is occasionally labeled Mystery or Fiction, and Gothics are designated as Romantic Suspense or even Alternative Reality or Paranormal. Once again, read for yourself and decide.

APPEAL

The particular appeal of the romantic mystery is to our innate sense of adventure, excitement, and mystery. From our earliest games of peekaboo and hide-and-seek to the telling of ghost stories around the campfire or at a slumber party, we all have enjoyed the vicarious delight of being frightened in safety. Most of us, however, do not lead lives in which danger and adventure are everyday realities. Indeed, if we did, most likely we would find being pursued by methodical murderers or haunted by shimmering specters unnerving and not at all exciting or romantic. We want our excitement, mystery, and romance, but we want it without the danger. This is just what the Romantic Mystery provides: the thrill of adventure, mystery, and terror, together with the guarantee (usually) of a happy, romantic ending—all without risk!

ADVISING THE READER

General readers' advisory information is provided in chapter 3; however, there are a few points that might be helpful for advising Romantic Mystery fans specifically.

- Many readers of Romantic Suspense also read Mystery-Suspense. A Mary Stewart fan might enjoy reading books by Helen MacInnes or even Agatha Christie or Patricia Wentworth.

- Conversely, people who enjoy Mystery-Suspense may also like Romantic Mysteries. Evelyn Anthony and Elizabeth Peters are often popular with both groups.

- A number of Romance and Romantic Suspense writers have begun to make forays into the Mystery-Suspense or Thriller genres (e.g., Iris Johansen, Tami Hoag, Eileen Dreyer, Nora Roberts as J. D. Robb), and readers familiar with these writers' other works may like their mysteries, as well.

- Readers who enjoy Gothics may also enjoy some of the Alternative Reality romances, especially those within the Paranormal subgroup. For example, Antoinette Stockenberg's "ghostly" romances have a definite Gothic feel, as do the vampire books of Lori Herter.

- It is also important to determine whether a reader likes all types of Romantic Mysteries or is partial to a particular variety. A confirmed Gothic fan may not enjoy Mysteries by Elizabeth Peters (perhaps preferring to read her alter-ego Barbara Michaels, instead), and a Romantic Suspense aficionado may detest Victoria Holt. In addition, a reader for whom a happy ending is essential may not care for some of Jane Aiken's work.

- For the reader who is new to the subgenre, recommend "tried and true" works by some of the major authors (e.g., early works by classic writers Mary Stewart, Phyllis Whitney, Victoria Holt, and the more recent Romantic Suspense novels of Sandra Brown, Nora Roberts, Karen Robards) and expand from there.

BRIEF HISTORY

Romantic mysteries have their particular historical origins in the late eighteenth century literary Gothics (see discussion in the "Gothic Romance" section). Inspired by Walpole's original Gothic novel, the chilling, supernatural *The Castle of Otranto* (1764), Ann Radcliffe in "The Mysteries of Udolpho" tempered the terror and horror with elements of romance and sentimentality, at the same time explaining away the supernatural happenings as the deliberate, "natural" work of the villain. She also may have been influenced in some degree by the work of Clara Reeve who emphasized the past, using its unfamiliarity to create an atmosphere of mystery and terror. Radcliffe's works were tremendously popular during her lifetime (late eighteenth century), influencing not only contemporary writers, but those who followed her as well.

Although a variety of forms of the Gothic novel flourished in late eighteenth- and early nineteenth-century England, it was those of the sentimental (à la Radcliffe) and historical (à la Reeve) types that found the most favor in the United States. The other major type, the terror Gothic (Walpole and a slightly later writer, Matthew "Monk" Lewis, were best known for this variety), held little appeal for the majority of Americans. Its elements were seen most often in the work of serious writers such as Edgar Allan Poe and Nathaniel Hawthorne. (Interestingly, it is the terror Gothic, through its influence on the development of the mystery/thriller and novels of detection, that is indirectly responsible for many aspects of the modern-day novels of Romantic Suspense.) Most popular Gothic Romances read in America were of British origin, although there were some local writers successfully working in the genre, such as Sally Wood and Isaac Mitchell. Eventually, interest in the Gothic began to wane both here and abroad, and its various conventions drifted into other literary genres. (Mysteries, Science Fiction, Melodrama, and even the Western all reflect the Gothic influence.)

However, it was the works of the American women writers of the mid-nineteenth century that most closely carried on the Gothic tradition within the United States. (The Gothic tradition in England was being continued by a number of writers, including the Brontës.) Although many of their novels were domestic-romantic as opposed to Gothic, works by such popular writers as E.D.E.N. Southworth often employed a number of Gothic elements, e.g., orphaned heroines, lost inheritances, mistaken identities, isolated castles, lecherous villains, dashing heroes, and contrived coincidences. Another popular writer of the period was Bertha M. Clay, who was not actually a person at all, but rather a group of people who produced Gothics for a popular dime novel series. Many of these novels still had European settings and characters (America obviously presented a problem in that it had no nobility and few castles). However, as time passed, local backgrounds and history began to be used more frequently, and by the end of the century, American history had achieved a validity of its own and its use in romantic novels was commonly accepted.

Although Gothic elements continued to be used in many popular romantic novels, it wasn't until the publication of *Rebecca* in 1938 by Britain's Daphne Du Maurier that the modern prototype for the contemporary Gothic novel appeared. *Rebecca* was popular and extensively read, but widespread interest in the Gothic Romance in general did not occur until the 1960s. Sparked by the 1960 publication of Victoria Holt's *Mistress of Mellyn* (an English Gothic romance highly reminiscent of *Rebecca*), the demand for Gothic Romances and other Romantic Mysteries increased dramatically in both England and America. Writers such as Mary Stewart, Phyllis Whitney, Dorothy Eden, and to some extent Anya Seton, who had already published novels of Romantic Suspense and Gothic Romance, found themselves caught up in this new wave of popularity. However, this movement not only renewed interest in the works of established authors, it also created a demand for new writers—launching the careers of a host of authors including Catherine Gaskin, Evelyn Anthony, and Susan Howatch.

After the 1960s the popularity of Romantic Mysteries diminished somewhat, and by the mid-1970s many people were predicting the total demise of the subgenre. But the Romantic Mystery did not die, and by the mid 1980s the Gothic was on the rise once more, this time in the form of the new sensual Gothic. Classic Gothic heroines, for all their spunk and curiosity, are a fairly timid breed—and reference to sex, other than for kisses, chaste embraces, and unexplained feelings of euphoria and lightheadedness, is strictly forbidden. Zeroing in on the fact that a growing number of romance readers enjoyed spicier books with more assertive heroines, Signet (New American Library) launched a new series of sexy Gothics in 1986. Romantic Suspense was also on the move, and by the end of the decade, interest was such that several publishers had added separate romance lines that featured romantic suspense plotlines (e.g., Harlequin Intrigue and Avalon Mystery Romance).

Interest in both Romantic Mystery subtypes continued into the 1990s, with several publishers adding Gothic Romance lines and most houses actively seeking even more Romantic Suspense manuscripts. The Gothic reached a high point in 1993 with the launching of Silhouette Shadows, a line of Gothically tinged romances, but the boom was short-lived and by the mid-1990s, interest had waned and most Gothic lines had been quietly discontinued. Romantic Suspense, on the other hand, continued to expand, and by the middle of the decade new writers were emerging, notable writers who had left the subgenre were returning (e.g., Mary Stewart), and a noticeable number of established romance writers were either crossing over to the subgenre itself or incorporating dashes of mystery or suspense into the romances they were already writing.

The situation today shows every sign of continuing along the same lines. However, while it might be tempting to say that the Romantic Suspense is hot and the Gothic is not, this would not be quite accurate, because despite the fact that the Gothic as a specific subgenre is no longer being published, many of its classic elements (e.g., isolated settings, old mysteries, family secrets, unexplained happenings, supernatural characters, a menacing or brooding atmosphere, a sense of impending doom) are alive and well in almost any other Romance subgenre you can name. For example, Regencies have been known to play host to vampires; psychics are routine in Romantic Suspense; ghosts and unexplained happenings appear in Paranormals; and isolated houses, brooding atmospheres, and other Gothic conventions are common in many Historical Romances and are found increasingly in Romantic Suspense. Obviously, the Gothic has not lost its appeal; it has simply reinvented itself—either by changing form (or in some cases merely changing its label to "Romantic Suspense") or by spinning off various components and letting them migrate into other subgenres. In any case, the elements of the Gothic are still there; they just are not always where you might expect to find them.

EARLY GOTHIC PROTOTYPES

Several of the early literary Gothics have been reprinted and make fascinating reading. Written two centuries ago in a different world for a very different group of readers, some of the characterizations, conventions, and assumptions implicit in them are alien to our contemporary culture. Essentially, these Gothic novels are not the Gothics of today. The study of psychology as we know it did not exist for Radcliffe and Walpole; the writers of today cannot remember when the ideas of Freud did not form the foundation for explaining every human thought, action, or reaction. Nevertheless, these works were extremely popular in their day and are still excellent examples of pure terror and suspense. The modern Romantic Mysteries owe them much.

These works have been reprinted in various editions and are all in print as of this writing. The dates listed immediately following the title are those of original publication.

Eberhart, Mignon Good
Beginning with *The Patient in Room 18* in 1929 until her final *Three Days for Emeralds* in 1988, Mignon Eberhart (d. 1996) produced approximately one novel of Romantic Suspense each year. Her well-crafted stories of detection often feature female protagonists (sleuths) and are noted for their appropriately sinister settings and suspenseful, often terrifying, atmosphere.

> **While the Patient Slept.** *Doubleday, 1930.* This classic (Eberhart's second book) established her reputation for creating chilling, Gothic settings. Her later books developed, balanced, and refined her style.

Lewis, Matthew Gregory. Ambrosio; or The Monk. (1795)
A true horror Gothic, this tale of clerical lust and murder was extremely popular in its day. While preaching purity and piety, Father Ambrosio (The Monk) plots to rape the innocent Antonia. At the same time, Lorenzo, who loves Antonia, helps his friend Raymond rescue his lover, Agnes, from the evil machinations of Ambrosio and the convent prioress. Filled with evil, sorcery, the supernatural, and ghoulishly graphic descriptions, this novel of mystery and terror has more in common with today's horror stories than with Gothic Romances. It is, however, an excellent example of the genre and does make interesting, if unsettling, reading.

Radcliffe, Ann. The Mysteries of Udolpho. (1794)

This is a popular example of what every young girl of the period was reading, much to the horror of parents and governesses. Orphaned, aristocratic Emily tries to foil Signor Montoni's plans to marry her off and steal her estate. In the process she solves several mysteries and is reunited with her lover. Although while at Montoni's castle, Udolpho, Emily experiences many strange happenings (talking shadows, bloody stairs, eerie noises, disappearances, etc.), all have rational explanations. Although stilted and unrealistic by today's standards, this widely read sentimental Gothic novel will appeal to many contemporary Gothic buffs. Incidentally, The "novels of Mrs. Radcliffe" are often mentioned in today's popular historical fiction (by Georgette Heyer and her imitators, for example), and devotees of the Regency might find it interesting to read what their favorite characters are said to be reading.

Walpole, Horace. The Castle of Otranto. (1764)

This is the original Gothic tale of love, castles, supernatural happenings, and good and evil. It is built around an incredible, convoluted plot in which a nobleman wants to divorce his wife and wed his dead son's fiancée. Replete with bleeding statues, praying skeletons, outsized armor and apparitions, pursuits through dank corridors, and startling revelations, this brief book makes interesting reading, if only for an idea of how Gothics got their start.

ROMANTIC SUSPENSE

The novel of Romantic Suspense is the feminine counterpart of the male adventure story. Deriving directly from mystery/detective and spy stories (which were influenced by the original horror Gothics), this subgenre is exemplified by fast-paced tales filled with action, mystery, suspense, and, of course, romance. A number of authors produced stories of this type during the first half of the twentieth century; however, it wasn't until the Romantic Mystery boom of the 1960s that the type achieved general popularity. Although there are several competent authors of Romantic Suspense, it is generally acknowledged that Mary Stewart set the standard for this subgenre. Even though the subgenre has evolved significantly since she first started writing, Stewart's works, especially the earlier ones, are considered classic examples of the type and are still the ones against which all others are judged.

In recent years, the Romantic Suspense subgenre has grown phenomenally. This may be due, in part, to the general surge of interest in the larger Mystery-Suspense genre. It may also be because a number of veteran romance writers decided to spread their wings and flew in the direction of Romantic Suspense. But whatever the reason, Romantic Suspense is currently popular with both writers and readers, and although the market will continue to have its ups and downs, the subgenre is important and is likely to remain in demand.

The recent tendency toward genreblending has added a bit of confusion to the scene by making it harder to distinguish between a Romantic Mystery and a Mystery-Suspense. Distinctions are also confused by the fact that a number of Romance writers are also making the leap to Mystery-Suspense, and although some writers totally change styles for their Mysteries, many do not, retaining strong romance plotlines and other Romance conventions. As a result, many of these works hover some-where between the genres, making it difficult to determine exactly where a book should be classified. An interesting sidelight to the genreblending phenomenon is that as Romance in-corporates elements from other genres, these genres are beginning to employ aspects of Ro-mance, blurring the distinctions even further. In fact, it is rumored that one noted mystery author was instructed to add some love interest to his popular mysteries. This is likely a re-action to the recent popularity of the Romance genre. It is also an indication that gen-reblending is increasing and is probably here to stay.

The following authors are known for their contributions to Romantic Suspense, al-though they may also write in and be noted for works in other subgenres. Only their Roman-tic Suspense novels are listed below; any other romance works included are discussed in the appropriate chapters.

Selected Romantic Suspense Bibliography

Aiken, Joan
Aiken's works are not all typical Romantic Suspense. Serious illness is often a factor, relatives are not necessarily nice and do not always get along, and the endings are not always happy. In addition, some of her novels are linked by the same character. Aiken is also noted for other works, including a large body of juvenile fiction. (*See also Gothic Bibliography and Regency bibliography.*)

Beware of the Bouquet. *Doubleday, 1966.* Published as *Trouble with Product X* by Gol-lancz, 1966.

The Crystal Crow. *Doubleday, 1968.* Originally published as *The Ribs of Death* by Gol-lancz, 1967.

The Embroidered Sunset. *Doubleday, 1970.* A poignant, bittersweet story of mystery, love, and death.

A Cluster of Separate Sparks. *Doubleday, 1972.* Originally published as *The Butterfly Picnic* by Gollancz, 1970. Hovers between the Gothic and Romantic Suspense genres.

Died on a Rainy Sunday. *Holt, Rinehart & Winston, 1972.*

Last Movement. *Doubleday, 1977.* Character links to *The Embroidered Sunset.*

The Five-Minute Marriage. *Gollancz, 1977.*

The Smile of the Stranger. *Gollancz, 1978.*

The Weeping Ash. *Doubleday, 1980.* Published as *The Lightning Tree* by Gollancz, 1980. Has character links to *The Smile of the Stranger.*

Anthony, Evelyn (Evelyn Ward-Thomas)
Anthony's first books were historical fiction. Later, she turned to Romantic Sus-pense of the thriller variety, specializing in well-crafted, compelling tales of inter-national crime, espionage, and intrigue. Although love is a strong motivating factor in most of her works, the stories don't always end happily. (Readers who enjoy An-thony may also like Helen MacInnes, a mystery-suspense writer not included in this guide.) Several of her more recent books are listed below. (*See also Historical Romance bibliography.*)

Davina Graham series

The Defector. *Hutchinson, 1980,* Coward, McCann & Geoghegan, 1981.

The Avenue of the Dead. *Hutchinson, 1981,* Coward, McCann & Geoghegan, 1982.

The Albatross. *Hutchinson, 1982,* Putnam, 1983.

The Company of Saints. *Hutchinson, 1983,* Putnam, 1984.

A Place to Hide. *Putnam, 1987.* When Claire sets out to find her missing brother Frank, she is pursued by both the IRA and British intelligence in a frightening journey through Ireland.

The Scarlet Thread. *Hutchinson, 1989,* Harper & Row, 1990. A "resurrected" first wife, a jealous second wife, and murder plans make for an exciting and suspenseful romantic adventure.

The Doll's House. *HarperCollins, 1992.* An undercover assignment leads Rosa Bennett into danger and unexpected love.

Exposure. *Bantam Books, 1993.* An investigative reporter runs into danger, adventure, and murder as her search to expose a media tycoon leads her to Germany and a deadly web of deceit and death that stretches back to the horrors of World War II.

Bloodstones. *HarperCollins, 1994.* The battle for control of a fabulous new Russian diamond mine creates chaos within the industry as well as deadly and intriguing problems for all involved.

Baxter, Mary Lynn

Hot Texas Nights. *Warner Books, 1996.* A reopened investigation into her husband's death ends up nearly costing Natalie Whitmore her daughter and her life as her efforts stir up family anger and greed—and a murderer's fears.

Lone Star Heat. *Harlequin, 1997.* A journalist heroine and her ex-husband are forced to work together in this fast-paced, steamy story of murder and deception.

Brent, Madeleine (Peter O'Donnell)

Brent specializes in strong, capable, and unusual heroines; far-flung settings; and plots that incorporate both Gothic and Romantic Suspense elements—all in a Victorian setting. In 1978 Brent won Britain's Romantic Novelists Association's Major Award.

Tregaron's Daughter. *Doubleday, 1971.*

Moonraker's Bride. *Doubleday, 1973.*

Stranger at Wildings. *Doubleday 1976.* Published as *Kirby's Changeling* by Souvenir, 1975.

Merlin's Keep. *Doubleday, 1978.* Souvenir, 1977.

The Capricorn Stone. *Doubleday, 1980.* Souvenir, 1979.

The Long Masquerade. *Doubleday, 1982.* Souvenir, 1979.

A Heritage of Shadows. *Doubleday, 1984.* Souvenir, 1983.

Stormswift. *Doubleday, 1985.* Souvenir, 1984.

The Golden Urchin. *Doubleday, 1987.* Souvenir, 1986.

Brown, Sandra

Although a noted writer of both historical and contemporary romance, Brown's passionate, action-filled novels of Romantic Suspense are some of her most popular. Southern settings, family secrets, and a bit of violence are often elements of her well-done stories. (*See also Basic Contemporary Romance bibliography.*)

Best Kept Secrets. *Warner Books, 1989.* An old murder and family secrets.

Mirror Image. *Warner Books, 1990.* Politics, assassination attempts, and revenge.

Breath of Scandal. *Warner Books, 1991.* Gang-rape, revenge, and retribution.

French Silk. *Warner Books, 1992.* Televangelism, lingerie, and murder.

Where There's Smoke. *Warner Books, 1993.* Politics, homosexuality, and treachery.

Clark, Mary Higgins

Although generally classified as straight Suspense or Mystery-Suspense, Clark's stories often have enough romantic interest or domestic appeal to satisfy readers of Romantic Suspense.

Coulter, Catherine

Coulter is a popular writer of Period Romance, Contemporary Romance, and some Romantic Suspense.

Beyond Eden. *E. P. Dutton, 1992.* A beautiful model with a difficult past becomes a killer's target. Family and abuse issues.

The Cove. *Jove, 1996.* A fugitive heroine, a mysterious small town along the Oregon coast, and a hero who is not quite what he seems combine in this fast-paced, chilling story.

The Maze. *Putnam, 1997.* A serial killer, brutal violence, and an avenging heroine in a San Francisco setting.

The Target. *Putnam, 1998.* Violence and a mute, abused child in the Colorado Rockies.

Cresswell, Jasmine

No Sin Too Great. *Mira Books, 1996.* On the run from the mob, Caroline ends up in the care of a sexy Episcopalian priest in this fast-paced, touching, and humorous story.

Dreyer, Eileen

Dreyer also writes award-winning contemporary romances as Kathleen Korbel. Her mysteries, while not romances, are well done; have an off-beat, quirky sense of humor; and may be of interest to readers who enjoy her Korbel books.

A Man to Die For. *HarperPaperbacks, 1991.*

If Looks Could Kill. *HarperPaperbacks, 1992.*

Nothing Personal. *HarperPaperbacks, 1994.*

Bad Medicine. *HarperPaperbacks, 1995.*

Brain Dead. *HarperCollins, 1997.*

Forster, Suzanne

Forster's stories tend to be fast-paced, sexy, intense, and occasionally dark.

Come Midnight. *Berkley, 1995.* A psychologist falls in love with the accused murderer she is supposed to be evaluating in this intense, passionate story.

Blush. *Berkley, 1996.* A scheme to arrange for her own kidnapping backfires, and spoiled brat "Gus" Featherstone ends up a prisoner of Jake Culhane. Jake is a man with vengeance on his mind, and they both get a bit more than they bargained for. Family secrets, betrayals, and suspense abound.

Gaskin, Catherine

Gaskin is noted for her strong, determined heroines; her detailed descriptions of the crafts and businesses discussed in her books; and her ability to combine romance with realism. Not always easy to categorize, her books combine Gothic and Romantic Suspense elements, employ both contemporary and historical settings, and could be legitimately classified within a number of romance subgenres. Some of her most notable stories include:

All Else Is Folly. *Harper, 1951.* The fashion industry is the backdrop for this story that is one of Gaskin's best.

The Tilsit Inheritance. *Doubleday, 1963.*

The File on Devlin. *Doubleday, 1965.*

The Property of a Gentleman. *Doubleday, 1974.* Art, skeletons, and a dash of violence.

Gilbert, Anna

Gilbert writes compelling, character-driven stories of Romantic Suspense set in rural Victorian England. Her remote settings, closed social environments, and occasional mysterious atmosphere lend a vaguely Gothic touch. Vivid descriptions, attention to detail, and carefully crafted writing make these classics of the genre.

Images of Roses. *Delacorte Press, 1974.*

The Look of Innocence. *St. Martin's Press, 1975.* Romantic Novelists Association Major Award winner.

Remembering Louise. *St. Martin's Press, 1978.*

The Leavetaking. *St. Martin's Press, 1980,* Hodder & Stoughton, 1979.

Flowers for Lillian. *St. Martin's Press, 1981.*

A Walk in the Wood. *St. Martin's Press, 1989.*

The Wedding Guest. *St. Martin's Press, 1993.*

Gordon, Deborah

Better known as contemporary series romance writer Brooke Hastings, Gordon writes Romantic Suspense and some Alternative Reality romances under her own name.

Beating the Odds. *HarperPaperbacks, 1992.*

Haley, Wendy

Shadow Whispers. *Zebra, 1992.* A bookstore owner almost becomes the victim of a serial killer when she tries to discover who killed her sister.

Dead Heat. *Zebra, 1994.* Arson and a firebug bent upon destruction draw the protagonists and their children together.

White Light. *Zebra, 1995.* The occult plays a part in this realistic tale of murder and suspense.

Hoag, Tami

Hoag has also written Contemporary Series Romances. Her most recent novels are in the Romantic Suspense or Mystery-Suspense modes.

Still Waters. *Bantam Books, 1992.* Murder and suspense in a small Amish community.

Cry Wolf. *Bantam Books, 1993.*

Dark Paradise. *Bantam Books, 1994.* Murders and mystery in rural Montana.

Night Sins. *Bantam Books, 1995.* State cop Megan O'Malley becomes involved in solving the kidnapping of a young boy in Deer Lake, Minnesota, in Hoag's first real thriller.

Guilty As Sin. *Bantam Books, 1996.* Attorney Ellen North flees Minneapolis for rural Deer Lake hoping for a change of pace. She ends up involved with a sick killer and a crime writer in this dark, convoluted mystery that continues where *Night Sins* left off.

A Thin Dark Line. *Bantam Books, 1997.*

Hodge, Jane Aiken

Primarily known for her exceptionally well-done period romances, Hodge has also written several contemporary novels in the Romantic Suspense genre.

Strangers in Company. *Coward, McCann & Geoghegan, 1973.*

One Way to Venice. *Coward, McCann & Geoghegan, 1975.*

Last Act. *Doubleday, 1979.*

The Lost Garden. *Coward, McCann & Geoghegan, 1982.*

Secret Island. *Putnam, 1985.*

Holt, Victoria (Eleanor Burford Hibbert)

Most of Holt's novels fall well within the Gothic subgenre; however, several exhibit enough fast-paced adventure (liberally laced with Gothic conventions) to appeal to readers of Romantic Suspense. Hibbert (d. 1993) was a prolific writer who produced romances under the pseudonyms Philippa Carr and Jean Plaidy, as well as Victoria Holt. *(See also Gothic and Historical Romance bibliographies.)*

The Pride of the Peacock. *Doubleday, 1976.*

The Judas Kiss. *Doubleday, 1981.*

The Time of the Hunter's Moon. *Doubleday, 1983.*

Hooper, Kay

Hooper often sprinkles mystery and suspense elements throughout her romances; however, those below are a bit more mystery than romance. Several of her more recent novels have been listed under Gothic Romance. *(See also Gothic and Alternative Reality bibliographies.)*

Crime of Passion. *Avon, 1991.*

House of Cards. *Avon, 1991.*

Howard, Linda (Linda Howington)

Howard writes Period Romance, Romantic Suspense, and Contemporary series romances. Her stories are often dark and sexy with an occasional touch of the paranormal. Her heroines are strong and capable, and her heroes are hard, occasionally brutal, and emotionally wounded. *(See also Western Romance bibliography.)*

After the Night. *Pocket Books, 1995.* A successful businesswoman returns to the Louisiana town that threw her out 12 years ago and stirs up old secrets, with dangerous results.

Dream Man. *Pocket Books, 1995.* A psychic heroine and a skeptical cop join forces in this dark, passionate tale of suspense.

Shades of Twilight. *Pocket Books, 1996.* A slightly Gothic story of old family secrets, murder, and betrayal in a contemporary southern setting.

Johansen, Iris

Johansen also has written Period and Contemporary Romances.

The Ugly Duckling. *Bantam Books, 1996.* In this chilling story, a woman who watched her husband and child brutally murdered is transformed through plastic surgery and sets about avenging their deaths.

Long After Midnight. *Bantam Books, 1997.* A geneticist is stalked to keep her from a major discovery.

And Then You Die. *Bantam Books, 1998.* Kidnapping with a Mexico setting.

Lee, Rachel

A Fateful Choice. *Mira Books, 1996.* When grieving attorney Jennifer Fox changes her mind after she arranges for her own murder, she is faced with the double problem of finding a murderer and evading her own assassin.

Maxwell, Ann

Maxwell also writes historical and contemporary romances as Elizabeth Lowell and in several other genres jointly with her husband Evan as A. E. Maxwell.

Tell Me No Lies. *Worldwide, 1986.* (As Elizabeth Lowell) One of her best.

The Diamond Tiger. *HarperCollins, 1992.* (With Evan Maxwell) An inherited diamond mine involves Erin in danger and intrigue, courtesy of a greedy diamond cartel and a Chinese tong.

The Secret Sisters. *HarperCollins, 1993.* (With Evan Maxwell)

Pappano, Marilyn

Pappano writes well-plotted, often dark and dangerous stories with mainstream tendencies.

In Sinful Harmony. *Warner Books, 1995.* When Will Beaumont returns to Harmony, Texas, things change drastically—including the life of one very bored librarian.

Passion. *Warner Books, 1996.* Danger, hidden identities, and insanity combine in a fast-paced story of intrigue and passion with a New Orleans setting.

Survive the Night. *Warner Books, 1996.*

Suspicion. *Warner Books, 1997.* Kate Edwards and Tucker Caldwell, each with excellent reasons for wanting cruel, wealthy Jason Trask dead, are the prime suspects in his unexpected murder. This gripping, passionate story of rape, power, and retribution is complex, fast paced, and hard-hitting.

Pence, Joanne

This lively, witty series of detective stories features journalist/sleuth Angie Amalfi and usually focuses on cooking, food, and cooks.

Something's Cooking. *HarperPaperbacks, 1993.*

Too Many Cooks. *HarperPaperbacks, 1994.*

Cooking Up Trouble. *HarperPaperbacks, 1995.*

Cooking Most Deadly. *HarperPaperbacks, 1996.*

Cook's Night Out. *HarperPaperbacks, 1997.*

Cooks Overboard. *HarperPaperbacks, 1998.*

Peters, Elizabeth (Barbara Mertz)

Also known for her Gothic romances written as Barbara Michaels, Elizabeth Peters offers a sense of humor and a kind of lighthearted believability—all tied together by a strong mystery plotline and thorough research. Most of her books feature one of three heroines (Amelia Peabody, Vicky Bliss, or Jacqueline Kirby), although several of her non-series books are also included below. Because the author is a scholar of Egyptology , a number of her novels are set in Egypt or the Middle East. More mystery than romance, Peters' novels appeal to readers of both genres.

The Dead Sea Cipher. *Dodd, Mead, 1970.*

Legend in Green Velvet. *Dodd, Mead, 1976.* Published as *Ghost in Green Velvet*, by Cassell and Collier Macmillan, 1977. An uncanny Scottish mystery.

The Love Talker. *Dodd, Mead, 1980.*

Jacqueline Kirby Series

Jacqueline Kirby, academic librarian, scholar, amateur sleuth, and eventually an inadvertent romance writer, is a modern-day counterpart of Peters's Amelia Peabody.

The Seventh Sinner. *Dodd, Mead, 1972.*

The Murders of Richard III. *Dodd, Mead, 1974.*

Die for Love. *Congdon and Weed, 1984.* A wild and wacky romance writers' conference is the unlikely, but delightful, setting for murder in this witty story that is a bit of a spoof and one of the author's best.

Naked Once More. *Warner, 1989.*

Vicky Bliss Series

This series features art professor Vicky Bliss.

Borrower of the Night. *Dodd, Mead, 1973.*

Street of the Five Moons. *Dodd, Mead, 1978.*

Silhouette in Scarlet. *Congdon and Weed, 1983.* Mystery with a Swedish setting.

Trojan Gold. *Atheneum, 1987.*

Night Train to Memphis. *Warner, 1994.*

Amelia Peabody Series

This entire series involves a marvelously anachronistic Victorian sleuth/heroine, pokes fun at Victorian novels, and is something of a spoof of the entire Romantic Suspense subgenre. The independent and intrepid archaeologist Amelia is generally considered to be Peters' most popular and best known heroine.

Crocodile on the Sandbank. *Dodd, Mead, 1975.* A classic.

The Curse of the Pharoahs. *Dodd, Mead, 1981.*

The Mummy Case. *Congdon and Weed, 1985.*

Lion in the Valley. *Atheneum, 1986.*

The Deeds of the Disturber. *Atheneum, 1988.*

The Last Camel Died at Noon. *Warner Books, 1991.*

The Snake, the Crocodile, and the Dog. *Warner Books, 1992.* An ancient Egyptian fairy tale, amnesia, and unexplained disappearances in an exotic Cairo setting.

The Hippopotamus Pool. *Warner Books, 1996.*

Seeing a Large Cat. *Warner Books, 1997.*

The Ape Who Guards the Balance. *Avon Books, 1998.*

Pozzessere, Heather Graham

Pozzessere also writes as Heather Graham and Shannon Drake. Her recent stories of Romantic Suspense include:

Slow Burn. *Mira Books, 1994.* A fast-paced contemporary story of a widow who returns to her Miami home to discover the truth about her husband's murder.

Eyes of Fire. *Mira Books, 1995.* A story of greed, murder, and sunken treasure with a Caribbean island setting.

If Looks Could Kill. *Mira Books, 1997.* Serial killer stalks women in Miami in this story with a psychic touch.

Never Sleep with Strangers. *Mira Books, 1998.*

Robards, Karen

Robards' stories are fast-paced, suspenseful, and often passionate with an emphasis on the romance.

One Summer. *Delacorte Press, 1993.* When Johnny Harris returns to town after serving a ten-year prison sentence for a murder he didn't commit, Rachel Grant, his former teacher, is the only one who believes he is innocent—and then another woman is killed.

Maggy's Child. *Delacorte Press, 1994.* Spousal abuse plays a part in this dark and suspenseful story of love and revenge among the Kentucky elite.

Walking After Midnight. *Doubleday, 1995.* Dashes of humor and a touch of whimsy lighten this fast-paced story of kidnapping, murder, and pursuit as Summer ends up falling in love with the "corpse" that kidnapped her.

Hunter's Moon. *Dell, 1996.* Molly Ballard is forced to make a dangerous deal with the FBI and ends up falling in love with Agent Will Lyman in this fast-paced, sexy adventure.

Roberts, Nora

Award-winning, best-selling Roberts is one of the genre's luminaries. She writes both contemporary series and single title romances. Her Romantic Suspense titles are chilling, suspenseful, and appropriately atmospheric. Like all her books, they are fast-paced and well written and feature well-developed, believable characters.

Hot Ice. *Bantam Books, 1987.*

Sacred Sins. *Bantam Books, 1987.*

Brazen Virtue. *Bantam Books, 1988.*

Sweet Revenge. *Bantam Books, 1989.*

Public Secrets. *Bantam Books, 1990.*

Carnal Innocence. *Bantam Books, 1991.* A concert violinist comes to Innocence, Mississippi, for peace and quiet, finding a serial killer instead.

Genuine Lies. *Bantam Books, 1991.* A biographer goes to Hollywood and becomes involved in the murder of the film star she is writing about.

Divine Evil. *Bantam Books, 1992.* A sculptor returns to her hometown to resolve some past issues and ends up unearthing an old, terrifying evil.

Honest Illusions. *Putnam, 1992.*

Private Scandals. *Putnam, 1993.* A Rita Award winner.

Hidden Riches. *Putnam, 1994.* An antique store owner and a former police officer find love amid a tangle of murder and art smuggling.

Sawyer, Meryl

Blind Chance. *Dell, 1989.* Past indiscretions lead to revenge and blackmail in this fast-paced romance.

Midnight in Marrakesh. *Dell, 1991.* Theft, drugs, and forgeries abound in this story set amid the glittering, deceptive world of high-priced art.

Promise Me Anything. *Dell, 1994.* Diamonds and adventure.

Kiss in the Dark. *Dell, 1995.* A journalist falls in love with the attorney who destroyed her family when she is forced to enlist his help in discovering who is trying to frame her for murder.

Tempting Fate. *Zebra, 1998.* Learning that her late husband has a son in an orphanage, journalist Kelly Taylor decides to find him, with romantic and almost deadly results.

Scott, Alicia

The Quiet One. *Silhouette, 1996.* An artist flees New York for a bit of small-town peace and quiet and ends up stalked by a killer, involved in a 25-year-old murder, and in love with the local sheriff. Chilling and well crafted.

Stewart, Mary

Stewart sets the standard for the Romantic Suspense genre. In addition to having been published individually, many of the novels listed below have also appeared in collections. *(See also Gothic Romance bibliography.)*

Madam, Will You Talk? *Hodder & Stoughton, 1955.* When Charity Selborne, a young widow, stumbles into danger, her vacation in the South of France becomes a nightmare of murder and deadly evil.

Wildfire at Midnight. *Appleton-Century Crofts, 1956.* The Isle of Skye promises to be a good spot to escape the rigors of work and a broken marriage. There, Gianetta Brooke finds mystery, murder, insanity and her ex-husband.

Thunder on the Right. *Hodder & Stoughton, 1957.* While searching for her missing cousin Gillian, Jennifer Silver is caught in a web of intrigue and smuggling in a convent in the French Pyrenees.

My Brother Michael. *William Morrow, 1959.* Camilla Haven, vacationing in Greece's Delphi, stumbles into a mystery that started with the Greek Resistance. Among the ruins she finds romance and a startling conclusion.

The Ivy Tree. *William Morrow, 1961.* Mary Grey, or is it Annabel Winslow, returns to her English farm only to discover that someone does not want her back home—at any cost. An unusual tale of deception and danger set in rural Northumberland.

The Moon-Spinners. *William Morrow, 1962.* While vacationing in Crete, Nicola Ferris becomes entangled in a murderer's vicious plot, the intrigue of stolen jewels, and an unlikely romance.

This Rough Magic. *William Morrow, 1964.* While visiting her sister on the island of Corfu, Lucy Waring innocently finds herself involved in a smuggling ring. The combination of Shakespeare's *The Tempest* and trained dolphins make for an amazing adventure.

Airs Above the Ground. *William Morrow, 1965.* Vanessa March does not question her husband's business trip. However, when he appears where he shouldn't be, she is plunged into a maze surrounded by the circus and the famous Lippizaner horses. A chilling tale of mystery and intrigue set in the famous Spanish Riding School in Austria.

The Gabriel Hounds. *William Morrow, 1967.* In a ruined castle in Lebanon, Christy Mansel learns a secret surrounding her missing great-aunt, only to find herself in the middle of murder and drug trafficking. Based on accounts of the life of Lady Hester Stanhope.

Thornyhold. *William Morrow, 1988.*

The Stormy Petrel. *Hodder & Stoughton, 1991.* When a poetry-writing professor leases a remote Scottish island for the summer, the last thing she expects is mystery, danger, or love. Naturally, she finds all three.

Rose Cottage. *William Morrow, 1997.*

Tillis, Tracey

Deadly Masquerade. *Dell, 1994.* A fast-paced mystery that moves from the Indiana slums to the Louisiana bayous as the protagonists search for some unexpected answers.

NightWatcher. *Bantam Books, 1995.* An investigative reporter ends up over her head in a dangerous situation.

Flashpoint. *Onyx, 1997.* Politics, race, and scandal in Atlanta.

Final Act. *Onyx, 1998.*

Whitney, Phyllis A.

Although most of her works for adults fall within the modern Gothic Romance subgenre, many of her novels have enough fast-paced action to appeal to readers of Romantic Suspense. *(See Gothic Romance bibliography.)*

Woods, Sherryl

Woods writes both Contemporary Series romance and single title Romantic Suspense. Her style is witty, often humorous, and fast paced with lively dialogue.

Molly DeWitt series

Molly is a specialist in public relations; her love interest is detective Michael O'Hara.

Hot Property. *Dell, 1992.*

Hot Secret. *Dell, 1992.*

Hot Money. *Dell, 1993.*

Hot Schemes. *Dell, 1994.*

Amanda Roberts series

Amanda is an investigative reporter; her love interest is former cop Joe Donelli.

Reckless. *Warner Books, 1989.*

Body and Soul. *Warner Books, 1989.*

Stolen Moments. *Warner Books, 1990.*

Ties That Bind. *Silhouette, 1991.*

Bank on It. *Warner Books, 1993.*

Hide and Seek. *Warner Books, 1993.*

Wages of Sin. *Warner Books, 1994.*

Deadly Obsession. *Warner Books, 1995.*

White Lightning. *Warner Books, 1995.*

GOTHIC ROMANCE

Although the roots of the Gothic novel are most often traced to the late eighteenth century, it is in *Jane Eyre* by Charlotte Brontë and *Rebecca* by Daphne Du Maurier that the modern Gothic Romance has its true antecedents. Note: This use of the term *Gothic* should not be confused with the Gothic time period of the late Middle Ages. This usage refers to works that have grotesque, macabre aspects and the typical novel often contained an abundance of castles or abbeys; specters; and other eerie, supernatural, or horrible (a la Monk Lewis) occurrences. The basic plot patterns of these works have been widely adapted, and their numerous variations form the framework for most contemporary Gothic Romances. *Jane Eyre* provides us with the poor-orphaned-governess-who-falls-in-love-with-the-man-of-the-house theme, and *Rebecca* contributes the hasty-marriage-to-a-mysterious-man-who- has-a-terrible-secret plotline. *Rebecca* also gives us Manderley, the first house to become a truly memorable character in a Gothic novel.

While both works exude a Gothic atmosphere and include a number of archetypal Gothic characters (the resentful housekeeper; the insane relative; the moody, secretive hero; etc.), it is another work, *Wuthering Heights* by Emily Brontë, that provides us with some of the more chilling elements of the genre—revenge, violence, insidious evil, the supernatural, and the general sense of impending doom. In addition, its isolated setting and the wild and stormy atmosphere, as well as certain characteristics of the brooding, haunted hero, Heathcliff, are widely imitated in many contemporary Gothics.

These three prototypes of the modern Gothic are now considered literary classics. All three are in print, all three have been made into major motion pictures, and all three make excellent reading.

Brontë, Charlotte

Jane Eyre. *(1847).* The classic "governess" tale making full use of family secrets, demented relatives, unexpected inheritances, and mistreated orphans.

Brontë, Emily

Wuthering Heights. *(1847).* An eerie tale of love and revenge set in the desolate, windswept English moors.

Du Maurier, Daphne

Rebecca. *(1938).* A gripping story of love, death, and deception employing a number of now-classic conventions such as the house-as-character; the vulnerable, isolated heroine; the precipitous marriage to a near stranger; the palpable influence of the dead first wife; old secrets; and first-person narrative by the heroine.

Although the Gothic Romance as a specific subgenre is considered by most to be in a state of decline, and certainly there is currently much less activity in this subgenre than in earlier years, the Gothic is still around, and it is still being requested and read. Older works are still in print, and many works that are no longer in print are still available in libraries or in individual private collections. Gothics by such luminaries as Victoria Holt, Phyllis Whitney, and Barbara Michaels have remained continuously in print, and Michaels and Whitney are still writing for the market. In addition, a number of recent romances, particularly those of the Romantic Suspense and Paranormal varieties, make use of enough Gothic conventions that they will not only appeal to Gothic readers, but in an earlier, more Gothic-friendly time, would even have been labeled as such.

The following authors are known for their contributions to gothic romance, although they may also write in and be noted for works in other subgenres. Only their Gothic Romance novels are listed below. For a more complete coverage of older works, consult *Happily Ever After: A Guide to Reading Interests in Romance Fiction* (Libraries Unlimited, 1987).

Selected Gothic Bibliography

Aiken, Joan

Aiken is an imaginative, literate writer whose works are not always easy to categorize. However, Gothic elements are present in many of her novels, including:

Castle Barebane. *Viking, 1976.*

The Weeping Ash. *Doubleday, 1980.* Published as *The Lightning Tree* in London by Gollancz, 1980.

The Haunting of Lamb House. *St. Martin's Press, 1993.* Cape, 1991. A multigenerational Gothic saga, complete with house-as-character and long kept secrets.

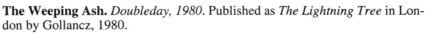

Berckman, Evelyn

Although noted for her well-crafted and painstakingly researched crime novels, Berckman's works often included Gothic, romantic, and historical elements. Her works are listed selectively.

The Heir of Starvelings. *Doubleday, 1967.*

The Victorian Album. *Doubleday, 1973.*

Brandewyne, Rebecca

Brandewyne has also written Contemporary and Period Romance.

Highclyffe Hall series

Upon a Moon-Dark Moor. *Warner Books, 1988.* A multi-family historical saga with definite Gothic tendencies.

Across a Starlit Sea. *Warner Books, 1989.* Continues *Upon a Moon-Dark Moor.*

Brandon, Beatrice (Robert W. Krepps)

The Cliffs of Night. *Doubleday, 1974.*

Court of the Silver Shadows. *Doubleday, 1980.* A modern-day Gothic of such purity that it is almost a parody.

Carr, Philippa (Eleanor Burford Hibbert, also writes as Victoria Holt and Jean Plaidy)

Carr's works are historical romances with a definite Gothic touch. However, because they all follow the lives of the various descendants of Bruno and Damask (of the first title, *The Miracle at St. Bruno's*), they are included in the Saga section of this book. (See chapter 10, "Sagas.")

Coffman, Virginia

An expert in creating appropriate atmosphere, Coffman has written more than 70 novels. She combines Gothic and detective conventions with historical settings, and her occasionally unconventional heroine does not always "get her man." Some of her books are linked (e.g., the Moura books), and Lucifer Cove is a true Gothic series. Many of her works are now out of print, although some can still be found in large public libraries. Coffman has also written historical romances of the Saga type. *(See also Saga and Period Romance bibliographies.)*

Moura. *Crown, 1959.*

The Beckoning. *Ace, 1965.* Published as *The Beckoning from Moura* by Ace, 1977.

The Devil Vicar. *Ace, 1966.* Revised edition published as *Vicar of Moura* by Ace, 1972.

The Dark Gondola. *Ace, 1968.* Published as *The Dark Beyond Moura* by Ace, 1977.

The Vampyre of Moura. *Ace, 1970.*

The Mist at Darkness. *New American Library, 1968.*

Lucifer Cove Series

The Devil's Mistress. *Lancer, 1969.*

Priestess of the Damned. *Lancer, 1970.*

The Devil's Virgin. *Lancer, 1970.*

Masque of Satan. *Lancer, 1971.*

Chalet Diabolique. *Lancer, 1971.*

From Satan, With Love. *Lancer, 1972.*

The Jewelled Darkness. *Severn House, 1989.*

The Jewels series
    Emerald Flame. *Severn, 1996.*
    The Wine-Dark Opal. *Severn, 1997.*

Conway, Laura (Dorothy Phoebe Ansle)

(also writes as Vicky Lancaster, Hebe Elsna, and Lyndon Snow) A prolific writer of more than 200 romances, Conway specializes in psychological tales that deal with the occult, reincarnation, travel between time periods, and similar supernatural topics. Mysterious unexplained happenings and other Gothic conventions—the "house-as-character" in particular—are common to her works.

Heiress Apparent. *Collins, 1966. McCall, 1970.*

A House Called Pleasance. *Dutton, 1975.* Originally published under the name Hebe Elsna by Hale, 1963.

Dark Symmetry. *Saturday Review Press, 1973.*

Crecy, Jeanne (Jeanne Williams)

Williams wrote several Gothics under this pseudonym, including:

Hands of Terror. *Berkley, 1972.* Published as *Lady Gift* by Hale, 1973.

The Evil Among Us. *New American Library, 1975.*

The Night Hunters. *New American Library, 1975.*

Crowe, Cecily

Crowe's well-crafted Gothics sparkle with humor and a sense of the ridiculous, displaying her unusually well-drawn characters to full advantage. Three of her most memorable are:

The Tower of Kilraven. *Holt, Rinehart & Winston, 1965.*

Abbygate. *Coward, McCann, & Geoghegan, 1977.*

The Talisman. *St. Martin's Press, 1979.*

Daniels, Dorothy

Daniels has produced approximately 150 romance novels, mostly of the Gothic variety. Her works exude appropriately Gothic atmosphere, and exotic settings abound. Supposed supernatural occurrences are commonplace but are always logically explained. Typical of many writers, Daniels' later books veer away from the Gothic and toward Romantic Suspense. Although many of her books are no longer in print, they may be of interest to some readers and should be available in larger public libraries.

Darty, Peggy

The Widowed Bride of Raven Oaks. *Zebra, 1989.*

The Wailing Winds of Juneau Abby. *Zebra, 1990.* A ghost, a murder, and the typical Gothic romantic "choice" (i.e., which man should she trust?) in an Alaskan setting.

The Crimson Roses of Fountain Court. *Zebra, 1991.* Curses, superstition, and danger in a New Orleans setting.

The Captured Bride of Aspenwood. *Zebra, 1992.*

The Precious Pearls of Cabot Hall. *Zebra, 1992.*

Eden, Dorothy

Eden is a renowned novelist in a number of romance subgenres. *(See Period Romance and Historical Novels bibliographies.)*

Crow Hollow. *Macdonald, 1950.* Ace, 1977.

Voice of the Dolls. *Macdonald, 1950.* Ace, 1973.

Listen to Danger. *Macdonald, 1958.* Ace, 1976.

The Sleeping Bride. *Macdonald, 1959.* Ace, 1976.

Samantha. *Hodder & Stoughton, 1960.* Published as *Lady of Mallow* by Coward, McCann, 1962.

Sleep in the Woods. *Hodder & Stoughton, 1960.* Coward, McCann, 1961.

Darkwater. *Coward, McCann, 1964.*

Ravenscroft. *Coward, McCann, 1965.*

Winterwood. *Coward, McCann, 1967.*

The Shadow Wife. *Coward, McCann, 1968.*

Waiting for Willa. *Coward, McCann, 1970.*

An Afternoon Walk. *Coward, McCann & Geoghegan, 1971.*

Elgin, Mary

Elgin's few Gothics are well written, appropriately set in the Scottish Highlands, and enhanced by a marvelous sense of whimsy and humor.

A Man from the Mist. *Mill, 1965.* Originally published as *Visibility Nil* by Hodder & Stoughton, 1963. Progress and newcomers create discord in a mysterious and wildly beautiful part of the Scottish Highlands.

Highland Masquerade. *Bantam Books, 1967.* Originally published as *Return to Glenshael* by Mills & Boon, 1965. When Aillie Rannoch returns incognito to the Highland community she had cursed when she left ten years earlier, she finds an attractive stranger installed in her family home and learns that she has "become" the legendary ghost who haunts the local glen. Links to *A Man from the Mist.*

Erskine, Barbara

Erskine's romances often contain supernatural, paranormal, or time travel elements. *(See also Alternative Realities bibliography.)*

House of Echoes. *Dutton, 1996.* An old inherited house and a family curse cause problems for the heroine and her family.

Distant Voices. *HarperCollins, 1996.*

Gaskin, Catherine

Gaskin is a noted writer in a number of romance subgenres. Many of her novels display Gothic characteristics. *(See also Romantic Suspense and Basic Contemporary Romance bibliographies.)*

Fiona. *Doubleday, 1970.*

Gellis, Roberta

Gellis is primarily noted for her well-researched historical romances with strong, fiery heroines. *(See also Romantic Historical and Saga bibliographies.)*

Sing Witch, Sing Death. *Bantam Books, 1975.* Has a touch of the Gothic in it.

Heyer, Georgette

Noted for her classic Regency romances, Heyer produced one true Regency Gothic. *(See also Regency Period bibliography.)*

Cousin Kate. *Bodley Head, 1968.* E. P. Dutton, 1969. What begins as merely a visit to her aunt's estate rapidly becomes a nightmare as Kate realizes what her relatives have in mind for her.

Hill, Pamela

Primarily noted for her well-crafted Historicals, Hill has produced some novels with decidedly Gothic characteristics, including:

The Devil of Aske. *Hodder & Stoughton, 1972.* St. Martin's Press, 1973. "Truly worthy of the name Gothic...." Victoria Holt

Whitton's Folly. *St. Martin's Press, 1975.*

Norah. *St. Martin's Press, 1976.* Published as *Norah Stroyan* by Hodder and Stoughton, 1976.

Fire Opal. *St. Martin's Press, 1980.*

The Sutburys. *St. Martin's Press, 1988.* Family feuds and curses.

Holland, Isabelle

Holland's psychological Gothics include occasional paranormal or psychic elements and make use of similar themes and plot patterns. Several of her later novels have a number of characters in common.

Kilgaren. *Weybright, 1974.*

Moncrieff. *Weybright, 1975.*

Tower Abbey. *Rawson Wade, 1978.*

A Lover Scorned. *Doubleday, 1986.*

Bump in the Night. *Doubleday, 1988.*

A Fatal Advent. *Doubleday, 1989.*

Holt, Victoria (Eleanor Burford Hibbert)

Although a prolific writer in several romance subgenres, Holt's Gothic Romances are some of her best. *Mistress of Mellyn*, in particular, is a modern classic in the field, and aspiring writers have used her early titles as models. After the first seven or so, her works are not so purely Gothic, even though they do contain many of the classic elements of the genre. In addition, the novels written toward the end of her career (she died in 1993), are not always up to her usual standard. She also has written biographical Romantic Historicals as Jean Plaidy and Romantic Historicals with strong Gothic elements as Philippa Carr. *(See also Romantic Suspense bibliography.)*

Mistress of Mellyn. *Doubleday, 1960.* A classic tale of mystery, terror, and suspense that started the Gothic craze of the 1960s.

Kirkland Revels. *Doubleday, 1962.* When young Catherine Rockwell comes to wild, beautiful, and legendary Kirkland Revels as a new bride, she has no idea that she will soon be fighting not only to save her marriage but her sanity, and possibly her life.

Bride of Pendorric. *Doubleday, 1963.* A young bride accompanies her husband to his Cornish castle, Pendorric, and is met by warmth and acceptance. She is also relentlessly stalked by someone who wants her to follow in the footsteps of the other brides of Pendorric—to her death.

The Legend of the Seventh Virgin. *Doubleday, 1965.* When Kerensa marries into the wealthy St. Larnston family, her future seems bright. But then things begin to go wrong, and when her husband finally disappears, she fears for her life.

Menfreya in the Morning. *Doubleday, 1966.* Published as *Menfreya* by Collins, 1966. Jealousy, fear, and suspicion torment Harriet as she wonders if she is doomed to repeat the terrifying "Legend of Menfreya."

The King of the Castle. *Doubleday, 1967.* When Dallas Lawson comes to Chateau Gaillard to restore the old paintings of the Comte de la Talle, she is met with suspicion and hostility. Nevertheless, she perseveres, solves an old mystery, and wins the love of the Comte.

The Shivering Sands. *Doubleday, 1969.* Jealousy, deceit, and quicksand make this an unforgettable tale of Gothic terror, even though Holt fans may figure out who the villain is early on.

The Secret Woman. *Doubleday, 1970.*

Shadow of the Lynx. *Doubleday, 1971.*

On the Night of the Seventh Moon. *Doubleday, 1972.*

Curse of the Kings. *Doubleday, 1973.*

The House of a Thousand Lanterns. *Doubleday, 1974.*

Lord of the Far Island. *Doubleday, 1975.*

The Spring of the Tiger. *Doubleday, 1979.*

The Mask of the Enchantress. *Doubleday, 1980.*

The Demon Lover. *Doubleday, 1982.*

The Landower Legacy. *Doubleday, 1984.*

The Road to Paradise Island. *Doubleday, 1985.*

Secret for a Nightingale. *Doubleday, 1986.*

The Silk Vendetta. *Doubleday, 1987.*

The India Fan. *Doubleday, 1988.*

The Captive. *Doubleday, 1989.* Having endured shipwreck, capture by pirates, and being sold to a Turkish pasha, Rosetta Cranleigh takes on another challenge. She heads home to England to find a murderer and prove the innocence of the accused man.

Snare of Serpents. *Doubleday, 1990.* Accused of patricide, Davina Glentyre heads for South Africa and finds herself involved in another strange death—and her reputation in shambles once again.

Daughter of Deceit. *HarperCollins, 1991.*

Seven for a Secret. *Doubleday, 1992.*

Hooper, Kay

Hooper writes short, contemporary series, alternative reality romances, and most recently, contemporary Gothics—although these are usually labeled "romantic suspense" by the industry. Her works are generally well written, peopled with memorable characters, sensual, and occasionally humorous. *(See also Alternative Reality Romance bibliography.)*

Amanda. *Bantam Books, 1995.* A long-lost heiress returns to the southern estate where she spent her early childhood and finds resentment, the answer to an old murder, and a killer. A classic contemporary Gothic.

After Caroline. *Bantam Books, 1996.* When a serious accident results in a bizarre paranormal link between Johanna and someone named Caroline, Johanna leaves Georgia and heads for a small town along the Oregon coast to find some answers. Murder and mystery with a Gothic touch.

Finding Laura. *Bantam Books, 1997.* An old mirror and a current murder make life more than interesting for aspiring artist Laura Sutherland as she tries to prove herself innocent of killing one of the wealthy Kilbournes, a family with a history of mysterious deaths.

Howatch, Susan

A writer of modern Gothics, historical sagas (some with Gothic overtones), and contemporary family sagas, Howatch is especially adept at drawing well-rounded, realistic characters. Her Gothic characters, in particular, are unusual in that they display a variety of characteristics, making them more complex and believable than the standard players in most Gothics. Her six Gothics still make interesting, if predictable, reading.

The Dark Shore. *Ace, 1965.* Stein and Day, 1972.

The Waiting Sands. *Ace, 1966.* Stein and Day, 1972.

Call in the Night. *Ace, 1967.* Stein and Day, 1973.

The Shrouded Walls. *Ace, 1968.* Stein and Day, 1971.

April's Grave. *Ace, 1969.*

The Devil on Lammas Night. *Ace, 1971.* Stein and Day, 1972.

Hylton, Sara

The Talisman of Set. *St. Martin's Press, 1984.*

The Whispering Glade. *St. Martin's Press, 1985.*

James, Margaret (Pamela Bennetts)

James writes chilling Gothics that leave the reader guessing until the end. Some are more thriller than romance. She also writes light romances as Helen Ashfield. Her works include:

The Haunting of Sara Lessingham. *St. Martin's Press, 1978.* Published as *The House in Candle Square* under the name Pamela Bennetts by Hale, 1977.

Footsteps in the Fog. *St. Martin's Press, 1979.*

A Voice in the Darkness. *St. Martin's Press, 1979.*

Johnston, Velda

Johnston writes in both romantic suspense and Gothic subgenres, using historical and contemporary settings. Her works include:

A Howling in the Woods. *Dodd, Mead, 1968.*

A Presence in an Empty Room. *Dodd, Mead, 1980.*

Voices in the Night. *Dodd, Mead, 1984.*

The Underground Stream. *St. Martin's Press, 1992.* An isolated old mansion and a bit of time travel add interest.

Lee, Elsie

Known primarily for her delightful Regencies, her earlier works include some well-crafted, modern Gothics, which are both more socially aware and somewhat more sensual than the norm for this subgenre. They also have assertive, intelligent heroines.

Wingarden. *Arbor House, 1971.*

The Passions of Medora Graeme. *Arbor House, 1972.*

Lofts, Norah

Although Lofts is essentially known for her historical and period romances, the two related books listed below focus on the haunting of a doomed house and display marked Gothic qualities.

Gad's Hall. *Doubleday, 1978.* Hodder & Stoughton, 1977.

The Haunting of Gad's Hall. *Doubleday, 1979.* Originally published as *Haunted House* by Hodder & Stoughton, 1978.

Marchant, Catherine (Catherine Cookson)

Noted primarily for her historical sagas and single volume stories featuring ordinary working-class protagonists (under the Marchant pseudonym), Cookson wrote a number of quite Gothically inclined romances, including:

The House on the Fens. *Lancet, 1965.* Published as *The Fen Tiger* by Macdonald, 1963.

Evil at Roger's Cross. *Lancet, 1965.* Published as *The Iron Facade* by Heinemann, 1976.

A Slow Awakening. *William Morrow, 1977.* Heinemann, 1976.

Maybury, Anne (Anne Buxton)

Maybury wrote many light contemporary romances before turning to the Gothic Romance subgenre. Her Gothic heroines are strong and independent, her settings are lavish (and deliciously described!), and the atmosphere is properly tense and threatening. Her works include:

The Terracotta Palace. *Random House, 1971.*

The Midnight Dancers. *Random House, 1973.*

Jessamy Court. *Random House, 1974.*

The Jewelled Daughter. *Random House, 1976.*

Melville, Jennie (Gwendoline Butler)

Melville, author of the Charmian Daniels series, writes exceptionally well-plotted, readable Gothics, including:

Ironwood. *Hodder & Stoughton, 1972.*

Raven's Forge. *Macmillan, 1975.*

Dragon's Eye. *Simon & Schuster, 1976.*

Axwater. *Macmillan, 1978.* Published as *Tarot's Tower* by Simon & Schuster, 1978.

Michaels, Barbara (Barbara Mertz)

This classic Gothic writer also writes Romantic Suspense as Elizabeth Peters. Many of her Gothics contain elements of the unexplained supernatural. They include:

The Master of Blacktower. *Appleton-Century Crofts, 1966.* A typical 1960s-type Gothic. Michael's first.

Ammie, Come Home. *Meredith, 1969.* Ancient spirits haunt an old Georgetown house and terrify the current inhabitants in this chilling tale of murder and passion. This classic set the pattern for many of the later novels and is one of the author's most memorable.

Dark on the Other Side. *Dodd, Mead, 1970.*

Crying Child. *Dodd, Mead, 1971.*

Greygallows. *Dodd, Mead, 1972.*

 6

Witch. *Dodd, Mead, 1973.*

House of Many Shadows. *Dodd, Mead, 1974.*

The Sea King's Daughter. *Dodd, Mead, 1975.*

Wait for What Will Come. *Dodd, Mead, 1978.*

The Walker in the Shadows. *Dodd, Mead, 1979.*

The Wizard's Daughter. *Dodd, Mead, 1980.*

Someone in the House. *Dodd, Mead, 1981.*

Black Rainbow. *Dodd, Mead, 1982.*

Here I Stay. *Congdon and Weed, 1983.*

Be Buried in the Rain. *Atheneum, 1985.*

Shattered Silk. *Atheneum, 1986.* Links to *Ammie, Come Home.*

Search the Shadows. *Atheneum, 1987.*

Smoke and Mirrors. *Simon & Schuster, 1989.* Politics, old tragedies, and no paranormal elements make this romance somewhat atypical of the author.

Into the Darkness. *Simon & Schuster, 1990.* Meg returns to New England and finds herself sharing ownership of her grandfather's jewelry store with a strange man and dealing with the fact that someone wants her to leave town. Suspense and old secrets.

Vanish with the Rose. *Simon & Schuster, 1992.* An attorney heroine poses as a rose expert to discover what has happened to her brother and finds mystery, romance, and danger on an old estate.

Houses of Stone. *Simon & Schuster, 1993.*

Stitches in Time. *HarperCollins, 1995.*

The Dancing Floor. *HarperCollins, 1997.*

Ogilvie, Elisabeth

Known for her Basic Contemporary Romances and Sagas set along the Maine coast, several of her works have definite Gothic tendencies, including:

Bellwood. *McGraw-Hill, 1968.*

The Devil in Tartan. *McGraw-Hill, 1980.*

O'Grady, Rohan (June O'Grady Skinner)

Highly reminiscent of the original literary Gothics, O'Grady's Gothic novels compellingly combine mystery, horror, and the supernatural.

Pippin's Journal: or Rosemary for Remembrance. *Macmillan, 1962.* Published as *Master of Montrolfe Hall* by Ace, 1965, and as *The Curse of the Montrolfes* by Second Chance Press, 1983.

Bleak November. *Dial, 1970.*

Randall, Rona

Noted for straight romances, Randall has written several in the Gothic mode.

Dragonmede. *Simon & Schuster, 1974.* One of the author's most important Gothic contributions.

Salisbury, Carola (Michael Butterworth)

Salisbury wrote chilling period Gothics, most of which are set during the nineteenth century. Well-developed plots; surprising twists; and intriguing, believable characters are characteristic. He was also a noted suspense writer, and his works include:

The Pride of the Trevallions. *Doubleday, 1975.* Published as *Mallion's Pride* by Collins, 1975.

Dark Inheritance. *Doubleday, 1975.*

The "Dolphin" Summer. *Doubleday, 1976.*

Count Vronsky's Daughter. *Doubleday, 1981.*

An Autumn in Araby. *Doubleday, 1983.*

The Woman in Grey. *Century, 1987.*

Seton, Anya

Noted for exceptionally well-written and researched historical novels about the lives of actual women, Seton has written one pure Gothic:

Dragonwyck. *Houghton Mifflin, 1944.*

Shayne, Maggie

Kiss of the Shadow Man. *Silhouette, 1994.* A heroine isolated through amnesia and the knowledge that someone is trying to kill her add to the Gothic feel of this Contemporary Romance.

Wings in the Night series

A series of linked books featuring vampires.

Twilight Phantasies. *Silhouette, 1993.*

Twilight Memories. *Silhouette, 1994.*

Twilight Illusions. *Silhouette, 1994.*

"Beyond Twilight." Novella in *Strangers in the Night* by Silhouette, 1995.

Born in Twilight. *Silhouette, 1997.*

Stevenson, Florence

Quick wit and an indomitable sense of humor characterize all Stevenson's works, including the Gothics. Some of her novels are close to graceful spoofs of the genre.

The Curse of the Concullens. *World, 1970.* One of the author's most memorable and a bit of a spoof.

Stewart, Mary

Noted for her stories of romantic suspense, Stewart has also written the following Gothics. *(See also Romantic Suspense bibliography.)*

Nine Coaches Waiting. *Hodder & Stoughton, 1958.* After a childhood as an orphan, Linda Martin looks forward to being governess in a French chateau. However, what awaits her is menacing evil as well as surprising romance. A chillingly suspenseful romance in the true Gothic tradition, many consider this one of Stewart's best.

Touch Not the Cat. *William Morrow, 1976.* Although this title could be considered Romantic Suspense, it contains enough Gothic elements (ancient family home, mazes, telepathic communications, a dark family secret, etc.) to place it within the boundaries of the Gothic subgenre.

Stuart, Anne

Stuart has written in most Romance subgenres, and many of her books have Gothic tendencies. She is particularly known for her dark heroes and high level of sensuality. The books listed here are particularly Gothic in feel.

Night of the Phantom. *Harlequin, 1991.* An intrepid heroine finds herself the prisoner of a mysterious and mesmerizing hero who appears only at night. A Beauty and the Beast romance with a touch of the paranormal.

A Dark and Stormy Night. *Harlequin, 1997.* A ghost, a recluse, and a Gothic mansion along the Irish coast make for a chilling tale.

Tattersall, Jill

Typical of the genre, Tattersall's well-written, entertaining Gothics are replete with plucky heroines, family secrets, sinister plots, and an occasional touch of the supernatural. Several of her more memorable titles include:

Enchanter's Castle. *Collins, 1966.*

Lyonesse Abbey. *William Morrow, 1968.*

Lady Ingram's Room. *William Morrow, 1981.* Originally published as *Lady Ingram's Retreat* by Collins, 1970.

Chanter's Chase. *William Morrow, 1978.*

Whitney, Phyllis A.

Although she no longer considers her works Gothics, the majority of Whitney's works are well within the limits of the contemporary Gothic Romance subgenre, and to many readers she is still the undisputed queen of that subgenre. Isolated mansions, family secrets, unprotected heroines, and more recently a bit of the supernatural are standard fare in these classics of the subgenre. Her earlier and mid-career works are some of her best. They include:

The Quicksilver Pool. *Appleton-Century Crofts, 1955.*

Skye Cameron. *Appleton-Century Crofts, 1957.*

The Moonflower. *Appleton-Century Crofts, 1958.*

Thunder Heights. *Appleton-Century Crofts, 1960.*

Window on the Square. *Appleton-Century Crofts, 1962.*

Seven Tears for Apollo. *Appleton-Century Crofts, 1963.*

Columbella. *Doubleday, 1966.*

Silverhill. *Doubleday, 1967.*

Hunter's Green. *Doubleday, 1968.*

The Winter People. *Doubleday, 1969.*

Listen for the Whisperer. *Doubleday, 1972.*

Snowfire. *Doubleday, 1973.*

The Turquoise Mask. *Doubleday, 1974.*

Spindrift. *Doubleday, 1975.*

The Golden Unicorn. *Doubleday, 1976.*

The Stone Bull. *Doubleday, 1977.*

The Glass Flame. *Doubleday, 1978.*

Domino. *Doubleday, 1979.*

Poinciana. *Doubleday, 1980.*

Vermilion. *Doubleday, 1981.*

Emerald. *Doubleday, 1983.*

Rainsong. *Doubleday, 1984.*

Dream of Orchids. *Doubleday, 1985.*

Flaming Tree. *Doubleday, 1986.* Vintage Whitney in a Carmel, California, setting.

Silversword. *Doubleday, 1987.* Mystery on Maui.

Feather on the Moon. *Doubleday, 1988.*

Rainbow in the Mist. *Doubleday, 1989.* A clairvoyant heroine, a missing woman, and a wonderful mountain setting combine in this mysterious—but not quite so Gothic as some—romance.

The Singing Stones. *Doubleday, 1990.* Murder, the paranormal, and romance in the Blue Ridge Mountains of Virginia.

A Mystery of the Golden Horn. *Fawcett, 1990.*

Woman Without a Past. *Doubleday, 1991.* A long-lost heiress is reunited with her family with deadly results.

The Ebony Swan. *Doubleday, 1992.*

Star Flight. *Crown, 1993.*

Daughter of the Stars. *Crown, 1994.*

Amethyst Dreams. *Crown, 1997.*

Chapter 7

Historical Romances

"Journalism allows its readers to witness history, fiction gives its readers an opportunity to live it."
John Hersey

"History never looks like history when you are living through it. It always looks confusing and messy, and it always feels uncomfortable."
John W. Gardner

DEFINITION

The most diverse of all the romance subgenres, the Historical Romance includes everything from Georgette Heyer's exquisite Regencies to Jean Plaidy's embroidered biographies to the steamy, Sweet/Savage Romances of Rosemary Rogers. However, as disparate as these seem, they are all, in essence, the same thing—love stories with historical settings. The design of the love story varies slightly according to specific type, but it is the historical setting and how it is used that is the critical element in this subgenre.

In the first place, not just any historical setting will do. In order to qualify, the historical period must be properly romantic, i.e., it must be far enough removed in time and place that it is surrounded by an aura of unfamiliarity and mystery. Even though any time preceding our own can be considered historical, it is rare that a Historical Romance will be set later than the Edwardian Period (1901-1910). This is partly because anything later than World War I is simply too recent to be considered romantic—or even historical—by current readers, many of whom have lived through those decades. Most people are not likely to consider as "historical" a time period they can actually remember. In addition—and this is a critical element in most historical romances, especially those of the Period variety—the Edwardian is the last period during which a good marriage was "officially" considered a woman's main objective in life and was her only practical alternative. With the coming of World War I, the existing social structure began to crumble as women, forced from the home into the workplace in unprecedented numbers, learned to become self-sufficient and gradually gave up their total dependence upon men. Of course there are exceptions, and writers have used the Roaring Twenties and the 1930s as successful settings. Nevertheless, these stories are rare, and Historicals set before the twentieth century are the norm. However, as we become more removed from the first half of the twentieth century, particularly after the millennium, it is likely that these years will begin to take on a more charming glow and lend themselves more easily to Romance. It will be interesting to see the trends that emerge.

On the other hand, the historical setting cannot be too unfamiliar, or the reader will not be able to identify with the protagonists. It is for this reason that certain periods and settings, especially those that are pre-medieval and non-Western, are not especially popular with today's romance readers and writers. They are simply too alien to allow for the necessary identification. One interesting exception to this rule is the interest in prehistoric times spawned by Jean Auel's best-selling Earth's Children series. Of course, these are not all considered romances even though many of them do contain a significant amount of love and sex. Following Auel's lead, several other writers produced novels with prehistoric settings (e.g., Joan Wolf, Linda Lay Shuler, and Theresa Scott), but their popularity was short lived and currently, Prehistoric Romances are not much in demand.

Given the stipulations, then, that historical romances be set in time periods that are distant and unusual enough to be perceived as romantic, yet similar enough to our own to allow for easy identification, it is easy to see why certain historical periods dominate this subgenre. Currently, the medieval, the Regency, the Georgian (eighteenth century), and the Victorian are particular favorites.

The Historical Romance subgenre can be divided into two basic types: those in which actual historical events and characters are essential to the plot (Romantic Historicals) and those in which they serve primarily as a background to the love story (Period Romances). Both types include well-written and diligently researched titles, as well as poorly crafted ones. While some readers may prefer one type over the other, this distinction is mainly structural and does not necessarily indicate quality.

Romantic Historicals provide accurate historical settings, information, atmosphere, and characters that are essential to the story, i.e., this particular story could not (or would probably not) take place in another period in history. A number of fictionalized biographies (done quite well by writers such as Jean Plaidy) fall into this category. However, though the historical figures may be central to the plot, the actual romantic interest is typically centered around an invented, or real but lesser-known, hero and heroine.

In novels of this type, the love relationship is, to a large extent, shaped by the actual historical events of the period. Lovers are generally kept apart by wars or political circumstances rather than simple misunderstandings or romantic entanglements. In addition, if the heroine is an actual historical figure, the story will not usually contradict *known* facts about her, although considerable liberty is usually taken with those areas of her life that have not been documented. For example, while it may be fact that a certain earl married a certain lady, the details of the courtship may be wholly at the discretion of the author. Even if the important characters are not actual historical figures, they must behave in accordance with and must be subject to the events of the time. In general, romances of this type are well researched and exhibit a relatively high quality of writing, although there are the inevitable exceptions.

The distinction between the Romantic Historical and the pure historical novel is a fuzzy one at best. Some have said that historical novels have more history and Romantic Historicals have more romance. This isn't far from the truth, although in this case, "romance" does not necessarily refer to a love interest. In general, although both types usually demonstrate a literary quality of writing and a high degree of historical research, historical novels tend to be slightly more serious about presenting pure history, using less fictionalization and greater breadth of focus. This is, however, not always the case, and many Historicals legitimately fall into both categories.

Because of the similarities between the historical novel and the Romantic Historical, it is not surprising that there is a significant crossover readership between the two. Those who like historical novels often read Romantic Historicals if the historical aspects are sufficiently accurate and well presented. Conversely, readers who prefer Romantic Historicals typically enjoy historical novels with interesting characters, lively dialogues, and intriguing plots.

7

The Period Romance, on the other hand, is essentially a generic love story in a historical setting, generally patterned after the boy-meets-girl, boy-and-girl-are mutually-attracted-but fight-it-or-are-kept-apart-by-misunderstandings, boy-gets-girl-at-last scenario. Although, like the Romantic Historical, this type provides genuine historical information, atmosphere, and even characters, the basic plot is not dependent upon the historical background and could easily be rewritten into any number of historical settings. However, if the actual facts of the political, economic, and military history are not overly important to readers of this genre, the historical atmosphere certainly is. They want to know exactly what it felt like to be living (and loving) during that particular period in history. In short, they want to escape into and actually experience the period. As a result, Period Romances abound in lengthy descriptions of the clothing, food, houses, countryside, entertainments, manners, customs, language, and other details of everyday life during the selected period. Some of the best examples of this are Georgette Heyer's Regencies. Her use of the language of the period is unequaled (despite a bit of twentieth century slang), her research impeccable, and her knowledge of the period so extensive that, despite an occasional detractor, critics note that her novels "will probably be consulted by future scholars as the most detailed and accurate portrait of Regency life anywhere."[1]

Diverse and abundant, Period Romances account for the majority of titles in the Historical Romance subgenre and can be organized in several ways. Most often they are divided along sensuality or topical lines, producing a number of intriguing and occasionally overlapping groups. A breakdown by sensuality level produces two broad, but increasingly less distinct, categories—the Innocent (usually called "Sweet" in the trade) and the Sensual. A topical breakdown results in a wide variety of specialized romances, including Western, Indian (Native American), Period Americana, Sweet/Savage, Period Inspirational, and Regency, among others.

The Innocent Period Romance, popularized by Barbara Cartland but refined and improved upon by many subsequent writers, is usually a simple straightforward love story complete with a spunky, resourceful, virginal heroine; strong, dashing, wealthy hero; and the usual assortment of ancient aunts, unscrupulous villains, conniving other women, and simpering cousins—all in a historical setting. While they can be intensely romantic and often display a high degree of sexual tension, these stories are never sexually explicit, and the romantic high point of the plot is usually the passionate kiss at the end of the book. Although there are exceptions, traditional Regency Romances (discussed in chapter 8), a number of Period Americanas, and Period Inspirationals (see the Inspirational Romance bibliography) are often of this type.

Prior to the early 1970s, Historical Romance of the innocent variety pre-dominated. However, with the entry of Kathleen Woodiwiss and Rosemary Rogers into the scene, Historicals with far more sensuality rapidly gained in popularity and for the past two decades have accounted for the majority of Historicals published. In fact, even though many Period Romances currently being written are only mildly sensual, for the reading public today, the phrase "Historical Romance" is still synonymous with a fast-paced, adventurous romance filled with wild, explicit sex.

The reason for this view is that early subsets within the Sensual Period Romance—most notably the Sensual Historical; the Sweet/Savage Romance; and its close relative, the Plantation Romance—are all characterized by action; adventure; and sensuous, explicit, occasionally brutal, sex. They are also usually set in exotic, romantic places such as pirate ships, medieval castles, Caribbean islands, and southern plantations. Although characteristics of these novels can be found in current romances, these specific subtypes have generally met their demise, and few of these novels are being written today. Nevertheless, some of the earlier works have been reprinted or are available on library shelves and in private collections, and some writers are still contributing new material. Because of their continuing availability and the profound influence they have had on the present genre, they are included in this guide.

The Sensual Historical, popularized in 1972 by Kathleen Woodiwiss's *The Flame and the Flower*, is typified by a heroine who remains faithful to the hero even though he rapes her (usually by mistake at the beginning of the story), ignores her, pursues her, and insults and humiliates her. She may also be the target of other men's sexual desires, but she always eludes them or is rescued from them, keeping herself for the hero only. In this type, as well as in the Sweet/Savage Romance, the heroine is often hiding from someone (almost always a man) in her past who seeks revenge and threatens her present relationship with the hero. Eventually, of course, all problems are solved and the couple is blissfully united. It is from this type of romance, with its emphasis on monogamy, that today's Sensual Period Romance is derived.

In the Sweet/Savage Romance, first written by Rosemary Rogers (*Sweet Savage Love,* 1974), the heroine experiences rape, abuse, humiliation, and various kinds of sexual encounters with a number of men. She usually ends up with the hero, but he may or may not have been the first man in her life.

Strictly speaking, the Plantation Romance is a highly specialized type of Sweet/Savage Romance. Replete with slave uprisings, miscegenation, incest, family rivalries, long-kept secrets, and violence, these steamy romances can be set anywhere slavery existed. (Lance

Horner used ancient Rome in his *Rogue Roman.*) However, the large plantations of the American South and the Caribbean are the settings most often used. (The warmer the climate, it seems, the hotter the historical.)

Plantation Romances contain elements of both the Saga and the Soap Opera in that the characters often continue into sequels, and the sins of the fathers (and mothers) usually return to haunt the children in full measure. Kyle Onstott launched this subgenre in 1959 with the publication of the now almost legendary *Mandingo,* and while novels of this type have fallen out of favor in recent years, its influence can be seen in some of the more exotic romances and Sagas today. For a selected bibliography of Plantation Romances, consult *Happily Ever After: A Guide to Reading Interests in Romance Fiction* (Littleton, CO: Libraries Unlimited, 1987) by Kristin Ramsdell.

Unquestionably, the Sensual Period Romances of today owe much to their predecessors, particularly their increased openness to sensuality. However, the rape, violence, and cruelty so common in the earlier novels are no longer acceptable, and a submissive, ineffective heroine is rare enough in a historical today to cause comment. In addition, the current emphasis is on a monogamous love relationship rather than the polygamous or serial monogamous relationships so common in the original Sweet/Savage Romances.

Today's Sensual Period Romances are diverse in both content and sensuality levels. Incredibly varied in their handling of sex, they run the gamut from the sweetly sensual (almost verging on the Innocent) to the overtly erotic (sometimes labeled "spicy" or "hot"), with the majority falling somewhere in between. Content and topic vary with the historical setting of the romance, and several of the more popular periods and their key features are discussed later in this section. However, several types of Period Romance are currently popular and deserve special mention. All are essentially American in setting (an interesting development in itself since it has been only recently that the United States has been considered old enough to be interesting historically), all have a particular focus, and some overlap.

The most generic and inclusive of these is the Western Period Romance. Set in the nineteenth-century American West (most often the last half), these stories revolve around the settling of America, usually west of the Mississippi, and can involve range wars, westward treks, gold or silver strikes, "cowboys and Indians" and "lawmen and outlaws" scenarios, and a number of typically "Western" themes and events. They are often action packed, fast paced, and sensual. Although one of the most popular romance types for a number of years, recently, this "rip-roaring" version of life in the Old West has been giving way to a gentler version in which the focus is on homesteading, family building, and relationships, much in keeping with Americana Period Romance described below.

The Native American (or "Indian" as it often is called in the trade) Period Romance is a subset of the Western Period Romance and focuses on Native American culture and characters, often in relation to the settling of the West. *(See also Ethnic and Multicultural Romance bibliography.)*

Americana Period Romance is the historical half of the Americana Romance subgenre and it focuses on everyday life in America, most often in the rural or small town in the nineteenth-century Midwest but occasionally in the Far West. The characters are ordinary people, the plots usually revolve around commonplace events and interpersonal relationships, and the sensuality levels vary.

Although it is debatable whether or not to consider it a true Period Romance, one more romance type must be considered in this section— the Fantasy of Passion. Although few, if any, Fantasy of Passion books are written today, the Sensual Period Romance and the Sweet/Savage Romance are direct descendants of these passionate, erotic stories that alternately enchanted and scandalized their avid readers. Although these books did not use historical backgrounds, their settings were so far removed from the experience of readers (mythical kingdoms, the Arabian Desert, etc.) that the appeal to the imagination was much the same as that of the Period Romance. The prototypes of this subgenre, *Three Weeks* (1907) by Elinor Glyn and *The Sheik* (1919) by Edith M. Hull, are read today primarily as Historicals.

Just as many readers selectively read both Historical Novels and Romantic Historicals, they may also read across the boundary between the Romantic Historical and the Period Romance, especially if the Period Romance makes better than average use of the historical background and characters. Interestingly, although readers often read nonselectively within either the Innocent and Sensual subdivisions (for example, choosing novels from a variety of historical periods), there does not seem to be the same crossover pattern between novels of the Innocent variety and those containing more explicit sex scenes. Although the lines between the types are much fuzzier than they have been in the past, readers often have definite ideas about the degree of sensuality they want in their books, and the reader who loves a sexy Western may be totally put off by a sweet Americana with a similar setting, or a devotee of the traditional Regency Romance may find Amanda Quick's lively Historical Regencies far too sensual. There is always the exception, of course: the reader who will read omnivorously.

APPEAL

The specific appeal of the historical romance is to our fascination with life in past times and to our not-so-latent yearning to escape, if only for a moment, to a time when life was simpler, better defined (especially regarding roles and rules), more exciting, and more romantic. From our earliest pleas of "Tell me about when you were a little girl, Mommy," or "What was it like in the olden days, Grandpa?" to our more adult interests in genealogy and family history, we have all enjoyed hearing about the past and wondering what it would have been like to have lived "way back then." With their ability to transport us to another period in history and allow us to become a part if it, Historical Romances satisfy our curiosity in a way that history books never can. They allow us to experience history with our senses and emotions rather than to just understand it with our minds. However, like all romances, Historicals are not totally realistic. For example, while it is true that eighteenth-century London stank, medieval castles were cold and drafty, and the personal hygiene of most people prior to the twentieth century was appalling by today's standards, these aspects may be mentioned but are rarely dwelt upon. Most authors and readers prefer to consider the jewel-encrusted ballgowns and the well-cut Weston coats rather than the unwashed bodies they covered.

Like memory, Historical Romances filter out many of the unpleasant, mundane, uncomfortable realities of everyday life and leave only the desirable, exciting, and romantic elements. Through them we are able to participate in the romance and adventure of the period without sharing in the inconvenient realities. These stories allow us to have it both ways: to have our historical cake and eat it too. Is it any wonder that they exist?

ADVISING THE READER

General readers' advisory information is provided in chapter 3. However, following are some points that might be helpful specifically for advising readers who enjoy Historical Romances.

- Many readers of Historical Romances also read Historical Novels. Rafael Sabatini attracts readers in both genres, and those who like Jean Plaidy may also enjoy reading Rosemary Sutcliffe. Likewise, devotees of Shellabarger and Yerby may also enjoy Forester and vintage Dumas.

- The reverse is also true; those who prefer Historical Novels may also enjoy some Historical Romances. Readers of Biographical Historicals may enjoy Jean Plaidy or Anya Seton's well-researched Historical Romances, and Georgette Heyer writes in and is read by those who enjoy both subgenres.

- Readers may also enjoy both Romantic Historicals and Period Romances, and readers of Sweet/Savage romances may enjoy its subset, the Plantation Romance. The same reader will probably enjoy both Kathleen Woodiwiss and Bertrice Small.

- Readers of Historical Romance may also enjoy Historical Gothics, Sagas, or Time Travel and other Alternative Reality Romances that are set in an appropriate historical period.

- Determining what particular type of Historical Romance the reader prefers—sweet, sensual, light, serious, biographical, etc.—is particularly important in such a diverse subgenre. Bertrice Small is not Georgette Heyer and Sir Walter Scott is not Barbara Cartland. If the reader enjoys Innocent Historicals, don't recommend *Skye O'Malley*. By the same token, don't suggest *Ivanhoe* to someone who wants a quick read.

- For the reader who is new to the Historical Romance subgenre, recommend some of the standard works by major authors (e.g., Georgette Heyer, Jean Plaidy, Rafael Sabatini, Carla Kelly, Roberta Gellis, Mary Jo Putney, Pamela Morsi, Betina Krahn, and Jo Beverley) and then branch out to others.

BRIEF HISTORY

Although elements of the Historical Romance can be found in earlier literary forms, it is generally considered that the genre achieved both definition and popularity with the novels of Sir Walter Scott. Already an acknowledged narrative poet, Scott turned to the newer and somewhat suspect form, the novel, and in 1814 *Waverly* was published anonymously. Scott's anonymity lasted for only 13 years, but his popularity endured well beyond his death in 1832 and continues, in a somewhat different form, into the present. Widely read on both sides of the Atlantic, Scott's imaginative and vigorous tales appealed directly to the current fascination for past times and vanished cultures, especially those of the Middle Ages. His works met the need admirably and, in many readers' opinions, satisfied public taste better than anything else available at the time. In fact, as James D. Hart observes, "Uniting the attributes of prose and poetry, his [Scott's] historical romances presented the pageantry of the past, the adventure of heroic life, the beauty of spacious scenery, and a dramatic conception of human relations, all more exuberantly and firmly realized than in any other contemporary works of literature."[2]

Scott's success encouraged a number of younger writers to follow in his footsteps, and a few even achieved a certain degree of fame. Three of the most important were Edward George Bulwer-Lytton, G. P. R. James, and Alexandre Dumas. Although sometimes criticized for his scandalously immoral novels, Bulwer-Lytton was quite popular with the fashionable readers of his time. He is best remembered today for his novel of ancient Rome, *The Last Days of Pompeii* (1834). While Bulwer-Lytton wrote in a number of fictional styles (not all of them historical), the exceptionally prolific James chose one and used it almost exclusively. Adventure, chivalry, and romance were all part of his formula, and his public loved it. The public also loved the works of another writer of action adventures, Alexandre Dumas. *The Three Musketeers* (1844) and *The Count of Monte Cristo* (1845) were widely read in America as well as in France and England, and both works, along with a number of his other novels, remain popular to this day.

Although American readers greatly enjoyed reading English, and some continental, authors, a spirit of nationalism developed after the War of 1812. People also began to want American-authored novels set in the American past. Of the many writers who subsequently began to publish American Historicals, James Fenimore Cooper was one of the first and probably remains the best known. Considered by many to be Scott's American counterpart, Cooper wrote more than 30 novels, often using pre- and post-Revolutionary War settings. His first success, *The Spy*, a tale of the American Revolution published in 1821, and his later *Leatherstocking Tales* are still considered American classics. Although his stories are actually more historical adventure than romance, romance authors owe him a great debt. By using American settings and history as a background for his highly popular stories, he firmly established the United States as an appropriate, acceptable, and even desirable place in which to set a novel.

At the same time Cooper was beginning his publishing career and Scott was enjoying extreme popularity, a group of romance writers, later known as the Domestic Sentimentalists, were beginning to make their presence felt. These women wrote many types of romance (domestic with Gothic overtones was a prevalent variety), and a number of them used historical settings. Although the settings of these early Historicals were often European, readers and authors were beginning to find early American history, particularly the Puritan period, intriguing. Some 30 novels set in this particular period appeared before the publication in 1850 of *The Scarlet Letter*, Hawthorne's Puritan classic. Among the earliest of these was *Hope Leslie* (1827) by Catharine Maria Sedgwick, whose works rivaled those of Cooper in popularity.

Historical romances continued to appear throughout the century, waxing and waning in numbers and popularity as public taste dictated. By the 1840s Historicals in the vein of Cooper and Scott had been supplanted by novels of a more sentimental, and in some instances sensational, nature. By the 1850s romantic literature was almost completely dominated by the Domestic Sentimentalists. Following the Centennial in 1876, there was a renewed interest in the American past, and historical novels and romances with American settings began to appear in greater numbers. In keeping with the general mood of the time, these novels tended to sentimentalize the past. Unfortunately, in doing so they often sacrificed accuracy for the sake of romance, creating a wealth of misconceptions that continued well into the next century. One of the earliest and most enduring of these Historicals was Helen Hunt Jackson's *Ramona* (1884), the classic story of love among the Native Americans of the early Southwest. By the end of the century, a number of authors were producing romances with American historical settings. One of the most popular was Virginia-born Mary Johnston. Of a number of romances set in early Virginia, *To Have and To Hold* (1900) is considered her most significant and enduring work.

This historical resurgence, however, was not limited to American themes. Romances of all types and historical persuasions abounded, including a number of novels with mythical settings. Although Robert Louis Stevenson wrote an early novel of this type, *Prince Otto* (1885), it was Anthony Hope's *The Prisoner of Zenda* (1894) and the mythical kingdom of Ruritania that enchanted the reading public and set the form for the rest of the decade. In 1901, George Barr McCutcheon produced *Graustark*, adding the *pièce de résistance*, an American self-made hero who marries the princess. Graustarkian romances became the new rage. Eventually, the form's popularity began to decline, and it might have totally died out had not Elinor Glyn added erotic sex to the basic formula and produced the sensational *Three Weeks* (1907). This fantasy of passion, along with *The Sheik* (1919) by Edith M. Hull, foreshadowed the sexier Historicals of the future. Indeed, *Forever Amber* (1944) and even the Sweet/Savage Romances of the 1970s might well trace their lineage to these pioneering works.

Through the 1890s and into the first decade of the twentieth century, historical fiction continued to be popular. Although infinite in variety, it was singular in appeal. As James Hart observes, "Sometimes the fiction dealt with wondrous far-off places of distant times where the reader might see knighthood in flower and ordinary Americans succeeding to the choicest blossoms; sometimes it dealt with a homely, happier, and simpler American day toward which the reader nostalgically turned backward glances. But whatever the subject, the mood was predominantly one of escape and the medium one of romance."[3]

The vogue for historical fiction declined somewhat during the second decade of the century but was revived during the 1920s by swashbuckling works such as *Scaramouche* (1921) and *Captain Blood* (1922) by Rafael Sabatini. However, Historical Romances achieved even greater popularity during the two decades that followed. Largely because of the social circumstances of the Great Depression and later World War II, readers were once again attracted to stories of a more pleasant and light-hearted past so that "every year from 1930 to 1948 brought forth a new and extremely popular romance of the past, each one cut in the same pattern."[4] Of particular importance were *Anthony Adverse* (1933) by Hervey Allen, *Gone with the Wind* (1936) by Margaret Mitchell, and *Forever Amber* (1944) by Kathleen Winsor.

Although *Anthony Adverse* was a lusty adventure tale with historical trappings rather than a true romance, it set the stage for one of the most important Historical Romances of the century, *Gone with the Wind.* Not only did Mitchell create a sweeping historical panorama, as did many earlier historical novelists, but she also invented believable, if not necessarily admirable, characters and let them behave more realistically than most Historical Romance novelists had done before. The unprecedented success of Mitchell's work precipitated a deluge of Historical Romances, and for the next decade the success of anything "historical" was virtually assured. While the popularity of many of these authors was transitory, several, including Samuel Shellabarger, Frank Yerby, Frances Parkinson Keyes, and Anya Seton, are still widely read today. Although many of these novels were patterned along traditional lines, the creation and public acceptance of a more "realistic" (i.e., egocentric, independent, and willful) heroine, gave authors more latitude in their characterizations, and gradually a new historical heroine began to evolve. One of the most notorious, although not the most typical, heroines of the period can be found in Kathleen Winsor's *Forever Amber.* Chaste in comparison with the heroines in today's Sensual Historicals, *Amber* nevertheless defies conventions, behaves outrageously, and pursues her man in a manner quite unusual for the 1940s. The book was highly controversial and sold unbelievably well.

Despite *Forever Amber*'s popularity, the Historical Romances of the next two decades were generally much tamer (Barbara Cartland's works, for example) and were somewhat overshadowed by other romance types, most notably the Gothic and Romantic Suspense subgenres. It wasn't until 1972 with the publication of *The Flame and the Flower* by Kathleen Woodiwiss that Historicals once again began to attract the attention of both readers and publishers. Two years later, Rosemary Rogers published *Sweet Savage Love* (1974), and the historical boom was on. These new novels, however, were not the Historicals of the immediate past. Appealing to the current, more open attitudes toward sexuality, these new Sensual Historicals offered their readers not only the adventure and romance of earlier Historicals, but also a high degree of sensuality and, in many cases, explicit sex. Other Historical Romance types, including Romantic Historicals and more innocent Period Romances, also benefited from this surge in reader interest, but it was clearly the sexier varieties of Historical Romance that were driving the market. Interest in Historicals peaked toward the end of the 1970s, and publishers and the reading public turned their attention in a more modern direction (the Contemporary Category Romance). Nevertheless, authors continued to write Historicals, readers continued reading them, and publishers continued offering them and keeping popular older Historicals in print. By the mid-1980s, interest in Historicals, particularly those with American settings, was once again on the rise. At the same time, American-set Sagas and series were also attracting some attention. This trend continued into the next decade, and despite a slight softening of the historical market in general (which may have had more to do with the shrinking midlist, distribution, and other industry problems than with reader demand), Historicals of all types remained popular.

Currently, the subgenre accounts for more than one-third of the romance titles published,[5] and at the moment seems to be holding its own. Historicals set in America are especially popular, particularly those of the Western and Americana varieties, and romances set in the British Isles continue to attract readers' interest. Favored time periods are the Medieval, Georgian, Regency, and Victorian, and currently Scotland is the locale of choice. All this, of course, is subject to the ups and downs of popular opinion, and the specifics will undoubtedly change. Nevertheless, the Historical Romance has been around in some form for a long time, and given its remarkable ability to adapt and change with the times, it is likely to continue to entertain readers for years to come.

HISTORICAL NOVEL

The principal requirement of a Historical Novel is that it be a fictional work set at some time in the past. Beyond that, limits are not usually specified, and, as a result, there is no one typical plot pattern that dominates this subgenre. However, the protagonist (most often male, but occasionally female) usually has a cause of some kind, which, in combination with the events of the period, motivates the story (e.g., the quest for political, social, or material success; revenge; the righting of an old family wrong; the settling of old debts; the clearing of a family name; and the regaining of a rightful heritage). In addition, there is usually some kind of romance plotline, which, though interesting, does not dominate the plot.

Just as there is not one mandatory plot type, neither is there a preferred historical time period. Historical novels have been set in almost every imaginable time and place. However, it is expected that the historical setting and events will be dealt with seriously and portrayed as accurately as possible.

Although straight historical novels are outside the scope of this guide, a number of them provide romance in sufficient amounts to appeal to many romance readers. Some examples are listed below. The older works listed first are still widely read, and most are generally available in both hardcover and paperback. Many of these are now considered classics, and several are staples in high school and college literature courses.

Selected Bibliography of the Nineteenth-Century Historical Novel

Cooper, James Fenimore

The Spy (1821). A tale of the Revolutionary War with some romance interest.

The Pathfinder (1840). The only one of the five *Leatherstocking Tales* in which Natty Bumppo, the protagonist, actually falls in love. Not a true romance.

Dickens, Charles

Although many of Dickens's novels are read today as "Historicals," he wrote about the times in which he lived and was, therefore, (like Jane Austen) writing contemporary novels.

A Tale of Two Cities (1859). Story of love and self-sacrifice set during the French Revolution. One of Dickens's true Historicals.

Dumas, Alexandre

The Three Musketeers (1844). Love, adventure, and espionage in seventeenth-century France during the time of Richelieu.

The Count of Monte Cristo (1845). Although not written as a true historical novel, it is read as such today. Dumas based his story on an actual incident that occurred during the first part of the nineteenth century.

Scott, Sir Walter

Often credited with beginning the historical novel, Scott's early Historicals were published anonymously. His works were immensely popular in both England and the United States.

Waverly (1814). A tale of romance and adventure centering around the Jacobite Rebellion of 1845. Scott's first historical novel.

Rob Roy (1818). Action and adventure in the Highlands of Scotland during the time of the Jacobites.

Ivanhoe (1819). A story of love and romance, knights and their ladies, honor and challenge set in England during the time of Robin Hood.

Selected Bibliography of the Twentieth-Century Historical Novel

Barnes, Margaret Campbell

Exquisite blends of British history and romance.

My Lady of Cleves. *Macrae Smith, 1946.*

The Tudor Rose. *Macrae Smith, 1953.*

Isabel the Fair. *Macrae Smith, 1957.*

The King's Bed. *Macrae Smith, 1961.*

Bryher (Annie Winifred Ellerman)

Bryher is noted for her strict attention to detail, excellent recreation of the period, and the ability to make the reader believe he or she is actually there.

The Fourteenth of October. *Pantheon Books, 1952.* A novel of the Battle of Hastings.

Roman Wall: A Novel. *Pantheon Books, 1954.* Concerns the fall of the Roman outpost Orba to the barbarians in the third century.

The Gate to the Sea. *Pantheon Books, 1958.* Considered by some to be her best novel. Set in fourth-century Greece.

Druon, Maurice

Druon is noted in particular for his The Accursed Kings series detailing the lives of 13 generations of the French House of Valois in the late Middle Ages beginning with King Philip IV and ending with the story of Edward III and Philip VI. The six-volume series begins with *The Iron King* (Charles Scribner's Sons, 1956) and ends with *The Lily and the Lion* (Charles Scribner's Sons, 1961).

Duggan, Alfred

A writer for both adults and children, Duggan is particularly known for his believable, well-drawn characters.

Besieger of Cities. *Pantheon Books, 1963.* A story of the third century B.C.

The Falcon and the Dove: A Life of Thomas Becket of Canterbury. *Pantheon Books, 1966.* Murder and intrigue in twelfth-century England.

Dunnett, Dorothy

Dunnett is especially known for her Lymond and Niccoló historical series. *(See also Saga bibliography.)*

King Hereafter. *Alfred A. Knopf, 1982.* A majestic reconstruction of the story of MacBeth of Scotland, historically based.

Fast, Howard

A prolific and competent writer of historical novels, Fast has most recently written generational family sagas beginning with *The Immigrants* (Houghton Mifflin, 1977). *(See also Saga bibliography.)*

Spartacus. *Crown, 1951.* This, possibly his most controversial novel, told of the Roman slave revolt of 71 B.C. It was made into a movie in 1960.

Feuchtwanger, Lion

A German playwright turned historical novelist, Feuchtwanger is noted for his concentration on the psychological aspects of the story. The trilogy listed here is based on the life of the Jewish historian Josephus who lived during the first century A.D.

Josephus: A Historical Romance. *Viking, 1932.*

The Jew of Rome. *Viking, 1936.*

Josephus and the Emperor. *Viking, 1942.*

Forester, C. S.

Although a prolific writer of a wide variety of historical novels, including *The African Queen* (1935), which was made into a movie in 1951, Forester is popularly known for his Hornblower series. Not written in chronological order, this series has been published in a number of different editions. Provided here is a selected listing of titles in the series. (The first three titles were published as *Captain Horatio Hornblower* in 1939.)

Beat to Quarters. *Little, Brown, 1937.*

Ship of the Line. *Little, Brown, 1938.*

Flying Colors. *Little, Brown, 1939.*

Lord Hornblower. *Little, Brown, 1946.*

Lieutenant Hornblower. *Little, Brown, 1952.*

Gavin, Catherine

Gavin is noted for accurate historical portrayals and her ability to combine history with romance. Her Second Empire series and her Second World War Trilogy are especially well known. *(See also Saga bibliography.)*

Second Empire series

Set during the turmoil of the Second Empire in the nineteenth century.

Madeleine. *St. Martin's Press, 1957.*

The Cactus and the Crown. *Doubleday, 1962.*

The Fortress. *Doubleday, 1964.*

The Moon into Blood. *Hodder & Stoughton, 1966.*

Second World War Trilogy
Possibly her best.

Traitor's Gate. *St. Martin's Press, 1976.*

None Dare Call It Treason. *St. Martin's Press, 1978.*

How Sleep the Brave. *St. Martin's Press, 1980.*

Gedge, Pauline
Gedge is an author particularly gifted at evoking a strong sense of time and place. The following take place in ancient Egypt.

Child of the Morning. *Dial Press, 1977.*

The Twelfth Transforming. *Harper & Row, 1984.*

George, Margaret
George writes serious, readable historical novels that immerse the readers in the lives and times of the characters.

The Autobiography of Henry VIII: With Notes by His Fool, Will Somers. *St. Martin's Press, 1986.*

Mary Queen of Scotland and the Isles. *St. Martin's Press, 1992.*

The Memoirs of Cleopatra. *St. Martin's Press, 1997.*

Graves, Robert
A noted writer of highly detailed historical novels, the two works listed below tell the story of Tiberius Claudius, Emperor of Rome. These books also formed the basis for the classic PBS television series, *I, Claudius.*

I, Claudius: From the Autobiography of Tiberius Claudius, Born B.C. 10, Murdered and Deified A.D. 54. *Smith & Haas, 1934.*

Claudius, the God and His Wife, Messalina. *Barker, 1934.* Smith & Haas, 1935.

Heyer, Georgette
Although noted for her period Regencies, Heyer also wrote historical novels. *(See also Regency Period Romance, and Period Romance bibliographies.)*

The Conqueror. *Heinemann, 1931.* E. P. Dutton, 1964. The story of William the Conqueror, spanning the years from his illegitimate birth to his coronation as King of England in 1066.

My Lord John. *E. P. Dutton, 1975.* In her last novel, Georgette Heyer tells the story of British King Henry IV's life, reign, and mysterious death as seen through the eyes of his youngest son, John. Violent and intriguing.

Oldenbourg, Zoe
Oldenbourg provides unsentimental and highly realistic novels of life in medieval France.

The World Is Not Enough. *Pantheon Books, 1948.*

The Cornerstone. *Pantheon Books, 1952.*

Renault, Mary
Renault is noted for her exceptionally well-researched and readable stories of the ancient world. Some of her works are appropriate for children and young adults.

Alexander the Great series

An engrossing, well-written account of the life of Alexander the Great with all its pageantry and splendor, reality and bloodshed.

Fire from Heaven. *Pantheon Books, 1969.*

The Persian Boy. *Pantheon Books, 1972.*

Funeral Games. *Pantheon Books, 1981.*

Theseus series

The King Must Die. *Pantheon Books, 1958.* A brilliant retelling of the legend of Theseus.

The Bull from the Sea. *Pantheon Books, 1962.* This sequel tells the love story of Theseus and Hippolyta.

Sabatini, Rafael

One of the most popular writers of historical fiction of this century, Sabatini wrote both historical novels and Romantic Historicals, all of which abound with swashbuckling adventure and romance. *(See also Romantic Historical bibliography.)*

Scaramouche: A Romance of the French Revolution. *Houghton Mifflin, 1921.* A tale of romance, adventure, and revenge set against the backdrop of the French Revolution. The hero is imaginary, but the background is real.

Stone, Irving

Stone was both a scholar of economics and political science and a best-selling author of biographical novels. His works are especially noted for their accurate research, attention to detail, and careful plotting.

Love Is Eternal. *Doubleday, 1954.* The story of Mary Todd and Abraham Lincoln.

Those Who Love. *Doubleday, 1965.* The story of Abigail and John Adams.

7

Sutcliffe, Rosemary

Many of Sutcliffe's novels are enjoyed equally by adults and young adults. Many of her stories are set in ancient England, and her Roman/British novels are considered especially well done. Her works are characterized by impeccable research and a graceful, readable style.

Lady in Waiting. *Coward-McCann, 1957.* Story of Sir Walter Raleigh's wife, Bess Throckmorton, and the political intrigue, drama, and tragedy that surrounds her.

The Sword at Sunset. *Coward-McCann, 1963.* Hodder & Stoughton, 1963. An intriguing version of the beginnings of Britain. Possibly the author's best.

Blood and Sand. *Hodder & Stoughton, 1987.* Based on the life of Englishman Thomas Keith and his journey to becoming the Emir of Medina.

Authurian Knights Trilogy

This lyrical, romantic trilogy details the lives of the legendary King Arthur and those around him. Although there is an element of fantasy in this trilogy, the historical foundation is sound.

A Light in the Forest: The Quest for the Holy Grail. *E. P. Dutton, 1980.* Bodley Head, 1979.

Trollope, Joanna

Trollope writes both historical and contemporary novels with strong romance plotlines. Her recent works are of the contemporary variety. *(See also Women's Romantic Fiction.)* She has also written Historicals as Caroline Harvey, most notably her linked stories included in two collections titled *Legacy of Love* (Octopus, 1983) and *A Second Legacy* (Doubleday, 1993).

Eliza Stanhope. *E. P. Dutton, 1979.* Hutchinson, 1978.

Mistaken Virtues. *E. P. Dutton, 1980.* Originally published as *Parson Harding's Daughter* by Hutchinson, 1979.

Leaves from the Valley. *St. Martin's Press, 1984.* Hutchinson, 1980.

The City of Gems. *Hutchinson, 1981.*

The Steps of the Sun. *St. Martin's Press, 1984.* Hutchinson, 1983.

Undset, Sigrid

Kristin Lavransdatter Trilogy

Now usually published in one volume, three novels detail the harsh conditions that existed in fourteenth-century medieval Norway. Titles include:

The Bridal Wreath. *Alfred A. Knopf, 1923.*

The Mistress of Husaby. *Alfred A. Knopf, 1925.*

The Cross. *Alfred A. Knopf, 1927.*

Yourcenar, Marguerite

Winner of the National Arts Club Medal of Honor for Literature, 1985.

The Memoirs of Hadrian. *Farrar, Straus and Young, 1954.*

ROMANTIC HISTORICALS

Because the Romantic Historical has a history-dependent plot, many authors use this to their advantage, setting their novels during periods of change, and general unrest. Revolutions, wars, and uprisings are especially popular, as are reigns of particularly controversial and flamboyant rulers. The idea, of course, is that exciting events make for exciting stories. While this is not always the case (we have all encountered at least one boring historical), it is generally true that dynamic stories more often than not have dynamic settings. Although most settings are based in historical reality, occasionally, as in the case of several of the early examples listed below, the writer chooses to use an imaginary setting. Whole countries are not usually invented (*The Prisoner of Zenda* is an exception), but nonexistent manor houses, castles, and families are commonplace in contemporary Romantic Historicals.

As with historical novels, there is not one particular plot pattern that is typical of Romantic Historicals. There are many, and the possibilities are endless, ranging from quiet, pastoral English tales to swashbuckling adventures on the high seas. In most cases, however, the protagonist (male or female) is faced with a particular problem, and the rest of the story describes the way in which he or she finds a solution to it. The historical circumstances play a large part both in creating the problem and in its solution. This is also one romance category in which the plot patterns exhibit some inconsistency with the general definition of a romance. Although there is usually a strong romance line in most Romantic Historicals, it is not always the most important aspect of the plot. In some titles that honor belongs to the solving of the original motivating problem, and in others, the two plotlines are equally important. This is especially true of fictionalized biographies or family dynasty tales that incorporate a large number of subplots, characters, and specific historical events. Admittedly, Romantic Historicals walk an uneasy line between the Historical Novel and the Period Romance, and many novels of this type are close enough to the edge to legitimately fall into either category. While this kind of ambiguity drives some organized types to distraction, most readers don't care. For them, the designation is unimportant; it is the story that counts.

Most of the prototypes and important examples listed below are still read today.

Selected Bibliography of Romantic Historical Prototypes

Allen, Hervey

Anthony Adverse. (1933). Rollicking story of action and adventure set in Napoleonic times. A rambling tale, reminiscent of the Victorian three-decker (a novel in three volumes).

Haggard, H. Rider

She. (1887). One of the original historical fantasy adventure stories involving an African sorceress, Ayesha, and a young Englishman who intends to avenge the death of an ancestor.

Hope, Anthony

The Prisoner of Zenda. (1894). Rudolf Rassendyll's resemblance to Rudolf, king of Ruritania, involves him in a dangerous scheme to outwit the king's half-brother, who is intent on usurping the throne. A romantic adventure story that is still popular today.

McCutcheon, George Barr

Graustark. (1901). This classic adds an American hero to the mythical romantic mix—and he ends up marrying the princess.

Mitchell, Margaret

Gone With the Wind. (1936). Beautiful, willful Scarlett O'Hara finds love, frustration, and tragedy in this classic romantic adventure set in Georgia during the Civil War and Reconstruction.

Winsor, Kathleen

Forever Amber. (1944). The lusty (for the times) story of an English country girl who eventually became the mistress of the king but couldn't forget the man she had first loved. Criticized, condemned, and banned, this lively romance might have been scandalous in the 1940s, but it is comparatively tame (but fun) reading today.

Selected Romantic Historical Bibliography

Anthony, Evelyn

Although better known today for her romantic suspense thrillers, Anthony began her career by writing Romantic Historicals. Although most are currently out of print, many are still available through libraries.

Anne Boleyn. *Thomas Y. Crowell, 1957.*

Victoria and Albert. *Thomas Y. Crowell, 1958.* Published as *Victoria* by Museum Press, 1959.

All the Queen's Men. *Thomas Y. Crowell, 1960.* Published as *Elizabeth* by Museum Press, 1960.

The Cardinal and the Queen. *Coward, 1968.* Published as *Anne of Austria by* Hurst & Blackett, 1968.

Belle, Pamela

Most of Belle's well-researched, fast-paced Historicals are set in seventeenth-century England. They are filled with strong heroines, charming children and animals, and details of everyday life. As a group, these could fall within the Saga subgenre.

The Goldhayes Trilogy

The Heron family and the English Civil War with a Royalist slant.

The Moon in the Water. *Berkley, 1984.* Pan, 1983.

Chains of Fate. *Berkley, 1984.*

Alathea. *Berkley, 1985.* A story of love and romance set in Restoration England.

The Lodestar. *St. Martin's Press, 1989.* Bodley Head, 1987. A fifteenth-century prequel to the Goldhayes Trilogy.

Wintercombe series

Seventeenth-century England from the Roundhead perspective.

Wintercombe. *St. Martin's Press, 1988.*

Herald of Joy. *St. Martin's Press, 1990.* Bodley Head, 1989.

A Falling Star. *Century, 1990.*

Treason's Gift. *Century, 1992.*

Bradshaw, Gillian

Beacon at Alexandria. *Houghton Mifflin, 1986.* The story of a woman who pretends to be a eunuch in order to study medicine. Set at the end of the Roman Empire.

Caldwell, Taylor

Her novels are not typical romances and they vary greatly in type. Her characters are strong, her themes are popular even though they can be depressing, her religious and moral views are often evident, and the endings are not necessarily happy.

The Arm of the Darkness. *Charles Scribner's Sons, 1943.*

Maggie, Her Marriage. *Fawcett, 1953.*

Dear and Glorious Physician. *Doubleday, 1959.* The story of Luke.

Captains and Kings. *Doubleday, 1972.* An Irish American family saga.

Ceremony of the Innocent. *Doubleday, 1976.* 1920s American setting.

Answer As a Man. *Putnam, 1981.*

Carr, Robyn

Carr's Historicals employ a variety of settings (most often medieval or Renaissance France or England), are intricately plotted, and feature strong heroines in difficult circumstances.

Chelynne. *Little, Brown, 1980.*

The Bellrose Bargain. *Little, Brown, 1982.*

The Braeswood Tapestry. *Little, Brown, 1984.*

The Troubadour's Romance. *Little, Brown, 1985.*

By Right of Arms. *Little, Brown, 1986.*

Woman's Own. *St. Martin's Press, 1990.* Three generations of Armstrong women struggle to survive in late nineteenth-century Philadelphia.

Cody, Denee

Court of Love. *Zebra, 1996.* Heroine is banished to the English court of Eleanor of Aquitaine and finds unexpected love.

Coffman, Virginia

Veronique. *Arbor House, 1975.* A story set during the Reign of Terror.

Costain, Thomas

Noted for his varied historical fiction, Costain has also written biographies and historical non-fiction.

For My Great Folly. *Putnam, 1942.* High seas adventure during the reign of James I.

The Black Rose. *Doubleday, 1945.* Medieval Chinese setting.

The Silver Chalice. *Doubleday, 1952.* Early Christian period.

Below the Salt. *Doubleday, 1957.* Medieval setting; time travel elements.

Donati, Sara

Into the Wilderness. *Bantam Books, 1998.* Elizabeth Bonner leaves England in 1792 to fulfill her dream of teaching children of all races and finds love and fulfillment with a frontiersman in the American wilderness.

Eden, Dorothy

(See also Period Romance and Gothic bibliographies.)

Never Call It Loving: A Biographical Novel of Katherine O'Shea and Charles Stewart Parnell. *Coward-McCann, 1966.*

Gartner, Chloe

Her well-researched, action-filled Historicals, peopled with both real and fictional characters, provide a detailed look at some of history's most exciting and violent times.

Drums of Khartoum. *William Morrow, 1967.*

The Woman from the Glen. *William Morrow, 1973.* A tale of love and adventure set in the Scotland of Bonnie Prince Charlie.

Mistress of the Highlands. *William Morrow, 1976.* Seventeenth-century Scotland during the bloody days of Cromwell and Charles I.

Gellis, Roberta

Gellis is noted for her careful research and strong, vibrant women. Most of her novels are set during the medieval period and many contain linked characters. She has also written The Roselynde Chronicles. *(See also Saga bibliography.)*

Bond of Blood. *Doubleday, 1964.*

Knight's Honor. *Doubleday, 1964.*

The Dragon and the Rose. *Playboy, 1977.*

The Sword and the Swan. *Playboy, 1977.*

A Tapestry of Dreams. *Berkley, 1985.*

The Rope Dancer. *Jove, 1986.* A departure from the usual historical tendency to dwell upon the aristocracy, this medieval romance tells the passionate story of Carys, a rope dancer, and Telor, a minstrel.

Masques of Gold. *Berkley, 1986.* A story of the guilds.

Fires of Winter. *Berkley, 1987.* Continues the story of *A Tapestry of Dreams.*

Grant, Maxwell

Blood Red Rose. *Macmillan, 1986.* A story of adventure, intrigue, and romance set in China during the 1920s.

Hardwick, Mollie

Noted for her meticulous research, Hardwick has also written plays and non-fiction. She also wrote a number of novels based on the characters from the television series *Upstairs, Downstairs* and a saga, *The Atkinson Heritage.* Also writes with her husband, Michael. *(See also Saga and Period Romance bibliographies.)*

Beauty's Daughter: The Story of Lady Hamilton's "Lost" Daughter. *Eyre Methuen, 1976.* Coward-McCann, 1977.

Charlie Is My Darling. *Coward-McCann, 1977.*

Hill, Pamela

Hill writes historical and period romances, many with Gothic tendencies. *(See also Gothic, Period, and Saga bibliographies.)*

The Crown and the Shadow. *Putnam, 1955.* Published in England as *Shadow of Palaces: The Story of Francoise d'Aubigne, Marquise de Maintenon* by Chatto and Wardue, 1955.

Marjorie of Scotland. *Putnam, 1956.*

The Green Salamander. *St. Martin's Press, 1977.*

Tsar's Woman. *Hale, 1977.*

Holland, Cecelia

The Firedrake. *Atheneum, 1966.*

Rakossy. *Atheneum, 1967.*

The Earl. *Alfred A. Knopf, 1971.*

City of God. *Alfred A. Knopf, 1979.*

The Sea Beggars. *Alfred A. Knopf, 1982.*

The Belt of Gold. *Alfred A. Knopf, 1984.* A novel of the violence and corruption of ninth-century Byzantium.

Pillar of the Sky. *Alfred A. Knopf, 1985.* Ancient Stonehenge setting.

The Bear Flag. *Houghton Mifflin, 1990.* A well-researched story of early California that focuses on the Bear Flag Revolt, the California Uprising, and other pre-statehood events, this is Holland's first venture into American history.

Holt, Victoria (Eleanor Burford Hibbert)

Noted for her pace-setting Gothics, Holt also wrote Period romances and Romantic Historicals.

The Devil on Horseback. *Doubleday, 1977.* A gripping tale of love, adventure, and suspense set during the French Revolution.

My Enemy the Queen. *Doubleday, 1978.* A fascinating story of the Elizabethan court as told from the viewpoint of Lettice Devereaux, the woman who thwarted the queen at every turn and stole from her the man she loved.

The Demon Lover. *Doubleday, 1982.* A story of intrigue, suspense, and romance set in Paris of the 1870s.

Jarman, Rosemary Hawley

Jarman is noted for her fifteenth-century historical romances and the events surrounding the War of the Roses.

We Speak No Treason. *Little, Brown, 1971.*

The King's Grey Mare. *Little, Brown, 1973.* Published as *Crown of Glory* by Berkley, 1987.

7

Crown in Candlelight. *Little, Brown, 1978.*

The Courts of Illusion. *Little, Brown, 1983.*

Kaufman, Pamela

Violence and romance in a medieval setting.

Shield of Three Lions. *Warner Books, 1984.*

Banners of Gold. *Crown, 1986.*

Kay, Susan

Legacy. *Crown, 1986.* An exceptionally well-done, award-winning novel about Elizabeth I.

Kaye, M. M.

Shadow of the Moon. Messner, 1957. 1857 Indian setting.

Trade Wind. *Coward-McCann, 1964.* Longman, 1963. Mid-nineteenth-century setting.

The Far Pavilions. *St. Martin's Press, 1978.* Indian setting.

Keyes, Frances Parkinson

I, The King. *McGraw-Hill, 1966.* The story of Philip IV of Spain and the women in his life.

Lambton, Antony

Elizabeth and Alexandra. *E. P. Dutton, 1986.* The stories of Queen Victoria's two granddaughters.

L'Amour, Louis

He is particularly known for his Sackett series.

The Walking Drum. *Bantam Books, 1984.* Set in twelfth-century Europe and Byzantium.

Lewis, Hilda

Wife to the Bastard. *David McKay, 1966.*

The Witch and the Priest. *David McKay, 1970.*

I Am Mary Tudor. *David McKay, 1971.*

Lide, Mary

Lide produces exceptionally well-written, highly sensual, and diligently researched historical romances.

Sedgemont Trilogy

Set in twelfth-century Britain, these novels center on the lives of Ann and Raoul and, eventually, their children.

Ann of Cambray. *Warner Books, 1984.*

Gifts of the Queen. *Warner Books, 1985.*

A Royal Quest. *Warner Books, 1987.* Published as *Hawks of Sedgemont* by Sphere, 1988.

Isobelle. *Warner Books, 1988.* Published as *Diary of Isobelle* by Grafton, 1988. A lyrical, exotic love story set in the Middle East.

Tregaran. *St. Martin's Press, 1989.* This and the book that follows are set in early twentieth-century Cornwall and deal with the long-standing difficulties between the Tregarans and the Tregarns.

The Legacy of Tregaran. *St. Martin's Press, 1991.* Published as *The Legacy* by Grafton, 1991.

Llywelyn, Morgan

Lion of Ireland: The Legend of Brian Boru. *Houghton Mifflin, 1979.*

Grania; She-King of the Irish Seas. *Crown, 1985.*

Lofts, Norah

Noted for her strong, interesting heroines; her gift of narrative; and her ability to establish a definite sense of time and place, Lofts produced historical novels about ordinary people of earlier times. She is also known for her biographical novels of women in history, e.g., *The Concubine: A Novel Based on the Life of Anne Boleyn*, and *The King's Pleasure* (Catherine of Aragon). Although a love story is present in most of her books, it rarely dominates, and while many readers consider her works within the romantic or Gothic genres, Lofts herself did not. Her career spanned more than 50 years. *(See also Saga bibliography.)*

Madselin. *Corgi, 1969.* Doubleday, 1983.

The Old Priory. *Doubleday, 1982.*

Pargeters. *Doubleday, 1986.*

Marshall, Edison

Marshall is noted for his adventurous, well-researched tales of sweeping scope.

Benjamin Blake. *Farrar and Rinehart, 1941.*

Yankee Pasha. *Farrar, Straus, 1947.*

The Viking. *Farrar, Straus, 1951.*

American Captain. *Farrar, Straus, and Young, 1954.*

Meade, Marion

Stealing Heaven. *William Morrow, 1979.* A retelling of the twelfth-century romance of Heloise and Abelard.

Newman, Sharan

Guinevere Trilogy

This trilogy tells the story of Guinevere, queen to Arthur, and also provides a new look at the often-told Arthurian legends.

Guinevere. *St. Martin's Press, 1981.*

The Chessboard Queen. *St. Martin's Press, 1983.*

Guinevere Evermore. *St. Martin's Press, 1985.*

Penman, Sharon Kay

The Sunne in Splendour. *Holt, Rinehart, & Winston, 1982.* A readable, well-researched story of the life of Richard III.

Here Be Dragons. *Holt, Rinehart & Winston, 1985.* Set in the days of King John of England.

Petrie, Glen

The Fourth King. *Atheneum, 1986.* Set in early nineteenth-century Russia

7

Plaidy, Jean (Eleanor Burford Hibbert)

(Also writes as Victoria Holt and Philippa Carr) Jean Plaidy is known for her historical novels of the lives of real people and is noted, in particular, for her series dealing with the various royal dynasties in England. Her work is well-researched, presented in a readable style, and it focuses on aspects of the characters and political situations that interest readers of romance fiction. Her series include: The Last of the Stuarts, The Victorian Saga, The Georgian Saga, The Plantaganet Saga, The Norman Trilogy, The French Revolution, The Queens of England, and a series on each of the following—Queen Victoria, Charles II, Catharine of Aragon, Louis XV, Catherine De'Medici, Lucrezia Borgia, Ferdinand and Isabella, and Mary Queen of Scots. Her works include:

The Norman Trilogy

One of her most popular series, this trilogy deals with England during the Norman Period.

The Bastard King. *Putnam, 1979.* Hale, 1974.

The Lion of Justice. *Putnam, 1979.* Hale, 1975.

The Passionate Enemies. *Putnam, 1979.* Hale, 1976.

The Queens of England series

My Self, My Enemy. *Putnam, 1984.* Hale, 1983.

Queen of This Realm: The Story of Queen Elizabeth I. *Putnam, 1985.* Hale, 1984.

Victoria Victorious. *Putnam, 1986.* Hale, 1985.

The Lady in the Tower. *Putnam, 1986.*

The Courts of Love. *Putnam, 1988.* Hale, 1987.

In the Shadow of the Crown. *Putnam, 1989.* Hale, 1988.

The Queen's Secret. *Putnam, 1990.* Hale, 1989.

The Reluctant Queen: The Story of Anne of York. *Hale, 1990.*

William's Wife. *Hale, 1990.*

Rofheart, Martha

Fortune Made His Sword. *Putnam, 1972.* A story of Henry V of England.

Glendower Country. *Putnam, 1973.* The story of the "last Welsh Prince," Owen Glendower.

Sabatini, Rafael

Sabatini is a past master of the novel of adventure and romance. His novels are historically accurate and filled with all the charm and "swash and buckle" of bygone eras. Many of his works have been reprinted or are available in public libraries. *(See also Historical Novel bibliography.)*

The Sea Hawk. *J. B. Lippincott, 1915.* Sir Oliver Tressilian, gentleman turned corsair, kidnaps the woman he loves and fights to keep her from ending up in the harem of the Basha.

Captain Blood, His Odyssey. *Houghton Mifflin, 1921.* First in the swashbuckling Captain Blood series.

Captain Blood Returns. *Houghton Mifflin, 1931.* Published as *The Chronicles of Captain Blood* by Hutchinson, 1932.

The Fortunes of Captain Blood. *Houghton Mifflin, 1936.*

Schoonover, Lawrence

The Queen's Cross. *William Sloane, 1955.* The story of Isabella of Spain.

Seton, Anya

Seton's historical novels are especially well researched, well written, and insightful.

My Theodosia. *Houghton Mifflin, 1941.* The story of Theodosia, the daughter of Aaron Burr.

Katherine. *Houghton Miflin, 1954.* Fourteenth-century English story of Katherine, wife of John of Gaunt.

The Winthrop Woman. *Houghton Mifflin, 1958.* Colonial American setting.

Devil Water. *Houghton Mifflin, 1962.* Set against the backdrop of the Jacobite Rebellions of the eighteenth century.

Avalon. *Houghton Mifflin, 1965.* Tenth-century adventure sweeping from England to Iceland and America.

Shellabarger, Samuel

Shellabarger's stories are meticulously researched, and many are set during times of change and are filled with excitement, violence, and adventure.

Captain from Castille. *Little, Brown, 1945.* Spain and Mexico during the time of Cortez. One of the author's best.

Prince of Foxes. *Little, Brown, 1947.* Classic story of intrigue, adventure, and romance in sixteenth-century Italy.

The King's Cavalier. *Little, Brown, 1950.* Published as *Blaise of France* by Hamish Hamilton, 1950.

Lord Vanity. *Little, Brown, 1953.* Set in Venice during the middle of the eighteenth century.

Tolbecken. *Little, Brown, 1956.* Set during the era of massive change that spans the years from 1898 to 1931.

Yerby, Frank

Yerby's fast-paced, adventurous novels are well researched and filled with conflict and colorful historical detail.

The Foxes of Harrow. *Dial Press, 1946.*

The Saracen Blade. *Dial Press, 1952.*

Judas, My Brother: The Story of the Thirteenth Disciple. *Dial Press, 1968.*

PERIOD ROMANCE

The Period Romance is basically a love story with a historical setting. It differs from the Romantic Historical and the Historical Novel in that, except for providing a few incidental historical characters and a backdrop for a traditional love story, the historical people and events of the period rarely affect the story line. The social history and customs of the time, however, have tremendous impact. Characteristically, a Period Romance recreates in great detail a romanticized version of a bygone era in which readers can immerse themselves, experiencing along with the heroine (or hero) the everyday life of that particular time in history. Therefore, the details of daily existence are of critical importance to the overall atmosphere of the story. There is a heavy emphasis on the description of clothes, food, houses and estates, and manners. It is not unusual, for example, to be given exact descriptions of the clothes of all the important characters (male and female) in attendance at a particular ball, of the refreshments that were served, and of the dishes the late evening supper included.

Although there are numerous variations, the typical plot introduces an attractive, independent, usually unconventional heroine to a strong, purposeful (often wealthy, successful, or titled) hero; places them in extreme opposition to each other; and then spends the rest of the book making sure that they fall in love and are altar-bound by the end. Of course, between their initial fiery meeting and their final embrace, any number of things can happen to keep the two main characters apart. But except for occasional historical interferences (the heroine temporarily loses the hero during the San Francisco earthquake and fire, for example), it is the personal relationship between the protagonists and the romantic tension that keep the plot moving and the story alive.

In addition to the obvious groupings by historical period (see descriptions that follow), Period Romances can also be divided by sensuality level. The resulting two types of Period Romances, the Innocent and the Sensual, differ in the use of explicit sex. Sensuals use it, Innocent Period Romances don't. However, the lines between the two are becoming increasingly fuzzy and less important as more and more Historicals and Period Romances regularly include some use of sex. Most other aspects of the stories, from the settings to the plot patterns, are remarkably similar. Often the settings for the Sensual Romances are more exotic and the action more violent than those of the innocent variety, but this is not always the case, and some very sexually innocent stories contain a great deal of bloodshed and gore.

Brief Historical Descriptions

Although it is possible for period romances to be set during any time in history, most authors make use of only a few favored periods. Some of the political realities, social conditions, and customs of several of the most popular periods are described below. Additional information can be found in most encyclopedias and by consulting the library catalog under the heading Social History and its various subdivisions: Social History—Medieval; Social History—17th Century; etc. In addition, if the catalog is computerized, a combination of relevant terms (e.g., Regency social customs) in a keyword search may produce good results—or try searching the Internet, via the World Wide Web.

Medieval

The Middle Ages, or the medieval period, lasted for approximately a millennium and filled the gap between the Classical Period and the Renaissance. Although the fifth through the fifteenth centuries are often cited as the limiting dates, these are approximate at best, and the actual beginning and ending of the period are still being debated by scholars. It is, however, generally accepted that far from either beginning or ending abruptly, the medieval period grew and developed as the old Classical World declined, flourished from the eleventh through the thirteenth centuries, and gradually gave way to the Renaissance during the fourteenth and fifteenth centuries. By the time Columbus discovered the New World in 1492, only a few remnants of medieval society remained.

The Middle Ages are characterized, in general, by the rising power and influence of the Christian church and the establishment, flowering, and decline of the feudal system. It was also the time of chivalry, courtly love, quests, the Crusades and other wars (including the Hundred Years War and the divisive War of the Roses), Viking raids, the development of trades and guilds, the building of many of Europe's greatest cathedrals, severe famines, and the devastating Black Death. (Europe lost almost 23 percent of its population to the plague, which lasted from 1348 to 1350.) This was also the time of the legendary Robin Hood.

The social structure during this period was relatively simple; it consisted of three groups—the clergy, the peasantry, and the nobility—although a small, trade-centered middle class began to develop late in the period. In general, the nobles lived in castles surrounded by their lands on which the peasants worked. The peasants provided labor, loyalty, and taxes, and the nobles provided protection from outside harm.

For the nobleman life consisted primarily of fighting and overseeing his estates, while noblewomen were concerned with managing the household affairs. However, household affairs of the Middle Ages were very different from those of today. In addition to supervising the creation and preparation of most of the food (cheese, bread, cured meats, wine, ale, etc.), the clothes they wore (which involved spinning, weaving, dying, etc.), and the herbs and medicines they needed to stay healthy, the medieval lady was also responsible for managing the estate when her husband was off in battle—which was most of the time. This meant that she understood feudal law and legal matters, agriculture, and economics, and was able to deal well with the peasant subjects. She was also expected to be able to entertain beautifully, take care of all personnel problems, and keep the accounts in order. The Middle Ages produced some very capable and independent women.

However, even though she had social standing, independence, and a certain amount of control over her own wealth, the average noblewoman had little control over her love life. Infant betrothals and early marriages (all arranged by parents) were common, and people usually married for political and social reasons, rarely for love. Occasionally, a woman would pay great sums of money for the right to choose her own husband, but this option was available only to the wealthy and influential.

Although the peasants far outnumbered the nobility, today's Period Romances generally deal with the upper levels of medieval society. The hero is most often a lord or a knight, and if the heroine is not a lady at the beginning of the story, she usually has become one by its conclusion. The hero and the heroine are also together and in love by the end of the book, something that was rare during that actual time. These stories can be set at any time during the medieval period, although the High Middle Ages, eleventh to the thirteenth centuries, are especially popular. Most reflect the violence and the general insecurity of the times and wars, sieges, and raids are common.

It is worth noting, however, that with the recent development of the Alternative Reality Romance subgenre, the medieval period has also become a favorite setting for romances with mystical or magical aspects, and even though there may still be a significant amount of realistic violence, some of the more recent romances set in this period have a lyrical quality that the earlier ones do not possess.

Sixteenth Century

This was the century of the Tudors, of Henry VIII and Elizabeth I, in particular. The War of the Roses was over, England was united and the Renaissance, which had begun in Italy two centuries earlier, had finally reached the British Isles.

Interest in the arts increased (Henry VIII was a noted patron), and luminaries such as Shakespeare, William Byrd, and Holbein (by way of Germany) were active during this period. Education and learning became important as people, in keeping with the humanistic thrust of the Renaissance, turned their attention to themselves and the world around them. This was also the era of the Reformation, the establishment of the Church of England, and the beginnings of British naval power. It was, in general, a time of growth and expansion, culturally and economically. It is often considered England's Golden Age.

Much of the activity during this period centered around the court of the reigning monarch, and many of the Period Romances set during this time take full advantage of this fact. Life at court was entertaining (Renaissance banquets and festivals are legendary), luxurious, and often dangerous. It was a time when an accepted method of dealing with one's enemies was to kill them, and both Henry and Elizabeth had several people executed simply because they considered them threats or inconveniences. Plots of stories set in this period are filled with political intrigue, adventure, and romance; and arranged marriages, plots against political rivals, and clandestine affairs are typical elements.

It is interesting to note that in addition to being the setting for a number of period romances, the sixteenth century is also popular as a setting for Romantic Historicals, especially in the area of fictionalized biographies. Henry VIII and Elizabeth I both make excellent background or primary characters, and their courts were large enough and interesting enough to include any number of suitable heroes and heroines, real or imaginary.

Seventeenth Century

Although the change from the Tudor to the Stuart dynasties was accomplished peacefully when James I ascended England's throne in 1603, the seventeenth century was marked by revolution and political and religious strife. This is the century of Oliver Cromwell and the Roundheads, the English Civil Wars, and the Restoration of the Monarchy. Throughout most of the century, England was plagued by a series of economic and political problems, but by its end the power of Parliament had been firmly established and the role of the reigning monarch more clearly defined. Agricultural and commercial advances had resulted in a thriving economy and increasing international trade, and England had firmly established its naval supremacy.

Many of the Period Romances set during this century focus either on the clashes between the Royalist and Cromwellian (Roundhead) factions or on the Restoration. As might be expected, because most of these stories deal with life among the noble and wealthy, the heroes and heroines are usually Royalists or Royalist sympathizers. Although many express a more moderate view of the political situation, rarely are they supporters of the radical Cromwell. Cromwell did win, however, and Charles I was executed as a traitor to the Commonwealth in 1649. Under Cromwell, England entered a much more austere and puritanical time, and the social activities (to say nothing of the wealth and power) of the upper classes were severely limited. When Charles II was restored to the throne in 1660, there was a change in the mood of the country, and people once again began to enjoy themselves. In reaction to the extremely oppressive rule of Cromwell and the Puritans during the Interregnum, a number of highly restrictive laws were passed against the Puritans, and the Court of Charles II gained a reputation for being one of the more extravagant and immoral courts in English history.

The plots of stories set before the Interregnum include much political intrigue and often center around outwitting the Cromwellians to save a known Royalist (typically the hero) from capture or death. Those set during the Restoration are usually lighter in nature, focusing on social rather than political aspects. In general, most romances set during this period make some use of the varying political situations, and they are usually characterized by an abundance of action, adventure, and romance.

This was also the century of the early colonization of America, and a number of romances have been set during the Puritan colonial times. These stories tend to center around the difficulties of not only living under primitive colonial conditions, but also putting up with the numerous strictures of Puritan society. Witchcraft can also be an issue. Often the heroine is rebellious and spends most of her time fighting the system. Usually she wins, but she often must leave the colony as a result.

Georgian Period (Eighteenth Century)

The Georgian Period, long and theoretically encompassing the reigns of the first four English kings named George (1714-1830), was marked by the Jacobite Rebellions, especially the ones led by Prince Charles Edward; the bloody Battle of Culloden; the French Revolution; the American Revolution; the War with France; and the beginnings of the Industrial Revolution. It was a transitional period from a more elegant, leisurely age into the faster-paced modern world of industry and democracy.

Although a number of Historicals have centered around the abortive attempt by Charles to take over the throne in 1745, many of the period romances known as Georgian are set during the reign of George III (1760-1820). (The last nine years of his reign are known as the Regency Period and are discussed in the next chapter.) Some of these are quite similar in tone to the Regency Romance—light, diverting, and full of witty conversation—and except for the dates of the settings, could be classified as such. However, an increasing number are more typical of the eighteenth century in general and, accordingly, are fast paced, adventurous, violent, licentious, and bawdy. Their plots usually deal with upper-class society; often focus on the French Revolution and rescuing French aristocrats from the guillotine; and involve smuggling, robbery by highwaymen (and women), and other quite illegal, but highly intriguing, activities.

A number of romances set during this time also deal with the American Revolution. American in both setting and point of view, these stories feature spies, secret missions, hair breadth escapes, and occasionally some battle action. The heroine is daring and independent and often becomes directly involved in the action. Although there is some mention of families divided against each other, this is not as important a feature in these stories as it is in the later stories of the Civil War. *(See Victorian description below.)*

Regency Period

Because of the large number of publications for this period and the fact that the Regency is actually a separate Romance subgenre, the Regency period is discussed in chapter 8.

Victorian Period (Mid- to Late-Nineteenth Century)

The Victorian Period, named for the British queen whose reign lasted from 1837 to 1901, is marked in England by increasing industrialization, rapid population and urban growth, the Crimean War, the Boer War, and worldwide colonization. The period was relatively peaceful, except for the Crimean War (1854-1856) and the Boer War (1899-1902), but they were fought far away and for relatively brief periods of time. For the English, it was an era of progress and achievement, and British power and world influence were at their height. In short, it was another Golden Age for the British Empire.

Because there were no major upheavals in Britain during this period, most of the romances set during this time center on society, family life, and the various effects of industrialization. One important event during Victoria's reign was the shift in power from the landed gentry and nobility to the industrial magnates and the moneyed middle class. This new group could no longer be ignored, and as a result, the *nouveau riche* came into increasing social contact with the old aristocracy. The newcomers, however, were not immediately recognized as true equals, and it often took several generations for a family to be truly accepted in all respects. These social position conflicts sometimes figure in period romances set during this time, and it is not unusual for a mother to deplore her titled daughter's wishing to marry a man "in the trades."

Just as social position was important in this era, so was conduct and decorum. And although proper etiquette had been an issue in past times, never was behavior expected to be so prim and prudish as during Victoria's reign. Fortunately, most of today's Victorian romance heroines are exceptions to this rule, and much of the action in stories occurs as they rebel valiantly against these strictures.

Although some Victorian Historicals deal with the needed social reforms of the day, most current Period Romances set during this time concentrate on the social and family life of the upper classes. The heroine is attractive and can be sensible and capable, or rebellious and improper, or sometimes a bit of both. These novels usually center around marriage and can range from a Regency-like focus on manners to a more serious focus on a variety of social issues along with the strong romance line.

Although many of the same conditions existed in the United States that were prevalent in England during Victoria's reign, the major event of this period for America was the Civil War. This conflict killed more Americans than any war in history, divided families, radically changed society, and caused deep wounds that still have not healed today. Novels set during this time often employ the same pattern as *Gone With the Wind*, beginning with the antebellum South, continuing through the violence and destruction of the war itself, and then finishing with the struggle of the Reconstruction era. Plots typically include such elements as brother-fighting-brother and Southern-heroine-in-love-with-Northern-hero (or vice versa), and certain stereotypical characters (the faithful old slave, the lecherous carpetbagger, etc.) are rarely omitted. Heroines of novels of this type sometimes appear fragile and weak in the beginning (Scarlett not withstanding), but their hidden strength and resourcefulness appear just when needed, and they usually turn out to be very strong and capable woman indeed.

Another American event that has provided fertile background for romance novels, particularly recently, is the Western Expansion. Novels set in the Old West make full use of devices such as Indian or outlaw raids, gunfights, severe weather conditions (e.g., a winter blizzard or the summer desert heat), mutiny among the members of the wagontrain, and numerous other hardships. The plots most often revolve around survival—either of the trip west or of the primitive, lawless conditions that the characters find once they get there. Success is usually achieved under extremely difficult conditions. The tone of these novels can range from violent and fast-paced to humorous and tender, and heroes and heroines alike are strong, determined individuals, capable of surviving and actually enjoying all the action that surrounds them. The American West is also often used as a setting for the Saga and for the period versions of the Inspirational and Americana Romance subgenres.

Edwardian Period

Situated between the death of Queen Victoria and the beginning of World War I, the Edwardian Period (roughly corresponding to the reign of Edward VII—1901-1910) was a time of reaction, transition, and growing political uneasiness. It was also a time of luxury and leisure that was previously unknown in modern times, and the members of the upper classes, especially in England, were busy enjoying it. This small, privileged group, newly released from the moral and social constraints of the Victorian era and wealthy enough to be unconcerned about finances on a day-to-day basis, turned its attention to the pursuit of pleasure. And pursue it the Edwardians did—methodically, consistently, and with great purpose. With productive labor increasingly considered unworthy and demeaning for the elite, it became their obligation to maintain a lifestyle of indulging in a constant variety of costly and elaborate entertainments.

Of all the numerous amusements, the Edwardian weekend house party was by far the most favored and the most famous. Held in the large, old, elegantly furnished and beautifully landscaped homes of the upper classes, these gatherings could include as many as 30 guests, mostly members of society, but occasionally including a well-known author, political figure, or popular hero.

Food played an especially important role in these weekend affairs, and indeed, in all of Edwardian life. Food of all kinds was available at most hours of the day and night, and both lunch and dinner consisted of anywhere from 8 to 12 courses. It is not surprising that this period is noted for its gourmands rather than its gourmets and that its members were inclined to vacation at continental spas to "take the waters" for their health.

Food, however, was not the only attraction at these weekend parties. It was an accepted fact that because of the strict behavioral code which absolutely forbade public scandal, these house parties were to provide opportunities for discreet romantic interludes. The facilitation of these interludes was considered one of the most important jobs of the weekend's hostess. Indeed, the reputation of an Edwardian hostess could rise or fall on how perceptively she arranged her guests' sleeping accommodations.

Fashion was another important aspect of Edwardian life. Both men and women spent a great deal of time choosing and changing their clothes, often several times a day. Dandyism among the men was common, and no Edwardian woman of consequence would travel anywhere for even a day without her assemblage of trunks and boxes, all containing clothes and accessories. This was the era of the S-shaped figure, the top hat, the pompadour, the walking stick, and the Gibson girl.

The Edwardian period has much in common with the Regency and Restoration periods. Social activity was at a high, leisure activities were all-important, and the pursuit of pleasure was almost mandatory.

Edwardian Romances, many of them resembling Regencies, usually take full advantage of these aspects of the period with social behavior and manners being of paramount importance. Typically, the plots revolve around the social scene and marriage and may include such elements as "upstairs downstairs" situations. They may also include references to events such as the sinking of the *Titanic* and the incidents leading up to World War I. In general, however, although they can deal with serious issues, Edwardian romances are light, witty, and above all entertaining. They are true to their aim of depicting what has sometimes been called the Last Golden Age.

Selected Period Romance Bibliography

The works listed here include examples of both Innocent and Sensual Period Romance and cover a variety of historical periods. They exhibit a number of literary styles, and range in sensuality level from the innocent to the explicit. Separate bibliographies and brief discussions are also included for several of the important earlier and currently popular Period Romance types. (Because they differ in several ways from Period fiction, the Regency Period Romance is discussed in chapter 8 and the Period Inspirational Romance is discussed in chapter 12.) Many of the authors listed below also write other types of romantic fiction.

Adler, Elizabeth

Leonie. *Villard, 1985.* Set in the frenzied glamour of turn-of-the-century Paris.

Aiken, Joan

Many of Aiken's Gothic and Romantic Suspense novels use historical settings. *(See also Gothic and Regency Period bibliographies.)*

The Girl from Paris. *Doubleday, 1982.* A story of love, scandal, and tragedy set in Victorian England.

Anthony, Evelyn

Anthony began her writing career with Romantic Historicals and period romances, although she is now best known for her romantic suspense thrillers.

Clandara. *Doubleday, 1963.*

The Heiress. *Doubleday, 1964.* Sequel to *Clandara*.

Valentina. *Doubleday, 1966.* A fast-moving romance set during Napoleon's invasion of Russia.

Ashfield, Helen (Pamela Bennetts)

The Royal Jewel series

Social differences and the struggles of the poor are often elements in this charming series set in nineteenth-century England.

Emerald. *St. Martin's Press, 1983.*

Ruby. *St. Martin's Press, 1984.*

Pearl. *St. Martin's Press, 1985.* Hale, 1984.

Sapphire. *St. Martin's Press, 1985.*

Garnet. *St. Martin's Press, 1985.*

Opal. *St. Martin's Press, 1986.*

Topaz. *St. Martin's Press, 1987.*

Crystal. *Hale, 1987.*

Balogh, Mary

Noted primarily for her innovative Regencies that often stretch the boundaries of the genre, Balogh also writes provocative Period Romances.

Deceived. *Onyx, 1993.* After an absence of seven years, the Earl of Trevelyan returns to England just in time to kidnap his ex-wife as she is about to remarry. This realistic Regency-set romance deals with some serious issues including divorce and rape recovery.

Tangled. *Topaz, 1994.* Believing that her soldier husband is dead, Rebecca reluctantly remarries. But when her husband shows up after having been imprisoned, she must deal not only with conflicting emotions, but also with revenge, murder, and other secrets that simmer beneath the surface of mid-nineteenth-century Victorian society.

Heartless. *Berkley, 1995.* In this dark Georgian romance, past secrets haunt a marriage between a resigned spinster and a duke who thought he would never marry.

Truly. *Berkley, 1996.* A story of conflict, rebellion, and love set in Wales in the 1840s.

Indiscreet. *Jove, 1997.* When a case of mistaken identity eventually ruins widowed Catherine's reputation, the nobleman responsible insists on marrying her, despite her objections.

Thief of Dreams. *Jove, 1998.*

Barbieri, Elaine

(See also Period Americana bibliography.)

Tattered Silk. *Zebra, 1991.* Italian immigrant seeks success in the fashion industry.

Only for Love. *Zebra, 1994.* Exotic Caribbean setting.

Midnight Rogue. *Zebra, 1995.* Kidnapping and piracy in early nineteenth-century Louisiana.

Barnett, Jill

Barnett writes light, whimsical Period Romances with an occasional touch of magic. *(See also Alternative Reality bibliography.)*

The Heart's Haven. *Pocket Books, 1990.*

Surrender a Dream. *Pocket Books, 1991.* A librarian and a drifter spar over the same California farm.

Just a Kiss Away. *Pocket Books, 1992.* A freedom fighter and a Southern belle find love in the Philippine jungle.

Bewitching. *Pocket Books, 1993.*

Dreaming. *Pocket Books, 1994.* A whimsical story of a dreamy debutante who pursues— and finally gets—the man of her dreams.

Carried Away. *Pocket Books, 1996.* When the MacLachlan brothers decide to marry, they do it in the traditional way: by kidnapping their women.

Wonderful. *Pocket Books, 1997.* A war-weary knight and the bride he hasn't seen in years struggle to find happiness in Camrose Castle in thirteenth-century England.

Becnel, Rexanne

Becnel writes in a number of romance subgenres. The first three Period Romances listed below are all set in medieval England. *(See also Basic Contemporary, Alternative Reality, and Western Romance bibliographies.)*

My Gallant Enemy. *Dell, 1990.*

The Rose of Blacksword. *Dell, 1992.*

A Dove at Midnight. *Jove, 1993.*

Dangerous to Love. *St. Martin's Press, 1997.* A charming bluestocking and a "gypsy" rakehell earl find love in late Georgian (post-Regency) England.

Benzoni, Juliette

Translated from the French, Benzoni's Catherine series (set in medieval France) and Marianne series (set in Napoleonic France) may be of interest to some readers.

Beverley, Jo

Noted for her beautifully crafted Regencies, Beverley also writes lively, sensual Period romances, primarily set in medieval, Georgian, or Regency England. She is a member of the Romance Writers of America Hall of Fame for her Regencies.

Malloren series

These sexy, bawdy stories focus on the Malloren siblings and their exploits.

 My Lady Notorious. *Avon Books, 1993.*

Tempting Fortune. *Zebra, 1993.*

Something Wicked. *Topaz, 1997.*

Lord of My Heart. *Avon Books, 1992.* Medieval romance

Dark Champion. *Avon Books, 1993.* More medieval romance.

Forbidden. *Zebra, 1994.* One of the Company of Rogues series set in Regency England.

Dangerous Joy. *Zebra, 1995.* Another of the Company of Rogues series set in Regency England.

The Shattered Rose. *Zebra, 1996.* A medieval knight, thought dead, returns from the Crusades to discover his castle under siege and his wife in a relationship with another man.

Lord of Midnight. *Topaz, 1998.* Yet more medieval romance.

Blake, Jennifer (Patricia Maxwell)

Blake is a popular writer in a number of romance subgenres and won the Romance Writers of America Golden Treasure Award (now called the Lifetime Achievement Award) in 1987. Most of her Period romances are set in Louisiana during the eighteenth and nineteenth centuries. *(See also Basic Contemporary and Sensual Historical and Sweet/Savage Romance bibliographies.)*

Love's Wild Desire. *Popular Library, 1977.*

Tender Betrayal. *Popular Library, 1979.*

The Storm and the Splendor. *Fawcett, 1979.*

Golden Fancy. *Fawcett, 1979.*

Midnight Waltz. *Fawcett Columbine, 1985.*

Royal Passion. *Fawcett, 1985.*

Prisoner of Desire. *Fawcett, 1986.*

Arrow to the Heart. *Fawcett, 1993.* The impotent Giles Castlereagh holds a "medieval tournament" (in antebellum Louisiana) and compels the victor to impregnate his young wife by locking them in a tower until they accomplish the task.

Silver-Tongued Devil. *Fawcett, 1996.*

Brandewyne, Rebecca

Brandewyne is a popular writer of poetic, often lyrical, highly detailed romances of various types. *(See also Western Period, Gothic, and Alternative Reality Romance bibliographies.)*

No Gentle Love. *Warner Books, 1980.* A forced marriage between cousins becomes one of love.

Forever My Love. *Warner Books, 1982.* Highland love during the reigns of James III and IV in fifteenth-century Scotland.

Love, Cherish Me. *Warner Books, 1983.*

Rose of Rapture. *Warner Books, 1984.* Set during the reign of Richard III.

Bristow, Gwen

Classic historical romances.

Jubilee Trail. *Thomas Y. Crowell, 1950.*

Celia Garth. *Thomas Y. Crowell, 1959.*

Calico Palace. *Thomas Y. Crowell, 1970.*

Brockway, Connie

Brockway produces well-written, compelling novels with occasionally dark and dangerous heroes.

Anything for Love. *Avon Books, 1994.*

Promise Me Heaven. *Avon Books, 1994.* An innocent, husband-hunting noblewoman seeks the help of a notorious rake to learn the art of seduction in this Regency-set historical.

A Dangerous Man. *Dell, 1996.* Heroine heads for England to find her brother and ends up battling a former gunslinger-turned-nobleman to accomplish her aims.

As You Desire. *Dell, 1997.*

All Through the Night. *Dell, 1997.* Demure widow by day and intrepid cat burglar by night, Anne Wilder meets her match when Colonel Jack Seward, Whitehall's Hound, sets out in pursuit.

Cameron, Stella

Cameron writes passionate, fast-paced romances that can be a bit dark. Most of her Historicals are set during the years just following the official British Regency Period. *(See also Basic Contemporary Romance bibliography.)*

Fascination. *Avon Books, 1993.* Deception has unintended results in this passionate, rather Gothic romance.

His Magic Touch. *Avon Books, 1994.* To avoid a distasteful marriage, the heroine asks the hero to compromise her—but she has no idea he has darker ulterior motives for doing so.

Charmed. *Avon Books, 1995.* A dispossessed heir returns to claim his heritage in late-Georgian (post-Regency) England.

Beloved. *Warner Books, 1996.* A mysterious "wounded" rake and a heroine with a secret scandalize society in this late-Georgian (post-Regency) romance.

Canham, Marsha

Canham's Historicals are fast paced, action filled, and peopled with memorable characters.

Through a Dark Mist. *Dell, 1991.* First of the Robin Hood Trilogy.

Under the Desert Moon. *Dell, 1992.* American West setting.

In the Shadow of Midnight. *Dell, 1994.* Second in the Robin Hood Trilogy.

Straight for the Heart. *Dell, 1995.*

Across a Moonlit Sea. *Dell, 1996.* Elizabethan pirates.

The Last Arrow. *Dell, 1997.* Conclusion of the Robin Hood Trilogy

Cartland, Barbara

One of the most prolific writers of this century, Cartland is best known for light, innocent Period Romances. Except for the historical settings, these frothy confections are similar in pattern to the original Harlequins, generally following the traditional boy-meets-girl, boy-loses-girl, boy-gets-girl formula. Because of the volume of her work (more than 500 titles as of this writing) and their accessibility through other sources, only her first romance is listed here. For a more complete listing of Cartland's works consult Aruna Vasudevan and Lesley Henderson's *Twentieth-Century Romance and Historical Writers*, 3rd edition (St. James Press, 1994). For those currently in print, consult *Books in Print* or any of the relevant online sources, e.g., www.amazon.com.

Jig-Saw. *Duckworth, 1925.* Cartland's first romance and one of her more important ones because it set the pattern for the hundreds to come.

Cates, Kimberly (Kim Ostrum Bush)

Cates uses a wide variety of historical settings for her warm, often humorous, romances. *(See also Alternative Reality bibliography.)*

To Catch the Flame. *Pocket Books, 1991.* A female highwayman and a British lord come to terms in this Georgian romance with a Pygmalion theme.

Crown of Dreams. *Pocket Books, 1993.* Georgian high adventure as protagonists raised as brother and sister discover there is more to their relationship than just friendship.

The Raider's Bride. *Pocket Books, 1994.* A British spy heroine falls in love with the enemy in Colonial America.

Angel's Fall. *Pocket Books, 1996.* A "good Samaritan" deed takes adventurer Adam Slade to London, into the life of activist Juliet Grafton-Moore and her home for fallen women in this romance that touches on some serious social issues.

Chase, Loretta (Loretta Chekani)

The Lion's Daughter. *Avon Books, 1992.* Esme and Varian find love as they work to find her missing father and rescue a cousin from kidnappers. A lively Regency-set historical that sweeps across both Italy and Albania.

Captives of the Night. *Avon Books, 1994.* An intrepid heroine seeks the help of a mysterious count to solve the murders of her father and her husband.

 Lord of Scoundrels. *Avon Books, 1995.* A spinster and an infamous nobleman spar charmingly in this unusual, well-done late-Georgian (post-Regency) romance that is laced with suspense and a dash of evil. A Rita Award winner.

Cleeve, Brian

Cleeve's unusual Historicals combine wit, social commentary, romance, adventure, and suffering with a wide variety of highly interesting characters. Most of these are set during the Regency period.

Kate. *Coward, McCann & Geoghegan, 1977.*

Judith. *Coward, McCann & Geoghegan, 1978.*

Hester. *Coward, McCann & Geoghegan, 1979.*

Coleman, Bob

The Later Adventures of Tom Jones. *Simon & Schuster, 1985.* Sequel to Henry Fielding's *Tom Jones.* Set in eighteenth-century England.

Cookson, Catherine

Both prolific and popular, Cookson produces compelling works that are generally filled with memorable characters, realistic settings and situations, and plots that focus on relevant social issues—particularly class differences. Her works often span decades and can be historical, contemporary, or both. *(See also Saga and Women's Romantic Fiction bibliographies.)*

Kate Hannigan. *Macdonald, 1950.* Bantam, 1972. This first novel, depicting the plight of a working-class girl who is impregnated by a middle-class man, set the pattern for the authors of many titles that followed. Set in the early twentieth century.

Coulter, Catherine

Coulter is a popular writer in a number of romance subgenres. Her romances are adventurous and often explore the darker, violent side of sex. They can contain elements of hero/heroine abuse, and they have definite Sweet/Savage elements. Many of her books are linked by theme, place, characters, or family.

Devil's Embrace. *New American Library, 1982.*

Devil's Daughter. *New American Library, 1985.* Features the daughter of the protagonists in *Devil's Embrace.*

Song Trilogy

Medieval setting.

Fire Song. *New American Library, 1985.*

Earth Song. *New American Library, 1990.*

Secret Song. *Onyx, 1991.*

Season of the Sun. *Dutton, 1991.* Viking violence with a captor/captive theme.

Bride Trilogy

Regency setting.

The Sherbrooke Bride. *Putnam, 1992.*

The Hellion Bride. *Putnam, 1992.*

The Heiress Bride. *Putnam, 1993.*

Legacy Trilogy

Regency Setting.

The Wyndham Legacy. *Putnam, 1994.*

The Nightingale Legacy. *Putnam, 1994.*

The Valentine Legacy. *Putnam, 1995.*

Cuevas, Judy

(See also Judith Ivory, this bibliography.)

Black Silk. *Berkley, 1991.* An elegant romance that explores the darker side of Victorian society.

Bliss. *Jove, 1995.* A young American helps a disillusioned French artist find love in this Edwardian romance.

Dance. *Jove, 1996.* Former lovers with diverse interests meet again in France in the early twentieth century and learn that love can be a common denominator.

De Blasis, Celeste

The Night Child. *Coward, McCann & Geoghegan, 1975.*

The Tiger's Woman. *Delacorte Press, 1981.* Love, sex, violence, and secrets in abundance in this story of a wealthy businessman and the woman who loves him. Pacific Northwest setting.

Deveraux, Jude (Jude Gilliam White)

Deveraux has been a popular historical romance writer since the 1970s, and although many of her early novels featured abductions and rapes typical of the decade's Sensual Historical and Sweet/Savage subgenres, her later ones generally do not. Her heroines are strong, usually monogamous, and rarely allow themselves to become victims. *(See also Western and Time Travel Romance bibliographies.)*

The Enchanted Land. *Avon Books, 1977.*

The Black Lyon. *Avon Books, 1979.*

Velvet series

This is one of her most widely read and remembered series.

The Velvet Promise. *Pocket Books, 1981.*

Highland Velvet. *Pocket Books, 1982.*

Velvet Angel. *Pocket Books, 1983.*

Velvet Song. *Pocket Books, 1983.*

James River Trilogy

Forced marriages are featured in each of these novels.

Counterfeit Lady. *Pocket Books, 1984.*

Lost Lady. *Pocket Books, 1985.*

River Lady. *Pocket Books, 1985.*

Dodd, Christina

Dodd's diverse Historicals are well written, display good character development (although the characters are not always likable), and are often highly sensual and action filled. However, they can also be humorous, tender, and occasionally a bit Gothic.

7

Candle in the Window. *HarperPaperbacks, 1991.* Tender story of two blind protagonists in twelfth-century England.

Priceless. *HarperPaperbacks, 1992.*

Castles in the Air. *HarperPaperbacks, 1993.*

The Greatest Lover in All England. *HarperPaperbacks, 1994.* Shakespeare, secrets, and a long-lost heiress.

Outrageous. *HarperPaperbacks, 1994.* Intrigue, danger, and humor in a Renaissance setting.

Move Heaven and Earth. *HarperPaperbacks, 1995.* Despondent, obnoxious, war-wounded hero is a challenge for the determined heroine in this Regency-set historical with a definite Gothic touch.

Once a Knight. *HarperPaperbacks, 1996.* A has-been knight is forced to become the hero he once was.

A Knight to Remember. *HarperPaperbacks, 1997.*

A Well Pleasured Lady. *Avon Books, 1997.* A bawdy, unconventional Georgian.

A Well Favored Gentleman. *Avon Books, 1998.* Links to *A Well Pleasured Lady.*

Domning, Denise

Domning's Historicals often provide an exceptional, realistic sense of time and place. The "Seasons" series is set in twelfth-century England.

Winter's Heat. *Topaz, 1994.*

Summer's Storm. *Topaz, 1994.*

Spring's Fury. *Topaz, 1995.*

Autumn's Flame. *Topaz, 1995.*

A Love for All Seasons. *Topaz, 1996.*

Lady in Waiting. *Topaz, 1998.* Dangerous Elizabethan court intrigue.

Eden, Dorothy

Eden is a renowned novelist in a number of romance subgenres. Her most memorable works include:

Sleep in the Woods. *Hodder & Stoughton, 1960.* Coward, 1961.

The Vines of Yarrabee. *Coward, 1969.*

Melbury Square. *Coward, 1970.*

Speak to Me of Love. *Coward, 1972.*

The Millionaire's Daughter. *Coward, 1974.*

The Storrington Papers. *Coward, McCann & Geoghegan, 1978.*

The American Heiress. *Coward, McCann & Geoghegan, 1980.*

An Important Family. *William Morrow, 1982.*

Elliott, Elizabeth

 The Warlord. *Bantam Books, 1995.* A Rita Award winner.

The Betrothed. *Bantam Books, 1995.*

Scoundrel. *Bantam Books, 1996.* British spy Lady Lily Walters is hard-pressed to keep her role hidden from a scandalous rake when he rescues her from a brutal attack.

Feather, Jane

Feather is a popular writer of sensual, fast-paced, descriptive Historicals that often feature adventurous heroines in intriguing, sometimes dark and dangerous, situations. Some of her more recent romances are listed here. Her "V" books are set primarily in Regency England.

Virtue. *Doubleday, 1993.*

Velvet. *Bantam Books, 1994.*

Vixen. *Bantam Books, 1994.*

Valentine. *Bantam Books, 1995.*

Vanity. *Bantam Books, 1995.*

Violet. *Bantam Books, 1995.*

The Diamond Slipper. *Bantam Books, 1997.* This is the first in Feather's latest series of books, which are linked by a series of heirloom charms.

The Silver Rose. *Bantam Books, 1997.*

The Emerald Swan. *Bantam Books, 1998.*

Feyrer, Gayle

Feyrer's romances are intricate, realistic, and fast paced.

The Prince of Cups. *Dell, 1995.* Intrigue in Renaissance Florence.

The Thief's Mistress. *Dell, 1996.* A new look at the Robin Hood legend.

Garwood, Julie

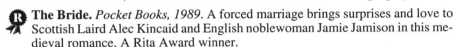

Garwood is a popular writer of lively, often witty and humorous, romances that are filled with appealing characters. Her favored settings are the British medieval and Regency periods and recently, Victorian America and the American West. *(See also Western Period Romance bibliography.)*

The Bride. *Pocket Books, 1989.* A forced marriage brings surprises and love to Scottish Laird Alec Kincaid and English noblewoman Jamie Jamison in this medieval romance. A Rita Award winner.

Guardian Angel. *Pocket Books, 1990.* A woman pirate and a noble spy find love in Regency England.

The Gift. *Pocket Books, 1991.* Kidnapped by her pirate husband after having been ignored for years, Sara nearly destroys the ship in her efforts to save her marriage. Contains character links to *Guardian Angel.*

The Prize. *Pocket Books, 1991.* The Saxon heroine eventually falls for the Norman nobleman who is charged with seeing her safely to William's London court.

The Secret. *Pocket Books, 1992.* A warm and unusual story of friendship and love.

Castles. *Pocket Books, 1993.* Links to *Guardian Angel* and *The Gift.*

Saving Grace. *Pocket Books, 1993.* A young widow learns that all men are not as cruel as her first husband when she weds Scottish laird Gabriel McBain to assure political stability. One of the author's best.

Golon, Sergeanne (Anne and Serge Golon)

Angelique series

The continuing stories of beautiful, golden-haired, green-eyed Angelique who blazes a trail through the seventeenth century from France to the New World in an amazing series of adventures. These are interesting classics of the genre that are still being read, reprinted, and translated into various languages. *Angelique* (J. B. Lippincott, 1958) is the first in the series, all of which have "Angelique" in the title.

Graham, Heather

A popular writer in many romance subgenres, Graham also writes as Heather Graham Pozzessere and Shannon Drake. Her stories make use of many different settings and time periods and are characterized by fast-paced, compelling action; a high degree of sensuality; and well-drawn, appealing characters. Her works include:

A Pirate's Pleasure. *Dell, 1989.* Fleeing an unwanted marriage, Skye Kinsdale heads for the American colonies and runs afoul of the pirate Silver Hawk.

The Viking's Woman. *Dell, 1990*. Rhiannon mistakenly attacks a visiting Viking leader and then is ordered by the king to make amends by marrying him. Ninth-century Ireland setting.

Civil War Trilogy

Details the fortunes of the Cameron siblings during and following the war.

One Wore Blue. *Dell, 1992.*

And One Wore Gray. *Dell, 1992.*

And One Rode West. *Dell, 1992.*

Captive. *Topaz, 1996*. A Southern belle and a half-Seminole hero find love and danger during the Seminole wars in Florida.

Rebel. *Topaz, 1997.*

Surrender. *Topaz, 1998.*

Hardwick, Mollie

Also writes Romantic Historicals and sagas. *(See Romantic Historical and Saga bibliographies.)*

Lovers Meeting. *St. Martin's Press, 1979.*

Willowwood. *St. Martin's Press, 1980.*

Monday's Child. *St. Martin's Press, 1982.*

The Shakespeare Girl. *St. Martin's Press, 1983.*

The Merry Maid. *St. Martin's Press, 1985*. Methuen, 1984.

The Girl with the Crystal Dove. *St. Martin's Press, 1985.*

Heath, Lorraine

(See also Western Romance bibliography.)

Always to Remember. *Jove, 1996*. Emotionally compelling story of a conscientious objector during the Civil War and the woman who loves him. A Rita Award winner.

Heyer, Georgette

Noted primarily for her delightful, standard-setting Regency romances, Heyer also wrote historical novels, period romances, and mysteries. *(See also Regency and Historical Novel bibliographies.)*

The Black Moth. *Constable, 1921*. An eighteenth-century romance of an earl's son turned highwayman and of the young lady he rescues from a would-be abductor.

The Great Roxhythe. *Small Maynard, 1923*. In the late 1660s, the Marquis of Roxhythe, a favorite of King Charles II, is embroiled in political intrigue while seeming to be a superficial fop. Primarily of interest because it is one of Heyer's earliest attempts at historical fiction.

Simon the Coldheart. *Small Maynard, 1925*. Simon of Beauvallet, a soldier of fortune in the fifteenth century, finally learns the importance of true love in this story of politics and romance set in England during the reigns of Henry IV and Henry V.

These Old Shades. *Small Maynard, 1926*. Although technically a Georgian period romance, this light, typically Heyer work has all the attributes of her Regencies. Set in eighteenth-century England and France, this novel describes the adventures of gamine Leonie and her protector (and future husband), the Duke of Avon.

The Masqueraders. *Heinemann, 1928.* Adventure and romance following the Jacobite uprising of 1745.

Beauvallet. *Heinemann, 1929.* Swashbuckling adventure of pirate Sir Nicholas Beauvallet who finds love and romance during the seventeenth century.

The Devil's Cub. *Heinemann, 1934.* Sequel to *These Old Shades.* Mary Challoner devises a plan to save her sister from seduction by the notorious young Marquis of Vidal, only to find herself forced aboard his yacht bound for France. Set in the eighteenth century.

The Convenient Marriage. *Heinemann, 1934.* To allow her eldest sister to marry the man she loves, Miss Horatia Winwood offers herself to the Earl of Rule in her sister's place. Soon all London is talking about the young countess's wild behavior. Set in the eighteenth century.

The Talisman Ring. *Heinemann, 1936.* When the irrepressible Eustacie escapes from her home in the dead of night to avoid marrying her prosaic cousin Tristam, she falls in with a band of smugglers led by none other than her unknown, romantic cousin Ludovic. Set in the eighteenth century.

Hill, Pamela

Hill's numerous historically set romances feature strong heroines, fast-paced action, intrigue and mystery, and Gothic overtones. *(See also Saga, Gothic, and Romantic Historical bibliographies.)*

The Malvie Inheritance. *St. Martin's Press, 1973.*

A Place of Ravens. *Hale, 1980.* St. Martin's Press, 1981.

Hodge, Jane Aiken

Hodge is noted for her period novels, many of which contain strong elements of romantic suspense. *(See also Romantic Suspense and Regency Period Romance bibliographies.)*

Here Comes a Candle. *Doubleday, 1967.*

The Winding Stair. *Doubleday, 1969.* Hodder & Stoughton, 1968.

Marry in Haste. *Doubleday, 1970.* Hodder & Stoughton, 1969.

Greek Wedding. *Doubleday, 1970.*

Savannah Purchase. *Doubleday, 1971.*

Shadow of a Lady. *Coward, McCann & Geoghegan, 1974.*

Rebel Heiress. *Doubleday, 1975.*

Runaway Bride. *Fawcett, 1975.*

Judas Flowering. *Doubleday, 1976.*

Red Sky at Night, Lovers' Delight. *Doubleday, 1978.*

Wide Is the Water. *Coward, McCann & Geoghegan, 1981.* Sequel to *Judas Flowering.*

The Lost Garden. *Coward, McCann & Geoghegan, 1982.*

Ibbotson, Eva

Ibbotson's few historical romances are charming, descriptive, and gently humorous. She has also written several children's stories.

A Countess Below Stairs. *Avon Books, 1981.*

Magic Flutes. *St. Martin's Press, 1982.*

A Company of Swans. *St. Martin's Press, 1985.*

Ivory, Judith (Judy Cuevas)

Beast. *Avon Books, 1997.* While aboard a ship headed for Europe to marry a "beastly" prince she has never met, the heroine is swept off her feet by the prince in disguise. But his plan backfires when he falls in love with the heroine. Definite Beauty and the Beast characteristics.

Sleeping Beauty. *Avon Books, 1998.* A beautiful, wealthy, and independent woman of the world is awakened to true love by a most unlikely hero in this compelling romance that takes a look at Victorian society values and finds them wanting.

Johansen, Iris

Johansen has written in a number of romance subgenres including contemporary, period, and most recently, romantic suspense. Her novels are typified by innovation, well-drawn characters, and compelling plots.

The Golden Barbarian. *Bantam Books, 1991.* In this novel that fills in the early history of the country of Sedikhan (the setting for some of Johansen's earlier contemporary novels), the sheik marries the spirited woman he has loved since she was a child. Then he must deal with her liberated attitudes and the effects they are having on the male-dominated society in Sedikhan.

Tiger Prince. *Bantam Books, 1993.* A determined businesswoman and a ruthless adventurer clash all the way from India to Scotland in a story that is as complex and thought-provoking as it is romantic.

The Beloved Scoundrel. *Bantam Books, 1994.* Kidnapped because she is suspected of holding secrets that could harm Napoleon, the stained glass artist heroine falls in love with the nobleman who holds her prisoner.

Midnight Warrior. *Bantam Books, 1994.* An eleventh-century Saxon healer helps a wounded Norman warrior and ends up attracting his romantic interest. Somewhat mystical.

Lion's Bride. *Bantam Books, 1996.* A twelfth-century tale of a runaway weaver and a mercenary who find a new life for themselves despite their separate enemies. Passionate, picaresque, and exotic.

Johnson, Susan

Although Johnson's highly erotic romances are some of the hottest in the genre, they are rarely cruel or sexually violent and do not contain the hero-to-heroine abuse necessary to place them within the Sweet/Savage subgenre. *(See also Ethnic Romance bibliography.)*

Russian Trilogy

An erotic series depicting the adventures of three generations of men in the Kuzan family.

Seized by Love. *Playboy, 1979.*

Love Storm. *Playboy, 1981.*

Sweet Love, Survive. *Playboy, 1985.*

Golden Paradise. *Harlequin, 1990.* A wealthy, bright, spoiled princess and an equally endowed prince fight their way to love amid the glitter of Tsarist Russia. Linked to the Kuzan books, but slightly less erotic.

Sinful. *Bantam Books, 1992.* When Chelsea schemes to avoid marriage by losing her virginity, she ends up married to the infamous Sinjin St. John, Duke of Seth. Exile and exotic adventures and love await.

Outlaw. *Bantam Books, 1993.* Kidnapping, treachery, and intrigue are all part of this passionate story with an eighteenth-century Scottish setting.

Brazen. *Bantam Books, 1995.* Star-crossed lovers in a lavish Victorian setting.

Taboo. *Bantam Books, 1997.* The wife of a notorious Russian general and a French general find love during war as they deal with an impossible situation. Set in late eighteenth-century Europe.

Johnston, Joan

Johnston writes in several romance subgenres. *(See also Western Romance Period Americana bibliographies.)*

The Inheritance. *Dell, 1995.* When Texas rancher Nicholas Calloway goes to England to claim and then quickly sell his inherited estate, he must deal with his cousin's widow, Daisy, who has ideas of her own.

After the Kiss. *Dell, 1997.* This charming Regency romp takes a spirited, disinherited debutante and an infamous rake, puts them in the hands of a determined amateur matchmaker, and lets nature take its course.

Kinsale, Laura

Kinsale's Historicals are well written, uncommon, thought provoking, and filled with imperfect characters.

Seize the Fire. *Avon Books, 1989.* An exiled princess and a reluctant hero find love in this unusual romance.

Prince of Midnight. *Avon Books, 1990.* A has-been highwayman with hearing and vertigo problems joins forces with an emotionally frozen heroine to foil a villain. A compelling story of healing and love.

The Shadow and the Star. *Avon Books, 1991.* A thief and a seamstress find love and adventure in some conventional and exotic places.

Flowers from the Storm. *Avon Books, 1992.* A Quaker heroine and a hero who has had a stroke find love and healing in this unusual and extremely well-crafted romance. Late Regency setting.

For My Lady's Heart. *Berkley, 1993.* Based on *Sir Gawain and the Green Knight*, this complex medieval tale features strong characters, political intrigue, and is laced with Middle English dialogue. One of the author's more controversial novels.

The Dream Hunter. *Berkley, 1994.* A legendary mare and an equally legendary lady are at the heart of this multidimensional story of love and adventure that moves from the deserts of Syria to the drawing rooms of England.

My Sweet Folly. *Berkley, 1997.*

Krahn, Betina

Krahn writes charming, witty, often humorous romances that address serious issues (especially the plight of women) with a light touch.

Caught in the Act. *Avon Books, 1990.* Elizabethan court intrigue.

Midnight Magic. *Zebra, 1990.* A "jinxed" heroine decides to marry someone who deserves all the bad luck that surrounds her. Funny and witty.

Behind Closed Doors. *Avon Books, 1991.* An "arranged" marriage has romantic results. Renaissance setting.

My Warrior's Heart. *Avon Books, 1992.* A warrior maiden and a pacifist hero find love in spite of their differences.

The Last Bachelor. *Bantam Books, 1994.* Heroine's campaign to obtain husbands for poor, but gently bred women results in an unusual challenge to one of the ton's most eligible bachelors. Serious issues charmingly handled.

The Perfect Mistress. *Bantam Books, 1995.* Raised by a delightful quartet of courtesans to be a "perfect mistress," Gabrielle wants a real marriage—and she finds one in a rather unexpected place. Addresses the serious issue of the vulnerability of women in Victorian society.

The Unlikely Angel. *Bantam Books, 1996.*

The Mermaid. *Bantam Books, 1997.* The heroine's unusual work with dolphins brings an icthyologist hero to her seaside home to validate her findings, with romantic results.

Laker, Rosalind (Barbara Ovstedal)

One of the best-known historical writers, Laker produces well-crafted, meticulously researched books. Her works include:

Banners of Silk. *NAL Signet, 1981.*

The Jewelled Path. *Doubleday, 1983.*

This Shining Land. *Doubleday, 1985.* One of the author's best.

Tree of Gold. *Doubleday, 1986.*

The Silver Touch. *Doubleday, 1987.*

Circle of Pearls. *Doubleday, 1990.*

The Golden Tulip. *Doubleday, 1991.* The heroine faces many obstacles in her struggle to become a master painter in seventeenth-century Holland.

The Venetian Mask. *Doubleday, 1992.* Music and intrigue in eighteenth-century Venice.

The Sugar Pavilion. *Doubleday, 1993.*

Lamb, Arnette

Most of Lamb's fast-paced, compelling romances are set in Scotland during the Georgian or medieval periods. Appealing characters, interesting situations, and humor are characteristics of her works.

Highland Rogue. *Pocket Books, 1991.*

The Betrothal. *Pocket Books, 1992.*

Border Bride. *Pocket Books, 1993.*

The Border Lord. *Pocket Books, 1993.*

Chieftain. *Pocket Books, 1994.*

Maiden of Inverness. *Pocket Books, 1995.*

MacKenzie Trilogy

Lachlan MacKenzie's daughters find love and adventure in eighteenth-century Scotland and America.

Betrayed. *Pocket Books, 1995.*

Beguiled. *Pocket Books, 1996.*

True Heart. *Pocket Books, 1997.*

Langan, Ruth

Captive of Desire. *Pocket Books, 1990.* Seventeenth-century Ireland with a captive-in-love-with-captor plot pattern.

Highland series

Highland Barbarian. *Harlequin, 1990.*

Highland Fire. *Harlequin, 1991.* Primarily set in mid-sixteenth-century Ireland.

Highland Heart. *Harlequin, 1992.* Scottish Highland love and adventure in the days of Mary, Queen of Scots.

Highland Heather. *Harlequin, 1991.*

The Highlander. *Harlequin, 1994.* Prequel to Langan's other Highland books.

Deception. *Harlequin, 1993.* Court intrigue and deception in mid-seventeenth-century England.

Layton, Edith

Layton's diverse historical romances are well crafted and filled with accurate historical detail.

Fireflower. *Signet, 1989.* A would-be prostitute finds love with her first customer in mid-seventeenth-century England.

The Crimson Crown. *New American Library, 1990.* Drama and court intrigue in the days of Henry VII.

The Guilded Cage. *New American Library, 1991.* The tawdry, glittery theatrical scene in New York of the late 1870s.

McCullough, Colleen

The Ladies of Missalonghi. *Harper & Row, 1987.* Early twentieth-century Australia.

McKinney, Meagan (Ruth Goodman)

Till Dawn Tames the Night. *Dell, 1991.* Pirates, passion, treachery, and revenge in an exotic early-nineteenth-century setting.

Lions and Lace. *Dell, 1992.* A story of dark revenge set among the New York elite. Early twentieth century. Links to *Fair Is the Rose. (See Western Romance bibliography.)*

The Ground She Walks Upon. *Delacorte Press, 1994.* An ancient Celtic cross is at the heart of this mystical story set in Ireland in the first half of the nineteenth century.

McNaught, Judith

McNaught writes both Contemporary and Period Romances and is noted for her independent, proactive heroines.

Whitney, My Love. *Pocket Books, 1985.* Heroine falls in love with the man she is forced to marry as payment for her father's debts in this Regency-set romance. One of the author's most popular.

Something Wonderful. *Pocket Books, 1988.*

A Kingdom of Dreams. *Pocket Books, 1989.*

Once and Always. *Pocket Books, 1987.*

Almost Heaven. *Pocket Books, 1990.* Regency heroine sets out to discourage suitors, with interesting results.

Medeiros, Teresa

Medeiros writes in a number of historical periods.

Lady of Conquest. *Berkley, 1989.* A realistic story of second century Ireland.

Shadows and Lace. *Berkley, 1990.* Revenge and love in a medieval setting.

Once an Angel. *Bantam Books, 1993.* A naked heroine on a New Zealand beach, a dashing guardian hero, and a bit of mystery add to this passionate, humorous romance.

Thief of Hearts. *Bantam Books, 1994.*

Fairest of Them All. *Bantam Books, 1995.*

Michaels, Kasey

Michaels writes in a wide variety of romance subgenres and is especially known for her earlier Regencies. Many of her period romances use the British Regency as a setting.

Legacy of the Rose. *Pocket Books, 1992.* A dark Gothic tale of a wounded war hero and the shattered, but eventually reclaimed life to which he returns.

Bride of the Unicorn. *Pocket Books, 1993.* A long-lost heiress is turned into a "lady" in a scheme of vengeance. Then her "creator" falls in love. Pygmalion elements.

The Illusions of Love. *Pocket Books, 1994.* Amnesia creates problems in this marriage-of-convenience story.

Masquerade in Moonlight. *Pocket Books, 1994.* A fast-paced, dark, and sensual story of two people seeking vengeance.

The Passion of an Angel. *Pocket Books, 1995.* A funny, romantic guardian/ward romance with distinct Regency touches.

Secrets of the Heart. *Pocket Books, 1995.*

The Homecoming. *Pocket Books, 1996.* An Irish immigrant finds love in Colonial America in this marriage-of-convenience romance.

The Untamed. *Pocket Books, 1996.* Follows *The Homecoming.*

The Promise. *Pocket Books, 1997.*

Miller, Linda Lael

Miller writes in a number of subgenres and is noted for her humorous, relatively sexually explicit romances. *(See also Time Travel and Paranormal and Western Romance bibliographies.)*

Taming Charlotte. *Pocket Books, 1993.*

Princess Annie. *Pocket Books, 1994.* Annie visits her best friend, Princess Phaedra, in Bavia and falls in love with the prince. Follows *Taming Charlotte.*

Mills, Anita

Fire series

Medieval setting.

Lady of Fire. *Onyx, 1987.*

Fire and Steel. *Onyx, 1988.*

Hearts of Fire. *Onyx, 1989.*

The Fire and the Fury. *Penguin Books, 1991.*

Winter Roses. *Signet, 1992.*

Autumn Rain. *Onyx, 1993.* Regency setting.

Falling Stars. *Topaz, 1993.* English heroine is disillusioned with Russian life.

Secret Nights. *Topaz, 1994.* Heroine offers herself as a mistress to the barrister hero if he will take her father's case. She ends up falling in love with the barrister in this realistic, dark Regency.

Monk, Karyn

Surrender to a Stranger. *Bantam Books, 1995.*

The Rebel and the Redcoat. *Bantam Books, 1996.*

Once a Warrior. *Bantam Books, 1997.* A disillusioned warrior helps the heroine save her clan.

The Witch and the Warrior. *Bantam Books, 1998.* Hero snatches heroine from the burning stake because he wants her to heal his sickly son—and falls in love with her.

Paisley, Rebecca

Paisley writes lively, sexy Historicals filled with off-beat humor and "down-home" language. *(See also Western Romance and Fantasy bibliographies.)*

Barefoot Bride. *Avon Books, 1990.* Hero brings an Appalachian bride back to his native Boston with interesting results.

Diamonds and Dreams. *Avon Books, 1991.* An American heroine causes problems and finds love in a small English village.

Midnight and Magnolias. *Avon Books, 1992.* Heroine heads for Aventine to "catch herself a prince."

Potter, Patricia

Potter has written in a number of romance subgenres and is noted for action-oriented, intense stories peopled with well-developed, often "wounded" characters. *(See also Western Romance bibliography.)*

7

Dragonfire. *Harlequin, 1990.* An unusual romance set in China during the Boxer Rebellion.

The Abduction. *Harlequin, 1991.* The "traditional" kidnapping of an English lord by a female Scottish chieftain results in love and peace, much to the dismay of those who prefer conflict. A passion romance with a sixteenth-century setting.

Rainbow. *Bantam Books, 1991.* A Southern belle with a mission and an undercover abolitionist riverboat owner eventually join forces in a romance set in the antebellum American South.

Lightning. *Bantam Books, 1992.* Lauren becomes a Union spy in order to avenge her twin brother's death and ends up in love with the blockade runner she considers responsible.

The Marshall and the Heiress. *Bantam Books, 1996.* Marshall Ben Masters takes his young ward to Scotland to claim her fortune and ends up in love with a horse-training noblewoman. A spin-off of Potter's *Diablo.*

Starcatcher. *Bantam Books, 1997.*

Putney, Mary Jo

Putney also has written Regencies and is a Rita Award-winning writer.

Dearly Beloved. *Topaz, 1990.*

Uncommon Vows. *Signet, 1991.* Love and amnesia with a medieval twist.

Silk Trilogy

Exotic, compelling trilogy set during the early Victorian period.

Silk and Shadows. *New American Library, 1991.*

Silk and Secrets. *Onyx, 1992.*

Veils of Silk. *Onyx, 1992.*

Thunder and Roses. *Topaz, 1993.* Heroine agrees to live temporarily with the notorious hero to save her village. Features a "wounded" hero and a Regency setting.

 Dancing on the Wind. *Topaz, 1994.*

River of Fire. *Signet, 1996.*

Shattered Rainbows. *Topaz, 1996.*

One Perfect Rose. *Fawcett Columbine, 1997.* Ostensibly doomed noble hero finds love and acceptance with a theater troop in the English countryside.

Quick, Amanda (Jayne Ann Krentz)

Quick's popular Historicals feature high-spirited, independent heroines in lively, humorous, sensual stories, often set during the Regency period.

Seduction. *Bantam Books, 1990.* The free-thinking Sophy is not quite the biddable wife Julian had in mind.

Surrender. *Bantam Books, 1990.*

Scandal. *Bantam Books, 1991.* A hero out for vengeance falls in love with the intelligent, red-haired, ostensibly "ruined" woman who is the means of his revenge.

Rendezvous. *Bantam Books, 1992.*

Ravished. *Bantam Books, 1992.* Archaeologist heroine and estate owner hero reluctantly join forces to deal with smugglers.

Reckless. *Bantam Books, 1992.*

Dangerous. *Bantam Books, 1993.*

Deception. *Bantam Books, 1993.*

Desire. *Bantam Books, 1994.* Medieval setting.

Mistress. *Bantam Books, 1994.* Out to trap a blackmailer, the heroine poses as the mistress of a dead earl. Then the earl walks in.

Mystique. *Bantam Books, 1995.* Medieval setting.

Mischief. *Bantam Books, 1996.*

Affair. *Bantam Books, 1997.*

With This Ring. *Bantam Books, 1998.* Widowed writer and reclusive earl team up to learn the truth about an ancient artifact.

Randall, Rona

Randall is a prolific writer of historical romances. *(See also Gothic Romance bibliography.)* Some recent examples are:

Drayton series

Series provides good detail about the historic English potteries.

The Drayton Legacy. *Hamish Hamilton, 1985.*

The Potter's Niece. *Hamish Hamilton, 1987.*

The Rival Potters. *Hamish Hamilton, 1988.*

Rice, Patricia

Rice writes lively, often humorous and witty stories in a number of historical romance subgenres. *(See also Western and Period Americana bibliographies.)*

Love Forever After. *New American Library, 1990.* Heroine turns her marriage of convenience into one of love in this Georgian-set romance with a dash of mystery.

Moon Dreams. *Onyx, 1991.* An heiress flees her greedy cousin and heads for America in this lively Georgian romance with a touch of the paranormal.

Rebel Dreams. *Onyx, 1991.* Compromised and then married, businesswoman Evelyn Wellington and investigator Alex Hampton find love despite a number of obstacles in this fast-paced Georgian tale.

Devil's Lady. *New American Library, 1992.* A disenfranchised Irish nobleman and an abused English noblewoman find love despite difficult circumstances.

Touched by Magic. *Onyx, 1992.* Unwanted marriages, guilt, and old secrets combine in this country-set romance with a Georgian touch.

Shelter from the Storm. *Onyx, 1993.* Abuse, old love, and a returning hero combine in this poignant story with mainstream elements.

The Marquess. *Topaz, 1997.*

Ripley, Alexandra

Ripley's novels are set primarily in the antebellum South.

Charleston. *Doubleday, 1981.*

On Leaving Charleston. *Doubleday, 1984.* Follows *Charleston.*

New Orleans Legacy. *Macmillan, 1987.*

Scarlett. *Warner Books, 1991.* Sequel to *Gone With the Wind.*

Robards, Karen

Morning Song. *Avon Books, 1989.* A steamy story of the antebellum American South.

Green Eyes. *Avon Books, 1991.* Emeralds, adventure, and passion in an exotic Ceylon setting.

This Side of Heaven. *Dell, 1991.* An English woman finds challenge and love with the Pilgrims in seventeenth-century America.

Nobody's Angel. *Delacorte Press, 1992.* When Susannah buys the indenture of an English convict, she is stunned to eventually discover she has "purchased" a British nobleman. A story that sweeps from the simplicity of eighteenth-century American colonies to the glitter of the British social scene.

Saunders, Jean

Saunders is a prolific writer of novels using a number of pseudonyms (Jean Innes, Sally Blake, Rowena Summers) for romances of various types. Her settings are primarily historical, her style realistic, and her research accurate. Her more recent works include:

All in the April Morning. *W. H. Allen, 1989.* Zebra, 1993. This story begins with the San Francisco earthquake and ends after World War II, sweeping its characters between the United States and Ireland.

The Bannister Girls. *Grafton, 1991.* A tale of three sisters and how World War I affects their lives and loves.

Stuart, Anne

Stuart is a Rita Award-winning writer and writes highly sensual romances in a variety of subgenres. Her heroes are often dark and dangerous.

A Rose at Midnight. *Avon Books, 1993.* A story of vengeance, passion, and forgiveness.

Shadow Dance. *Avon Books, 1993.* Abuse, deception, and murder.

To Love a Dark Lord. *Avon Books, 1994.* Hero saves the heroine from being accused of murder and ends up in love with her.

Prince of Swords. *Zebra, 1996.*

Lord of Danger. *Zebra, 1997.* A mysterious sorcerer and an outwardly gentle noblewoman find love in this dark and passionate medieval romance.

Stuart, Elizabeth

Stuart's medieval romances are well written and well researched.

 Where Love Dwells. *St. Martin's Press, 1990.* Welsh heroine and English hero find love amid conflict.

Without Honor. *St. Martin's Press, 1993.*

Bride of the Lion. *St. Martin's Press, 1995.* English heroine and Norman hero resolve conflicts and find love.

Taylor, Janelle

Primarily noted for her passionate Native American and Western romances, Taylor has also written Historicals in several other settings.

Wild Is My Love. *Bantam Books, 1987.* Love and romance in early Britain.

Wild Sweet Promise. *Bantam Books, 1989.* Linked to *Wild Is My Love.*

Whispered Kisses. *Zebra, 1990.* The protagonists find mystery, danger, and love during an African safari.

Promise Me Forever. *Zebra, 1991.* Widowed for the third time, Rachel McCandless is determined to clear her name and solve a few mysteries in this late-Victorian period romance that makes use of both Georgian and Cuban settings.

Thornton, Elizabeth

Thornton writes adventurous, fast-paced stories that are most often set in the eighteenth and nineteenth centuries.

Scarlett Angel. *Pinnacle, 1990.*

Tender Is the Storm. *Pinnacle, 1991.*

Velvet Is the Night. *Pinnacle, 1992.*

Dangerous to Love. *Bantam Books, 1994.*

Highland Fire. *Pinnacle, 1994.*

Dangerous to Kiss. *Bantam Books, 1995.*

Dangerous to Hold. *Bantam Books, 1996.*

The Bride's Bodyguard. *Bantam Books, 1997.*

Veryan, Patricia

Veryan writes well-researched, deftly plotted Regency and Georgian period romances filled with believable characters and situations. *(See also Regency bibliography.)*

Golden Chronicles series

This series is set in Scotland during the Georgian period and deals with the struggle of Bonnie Prince Charlie to gain the English throne.

Practice to Deceive. *St. Martin's Press, 1985*

Journey to Enchantment. *St. Martin's Press, 1986.*

The Tyrant. *St. Martin's Press, 1987.*

Love Alters Not. *St. Martin's Press, 1987.*

Cherished Enemy. *St. Martin's Press, 1988.*

The Dedicated Villain. *St. Martin's Press, 1989.*

Ware, Ciji

(See also Saga bibliography.)

Island of the Swans. *Bantam Books, 1988.* A sweeping Georgian tale spanning several decades of the last half of the eighteenth century. Filled with misty Scottish castles; glittering ballrooms; and admirable, appealing characters.

Wiggs, Susan

Wiggs writes romances set in a number of historical periods (sixteenth-century England is a favorite) filled with appealing characters; colorful, well-described settings; and fast-paced action.

The Lily and the Leopard. *HarperPaperbacks, 1991.*

The Raven and the Rose. *HarperPaperbacks, 1992.*

The Mist and the Magic. *HarperPaperbacks, 1993.* A Rita Award winner.

Circle in the Water. *HarperPaperbacks, 1994.*

Vows Made in Wine. *HarperPaperbacks, 1995.*

Winds of Glory. *HarperPaperbacks, 1995.*

Dancing on Air. *HarperPaperbacks, 1996.*

Miranda. *HarperPaperbacks, 1996.*

The Lightkeeper. *Mira Books, 1997.*

The Drifter. *Mira Books, 1998.*

Williamson, Penelope

Many of Williamson's romances, especially the recent ones, have a mainstream quality. *(See also Alternative Reality and Western Romance bibliographies.)*

A Wild Yearning. *Avon Books, 1990.* A Rita Award winner.

Once in a Blue Moon. *Dell, 1993.*

The Passions of Emma. *Warner Books, 1997.*

Winston, Daoma

Winston is a solid, dependable writer of Period Romances, Sagas, and some early Gothics. Her stories feature strong heroines, focus on family, and are often set in the Washington, D. C. area or along the East Coast. *(See also Saga bibliography.)*

The Haversham Legacy. *Simon & Schuster, 1974.*

Gallow's Way. *Simon & Schuster, 1976.*

The Adventuress. *Simon & Schuster, 1978.*

Wolf, Joan

Wolf has written well-crafted romances in a variety of subgenres. Her most recent books are set during the Regency period.

Chronicles of the Dark Ages

Road to Avalon. *New American Library, 1988.*

Born of the Sun. *New American Library, 1989.*

Edge of Light. *New American Library, 1990.*

Prehistoric Trilogy

Set in prehistoric France.

Daughter of the Red Deer. *E. P. Dutton, 1991.*

The Horsemasters. *E. P. Dutton, 1993.*

The Reindeer Hunters. *E. P. Dutton, 1995.*

The Deception. *Warner Books, 1996.*

The Arrangement. *Warner Books, 1997.*

The Gamble. *Warner Books, 1997.*

The Guardian. *Warner Books, 1997.*

Sensual Historical and Sweet/Savage Romance

Similar in type—in fact, regarded as identical by some—Sensual Historicals and Sweet/Savage Romances are sexy, fast-paced, and adventurous. They are responsible for one of the more significant changes within the Romance genre and are the forerunners of today's Sensual Period Romance. These stories employ a wide variety of exotic settings, (e.g., tropical islands, pirate ships, lush plantations, moldering castles), adventurous action, and passionate lovemaking. The plot usually features a beautiful, independent heroine and a dashing, ruthless hero; places them in opposition to each other in adventurous situations; and manages to have them fall in love with each other by the end of the book. However, in the Sensual Historical the heroine remains true to the hero. In the Sweet/Savage, she may have any number of sexual encounters with any number of different partners.

An interesting point is that the heroine in these erotic tales, far from being the submissive, my-life-is-incomplete-without-a-man type of woman found in some other romance subgenres, is usually fiercely independent and capable. Her attitudes and behavior often reflect contemporary feminist thinking, especially in the areas of choice and self-determination, and although she often battles with the hero over her "revolutionary" ideas, he usually comes to see things her way in the end. However, the concept that romance heroines were "living" feminist ideals was controversial, to say the least, and was the subject of a number of articles. One of the earliest discussions of this viewpoint was in "Supermarket Erotica: 'Bodice-busters' Put Romantic Myths to Bed" by Carol Thurston and Barbara Doscher in *The Progressive* (April 1982) 46: 49–51.

Although both the Sensual Historical and the Sweet/Savage Romance types trace their ancestry from works such as *Forever Amber, Three Weeks,* and even *Gone With the Wind,* it wasn't until 1972 that the prototypes for the current form appeared. The Sensual Historical *The Flame and the Flower* by Kathleen Woodiwiss was the first. Two years later Rosemary Rogers produced the first Sweet/Savage title, *Sweet Savage Love,* and the Sensual Period Romance genre was born. Many authors produced novels of this type during the 1970s (e.g., Johanna Lindsey, Laurie McBain, and Shirlee Busbee), and for a while this variety of historical was truly hot. However, interest inevitably declined, and by the early 1980s the genre was almost cold—even though writers continued to produce. Eventually, Historicals began attracting attention once again. However, tastes and perceptions had changed, and previously accepted elements of the Sweet/Savage and Sensual Historical subgenres (e.g., rape; female subservience/male dominance; and physical, emotional, and sexual abuse of women) were no longer tolerated. As a result, the Sweet/Savage Romance is now more of an artifact than a viable form.

The Sensual Historical met a similar fate. However, it is from the Sensual Historical, with its monogamous emphasis, that the current Sensual Period Romance subgenre derives, and even though many of the older romances are dated and jarring, their legacy is alive and well in today's version of the genre.

Some readers may be interested in a parody of the subgenre, *Love's Reckless Rash* (St. Martin's Press, 1984) by Rosemary Cartwheel. This hilarious tale describes the adventures and misadventures of Lady Vanessa Sherwin-Williams and her "one true love," the Duke of Earl, as they romp their way through nineteenth-century England, New Orleans, and other assorted locales.

Selected Sensual Historical and Sweet/Savage Romance Bibliography

The works listed here are selective examples of both the Sensual Historical and the Sweet/Savage types. (For a more complete, older list, consult *Happily Ever After.* Littleton, CO: Libraries Unlimited, 1987.)

Blake, Jennifer (Patricia Maxwell)

Although some of Blake's early romances feature the "accidental" rape of the heroine (e.g., *Tender Betrayal.* Warner Books, 1984.) by today's standards most of her works do not fall within the Sweet/Savage category. *(See also Basic Contemporary Romance bibliographies.)*

Blake, Stephanie (Jacques Bain Pearl)

Blake's fast-paced romances are filled with sex, sin, and fiery passion. They often feature aggressive, adventurous heroines. Titles are typically steamy and include:

Flowers of Fire. *Playboy, 1977.*

Daughter of Destiny. *Playboy, 1977.* Continues *Flowers of Fire.*

Blaze of Passion. *Playboy, 1978.*

So Wicked My Desire. *Playboy, 1979.*

Wicked Is My Flesh. *Playboy, 1980.*

Burford, Lolah

The major element in her books is sex—constant and in endless variety. *(See also Gay Romance bibliography.)*

Vice Avenged: A Moral Tale. *Macmillan, 1971.*

The Vision of Stephen: An Elegy. *Macmillan, 1972.*

MacLyon. *Macmillan, 1974.*

Alyx. *New American Library, 1977.*

Busbee, Shirlee

One of the original "Avon Ladies," Busbee writes fast-paced, passionate, complex, adventurous romances filled with well-drawn characters, some of whom appear in several novels.

Gypsy Lady. *Avon Books, 1977.*

Lady Vixen. *Avon Books, 1980.*

While Passion Sleeps. *Avon Books, 1983.*

Deceive Not My Heart. *Avon Books, 1984.*

The Tiger Lily. *Avon Books, 1985.*

The Spanish Rose. *Avon Books 1986.*

Midnight Masquerade. *Avon Books, 1988.*

Whisper to Me of Love. *Avon Books, 1991.* An heiress grows up as a pickpocket in Regency London only to be "rescued" by one of her intended victims, with romantic and eventually life-changing results.

Each Time We Love. *Avon Books, 1993.*

Love a Dark Rider. *Avon Books, 1994.* Murder, intrigue, and family conflict abound in this passionate romance set in Texas during the 1860s.

Devine, Thea

Devine was not among the original writers of hot Historicals, but her current romances are erotic and explicit with definite Sweet/Savage elements. The following example is typical.

Sinful Secrets. *Zebra, 1996.* The heroine is kidnapped and forced to become a harem slave in this sexy, steamy story of love in an exotic setting.

Esler, Anthony

Esler writes well-researched, swashbuckling Historicals, many in the Sweet/Savage vein.

The Blade of Castlemayne. *William Morrow, 1974.*

Lord Libertine; Or the Memoirs of a Gentleman of Pleasure. Being a Rake's Progress from London to Paris in the Revolutionary Year of 1792. *William Morrow, 1976.*

For Love of a Pirate. *William Morrow, 1978.*

Gallagher, Patricia

Gallagher writes well-plotted, realistically descriptive stories that have more to say than the average romance.

Castles in the Air. *Avon Books, 1976.* One of the author's best-known books.

No Greater Love. *Avon Books, 1979.* Follows *Castles in the Air.*

Gluyas, Constance

Gluyas writes action-oriented tales, filled with violence, torture, and passion in the Sweet/Savage mode. Some of her more popular titles include:

The King's Brat. *Prentice-Hall, 1972.* The author's first.

Savage Eden. *New American Library, 1976.*

 Rogue's Mistress. *New American Library, 1977.*

Joyce, Brenda

Although not one of the "Hot Historical" writers of the 1970s, Joyce writes dark, sexy, often brutal, romances that are filled with action, fire, and definite Sweet/Savage tendencies. She regularly uses both American and European settings, and her Victorian Bragg Family Saga is set on both sides of the Atlantic. *(See also Western Period Romance bibliography.)*

The Conqueror. *Dell, 1990.* Passion, violence, and illicit love in eleventh-century England.

Dark Fires. *Dell, 1991.* A Bragg Family Saga.

Scandalous Love. *Avon Books, 1992.* Scandal and passion in late Victorian England. Continues the Bragg Family Saga.

The Promise of the Rose. *Avon Books, 1993.* Follows *The Conqueror.*

Beyond Scandal. *Avon Books, 1995.* Anne has finally recovered from her husband's cruelty and abandonment—and then he returns. Dark and somewhat Gothic.

The Game. *Avon Books, 1995.* Kidnapping, pirates, and court intrigue keep things interesting for the heroine in this novel set in Elizabethan England and Ireland.

The Finer Things. *Avon Books, 1997.* Poor heroine realizes some of her dreams in this rags-to-riches Cinderella story set in nineteenth-century London.

Splendor. *St. Martin's Press, 1997.* When an enlightened bookseller's daughter lampoons a visiting Russian prince in her political column, he discovers her identity and begins a deceptively dangerous game of cat and mouse.

7

Lindsey, Johanna

Lindsey was one of the original "Avon Ladies" and continues to be an extremely popular romance author today. Her works feature well-developed characters, compelling action, and accurate, vivid descriptions as well explicit sensuality with an emphasis on its darker side. Rape, sexual violence, and the use of sex as a weapon or means of punishment all have a place in Lindsey's fast-paced romances, many of which favor the captive-in-love-with-captor plot pattern. *(See also Western Period and Futuristic Romance bibliographies.)*

Captive Bride. *Avon Books, 1977.* One of the many descendants of *The Sheik.*

A Pirate's Love. *Avon Books, 1978.*

Fires of Winter. *Avon Books, 1980.*

Paradise Wild. *Avon Books, 1981.*

A Gentle Feuding. *Avon Books, 1984.*

When Love Awaits. *Avon Books, 1986.*

Defy Not the Heart. *Avon Books, 1989.* An abduction eventually results in love in another fast-paced romance with a twelfth-century England setting.

Gentle Rogue. *Avon Books, 1990.* Jilted by her English fiancé, Georgina returns home to America disguised as a cabin boy and finds love with the ship's virile captain, James Malory. Regency time period.

Prisoner of My Desire. *Avon Books, 1991.* The heroine captures the hero for heir-producing purposes and ends up kidnapped in return, with romantic results.

Once a Princess. *Avon Books, 1991.* A Cinderella story with a twist.

Man of My Dreams. *Avon Books, 1992.*

The Magic of You. *Avon Books, 1993.* Amy Malory pursues and finally captures the love of her cousin Warren when they are abducted and find themselves on a ship headed for America. Another of Lindsey's stories about the fascinating Malory family.

Surrender My Love. *Avon Books, 1994.* Viking passion flares in ninth-century England.

Love Me Forever. *William Morrow, 1995.* A forced marriage turns into one of love in this romance set in nineteenth-century Scotland.

Say You Love Me. *William Morrow, 1996.* When she sells herself as a mistress to save her family's estate, innocent Kelsey Langton is bought by the notorious Lord Derek Malory, who eventually falls in love with his purchase.

Matthews, Patricia

Matthews was a staple of Sweet/Savage Romances. Her stories are lusty and fast paced, her heroes often brutal and sadistic, and her heroines incredibly resilient. Her titles are characteristic of the type and most include some variation of the word "love." *Love's Avenging Heart* (Pinnacle, 1977), *Love's Raging Tide* (Pinnacle, 1980), and *Love's Sweet Agony* (Pinnacle, 1980) are typical examples.

McBain, Laurie

A popular writer of sensual Historicals with adventurous heroines and exotic settings. One of the original "Avon Ladies."

Devil's Desire. *Avon Books, 1975.*

Moonstruck Madness. *Avon Books, 1977.*

Tears of Gold. *Avon Books, 1979.*

Chance the Winds of Fortune. *Avon Books, 1980.* Follows *Moonstruck Madness.*

       Dark Before the Rising Sun. *Avon Books, 1982.* Follows *Chance the Winds of Fortune.*

       Wild Bells to the Wild Sky. *Avon Books, 1983.*

       When the Splendor Falls. *Avon Books, 1985.*

Michaels, Fern (Roberta Anderson and Mary Kuczkir)

Michaels's early works featured explicit sensuality, fast-paced adventures, and assertive, determined heroines who are a cut above the norm. Currently, she is better known for her glitzy, more contemporary Texas and Vegas series. *(See also Soap Opera bibliography.)*

       Vixen in Velvet. *Ballantine Books, 1976.*

       Captive Passions. *Ballantine Books, 1977.*

       Captive Embraces. *Ballantine Books, 1979.*

       Captive Splendors. *Ballantine Books, 1980.*

       Captive Innocence. *Ballantine Books, 1981.*

       Captive Secrets. *Ballantine Books, 1991.* By Mary Kuczkir only.

Peters, Natasha (Anastasia Cleaver)

Peters uses improbable plots, vivid settings, crude language, and detailed sex. She has also written similar stories with twentieth-century settings.

       Savage Surrender. *Ace, 1977.*

       Dangerous Obsession. *Ace, 1978.*

       The Masquers. *Ace, 1979.*

       Darkness into Light. *Fawcett, 1984.*

Riefe, Barbara (Alan Riefe)

Dandridge Trilogy

       This Ravaged Heart. *Playboy, 1977.* Considered by some to be Riefe's best romance.

       Far Beyond Desire. *Playboy, 1978.*

       Fire and Flesh. *Playboy, 1978.*

Rogers, Rosemary

Another "Avon Lady," Rogers founded the Sweet/Savage Romance subgenre. Fast action, historical color, and often rape and violent sex form the basis for these novels. Her few contemporary novels also display Sweet/Savage aspects.

       Sweet Savage Love. *Avon Books, 1973.* The novel that gave the subgenre its name. Rogers's first book introduces Virginia Brandon and Stephen Morgan, who travel through Paris, post-Civil War New Orleans, and end up in Mexico.

       The Wildest Heart. *Avon Books, 1974.* This historical epic covers the time period from 1872 in India to 1878 in Silver City, New Mexico. It revolves around Lady Rowena Dangerfield and Lucas Cord. Action-filled with a bit of mystery.

Dark Fires. *Avon Books, 1975.* Sequel to *Sweet Savage Love.*

Wicked Loving Lies. *Avon Books, 1976.* One of her longest books, this is the passionate story of Marisa de Castellanos y Gallardo and Dominic Challenger. It sweeps from convents in Spain to Napoleon's France and Louisiana. The characters endure revolutions, treachery, and captivity before finally admitting their love for each other.

Lost Love Last Love. *Avon Books, 1980.* The third in the Virginia Brandon-Stephen Morgan series.

Surrender to Love. *Avon Books, 1982.* This historical epic is a long, satisfying intricate book that takes Alexa Howard and Nicholas Dameron from Ceylon to Naples, Rome, Paris, and London.

The Wanton. *Avon Books, 1985.* Characters Trista and Blaze battle out their love during the Civil War in a story that is much shorter and less well developed than Rogers's earlier works.

Bound by Desire. Avon Books, 1988. Laura, the lovely and passionate daughter of Ginny and Steve, continues the Brandon-Morgan series and finds love and adventure with Trent Challenger.

The Tea Planter's Bride. *Avon Books, 1995.* A Ceylon-bred heroine finds passion when she goes to England.

A Dangerous Man. *Avon Books, 1996.* An independent heroine and an ex-Texas ranger find love along the trail.

Midnight Lady. *Avon Books, 1997.* A contested English inheritance provides the conflict for the hero and heroine in this fast-paced, passionate romance.

The following are books by Rogers in the Contemporary Romance subgenre.

The Crowd Pleasers. *Avon Books, 1978.* The author's first contemporary novel involves Anne Reardon and Webb Carnahan. Good characterizations, a fast-moving plot, and hidden mysteries make this book comparable to Rogers's historical epics.

The Insiders. *Avon Books, 1979.* This novel involves Eve, a TV anchorwoman, and Brant, an evil international playboy. Shorter than her earlier works, this is still all-engrossing and has unexpected plot developments.

Love Play. *Avon Books, 1981.* Sara, the daughter of an actress, and Marco, an Italian Duke, play at love in this, the least adventuresome of Rogers's novels.

Ryan, Nan

Although not one of the original "Hot Historical" writers of the 1970s, Ryan's books often exhibit similar qualities. *(See also Western Period Romance bibliography.)*

Sherwood, Valerie (Jeanne Hines)

Sherwood's passionate stories do not usually include rape or violence. Her titles are characteristic of the subgenre.

This Loving Torment. Warner *Books*, 1977.

The Imogene and Georgiana Quartet

The passionate adventures of Imogene and later her daughter, Georgiana.

Bold Breathless Love. *Warner Books, 1981.*

Rash Reckless Love. *Warner Books, 1981.*

Wild Willful Love. *Warner Books, 1982.*

Rich Radiant Love. *Warner Books, 1983.*

Lovely, Lying Lips. *Warner Books, 1983.*

Tales of the Silver Wench Trilogy

The adventures of the dashing Irish buccaneer Kells and the spirited Carolina.

Lovesong. *Pocket Books, 1985.*

Windsong. *Pocket Books, 1986.*

Nightsong.. *Pocket Books, 1986.*

To Love a Rogue. *New American Library, 1987.*

Small, Bertrice

One of the original "Avon Ladies," Small is still writing fast-paced, erotic books that attract readers.

The Kadin. *Avon Books, 1978.*

Love Wild and Fair. *Avon Books, 1978.* One of the author's best.

O'Malley series

Skye O'Malley. *Ballantine Books, 1980.* The black haired, green-eyed, sixteenth-century heroine is one of the most dashing and best known of the genre.

All the Sweet Tomorrows. *Ballantine Books, 1984.*

This Heart of Mine. *Ballantine Books, 1985.*

A Love for All Time. *New American Library, 1986.*

Lost Love Found. *Ballantine Books, 1989.*

Wild Jasmine. *Ballantine Books, 1992.* Last in the O'Malley series, this tells of the exotic, erotic adventures of Skye's granddaughter, Jasmine, who proves to be cut in her grandmother's image.

To Love Again. *Ballantine Books, 1993.* A Celtic captive finds love with a Saxon warrior in the fifth century.

The Love Slave. *Ballantine Books, 1995.* A kidnapped concubine-in-training falls in love with her "teacher."

The Hellion. *Ballantine Books, 1996.*

Betrayed. *Fawcett, 1998.* Passion and political intrigue sweep Fiona and Angus together and then apart in a sexy, fast-paced sorty set during the reign of James I of Scotland.

Deceived. *Kensington, 1998.* Deception, tragedy, and passion abound in this story that sweeps its characters from Georgian England to a lush, tropical paradise.

Winsor, Kathleen

Winsor has written several works; unfortunately, none of them comes up to the standard she set in her sensational landmark, *Forever Amber.*

Robert and Arabella. *Harmony/Crown, 1986.*

Woodiwiss, Kathleen E.

The publication of Woodiwiss's first book is credited with starting the boom in historical sensual fiction. She is one of the six original Avon Ladies.

The Flame and the Flower. *Avon Books, 1972.* The story of Heather and Brandon, their loves, hates, and struggles on a Carolina plantation at the turn of the nineteenth century.

The Wolf and the Dove. *Avon Books, 1974.* Defiant and beautiful Aislinn must deal with her growing feelings for Wulfar, a conquering Norman who has destroyed everything she holds dear.

Shanna. *Avon Books, 1977.* When Shanna marries a man destined for the gallows to avoid a real marriage, she cannot know that he will live to pursue and claim her for his own.

Ashes in the Wind. *Avon Books, 1979.* When beautiful Southerner Alaina MacGaren escapes to New Orleans, she is forced to come to terms with her growing passion for a young Yankee doctor.

A Rose in Winter. *Avon Books, 1982.* A story of love, jealousy, and vengeance in which Erienne must choose between her husband and the man she loves.

Come Love a Stranger. *Avon Books, 1984.* Amnesia, murder, and passion combine in this sensual historical set in the pre-Civil War South.

So Worthy My Love. *Avon Books, 1989.* Revenge, politics, and abduction are all part of this novel that sweeps its characters through sixteenth-century England and Germany.

Forever in Your Embrace. *Avon Books, 1992.* A romance of seventeenth-century Tsarist Russia.

Petals on the River. *Avon Books, 1997.* Sent as an indentured servant to colonial Virginia, the heroine is purchased as a nanny to a small boy and ends up in love with his father.

Western Period Romance

Set in the American West, usually west of the Mississippi and during the second half of the nineteenth century, these stories are the Romance genre's version of the Western. Plots are wide-ranging and focus on survival and the taming of the West. They can include trail drives, homesteading, bank robberies, showdowns, chases, range and Indian wars, and anything else appropriately Western. Characters vary, but gunslingers, ranchers, outlaws, lawmen, saloon hostesses, schoolmarms, pioneers, and other assorted people of the frontier are favorites. Styles can be rough and fast paced or gentle and tender; and while all levels of sensuality are represented, these stories are often quite sensual, with some bordering on the Sweet/Savage. Some romances of this type, especially the gentler ones with small-town settings, could also fall within the Period Americana subgenre discussed below. The books listed here are only a few examples of the many romances of this variety.

Anderson, Catherine

Anderson's romances often deal with abuse and healing.

Coming Up Roses. *HarperPaperbacks, 1993.* A Janet Dailey Award winner.

Cheyenne Amber. *HarperPaperbacks, 1994.* Raised by the Cheyenne, Deke Sheridan agrees to help abuse victim Laura Cheney regain her baby who has been kidnapped by Comancheros.

Annie's Song. *Avon Books, 1996.* Deaf and considered to be mentally retarded, gentle Annie is brutally raped but eventually finds love with the brother of her attacker.

Keegan's Lady. *Avon Books, 1996.* Out for vengeance, Ace Keegan ruins the reputation of the daughter of the man he is seeking, and they are forced to wed.

Becnel, Rexanne

Becnel writes both historical and contemporary romances.

Thief of My Heart. *Dell, 1991.* When Lacie pretends to be the widow of the late schoolmaster in order to keep the school open, she doesn't count on her "brother-in-law" arriving to disprove her story.

When Lightning Strikes. *Dell, 1995.* A bounty hunter falls in love with the woman he has been hired to find.

Bittner, Rosanne

Bittner writes realistic Western romances, some of which are of saga proportions. *(See also Saga and Ethnic Romance bibliographies.)*

Montana Woman. *Bantam Books, 1990.* Widowed by the Civil War, Joline heads for Montana to build a new life with settler Clint Reeves.

Embers of the Heart. *Bantam Books, 1990.* A war widow succeeds in rebuilding her life in post-Civil War Kansas. Then her husband reappears as one of Quantrell's violent raiders. Links to *Montana Woman.*

Sweet Mountain Magic. *Zebra, 1990.* A mute heroine with amnesia eventually finds love with her rescuer, but not before her past interferes.

Outlaw Hearts. *Bantam Books, 1993.* Two people both linked and separated by circumstance must come to terms with their past before they can find happiness together.

Brandewyne, Rebecca

Brandewyne also writes Contemporary and Period Romance with non-Western settings.

Heartland. *Warner Books, 1990.* The guardian of seven children has her hands full when the children's gunslinging uncle comes to town.

Rainbow's End. *Warner Books, 1991.* A would-be nun heads for Colorado to claim her late father's mine and falls in love instead.

Desperado. *Warner Books, 1993.* A stormy, fast-paced tale set during Mexico's pre-Revolutionary era.

Brown, Sandra

Primarily known for her Contemporary Romances and more recent novels of Romantic Suspense, Brown has also written several Period Romances.

Sunset Embrace. *Bantam Books, 1984.*

Another Dawn. *Bantam Books, 1985.* Follows *Sunset Embrace.*

Camp, Deborah

Fallen Angel. *Avon Books, 1989.* An actress turns to prostitution to survive and ends up working with a Pinkerton agent in this fast-paced, Western romance.

Black-Eyed Susan. *Avon Books, 1990.* A young woman goes to Oklahoma to care for her late sister's two children and ends up in a marriage of propriety that eventually turns into the real thing.

Lady Legend. *Avon Books, 1992.*

Cates, Kimberly

Cates writes romance in several historical periods.

Only Forever. *Pocket Books, 1992.* A religious novice steals a chalice to save a group of children in a story that sweeps from Ireland to Texas as they search for a place to call home.

Chastain, Sandra

Chastain's Westerns are often fast paced and very sensual.

Rebel in Silk. *Bantam Books, 1994.* While secretly searching for her brother's killers, newspaper editor/detective Dallas Banning tries to keep peace between the immigrants and the ranchers.

The Redhead and the Preacher. *Bantam Books, 1995.* A case of mistaken identity causes problems for the protagonists as they are mistaken for the new pastor and his wife in the small town of Heaven, Kansas.

Shotgun Groom. *Bantam Books, 1998.* A Southern belle ends up as a mail-order bride for the Texas rancher she has loved since childhood.

Coffman, Elaine

Escape Not My Love. *Dell, 1990.* A father sends a lawman to bring home his daughter who is teaching in Mexico. During the journey home, the two fall in love.

Angel in Marble. *Dell, 1991.* An unwed mother eventually learns to trust enough to find love. The first of the MacKinnon series.

For All the Right Reasons. *Dell, 1991.* A strong, independent woman eventually finds love in this sequel to *Angel in Marble*.

Somewhere Along the Way. *Dell, 1992.* Another in the MacKinnon series, this story sends a Texas man back to Scotland to claim his rightful heritage, with romantic results.

Copeland, Lori

Copeland's historical and contemporary romances are humorous and fast paced.

Fool Me Once. *Dell, 1989.* When Tom convinces amnesia victim Gideon that she is the new schoolteacher to save his lumber company, she believes and learns to love him. But when she learns the truth, their relationship suffers.

Sweet Hannah Rose. *Dell, 1991.* Two young lovers help their feuding families settle their differences so they can be together in this Texas-style Romeo and Juliet romance.

MacDougal Sisters Trilogy

The three infamous MacDougal sisters are the focus of the following fast-paced romances.

Promise Me Today. *Fawcett Gold Medal, 1992.*

Promise Me Tomorrow. *Fawcett Gold Medal, 1993.*

Promise Me Forever. *Fawcett Gold Medal, 1994.*

Coulter, Catherine

Coulter's period romances display a wide range of settings (most often English) and may include some sexual violence. This trilogy has a Western setting.

Star Trilogy

Midnight Star. *New American Library, 1986.*

Wild Star. *Onyx, 1986.*

Jade Star. *New American Library, 1987.*

Criswell, Millie

Criswell's romances tend to be funny and fast paced.

California Temptress. *Zebra, 1991.*

Temptation's Fire. *Zebra, 1992.* A spinster finally finds love and then is torn between husband and father.

Diamond in the Rough. *HarperPaperbacks, 1994.* An independent female rancher and a macho drifter find love while taking on the other local ranchers.

Mail Order Outlaw. *HarperPaperbacks, 1994.* A socialite and an outlaw agree to a marriage of convenience, but he wants something more. A story of pride, treachery, and love.

Flowers of the West series

The Martin women find love in a variety of places.

Wild Heather. *Warner Books, 1995.*

Sweet Laurel. *Warner Books, 1996.*

Prim Rose. *Warner Books, 1997.*

Deveraux, Jude

Deveraux is a popular romance writer and has contributed to most of the genre's subtypes, including the Western Period Romance. Some of her recent books have combined a Western setting with reincarnation or time travel elements. Most are lively, energetic, and filled with an underlying, often subtle, sense of fun.

Mountain Laurel. *Pocket Books, 1990.* An opera singer searches the Rockies for her sister and finds love in the process.

Eternity. *Pocket Books, 1991.* A domestically incompetent proxy bride wins over her new husband and his children with her loving ways and her organizational skills.

Dodd, Christina

Treasure of the Sun. *HarperPaperbacks, 1991.* A widowed Easterner finds herself dependent upon her late husband's best friend, a proud, macho Californio, in this realistic story of pre-gold rush California.

Garlock, Dorothy

Garlock writes realistic, occasionally dark, sometimes humorous, stories of the American West and Midwest, many of which could be classified as Period Americana Romances.

Midnight Blue. *Warner Books, 1989.* A determined woman must oust a few villains when she returns to take control of her Wyoming ranch.

Nightrose. *Warner Books, 1990.* A spinster and stranger find love in a Montana ghost town.

Homeplace. *Warner Books, 1991.* A widow coming to the aid of her teenaged stepdaughter, finds herself caught in a web of abuse and incest in this dark, but romantic, love story.

Sins of Summer. *Warner Books, 1994.* An unwed mother finds happiness with a gentle man who sees beyond the surface in this realistic, sometimes brutal, romance.

The Listening Sky. *Warner Books, 1996.* A fiery settler and a local mill owner find love despite conflict, deception, and danger.

Larkspur. *Warner Books, 1997.*

Sweetwater. *Warner Books, 1998.* City-bred Jenny battles greed and violence as she fights for her family and her future in the Wyoming Territory. She discovers friendship and love as well.

Garwood, Julie

Garwood is a best-selling writer of lively, witty Period Romance, many of which are set in England. Those that follow are set primarily in the American West and could also be classified as Period Americana.

Prince Charming. *Pocket Books, 1994.* To save her two young nieces from their uncle, Lady Taylor marries American Lucas Ross and ends up in the Montana wilderness, married to the kind of man she has always dreamed of—a real, live, "mountain man."

For the Roses. *Pocket Books, 1995.* When some homeless street urchins find a baby girl in a New York trashbin, they decide to make a better life for Mary Rose and head for Montana. The three novellas that follow tell the love stories of three of Mary Rose's adopted brothers.

One Pink Rose. *Pocket Books, 1997.*

One Red Rose. *Pocket Books, 1997.*

One White Rose. *Pocket Books, 1997.*

Come the Spring. *Pocket Books, 1997.* Culminating volume of the series that began with *For the Roses* that ties up a number of loose ends.

Greenwood, Leigh

Seven Brides series

Rose. *Leisure, 1993.*

Fern. *Leisure, 1994.*

Iris. *Leisure, 1994.*

Laurel. *Leisure, 1995.*

Daisy. *Leisure, 1995.*

Violet. *Leisure, 1996.*

Lily. *Leisure, 1996.*

Gregory, Jill

Lone Star Lady. *Jove, 1990.* Heroine survives pregnancy, abandonment, and treachery in this story set in Texas during the second half of the nineteenth century. Mainstream elements.

Cherished. *Dell, 1992.*

Heath, Lorraine

Heath writes emotionally involving, character-driven stories, many of which have a definite Period Americana flavor. *(See also Period Romance bibliography.)*

Parting Gifts. *Diamond, 1994.*

Sweet Lullaby. *Diamond, 1994.* A marriage of convenience becomes one of love when the hero and heroine (pregnant by another man) come to understand what love really is.

The Ladies' Man. *Jove, 1995.*

      Texas Destiny. *Topaz, 1997.*

      Texas Glory. *Topaz, 1998.*

Henke, Shirl

Henke has written both Contemporary and Period Romances using a variety of settings. Her stories are sensual and can deal with serious social issues.

      Night Flower. *Warner Books, 1990.*

      Night Wind's Woman. *Leisure, 1990.*

      Terms of Love. *Leisure, 1992.*

      A Fire in the Blood. *Leisure, 1994.*

Howard, Linda

Howard is a popular writer in a number of romance subgenres. Her work features strong, usually larger-than-life characters and compelling action Westerns that are realistic and can be dark.

      A Lady of the West. *Pocket Books, 1990.* Heroine marries for security and ends up in a violent, abusive situation. New Mexico ranch setting.

      Angel Creek. *Pocket Books, 1991.* Violence and passion over water rights in a Colorado setting.

      The Touch of Fire. *Pocket Books, 1992.* Fugitive abducts doctor heroine and ends up in love. Arizona setting.

 7

Johnson, Susan

Johnson's Western romances generally include Native American characters and are listed in chapter 13 on Ethnic Romance. *(See also Period Romance bibliography.)*

Johnston, Joan

Johnston writes in a number of romance subgenres. Her Historicals have a generally light, lively, often humorous touch. *(See also Period Americana bibliography.)*

      Outlaw's Bride. *Dell, 1993.*

      Kid Calhoun. *Dell, 1993.* Cross-dressing, gun-slinging heroine is out for revenge.

      Maverick Heart. *Dell, 1995.* Rekindled love in a western setting.

Joyce, Brenda

Joyce writes dark, sexy, often brutal, romances that are filled with action, fire, and definite Sweet/Savage tendencies. She uses American and European settings.

Bragg Family Saga

      Firestorm. *Avon Books, 1988.*

      Innocent Fire. *Avon Books, 1988.*

      Violet Fire. *Avon Books, 1989.*

      The Fires of Paradise. *Avon Books, 1991.*

      Secrets. *Avon Books, 1993.*

      Darkest Heart. *Dell, 1989.*

Lindsey, Johanna

Lindsey's fast-paced, sexy Historicals are popular and well conceived. She is a veteran romance writer and writes in a number of other romance subgenres as well. *(See also Futuristic, Ethnic/Multicultural, and Sensual Historical and Sweet/Savage Romance bibliographies.)* Her Western-set romances include:

Heart of Thunder. *Avon Books, 1983.*

Brave the Wild Wind. *Avon Books, 1984.*

Tender Is the Storm. *Avon Books, 1985.*

Love Only Once. *Avon Books, 1985.*

A Heart So Wild. *Avon Books, 1986.*

Tender Rebel. *Avon Books, 1988.*

Angel. *Avon Books, 1992.* A gunfighter (who had a small part in *Savage Thunder*) is the hero in this lively, occasionally funny romance. A toe-chewing black panther is especially memorable.

Lowell, Elizabeth

Lowell writes in a variety of romance subgenres. She also writes novels under her own name, Ann Maxwell, and as A. E. Maxwell in conjunction with Evan Lowell Maxwell. Her Western Historicals are usually fast-paced, sensual stories featuring strong, independent heroines and wounded, cynical heroes.

"Only" series

This set of stories revolves around the lives of related characters and is set primarily in Colorado following the Civil War.

Only His. *Avon Books, 1991.*

Only Mine. *Avon Books, 1992.*

Only You. *Avon Books, 1992.*

Only Love. *Avon Books, 1995.*

Autumn Lover. *Avon Books, 1996.*

Winter Fire. *Avon Books, 1996.* Vengeance, abuse, and fast-paced action are part of this passionate Western.

McKinney, Meagan

(See also Period Romance bibliography.)

Fair Is the Rose. *Dell, 1993.* Heroine escapes from an asylum and heads for Wyoming only to be taken hostage by an outlaw who is not quite what he seems. Links to *Lions and Lace (Dell, 1992).*

Miller, Linda Lael

Miller writes in a number of romance subgenres and is noted for her humorous, relatively sexually explicit romances. *(See also Time Travel, Paranormal, and Period Romance bibliographies.)*

Corbin series

Banner O'Brien. *Pocket Books, 1984.*

Corbin's Fancy. *Pocket Books, 1985.*

Memory's Embrace. *Pocket Books, 1986.*

My Darling Melissa. *Pocket Books, 1990.*

Orphan Train Trilogy

 Lily and the Major. *Pocket Books, 1990.*

 Emma and the Outlaw. *Pocket Books, 1991.*

 Caroline and the Raider. *Pocket Books, 1992.*

 Yankee Wife. *Pocket Books, 1993.*

Osborne, Maggie

Osborne's Westerns are unusual. They are action filled and humorous as well as sensitive and moving as they take on some serious issues.

 The Brides of Bowie Stone. *Warner Books, 1994.* When unconventional Rosie Mulvehey marries condemned murderer Bowie Stone, it seems like a great plan—she needs help on her ranch, he needs rescuing from the gallows. The problem? Bowie is already married.

 The Seduction of Samantha Kincade. *Warner Books, 1995.* Being on the trail of the same man causes problems for two bounty hunters, especially since one of them is a woman.

 The Brides of Prairie Gold. *Warner Books, 1996.* Twelve mail-order brides head west along the Oregon Trail.

  The Promise of Jenny Jones. *Warner Books, 1997.* Mule skinner Jenny keeps a promise to a dying mother and discovers love, as well as another dimension to her character. A Rita Award winner.

 The Best Man. *Warner Books, 1998.*

 7

Paisley, Rebecca

Paisley writes lively, sexy Historicals filled with off-beat humor and down-home language. *(See also Period Romance and Fantasy bibliographies.)*

 Moonlight and Magic. *Avon Books, 1990.* A witch, a cowboy, some orphans, and a dash of magic.

 Rainbows and Rapture. *Avon Books, 1992.* A prostitute and a gunslinger find love in the Old West.

 Heartstrings. *Avon Books, 1994.* Determined to be a surrogate mother for her barren sister, the heroine sets out to find the ideal father—with funny, romantic results.

Potter, Patricia

Potter has written in a number of romance subgenres and is noted for action-oriented, intense stories peopled with well-developed characters, often of the emotionally wounded variety. *(See also Period Romance bibliography.)*

 Lawless. *Doubleday, 1991.* A gunfighter comes to the aid of a young school-marm/rancher and her adopted children.

 Notorious. *Bantam Books, 1993.*

 Renegade. *Bantam Books, 1993.*

 Defiant. *Bantam Books, 1995.* A physically and emotionally wounded hero finds love with a young widowed rancher who also has past issues to deal with.

Diablo. *Bantam Books, 1996.* A hardened, convicted killer agrees to locate an outlaw stronghold in exchange for his friend's life and finds redemption and love in the process.

Rice, Patricia

Rice writes lively, often humorous and witty, stories in a number of romance sub-genres. *(See also Period Americana and Period Romance bibliographies.)*

Cheyenne's Lady. *New American Library, 1989.* A gunslinger finds himself helping the daughter of his late friend deal with some difficult local problems.

Texas Lily. *Topaz, 1994.* Widowed rancher Lily Brown and her foreman, Cade de Suela deal with greedy relatives, prejudice, and a war as they fight for their love and their land.

Denim and Lace. *Topaz, 1996.* A quest for vengeance turns a tomboy into a lady in this lively romance.

Ryan, Nan

Ryan's romances are fast paced and often feature graphic sex, an occasional rape, and definite Sweet/Savage elements.

Sun God. *Dell, 1990.* Rekindled love with steamy sex and a dash of Aztec mysticism.

The Legend of Love. *Dell, 1991.* The protagonists share a night of passion, separate, and meet again under very different circumstances. Passion and action in the Old West.

Written in the Stars. *Dell, 1993.* Heroine is kidnapped by a Wild West show Indian and ends up in love with him in this captive-in-love-with-captor romance.

A Lifetime of Heaven. *Dell, 1994.* Saloon owner and crusading Salvation Army captain clash and then fall in love.

Love Me Tonight. *Topaz, 1994.* Southern widow and Yankee officer find love and healing despite prejudice and shunning by the local townspeople.

Because You're Mine. *Topaz, 1995.* A calculating heroine ends up in love with the rancher she intends to destroy. Features an 1880s California setting.

You Belong to My Heart. *Harper, 1996.* A passionate story of love during the Civil War.

Taylor, Janelle

Although Taylor is best known for her Native American romances, especially her Ecstasy series, she has also written other types of romance, including the more traditional Western. Her stories are usually passionate and filled with action.

First Love, Wild Love. *Zebra, 1984.* Heroine heads for Texas to find her long-lost father and finds love in the process.

Passions Wild and Free. *Zebra, 1988.* Heroine seeking vengeance hires a gunman who is after the same outlaw gang for reasons of his own.

Kiss of the Night Wind. *Zebra, 1989.* A gunfighter and a schoolmarm flee their separate pasts and eventually find love with each other.

Follow the Wind. *Zebra, 1990.* Heroine fights to save her ranch with the help of a dangerous gunfighter.

Chase the Wind. *Zebra, 1994.* Disillusioned by love, a pair of undercover agents agree to a temporary marriage and head for Arizona to stop some gunrunners and the sure-to-follow confrontation with Geronimo.

Williams, Jeanne

Williams is primarily known for her Westerns, many of which are also appreciated by romance readers.

A Lady Bought with Rifles. *Coward, McCann, 1976.*

A Woman Clothed in Sun. *Coward, McCann, 1977.*

Bride of Thunder. *Pocket Books, 1978.*

Daughter of the Sword. *Pocket Books, 1979.*

Williamson, Penelope

Heart of the West. *Simon & Schuster, 1995.*

Native American or "Indian" Romance

A subset of both the Western and the Ethnic Romance, these stories generally focus on Native American characters in the Old West. The hero, heroine, or both, may be full- or half-blooded Native Americans, and the stories often revolve around cultural difference issues, prejudice, and the destruction of the tribal way of life. Although most of these stories take place in the American West, these romances can also be set in other times and in other parts of America. For example, Colonial New England or eighteenth-century Minnesota.

Books of this type are included in the bibliography in chapter 13, "Ethnic and Multicultural Romance," in the Native American section. The authors listed here are only a few writers of this type.

7

Anderson, Catherine

Baker, Madeline

Bittner, Rosanne

Dellin, Gennell

Gentry, Georgina

Johnson, Susan

Lindsey, Johanna

Taylor, Janelle

Period Americana Romance

Part of the larger Americana Romance subgenre, these stories focus on everyday life in the American past. Often making use of small-town or rural settings, these stories feature down-to-earth characters involved in ordinary situations and are generally driven by the relationships between the characters. This is not a subgenre of violence, wild adventure, or fast-paced action, although there may be a mystery or disaster that needs to be taken care of. Rather, these stories focus on the everyday and the ordinary. The domestic side of life—family, children, and marriage—is important and often highlighted. These romances can be both practical and charmingly nostalgic, and humor and warmth are often part of their appeal. Similar to the rest of the historical romance subgenre, most Period Americana Romances are single titles; however, several series (e.g., Jove's Our Town and Homespun Romances) do feature romances of this type. Many Period Americana authors write in other romance subgenres as well.

Barbieri, Elaine

Wings of a Dove. *Jove, 1990.* Two survivors of the orphan train are separated but eventually find each other and love.

Wishes on the Wind. *Berkley, 1991.* A mine owner's son and miner's daughter find love during the days of the Mollie Maguires.

More Precious Than Gold. *Zebra, 1992.* Saga-like story of love and success in the Old West.

Camp, Candace

Rosewood. *HarperPaperbacks, 1991.* A spinster finds unexpected love with a newspaperman in small-town Texas.

Heirloom. *HarperPaperbacks, 1992.* A domestically challenged former actress finds love with a taciturn Nebraska farmer.

Garlock, Dorothy

With Hope. *Warner Books, 1998.* First of a trilogy. Set in 1930s Oklahoma.

Hannah, Kristin

Although most of Hannah's books have some kind of paranormal or mystical element, several of them also have Americana elements.

A Handful of Heaven. *Fawcett, 1991.* Although perhaps more properly labeled "Period Canadiana," this story of the two co-owners of a store in the Yukon Territory has an appeal similar to Period Americana.

Once in Every Life. *Fawcett, 1993.* A bit of time travel sets the stage for this romance set on a sheep ranch in Washington.

If You Believe. *Fawcett, 1994.* With the help of an orphan, a drifter and a reclusive spinster find love among the Washington apple blossoms.

Hatcher, Robin Lee

Promise Me Spring. *Leisure, 1991.* A woman goes to an Idaho ranch as a governess and struggles with a dying woman's request to marry her husband and be a mother to her two daughters.

Where the Heart Is. *Leisure, 1993.* A schoolteacher finds love in Idaho.

Liberty Blue. *HarperPaperbacks, 1995.* Sheep rancher Libby Blue's peace is threatened when her autocratic, aristocratic father sends a detective to Idaho to find her.

Holm, Stef Ann

Firefly. *Leisure, 1990.* A fur trader and a farmer find love in the Minnesota wilderness.

Weeping Angel. *Pocket Books, 1995.* A piano brings a spinster and a saloon owner together with romantic results.

Harmony. *Pocket Books, 1997.* A schoolmarm and an outdoorsman end up owning the same piece of Montana property and must reconcile both their opposing plans for its use and their feelings for each other.

Johnston, Joan

Sweetwater Seduction. *Dell, 1991.* To get the men of the town to stop feuding, a spinster schoolteacher convinces the women to withhold marital rights from their husbands. However, the men plan a seduction—with some rather unexpected results.

The Barefoot Bride. *Dell, 1992.* Mail-order bride and Montana doctor find love, despite objections from his ten-year-old daughter.

Landis, Jill Marie

Sunflower. *Jove, 1988.*

Rose. *Jove, 1990.* A young bride from Italy arrives in Wyoming only to learn she is a widow. Against the local sheriff's advice, she decides to open a restaurant and make it on her own.

 Come Spring. *Jove, 1992.* Mistaken for a mail-order bride, Annika is whisked away to a trapper's mountain cabin where she lives with him and his young daughter until spring. A Rita Award winner.

Until Tomorrow. *Jove, 1994.* When Dake Reed promises he will take a dying woman's baby to her Alabama family, he ends up with more on his hands than just a baby.

After All. *Jove, 1995.* A former dancer (with no domestic skills) ends up as a ranch cook, and has to deal with an obnoxious teenager and a hero with a past.

Last Chance. *Jove, 1995.* A young widow (and former teacher) shocks the town when she dances with one of her former students, now a notorious gunfighter, at a local celebration.

Law, Susan Kay

Home Fires. *HarperCollins, 1995.* Fleeing from an abusive husband, Amanda and her stepson leave New York and settle in New Ulm, Minnesota. She finds love with a local brewer, but must deal with her husband before she can put the past behind her.

Morsi, Pamela

Heaven Sent. *Doubleday, 1990.* A spinster and a moonshiner end up forced into a marriage that eventually becomes real love.

Courting Miss Hattie. *Bantam Books, 1991.* Charming story of a young man who decides to court his spinster rancher boss, despite their long-standing friendship, their difference in age, and the public reaction.

Garters. *Jove, 1992.* The enterprising daughter of the local "good-for-nothing" decides she is going to marry the owner of the general store. Then, of course, she has to make it happen.

Wild Oats. *Berkley, 1993.* A divorcée and an undertaker must deal with small-town opinion in this Oklahoma-set romance.

Marrying Stone. *Jove, 1994.* A determined young woman and a serious music scholar end up accidentally married—and then their roles switch.

Runabout. *Jove, 1994.* A pretend courtship eventually becomes the real thing.

 Something Shady. *Jove, 1995.* A Rita Award winner.

The Love Charm. *Avon Books, 1996.* Despite their obvious differences—she's beautiful and flighty, he's intelligent and plain—Aida and Armand fall in love in this romance with a Cajun flair.

Simple Jess. *Jove, 1996.* A widow and a mentally handicapped man find happiness despite public opinion.

No Ordinary Princess. *Avon Books, 1997.*

Palmer, Diana

Noelle. *Ivy, 1995.* A gunslinging attorney returns home to make sure his grandmother isn't being taken advantage of by her new young companion and ends up falling in love.

Rice, Patricia

Rice writes lively, often humorous and witty, stories in a number of romance subgenres. *(See also Western and Period Romance bibliographies.)*

Paper Trilogy

Although the first book is more in the Western mode, the series has an overall Americana flavor.

Paper Roses. *Topaz, 1995.*

Paper Tiger. *Topaz, 1995.*

Paper Moon. *Topaz, 1996.*

Simon, Laura

Garden of Dreams. *Berkley, 1992.* This "East Coast immigrant experience" Americana romance focuses on Nina and Wim as their love for growing things eventually turns into love for each other.

Spencer, LaVyrle

(See also Basic Contemporary Romance bibliography.)

The Fulfillment. *Avon Books, 1979.* In the early 1900s, two brothers who are farming partners test their family ties with crises of infidelity and childlessness.

The Endearment. *Pocket Books, 1982.* Can a mail-order bride find happiness with a man who is less experienced than she?

Hummingbird. *Berkley, 1983.* Abigail McKenzie finds herself nursing two men injured in a train robbery. David, gentle and upstanding, is the answer to a woman's prayers, and Jesse, rude and handsome, stirs the depths of her soul.

Loved. *Berkley, 1984.* After five years of grieving for her husband lost at sea, Laura turns to another for love and support. Who could ever know that her husband would return?

Years. *Berkley, 1986.* Eighteen-year-old Linnea Brandonberg comes to North Dakota and steps into a totally new life on a farm. Through the harsh time of World War I, Linnea and Teddy grow in their love for each other.

The Gamble. *Berkley, 1987.* Proper Agatha and happy-go-lucky Scott take a chance and discover love through a child's innocence and in each other's arms. Late-1800s, small-town Kansas setting.

Vows. *Berkley, 1988.* Engaged to a man she doesn't love, Emily, a lifelong tomboy, is unaware of her femininity until Tom Wolcott comes to town and ignites a spark.

 Morning Glory. *Putnam, 1989.* When Lonely Will Parker answers an ad to work for the "Widow Dinsmore," he gets more than he has ever dreamed of in this romance set in the early 1940s.

Forgiving. *Putnam, 1991.* In the Dakota Territory of the 1870s, Sarah Merritt sets out to rescue her runaway sister Addie when their father dies. She and strong-willed Sheriff Noah Campbell butt heads, but they work together to save Addie.

November of the Heart. *Putnam, 1993.* Lorna and Jens must overcome the staggering odds of different backgrounds and objecting families before their love can prevail.

That Camden Summer. *Putnam, 1996.* In Maine 1916, newly divorced Roberta Jewett returns home from Boston with her three daughters. Her struggle to overcome narrow attitudes and raise her daughters to be independent and forward-thinking provides a satisfying story.

Then Came Heaven. *Putnam, 1997.* During the 1950s in small-town Minnesota, a nun struggles with her feelings for a widower and his daughters. Note: Spencer announced her retirement with the publication of this novel.

Thomas, Jodi

Thomas writes tender, sensual, sometimes humorous, romances with a Period Americana feel.

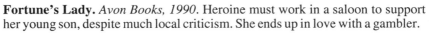 **The Tender Texan.** *Diamond, 1991.* A temporary marriage of convenience between a widowed immigrant and a cowboy eventually turns into the real thing.

Forever in Texas. *Jove, 1995.* A new "schoolteacher" livens things up in Saints Roost, Texas, especially for the school board member who hired her.

Thompson, Victoria

Many of Thompson's Western-set romances will appeal to those who enjoy Period Americana.

Fortune's Lady. *Avon Books, 1990.* Heroine must work in a saloon to support her young son, despite much local criticism. She ends up in love with a gambler.

Playing with Fire. *Avon Books, 1990.* A naive Eastern schoolteacher goes to woman-deprived Bittercreek, Texas, and ends as the prize in a local lottery in this warm, humorous, gentle romance.

Wild Texas Wind. *Zebra, 1992.* Heroine, who was a captive of the Cheyenne for seven years, must face the town's prejudice toward herself and her biracial son.

Winds of Destiny. *Zebra, 1994.* An independent, activist heroine and a Texas Ranger eventually find love.

Williamson, Penelope

The Outsider. *Simon & Schuster, 1996.* When Rachel Yoder offers aid to a wounded gunslinger, her rigid religious community is appalled. The widely divergent values and lifestyles of the hero and heroine drive the plot of this romance that verges on mainstream.

NOTES

1. "Rakes and Nipcheeses," *Time*, (February 21, 1964): 102.

2. Ibid., 73.

3. Ibid., 200.

4. Ibid., 261.

5. Shirley Hailstock, "1996 ROMSTAT Report," *RWR: Romance Writer's Report* (June 1997): 12.

Chapter 8

Regency Period Romance

"It is a truth universally acknowledged, that a single man in possession of a good fortune, must be in want of a wife."

Jane Austen

DEFINITION

Considered by many to be the most elite and intellectually appealing of the romance subgenres, the Regency Romance (primarily set during 1811–1820) is essentially a novel of manners and social custom. The emphasis is on the characters, their relationships, and their places within a highly structured society in which social position and consequence are all-important; and in a true Regency, Society itself functions as a character. Set within the limited sphere of London High Society, these charming confections describe a glittering, aristocratic world in which one's place in Society and acceptance by the *ton* are Everything. Indeed, an aspiring young lady's career can be left in Ruins by a chance remark, an objectionable manner, or even her choice of gowns. (The heroine is rarely one of these unfortunate damsels; but if she is, through a combination of spunk, charm, and strength of character, she usually manages to have both the hero and the rest of the socially elite at her feet by the end of the story.)

These stories typically take place in London during The Season (that is, the "social season" lasting from when the Parliament came into session until late spring and aimed at marrying off eligible daughters), on lavish country estates, and at fashionable resorts such as Brighton or Bath; and the social whirl, including clothes, food, surroundings, and customs, is described in great detail. Overflowing with aristocrats, royalty, and the wealthy, most of these stories make at least passing reference to a number of actual historical figures. Prinny (the Prince Regent), Beau Brummel, Napoleon, Byron, and the Patronesses of Almack's (especially the Ladies Jersey, Cowper, Sefton, and Castlereagh) are particular favorites. Also, current events (e.g., Waterloo, Peninsular Wars, politics, scandals) can be topics of conversation and are occasionally woven into the plot.

Although high levels of skill in accomplishments such as curricle-racing, horsemanship, or boxing are admired in the Regency hero, these are not novels of action. In spite of the fact that a "race to Gretna Green" (usually with the hero in hot pursuit of the villain who has abducted the heroine) is a fairly commonplace event in these stories, most of the real action is verbal and takes place at the numerous social functions—balls, routs, country weekends, nights at the opera, dinner parties, picnics—where the characters engage in the verbal repartee so important to this subgenre. The language is one of the delights of the Regency, and readers who are addicted to them occasionally report phrases such as "It doesn't signify!" or "How Gothick!" accidentally creeping into their everyday vocabularies. In addition, the classic Regency contains no explicit sex, and sensuality in general is often totally ignored.

The traditional Regency plot revolves around a young lady's entrance into high society, her adventures therein, and her courtship and eventual engagement to the hero. The heroine can be sprightly and impulsive or reserved and capable, but she is usually unconventional and is always independent. The hero, usually titled, wealthy, and Extremely Eligible, is initially captivated or repelled by the heroine and spends the rest of the story either convincing her that she is the only woman in the world for him or coming to that conclusion himself. The heroine, however, is not just sitting idly by. On the contrary, she has problems of her own, often related to the social whirl into which she has been thrown. Sometimes she is busy trying to decide how to avoid marrying someone just to save the family finances. Sometimes she must extricate a younger brother or cousin from the clutches of the moneylenders or creditors. Sometimes she must try to save a younger sister's reputation. As a result, she gets into situations from which she is either rescued by the hero, or more recently, escapes through her own efforts. In the end, of course, all wrongs are righted, all villains punished, all misunderstandings explained, and all couples properly aligned. Interestingly, the predictability of these plots does not detract from the Regency's overall charm. But then, Regencies are not read for their plots; they are read for their style, humor, wit, characterizations, and, especially, for their delightful use of language.

THE CHANGING REGENCY

The traditional Regency as described above is still being produced today. However, its style is changing. For the past few years, Regency writers have been pushing at the edges of the genre both sexually and socially, and while traditional, youthful debutantes and dashing noblemen are still the norm, older, more experienced heroines and less-than-perfect heroes are making their way into the subgenre. Darker, more realistic plots, often focusing on social abuses of the period, are also emerging. In addition, despite the traditional taboos against sex in this subgenre, Regencies are becoming much more sensual, and they are occasionally overtly sexual.

These trends have caused confusion. As the subgenre incorporates more changes, the lines defining it are blurring, and a question being asked more and more frequently is: What is the difference between a Regency and a Historical set during the Regency period? Despite the growing tendency of some to call any romance set during the Regency period a "Regency," most readers and writers agree that there is a difference. Basically, it is a difference in focus. As mentioned above, Regencies concentrate on the manners, language, customs, and social doings of the period, essentially recreating the period in minute detail for the reader. The action is verbal and social rather than physical, and the emphasis is on the characters, society, and their relationships rather than physical action or plot. Social consequence and outward appearance are all-important, often driving the plot and determining the course of action.

Historicals, on the other hand, tend to be more action oriented and concerned with larger issues than societal acceptance. Although some Historical writers are good with period detail, the focus is more on the plot and action rather than on recreating the period. However, while it would be simple to say that Historicals are plot driven and Regencies are character or period driven, it would not be accurate; there are too many Historicals with wonderful characters and too many Regencies with interesting plots to make that generalization.

In addition, there are "space" differences—both physical and social. The world of the Regency is small, focusing primarily on friends, family, and the social milieu of the period, while the scope of the Historical can be global. A typical Regency can easily take place within the confines of a single house or estate. In fact, in some the characters never set a foot outside, unless it is to walk in the garden! However, it would be a rare Historical that did not require a much larger theatre for its activities. Finally, there is the matter of sex. In the past, one could say that Regencies don't have sex and Historicals do. Now, it is not so easy. In fact, some current Regencies have more sex in them than some Historicals, and almost all Regencies (with a few chaste exceptions) have much more sensuality and sexual tension in them than ever before. Regencies are now on a continuum in regard to sex—none to some—and while this is still an issue for purists, for a growing number of readers, sex is no longer the defining feature it once was.

8

THE REGENCY PERIOD

The Regency Period began in 1811 when George III of England was declared insane and the Prince of Wales ("Prinny") became Prince Regent. The Regency lasted until George III died in 1820, and "Prinny" was crowned George IV in 1821. Although the official period lasted for only nine years, the flavor of the Regency is evident in works set both before and after these dates. While most Regencies are set within the traditional nine-year parameters, it is really the *tone* of the novel that defines it as a Regency, and a number of novels of this type (including many classics by Georgette Heyer) have been set either before or after the official Regency decade. (Novels of this kind are sometimes referred to as "Regency-type" romances.)

Politically, the period saw several conflicts, including the War of 1812 and the Battle of Waterloo. These conflicts, however, did not take place on English soil and except for a few casual references, they are not part of the story line of most Regencies. Occasionally, a book with a definite Regency flavor is set outside the boundaries of the period, (e.g., *The Scarlet Pimpernel* set during the French Revolution) and includes more specific references to the hostilities; but in general, wars and other political realities simply serve as background and are peripheral to the Regency Romance.

The social climate of the period was educated, permissive, and dissolute, at least for the upper class. People of the aristocracy had a great deal of leisure time, and their major task was to entertain themselves. They succeeded admirably. (There is a striking similarity between the Edwardian and the Regency periods in this respect.) Gambling was a great pastime among the men, and bets were routinely placed on everything from the results of a horse race to the sex of the next child of a local peeress. Visiting their private clubs, attending sporting events (including illegal prizefights), and hunting were also popular among men. Women planned social events, gambled occasionally (usually only at a game called silver loo), and also had discreet affairs. In general, women did not enjoy the freedom of men, especially before they were married. Both sexes enjoyed playing cards, horseback riding, and dancing. The high point of the Regency social calendar was the Season, which took place during the late winter months into the spring. During this time, dances (especially those held at Almack's under the sponsorship of the Patronesses every Wednesday night), routs, balls, and dinner parties were extremely popular. It was during the Season that a young lady was first introduced into society and expected to "make a match." If she didn't "take" in her first season, she returned to enjoy several more. However, if she were not married by her early mid-20s, she was considered a spinster and "on the shelf."

Social standing was always a consideration, whether for composing guest lists or deciding which suitor to marry. It was always thought better to marry "up," so young women were always "setting their caps" for men with titles or fortunes superior to their own. People engaged in commerce or the trades were rarely admitted to the social circles of the elite, and even though these "cits" were becoming an economic force in Regency England, the aristocracy ignored them for as long as they could.

Manners and language were of particular importance. Indeed, the way in which something was said was often more important than actual content, and being able to converse wittily was imperative to social success. In the same vein, a proper outward image was more important than what one actually did—for example, affairs were tolerated as long as the participants were discreet.

In general, the primary purpose of the Regency aristocracy was to enjoy itself, and this it did with abandon. It is this carefree, luxurious lifestyle that is the basis of today's Regency romances.

Although many books have been written about Regency England, the one cited below might be of particular interest to Regency readers, especially fans of Georgette Heyer.

Chris, Teresa.

> **Georgette Heyer's Regency England**. *London: Sidgwick & Jackson, 1989.* Illustrations by Arthur Barbosa. Filled with liberal references to Heyer's stories and characters, this readable work takes Regency fans on a delightful tour of the England depicted in Georgette Heyer's Regency romances. A number of walking tours are suggested, complete with commentary, and topics and places are covered in chapters with such intriguing titles as "Male Preserves: The St. James's Area," "Where Not To Live: The Fringes of Society," "Pleasure Jaunts: Escaping from the Heart of London," and "Pump and Circumstance: South-East Bath." Most useful to travelers in England, but interesting for all Regency readers.

APPEAL

The general appeal of the Regency Romance is the same as for any historical or period romance: It indulges our fascination with life in past times and allows the reader to experience what life was like "back then." However, the specific appeal of the Regency is more focused. Sparkling language, witty repartee, meticulous historical detail, and good writing are hallmarks of the subgenre and attract many readers. It is also a comfortable subgenre for its fans. That is, because the Regency time period is so limited (less than a decade) fans are familiar with the details of the period. As a result, reading a Regency is a little bit like coming home; it is a comfortable, predictable setting in which only the plots and characters change. It is also the world of Jane Austen, a fact that appeals to many readers.

ADVISING THE READER

  8

Although readers' advisors should consult both the general advisory section and the specific advisory section for Historical Romances, there are a few points that might be helpful for advising Regency readers.

- Readers who enjoy Jane Austen might also like some of the better contemporary Regency authors, and vice versa.

- Readers who particularly enjoy the Regency period might also enjoy Period Romances set during the same time, and vice versa.

- Readers who have favorite Regency authors might also enjoy these writers' Period romances (e.g., Jo Beverley, Mary Jo Putney, Kate Moore).

- Be aware that some recent Regencies are more sensual than the traditional ones, and make recommendations accordingly.

ORIGINS AND BRIEF HISTORY OF THE REGENCY ROMANCE

The origins of the Regency romance are often traced to Jane Austen, who in writing about the life and people she knew, set the style for the Regencies of today. However, several of her near-contemporaries also influenced the direction of today's

Regency genre, and while they are no longer often read, their contributions cannot be ignored. A generation before Austen, Fanny Burney in her *Evelina: Or, The History of a Young Lady's Entrance into the World* (1778) captured a quality and described a social scene that was decidedly Regency in flavor if not in fact; and Edward Bulwer-Lytton, who wrote after the Regency, achieved a properly scandalous tone in his *Pelham: Or, Adventures of a Gentleman* (1828).

Although Austen is widely read today and is currently enjoying a popular revival (due in part to recent, well-received film versions of several of her novels), it is Georgette Heyer who is the acknowledged doyenne of the modern traditional Regency. Influenced by turn-of-the-century writer Jeffery Farnol as well as the earlier Regency writers, Heyer employs exquisite language, attention to detail, knowledge of the period and its society, and an ability to create a vivid sense of place to set the standard for the modern Regency. While she has many imitators, she has few equals, and her books are still widely read today.

Over the past decade, there has been a gradual, definite improvement in both quality and variety within the subgenre. Dedicated, knowledgeable, and highly critical Regency readers are quite serious about their books, often demanding more of their subgenre than readers of any of the other romance types. Historical accuracy and strict attention to detail are essential, and because many readers are near-experts on the period, discrepancies are quickly noted—and rarely forgiven. The authors have responded, and many of today's Regencies are some of the best-written, most carefully crafted stories in the romance genre. Despite this, the subgenre has periodically been threatened by cutbacks, primarily because of bottom-line issues, the niche nature of the subgenre, and, most recently, the changes in the distribution system affecting all mass market fiction. Nevertheless, the Regency readership is stable, committed, and militant; and while the subgenre may suffer an occasional setback and evolve in unexpected ways, it is unlikely to meet its demise anytime soon.

The prototypes cited below (except for those by Farnol) are not actually Historical Romances; they are, instead, contemporary romances written in a historical period. Their authors were not writing about a distant romantic past; they were writing about the world they knew and lived in. For them, the setting was the reality of the here and now, not the romance of the there and then. Although Jane Austen's novels are the only ones actually written during the Regency, the others exhibit the characteristic Regency flavor of elegance, wit, and licentiousness.

Austen, Jane

Although she wrote relatively few novels, Austen enjoys the rare privilege of being both read by romance readers and studied by literary critics. In addition, sequels to a number of her novels have been produced and several of her unfinished works have been completed by other writers. For example, *The Watsons* was "continued and completed by John Coates" in *The Watsons* (Crowell, 1958) and also by Joan Aiken in *Emma Watson: The Watsons Completed* (St. Martin's Press, 1996); *Sanditon* was completed by Another Lady (Anne Telscombe) and was published by P. Davis in 1975. Examples of the sequels to her published novels are included in the bibliography below. Most of Austen's books have been made into films, and all are currently in print. The imprints following the original dates of publication are merely samples of the many editions of her works available.

Sense and Sensibility. *(1811). Oxford University Press, 1980.* Joan Aiken continues this story in her sequel, *Eliza's Daughter* (St. Martin's Press, 1994).

Pride and Prejudice. *(1813). Penguin, 1972.* Probably Austen's most famous and most widely read novel. Several sequels have been written, including *Pemberley: A Sequel to Pride and Prejudice* (Hodder & Stoughton, 1993) and *An Unequal Marriage: Or, Pride and Prejudice Twenty Years Later* (St. Martin's Press, 1994) both by Emma Tennant.

Mansfield Park. *(1814). New American Library, 1964.* Using a number of Austen's original characters, Joan Aiken wrote a sequel to this story, *Mansfield Revisited* (Doubleday, 1985).

Emma. *(1814). Norton, 1972.* Emma Tennant continues the story of Austen's meddling heroine with *Emma in Love: Jane Austen's Emma Continued* (Fourth Estate, 1996), and Joan Aiken presents a different perspective in *Jane Fairfax: Jane Austen's Emma through Another's Eyes* (Gollancz, 1990).

Northanger Abbey. *(1818). Buccaneer Books, 1986.* A delightful parody of the Gothic novels so popular during that period. A sequel to this story is *Uninvited Guests* (Janus, 1994) by Jane Gillespie.

Persuasion. *(1818). Bantam Books, 1984.*

Bulwer-Lytton, Edward

Bulwer-Lytton's writing career was varied and spanned almost 50 years.

Pelham: Or, Adventures of a Gentleman. *(1828). University of Nebraska Press, 1972.* This novel with both Regency and Gothic characteristics was his first popular success.

Burney, Fanny

Although she wrote several others, her first book is considered her best.

Evelina: Or, The History of a Young Lady's Entrance into the World. *(1778). Norton, 1965.*

Farnol, Jeffery

He wrote numerous popular novels, but the early novels are his best. Georgette Heyer was influenced greatly by his works.

The Broad Highway. *(1910). Buccaneer Books, 1975.*

The Amateur Gentleman *(1913). Buccaneer Books, 1975.*

SELECTED REGENCY PERIOD ROMANCE BIBLIOGRAPHY

Following are some contemporary examples of the traditional Regency Romance. Note that Historical set during the Regency period are included in the section on Period Romance.

Aiken, Joan

The Five-Minute Marriage. *Gollancz, 1977.* A Regency romance with Gothic and romantic suspense overtones.

The Smile of the Stranger. *Gollancz, 1978.*

If I Were You. *Doubleday, 1987.* Two look-alike girls trade places in this witty Regency.

Balogh, Mary

Balogh is a highly respected writer of innovative, character-driven Regencies that push the edges of the genre both in sensuality and subject. Her characters and their relationships are often complex, and her heroines unconventional and experienced. *(See also Period Romance bibliography.)*

Promise of Spring. *Signet, 1990.* Features an older heroine with a past, an honorable hero, and a marriage of convenience.

The Secret Pearl. *Signet, 1991.* An impoverished gentlewoman is rescued from prostitution by her first client, the unhappily married Duke of Rideway. She ends up as a governess to his child and in love with him—a situation that seems to have no happy solution.

The Snow Angel. *Signet, 1991.* A nobleman intent on a final bachelorhood fling and a rebellious young widow end up snowbound together in this Regency that pushes the envelope of the subgenre.

The Notorious Rake. *Signet, 1992.* A walk in the garden and a surprise thunderstorm bring unexpected, romantic changes to the lives of the respectable Lady Mary and the infamous Lord Waite.

Christmas Belle. *Signet, 1994.* An aristocratic hero and an actress heroine who was once his mistress unexpectedly meet again at his grandparents' estate, with romantic results.

Dancing with Clara. *Signet, 1994.* An invalid heiress, an immature rake, and a marriage of convenience on the rocks drives the plot of this romance with a serious side.

Lord Carew's Bride. *Signet, 1995.* Samantha wants a companion, not a husband, and Mr. Wade seems made to order in this novel that features deception, dark pasts, and difficult present realities.

The Famous Heroine. *Signet, 1996.* The lively, tomboyish daughter of a wealthy "cit" finds social fame and romance within the stifling London social scene.

The Plumed Bonnet. *Signet, 1996.* Mistaken for a "ladybird" while stranded along a country road, a vicar's daughter attracts the advances, and eventually the heart, of a jaded aristocrat.

The Temporary Wife. *Signet, 1997.*

Barbour, Anne (Barbara Yirka)

Barbour's Regencies are well written, witty, and intriguing.

A Talent for Trouble. *Signet, 1992.* A poor, talented artist collaborates with a rich, noble, engaged author on a controversial satire, with romantic and slightly dangerous results.

Kate and the Soldier. *Signet, 1993.* Returning home to his father's deathbed, wounded soldier David Merritt finds hostility, love, and a surprise.

Lord Glenraven's Return. *Signet, 1994.* A run-down estate, a lovely widow, and an incognito lord combine in this witty and charming Regency.

A Dangerous Charade. *Signet, 1995.* A companion with a secret and a suspicious nephew propel the plot of this slightly mysterious romance.

My Cousin Jane. *Signet, 1995.* Jane masquerades as the unattractive chaperone for her young cousin's Season and ends up capturing the affections of her young charge's guardian.

A Rake's Reform. *Signet, 1996.* A runaway ward, an ardent feminist, and a noble rake combine in a well-crafted Regency that offers an intriguing glimpse into women's issues of the period.

A Step in Time. *Signet, 1996.* A light and lively Time Travel Regency laced with humor and interesting culture clashes.

A Dedicated Scoundrel. *Signet, 1997.*

Lady Hilary's Halloween. *Signet, 1998.*

Bennett, Janice

(See also Time Travel bibliography.)

A Dangerous Intrigue. *Zebra, 1992.*

A Lady's Champion. *Zebra, 1994.*

A Desperate Gamble. *Zebra, 1995.*

Beverley, Jo

Beverley is a popular writer of lively, humorous, historically accurate, well-written Regencies. She is a multiple Rita Award winner and a member of the Romance Writers of America Hall of Fame. Her Company of Rogues series is more sensual, and the more recent stories in the series have been published as Historicals. *(See also Period Romance bibliography.)*

The Staniforth Secrets. *Walker, 1989.* An isolated estate provides a Gothic twist.

An Arranged Marriage. *Zebra, 1991.* This unusual Regency begins with the rape of the heroine. First in the Company of Rogues series. Rather sensual.

 Emily and the Dark Angel. *Walker, 1991.* When the infamous Dark Angel moves into the neighboring estate, Emily Grantwick knows she should avoid him, but fate has other plans. A Rita Award winner.

 The Christmas Angel. *Zebra, 1992.* The Christmas holidays provide the backdrop for this warm and witty story of a hero who wants to settle down and a young widowed mother who doesn't want to give up her independence. A Company of Rogues title. Sensual.

 An Unwilling Bride. *Zebra, 1992.* Forced into marriage by the Duke of Belcraven, Beth Armitage and Lucien De Vaux, the Duke's heir, eventually find love. A Company of Rogues title. Sensual. A Rita Award winner.

 Dierdre and Don Juan. *Avon Books, 1993.* A rake in need of an heir and a debutante who has ideas of her own (and they don't include marriage to someone like "Don Juan") reconcile their differences in this witty, humorous story. A Rita Award winner.

Carroll, Susan (Susan Coppula)

Carroll has won two Rita Awards in the Regency category.

 Sugar Rose. *Fawcett Crest, 1987.* A Rita Award winner.

Brighton Road. *Fawcett Crest, 1988.* A Rita Award winner.

The Bishop's Daughter. *Fawcett Crest, 1990.*

 Christmas Belles. *Fawcett Crest, 1992.* Chloe Waverly sets out to save her older sister from a forced marriage and ends up as the bride instead.

Mistress Mischief. *Fawcett Crest, 1992.* Failing as a gambler, impoverished Frederica sets out to become her rich cousin's mistress, with lively, romantic results.

 Miss Prentiss and the Yankee. *Fawcett Crest, 1993.*

The Valentine's Day Ball. *Fawcett Crest, 1994.*

Chase, Loretta

Isabella. *Walker, 1987.*

Viscount Vagabond. *Walker, 1988.*

The English Witch. *Avon Books, 1989.* Funny, fast-paced dialogue, with intriguing characters. One of the author's best.

Knave's Wager. *Walker, 1990.*

 The Sandalwood Princess. *Walker, 1990.* A Rita Award winner.

Chesney, Marion

Chesney is a popular, prolific writer of Regencies. Her contributions are typically light, lively, and relatively short. She knows the period, and her stories are charming reads. They are also a bit unusual in that she often uses upstairs/downstairs themes and gives sympathetic attention to the working classes and the poor. Although she has written many individual Regencies, her series are some of her most popular works. She also writes under several pseudonyms and currently is writing mysteries as M. C. Beaton.

Six Sisters saga

Each book is devoted to the courtship of one of the Armitage sisters.

Minerva. *St. Martin's Press, 1982.*

The Taming of Annabella. *St. Martin's Press, 1983.*

Dierdre and Desire. *St. Martin's Press, 1983.*

Daphne. *St. Martin's Press, 1984.*

Diana the Huntress. *St. Martin's Press, 1985.*

Frederica in Fashion. *St. Martin's Press, 1985.*

A House for the Season series

A series in which each book tells the story of a different group of occupants of the unlucky house at 67 Clarges. The staff remains the same, and they, as well as the house, form the unifying link in the series. Rainbird, the butler, is especially memorable.

The Miser of Mayfair. *St. Martin's Press, 1986.*

Plain Jane. *St. Martin's Press, 1986.*

The Wicked Godmother. *St. Martin's Press, 1987.*

The Adventuress. *St. Martin's Press, 1987.*

Rainbird's Revenge. *St. Martin's Press, 1988.*

Milady in Love. *St. Martin's Press, 1989.*

School for Manners series

Refining Felicity. *St. Martin's Press, 1988.*

Finessing Clarissa. *St. Martin's Press, 1989.*

Perfecting Fiona. *St. Martin's Press, 1990.*

Enlightening Delilah. *St. Martin's Press, 1990.*

Animating Maria. *St. Martin's Press, 1990.*

Marrying Harriett. *St. Martin's Press, 1990.*

The Daughters of Mannerling series

The Banishment. *St. Martin's Press, 1995.*

The Intrigue. *St. Martin's Press, 1995.*

The Deception. *St. Martin's Press, 1996.*

The Folly. *St. Martin's Press, 1996.*

The Romance. *St. Martin's Press, 1996.*

Comstock, Mary Chase

(See also Paranormal bibliography.)

An Impetuous Miss. *Zebra, 1993.* An unconventional, independent heroine and a helpful old friend find love where they least expect it.

Fortune's Mistress. *Zebra, 1996.* Pregnant and alone, Marianne Gardiner leaves her past behind her and heads for the country to raise her child and make a new life for them both. Darker and more serious than Comstock's other Regencies.

Cummings, Monette

See No Love. *Walker, 1983.*

Lady Shiela's Groom. *Walker, 1984.*

The Beauty's Daughter. *Walker, 1985.* A Rita Award winner.

A Husband for Holly. *Diamond, 1990.*

Scarlet Lady. *Diamond, 1991.*

The Wicked Stepdaughter. *Diamond, 1992.*

Crossed Hearts. *Zebra, 1993.*

Loving Spirit. *Zebra, 1994.*

Darcy, Clare

Darcy is one of the first writers to attempt to assume the Regency mantle of Georgette Heyer. Her works, especially her earlier ones, are noted for historical accuracy and exceptionally well-drawn historical characters.

8

Georgina. *Walker, 1971.*

Cecily: or A Young Lady of Quality. *Walker, 1972.*

Lydia: or Love in Town. *Walker, 1973.*

Victoire. *Walker, 1974.*

Allegra. *Walker, 1975.*

Lady Pamela. *Walker, 1975.*

Regina. *Walker, 1976.*

Elyza. *Walker, 1977.*

Cressida. *Walker, 1977.*

Eugenia. *Walker, 1977.*

Gwendolen. *Walker, 1978.*

Rolande. *Walker, 1978.*

Letty. *Walker, 1980.*

Caroline and Julia. *Walker, 1982.*

Devon, Marian

Miss Osborne Misbehaves. *Fawcett, 1990.* Eliza befriends former Newgate prisoner, solves a mystery, and gains a love.

Lady Harriet Takes Charge. *Fawcett, 1991.*

Lord Harlequin. *Fawcett, 1994.* Theatrics, disguises, and a murder mystery.

The Widow of Bath. *Fawcett, 1994.*

Deck the Halls. *Fawcett, 1995.* Sir Jervis Brougham's deathbed summons brings his family home for the holidays, with romantic results. Traditional Regency holidays-in-the-country fun.

Miss Kendal Sets Her Cap. *Fawcett, 1996.* Events take an interesting, and quite romantic, turn when impetuous Freddie Kendal announces she is setting her cap for a returning war hero.

Dolan, Charlotte Louise

Three Lords for Lady Anne. *Signet, 1991.*

The Substitute Bridegroom. *Signet, 1991.* A disfiguring accident, a broken engagement, and a marriage of obligation drive the plot in this traditional, but unusual, Regency.

The Black Widow. *Signet, 1992.* Someone wants to keep charming Meribe from marrying, and the hero is determined to discover who and why.

Fallen Angel. *Signet, 1993.* Family members cause their share of problems in this witty Regency.

The Counterfeit Gentleman. *Signet, 1994.* A former smuggler's timely rescue of a nearly drowned heiress draws him into a dangerous game, despite his intentions not to get involved.

Dunn, Carola

 The Miser's Sister. *Walker, 1984.* A Rita Award winner.

Lord Iverbrook's Heir. *Walker, 1986.*

The Man in the Green Coat. *Walker, 1987.*

Two Corinthians. *Walker, 1989.*

A Susceptible Gentleman. *Harlequin, 1990.*

The Fortune-Hunters. *Harlequin, 1991.*

My Lord Winter. *Harlequin, 1992.*

The Captain's Inheritance. *Zebra, 1994.*

His Lordship's Reward. *Zebra, 1994.*

The Lady and the Rake. *Zebra, 1995.* Miles and Nerissa must behave for six months in order to inherit a fortune. A ghost adds to the fun.

The Tudor Secret. *Zebra, 1995.* Smuggling and intrigue lend spice to this traditional Regency.

Scandal's Daughter. *Zebra, 1996.*

Eagle, Sarah

The Reluctant Suitor. *Jove, 1991.*

The Marriage Gamble. *Jove, 1992.*

The Bedeviled Baron. *Jove, 1994.* Determined to scorn all potential brides his mother suggests, Bramwell finds himself in a difficult position when he finally sees the woman of his dreams and then learns she is one of his mother's choices.

Eastwood, Gail

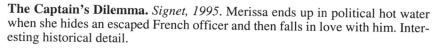

A Perilous Journey. *Signet, 1994.*

The Captain's Dilemma. *Signet, 1995.* Merissa ends up in political hot water when she hides an escaped French officer and then falls in love with him. Interesting historical detail.

The Persistent Earl. *Signet, 1995.* Resigned to spinsterhood, Phoebe is jolted out of her complacency when she ends up caring for the wounded Earl of Devenham. Compelling characters and nicely handled sexual tension.

An Unlikely Hero. *Signet, 1996.* A quiet, scholarly nobleman finds romance at a house party in the country.

Edghill, Rosemary

Turkish Delight: The Earl and the Houri. *St. Martin's Press, 1987.* Typical Regency involving an atypical heroine—one who was raised in a seraglio.

Two of a Kind: An English Trifle. *St. Martin's Press, 1988.*

The Ill-Bred Bride. *St. Martin's Press, 1990.* A marriage of convenience between an impoverished nobleman and a common heiress solves their immediate problems, but creates a few others.

Fleeting Fancy. *Fawcett, 1993.* A prodigal nobleman gets his just deserts from the woman he compromised ten years earlier. Witty and unique.

Ewing, Jean R.

Scandal's Reward. *Zebra, 1994.*

Rogue's Reward. *Zebra, 1995.* Blackmail, mystery, and deception are part of this fast-paced, witty Regency.

Virtue's Reward. *Zebra, 1995.* A dying soldier's request nets Captain Richard Acton a surprise bride and danger.

Valor's Reward. *Zebra, 1996.* A notorious rake shoots and then rescues a classics scholar, with surprisingly romantic results.

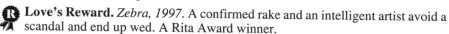

Folly's Reward. *Zebra, 1997.* A governess is determined to save her young charge from his evil guardian. Romance follows.

Love's Reward. *Zebra, 1997.* A confirmed rake and an intelligent artist avoid a scandal and end up wed. A Rita Award winner.

Fairchild, Elisabeth (Donna Gimarc)

The Counterfeit Coachman. *Signet, 1994.*

The Silent Suitor. *Signet, 1994.* A blind, protected heroine must choose between safety and love in this Beauty and the Beast romance.

Lord Endicott's Appetite. *Signet, 1995.*

The Love Knot. *Signet, 1995.* Aurora will teach Miles how to manage his estate; Miles will instruct Aurora in the art of catching a husband. Of course, the husband she catches is Miles.

Miss Dornton's Hero. *Signet, 1995.*

A Fresh Perspective. *Signet, 1996.*

Lord Ramsey's Return. *Signet, 1996.* Prudence Stanhope is shocked to learn that she was tended by the infamous Rash Ramsey while in Mohamed's Baths in Brighton, but she can't forget him.

The Rakehell's Reform. *Signet, 1997.*

Harbaugh, Karen

(See also Paranormal Romance bibliography.)

The Marriage Scheme. *HarperMonogram, 1994* (as Kathleen Elliott).

A Special License. *HarperMonogram, 1995* (as Kathleen Elliott).

The Reluctant Cavalier. *Signet, 1996.* The heroine's search for the man who rescued her and her sister during a masked ball is hampered by the fact that he is a most unlikely hero.

Heath, Sandra

Heath is a popular, prolific Regency author. Only her recent Regencies are listed. *(See also Paranormal and Time Travel Romance bibliographies.)*

A Scandalous Publication. *Signet, 1986.*

The Absent Wife. *Signet, 1987.*

The Pilfered Plume. *Signet, 1989.*

A Country Cotillion. *Signet, 1992.*

Cruel Lord Cranham. *Signet, 1993.*

Hendrickson, Emily

Queen of the May. *Signet, 1989.* A complex Regency featuring an adventurous heroine; a marquess with a secret; and a plot filled with mystery, excitement, and danger.

The Gallant Lord Ives. *Signet, 1989.* An accident, a charming heroine, and a responsible nobleman combine in a tale that features likable characters and an intriguing glimpse into the sport of falconry.

Miss Wyndham's Escapade. *Signet, 1990.* An eccentric hero, a schoolmistress heroine, and a sapphire necklace make for an intriguing Regency mystery.

A Scandalous Suggestion. *Signet, 1991.* A shy gentleman saves a charming stranger from drowning herself and ends up meeting her again when their mothers do a bit of matchmaking.

The Wicked Proposal. *Signet, 1992.*

Elizabeth's Rake. *Signet, 1993.* Elizabeth heads to the country to rest and escape the charms of an all too attractive rake only to find him there. Valentine's Day tie-in.

Miss Cheney's Charade. *Signet, 1994.* A cross-dressing heroine, a historian hero, and an ancient mummy propel the plot of this lively Regency.

The Rake and the Redhead. *Signet, 1994.* A scrappy, determined young woman goes to the defense of an entire village and ends up in love with its arrogant owner.

The Scoundrel's Bride. *Signet, 1994.* In the process of teaching naive Lady Chloe how to "go on" in Society, an experienced rake falls in love with his "creation."

The Contrary Corinthian. *Signet, 1995.* A charming governess, young twins, and a suspicious nobleman result in a light, satisfying romance.

The Debonair Duke. *Signet, 1996.* A mysterious sapphire necklace causes all sorts of problems, romantic and otherwise, for Lady Pamela Taylor and the Duke of Wexford.

Harriet's Beau. *Signet, 1997.*

Hern, Candice

A Change of Heart. *Signet, 1995.* When the highly unconventional Lady Mary offers to help the Marquess of Pemberton find a wife, she has no idea that she will eventually fill that role.

A Proper Companion. *Signet, 1995.* An heiress who must marry to gain her inheritance, falls in love with an unavailable man in this light, lively romance laced with a bit of greed and a lot of charm.

An Affair of Honor. *Signet, 1996.* A curricle accident places a noble rake in the care of the same woman he saved from being a wallflower at a society ball six years earlier—but the gawky duckling has turned into a glorious swan. Contains a touch of mystery.

A Garden Folly. *Signet, 1997.* A heroine falls in love with the gardener, never realizing that he is actually the lord of the manor. Charming and well written.

Heyer, Georgette

Best known of all the Regency writers and, indeed, the standard-setter for the genre, Heyer's Regencies are generally historically accurate, light, witty, and noted for their excellent use of Regency period language. Her earlier works contain the kind of historical detail that makes them excellent sources for those researching the period.

Powder and Patch: The Transformation of Philip Jettan. *Heinemann, 1930.* Originally published in 1923 by Mills and Boon as *The Transformation of Philip Jettan* by Stella Martin. When Cleone Charteris finds herself out of her element in London society and engaged to two men simultaneously, only Philip Jettan can unravel the tangle.

8

Regency Buck. *Heinemann, 1935.* When Judith Taverner and her brother Peregrine travel to London to meet their guardian, the elegant and haughty Lord Worth, romance and adventure lurk just around the corner.

The Corinthian. *Heinemann, 1940.* Published as *Beau Wyndham* by Doubleday, in 1941. Lovely Penelope Creed and Sir Richard Wyndham meet as she is climbing out of her aunt's window and discover that they have the same problem—both are being forced into marriage.

Faro's Daughter. *Doubleday, 1942.* Heinemann, 1941. Working in her aunt's elegant gaming house, Deb Grantham is used to slights. But when the rich Mr. Ravenscar offers her an intolerable insult, Deb vows to teach him a lesson.

Friday's Child. *Putnam, 1946.* Heinemann, 1944. When Lord Sheringham is rejected by the beautiful Miss Milborne, he vows to marry the first woman he sees. She is Miss Hero Wantage, a very young and unsophisticated orphan with no notion of how to behave in her new life.

The Reluctant Widow. *Putnam, 1946.* Elinor Rochdale, on her way to a new position as governess, takes the wrong carriage and ends up marrying Lord Carlyon's wealthy cousin, Eustace, on his deathbed. Then the adventure really begins.

The Foundling. *Putnam, 1948*. The Duke of Sale, known as Gilly to his friends, finds adventure and romance with Belinda, a beautiful and endearing foundling.

Arabella. *Putnam, 1949*. When Arabella Tallant, a lovely country vicar's daughter, travels to London to spend the Season with her godmother, the handsome, eligible Robert Beaumaris finds his life changed forever.

The Grand Sophy. *Putnam, 1950*. Lord Ombersley's orderly life is turned upside down with the arrival of his wife's niece, Sophy Stanton-Lacy.

The Quiet Gentleman. *Putnam, 1952*. Heinemann, 1951. When Gervase Frant returns home after the Napoleonic Wars to claim his inheritance, he discovers that his widowed stepmother would rather he had died in battle.

Cotillion. *Putnam, 1953*. When Kitty Charing engineers an engagement to Freddy Standen to make Jack Westruther jealous, she gets more than she bargained for.

The Toll-Gate. *Putnam, 1954*. When Captain John Staple stops at an unattended toll-gate for the night, he lands in a mystery of murder and missing gold and finds the bride of his dreams.

Bath Tangle. *Putnam, 1955*. Lady Serena Carlow is outraged to learn that her father has left her inheritance in trust to the Marquis of Rotherham. He is the man she jilted several years before, and he must approve of the man she marries. When an old suitor unexpectedly appears in Bath, Serena vows to break the trust.

Sprig Muslin. *Putnam, 1956*. Coming upon Amanda unattended in a common inn, Sir Gareth Ludlow decides to restore her to her family. But he reckons without Amanda's determination and lively imagination.

Sylvester, or the Wicked Uncle. *Putnam, 1957*. By anonymously writing a novel that accidentally describes real society people, Phoebe sets the *ton* in a whirl and creates all kinds of problems for her villain, Sylvester.

April Lady. *Putnam, 1957*. When Lady Nell Cardross finds herself in financial peril because of her extravagant spending and overly generous nature, she must discover a solution or risk marital unhappiness with her husband Lord Giles.

Venetia. *Putnam, 1959*. Heinemann, 1958. Beautiful, well-read Venetia Lanyon knows little of the world beyond her dull Yorkshire home until the intrusion into the neighborhood of the notorious Lord Damerel.

The Unknown Ajax. *Putnam, 1960*. Heinemann, 1959. When the son of a common weaver's daughter unexpectedly becomes his heir, Lord Darracott decides his unmarried granddaughter will make his heir a suitable wife. But the strong-minded Anthea has other ideas.

A Civil Contract. *Putnam, 1962*. Heinemann, 1961. Inheriting his father's staggering debts as well as his title, the new Viscount Lynton must give up all thought of marriage to Julia Oversley. His only hope of saving his home and providing for his sisters lies in a marriage of convenience to a girl as plain as Julia is beautiful.

The Nonesuch. *E. P. Dutton, 1963*. Heinemann, 1962. Ancilla Trent has her hands full as governess, and the presence of Sir Waldo Hawkridge, a handsome Corinthian, is certainly distracting.

False Colours. *E. P. Dutton, 1964*. Bodley Head, 1963. A charming comedy of manners that finds the Earl of Denville and his twin brother, Kit, attempting to unravel their mother's confused finances by proposing marriage to the wealthy Cressida Stavely.

Frederica. *E. P. Dutton, 1965*. When Frederica Merriville applies to the bored and cynical Marquis of Alverstoke for help in launching her beautiful sister into society, the marquis little guesses how completely the exuberant Merriville family will win his heart.

Black Sheep. *E. P. Dutton, 1967.* Bodley Head, 1966. High-spirited Abigail Wendover's objections to a fortune hunter's designs on her niece are heightened by the arrival of the young man's black sheep uncle.

Charity Girl. *E. P. Dutton, 1970.* Cherry Steane elicits strong feelings of chivalry in Lord Desford when he finds her at the mercy of a miserly grandfather and an irresponsible father.

Lady of Quality. *E. P. Dutton, 1972.* When Miss Annis Wynchwood takes charge of Lucilla Carleton, an appealing 17-year-old heiress, she hasn't yet met Lucilla's guardian, Mr. Oliver Carleton, known by all as the rudest man in London. Set in Bath.

Hodge, Jane Aiken

Although many of her well-written, historically accurate books are set during the late 1700s–early 1800s, not all fall within the Regency camp.

Runaway Bride. *Fawcett Crest, 1975.*

Kelly, Carla

Kelly produces well-crafted, emotionally involving Regencies and is a Rita Award winner in the Regency category.

Miss Chartley's Guided Tour. *Signet, 1989.*

Summer Campaign. *Signet, 1989.*

Marian's Christmas Wish. *Signet, 1989.*

Libby's London Merchant. *Signet, 1991.*

Miss Grimsley's Oxford Career. *Signet, 1992.*

Miss Billings Treads the Boards. *Signet, 1993.* A funny and witty tale of a governess and a nobleman involved in a traveling theatre company.

Miss Whittier Makes a List. *Signet, 1994.* Wit and romance on the high seas.

R Mrs. Drew Plays Her Hand. *Signet, 1994.* A warm, sensitive story of a vicar's widow who finds security for her family and love for herself in the arms of the Marquess of Winn. Emotionally involving.

Reforming Lord Ragsdale. *Signet, 1995.* Considered one of the author's best.

R The Lady's Companion. *Signet, 1996.* Rather than become dependent upon relatives, Susan Hampton chooses to become a companion to a legendary, aging adventuress. Exceptional depiction of the truly important things in life in a period that valued superficiality of appearance.

With This Ring. *Signet, 1997.*

Kerstan, Lynn

A Spirited Affair. *Zebra, 1993.* When Jill applies to her guardian, the Earl of Coltrane, for money to save her beloved sheep farm, he decides she needs to be "launched" into society instead.

R Gwen's Christmas Ghost. *Zebra, 1995.* A ghostly hero with a mission changes the lives of his future generations and unexpectedly finds a reason to live. Co-authored with Alicia Rasley. A Rita Award winner.

Francesca's Rake. *Fawcett Crest, 1997.* A disreputable rake and a tarnished bluestocking find love.

Kihlstrom, April

The Scholar's Daughter. *Signet, 1989.*

The Reckless Wager. *Signet, 1991.*

Dangerous Masquerade. *Signet, 1992.* An American heiress is betrayed by her British relatives and ends up a servant in the house of the hero. Laced with suspense and wicked villains.

Earl of Westcott's Daughters series

The Wicked Groom. *Signet, 1996.* The heroine is attracted to a new stable groom who, of course, turns out to be the hero.

The Widowed Bride. *Signet, 1996.* Raped and widowed on her wedding day, Annabelle is aided by the new heir to her late husband's estate. However, there is still a dangerous mystery to be solved.

An Honorable Rogue. *Signet, 1997.* A daring wager and too much brandy result in seduction, compromise, and, eventually, love for the fiery Lady Barbara.

Miss Tibble's Folly. *Signet, 1998.* A starchy governess and a retired army officer find love, despite society's conventions and a bit of family opposition.

Kingsley, Katherine

A Natural Attachment. *Signet, 1990.* A naive heiress and a less-than-honest hero drive the plot in this marriage-of-convenience story.

King of Hearts. *Signet, 1993.* When the new heir to his uncle's estate arrives to find the tenants celebrating the late earl's death, he realizes he has amends to make and people to provide for—including the heroine.

Kingsley, Mary

A Gentleman's Desire. *Zebra, 1991.* An irresponsible earl, a responsible heroine, and a compromising situation result in a marriage that eventually brings the hero to his senses.

The Rake's Reward. *Zebra, 1991.* A rake finds himself attracted to the woman he thinks might be responsible for a murder and assassination plot.

A Maddening Minx. *Zebra, 1992.* A magical Beauty and the Beast-type Regency.

An Intriguing Affaire. *Zebra, 1993.*

Scandal's Lady. *Zebra, 1994.* A governess and a newly titled lord are placed in a difficult position because they are childhood friends.

Lane, Allison

The Impoverished Viscount. *Signet, 1996.* Lady Melissa Stapleton agrees to pose as the fiancée of the Viscount Rathbone so he can retain his inheritance—but the pretence soon takes on an unintended life of its own.

The Prodigal Daughter. *Signet, 1996.* A fire at the local inn introduces a take-charge healer and an arrogant nobleman, and the sparks fly between them. Detailed and slowly paced.

The Rake's Rainbow. *Signet, 1996.* Although compromised and forced to marry, Caroline sets out to turn her marriage into the real thing—and succeeds. Interesting characters.

The Earl's Revenge. *Signet, 1997.*

Layton, Edith

The Disdainful Marquis. *Signet, 1983.*

The Abandoned Bride. *Signet, 1985.*

Love in Disguise. *Signet, 1987.*

A Love for All Seasons. *Signet, 1992.* A well-crafted collection of five Regency novellas, each focusing on a different season of the year.

Ley, Alice Chetwynd

Although not as well known as some, Ley's work is reminiscent of Heyer's and features well-developed characters and skillful recreations of the historical periods. Several of her titles take place during the Georgian period; however, they all share the Regency flavor. Several of her more recent works include:

A Fatal Assignation. *St. Martin's Press, 1987.*

Masquerade of Vengeance. *Severn House, 1989.*

London, Laura (Thomas Dale Curtis and Sharon Curtis)

These delightful Regencies are almost spoofs of the genre.

A Heart Too Proud. *Dell, 1978.*

The Bad Baron's Daughter. *Dell, 1978.*

Moonlight Mist. *Dell, 1979.*

Love's a Stage. *Dell, 1980.*

The Gypsy Heiress. *Dell, 1981.*

Malcolm, Anthea (Tracy and Joan Grant)

Malcolm's Regencies are well researched and complex.

Frivolous Pretense. *Zebra, 1990.*

Counterfeit Heart. *Zebra, 1991.* Two cousins in search of love end up with a host of other problems.

A Touch of Scandal. *Zebra, 1991.*

The Improper Proposal. *Zebra, 1992.*

A Sensible Match. *Zebra, 1993.*

8

Metzger, Barbara

Metzger's highly popular Regencies are light, witty, and liberally laced with humor.

My Lady Innkeeper. *Walker, 1985.*

Rake's Ransom. *Walker, 1986.*

The Luck of the Devil. *Fawcett Crest, 1991.* Separated by circumstances, Rowanne and Carey eventually renew their acquaintance, with romantic results.

Minor Indiscretions. *Fawcett Crest, 1991.*

An Affair of Interest. *Fawcett Crest, 1992.*

Lady in Green. *Fawcett Crest, 1993.* Disguised as an old housekeeper, the heroine makes the resident earl's romantic life a bit difficult.

A Loyal Companion. *Fawcett Crest, 1993.* A "love" of a dog makes this Regency unforgettable.

An Angel for the Earl. *Fawcett Crest, 1994.* Lucinda must reform a notorious rake if she is going to get into heaven. Light fantasy elements.

A Suspicious Affair. *Fawcett Crest, 1994.* A widow, a baby, and an impatient hero in a romance that combines humor, murder, and witty dialogue.

Father Christmas. *Fawcett Crest, 1995.* A profligate duke in need of an heir, a pair of lively three-year-old twins, and a furious mother eventually become a family.

An Enchanted Affair. *Fawcett Crest, 1996.* A fey heroine and a debt-laden hero strike a romantic bargain to save the forest that houses her fairy friends.

The Primrose Path. *Fawcett Crest, 1997.*

Snowdrops and Scandalbroth. *Fawcett Crest, 1997.*

Michaels, Kasey (Kathryn Seidick)

Michaels is a Rita Award-winning author.

 The Lurid Lady Lockport. *Avon Books, 1984.* A Rita Award winner.

The Questioning Miss Quinton. *Avon Books, 1987.*

The Mischievous Miss Murphy. *Avon Books, 1987.*

The Haunted Miss Hampshire. *Avon Books, 1992.* An arrogant hero and a lively but haunted heroine are forced to share the estate of her late aunt.

The Anonymous Miss Addams. *Avon Books, 1993.* Amnesia, suspense, and an assassination plot.

Moore, Kate

Moore's Regencies are exceptionally well researched and well written.

The Mercenary Major. *Avon Books, 1993.*

Sweet Bargain. *Avon Books, 1993.* Rumors and poisoned fish prove problematic in this country romance that features a family of interesting characters.

An Improper Widow. *Avon Books, 1995.* Stolen calling cards, an unusual highwayman, and a plot based on the Homer's *Odyssey.*

Oliver, Patricia

The Runaway Duchess. *Signet, 1993.*

Lord Harry's Angel. *Signet, 1993.*

Lord Gresham's Lady. *Signet, 1994.*

Miss Drayton's Downfall. *Signet, 1994.* When the heroine's lover dies, leaving her pregnant, her would-have-been-brother-in-law does the honorable thing and marries her, with romantic results.

An Immodest Proposal. *Signet, 1995.*

Roses for Harriet. *Signet, 1995.*

The Colonel's Lady. *Signet, 1996.*

An Unsuitable Match. *Signet, 1997.*

Overfield, Joan

Many of Overfield's Regencies have a dash of the paranormal. *(See also Time Travel bibliography.)*

Journals of Lady X. *Pageant Books, 1989.*

Bride's Leap. *Fawcett Crest, 1991.* A haunted estate, an independent heroine, a recovering spy hero, and a mystery are featured in this Gothic Regency. Sequel to *Journals of Lady X.*

A Spirited Bluestocking. *Zebra, 1992.* An old estate, an intrepid bluestocking heroine, and a real ghost make for lively reading.

The Viscount's Vixen. *Avon Books, 1992.* A wager brings an activist bluestocking and a dashing viscount together.

A Proper Taming. *Avon Books, 1994.*

The Learned Lady. *Avon Books, 1996.*

Pianka, Phyllis Taylor

Dame Fortune's Fancy. *Harlequin, 1987.*

The Tarte Shop. *Harlequin, 1989.*

The Calico Countess. *Harlequin, 1990.*

The Lark's Nest. *Harlequin, 1991.*

Coventry Courtship. *Harlequin, 1992.*

The Thackery Jewels. *Harlequin, 1994.* The story of the three Thackery girls and their romances, this book is actually three novellas in a single volume.

Putney, Mary Jo

Putney is a Rita Award-winning author. *(See also Period Romance bibliography.)*

The Diabolical Baron. *Signet, 1987.*

The Controversial Countess. *Signet, 1988.* Rewritten as the Historical *Petals in the Storm* (Topaz, 1993).

The Would-Be Widow. *Signet, 1988.*

Carousel of Hearts. *Signet, 1989.*

8

The Rake and the Reformer. *Signet, 1989.* Deciding to reform his profligate ways, Reggie Davenport returns to his recently inherited childhood home and is stunned that its steward is a woman of noble birth. The hero is the villain in *The Diabolical Baron.* A Rita Award winner.

Rasley, Alicia

Rasley is a Rita Award-winning writer.

A Midsummer's Delight. *Zebra, 1993.*

Poetic Justice. *Zebra, 1994.* A determined heroine saves her beloved rare book collection with the help of a book dealer. Well written and researched.

Gwen's Christmas Ghost. *Zebra, 1995.* A ghostly hero with a mission changes the lives of his future generations and unexpectedly finds a reason to live. Coauthored with Lynn Kerstan. A Rita Award winner.

Richardson, Evelyn (Cynthia Johnson)

Warm, intelligently written Regencies.

The Bluestocking's Dilemma. *Signet, 1992.*

The Willful Widow. *Signet, 1994.* An independent widow who wants to be left alone and a hero determined to save his young nephew from her end up falling in love themselves.

Lady Alex's Gamble. *Signet, 1995.* Taking on her twin brother's identity in a last-ditch effort to save their estate, Lady Alex goes to London to win at cards and ends up winning more than she'd bargained for.

The Reluctant Heiress. *Signet, 1996.* Lady Sarah's surprise inheritance causes her spendthrift brother and his wife to return to the family estate, causing Sarah no end of trouble when they decide to maintain their social schedule—but without money or expertise.

Savery, Jeanne

Savery's Regencies are generally well researched and detailed.

Last of the Winter Roses. *Zebra, 1991.* Happily single Lady Ardith doesn't intend to marry, and then she shelters a long-time friend and changes her mind.

A Handful of Promises. *Zebra, 1992.*

A Christmas Treasure. *Zebra, 1994.* Set in Portugal during the Peninsular Wars. Interesting detail.

A Reformed Rake. *Zebra, 1994.* Features a rake, an attempted abduction in the Alps, and a resistive heroine. Complex and detailed.

A Lady's Deception. *Zebra, 1995.*

A Springtime Affair. *Zebra, 1995.*

Cupid's Challenge. *Zebra, 1996.* A paralyzed heroine, a caring hero, and interesting scientific and medical detail result in a well-crafted Regency that deals with some dark social issues.

Lady Stephanie. *Zebra, 1996.*

A Timeless Love. *Zebra, 1997.*

Scott, Amanda

Scott is a Rita Award-winning author.

The Battling Bluestocking. *Signet, 1985.*

 Lord Abberley's Nemesis. *Signet, 1986.* A Rita Award winner.

The Dauntless Miss Wingrave. *Signet, 1989.* A kiss stolen years earlier causes problems between the heroine and her noble hero cousin.

The Madcap Marchioness. *Signet, 1989.*

Bath Charade. *Signet, 1991.* Young Caroline Hardy learns that real heroes aren't necessarily like those in her favorite books.

The Fickle Fortune Hunter. *Signet, 1993.*

Simonson, Sheila

Simonson's Regencies are gems, true to the form and sparkling with humor and authentic, witty dialog.

A Cousinly Connexion. *Walker, 1984.*

Lady Elizabeth's Comet. *Walker, 1985.*

The Bar Sinister. *Walker, 1986.*

Love and Folly. *Walker, 1988.*

Smith, Joan

Smith writes witty, amusing Regencies, highly derivative of Georgette Heyer and filled with interesting characters and bright, verbally quick protagonists. Her earliest works are among her best.

An Affair of the Heart. *Fawcett, 1977.*

Imprudent Lady. *Walker, 1978.*

Endure My Heart. *Fawcett, 1980.*

Madcap Miss. *Fawcett Crest, 1989.* Fun and deception.

Cousin Cecelia. *Fawcett Crest, 1990.* A matchmaking heroine falls in love with the nobleman who is influencing the local young men not to marry.

The Spanish Lady. *Fawcett Crest, 1993.* The hero resists serving as escort for his lovely cousin, only to eventually fall in love with her.

The Kissing Bough. *Fawcett Crest, 1994.* A returning war hero, his vulgar fiancée, and a gentle heroine spend a country Christmas together.

A Christmas Gambol. *Fawcett Crest, 1996.* When a budding novelist pretends to be the author of a bad book, simply for an entrée into the London publishing world, she furthers her romantic situation as well as her career.

A Tall, Dark Stranger. *Fawcett Crest, 1996.* Murder in a country setting.

An Infamous Proposal. *Fawcett Crest, 1997.*

Petticoat Rebellion. *Fawcett Crest, 1997.*

Stratton, Penelope

The Unromantic Lady. *Fawcett, 1996.* A heroine who doesn't believe in love finally sorts out her feelings for her husband. Amusing and quite sensual for a traditional Regency.

8

Veryan, Patricia

Veryan writes intriguing, action-filled Regency and Georgian Period Romances. Her linked books are especially popular.

Sanguinet saga

Nanette. *Walker, 1981.*

Feather Castles. *St. Martin's Press, 1982.*

Married Past Redemption. *St. Martin's Press, 1983.*

The Noblest Frailty. *St. Martin's Press, 1983.*

Sanguinet's Crown. *St. Martin's Press, 1985.*

Give All to Love. *St. Martin's Press, 1987.*

Lanterns. *St. Martin's Press, 1996.* Moving into the dower house on an abandoned estate to keep her family clothed and fed, Marietta soon discovers that the estate is not so deserted as she thought. Mystery, intrigue, and adventure.

Logic of the Heart. *St. Martin's Press, 1990.* When the hero and heroine claim the same cottage, the scene is set for delightful action. Inheritances, difficult relatives, and crooks add to the mix.

Tales of the Jewelled Men series

Time's Fool. *St. Martin's Press, 1990.*

Had We Never Loved. *St. Martin's Press, 1991.*

Ask Me No Questions. *St. Martin's Press, 1993.*

The Mandarin of Mayfair. *St. Martin's Press, 1995.*

Walsh, Sheila

Walsh writes traditional Regencies in the manner of Georgette Heyer, featuring self-reliant, resilient heroines and cynical heroes who evolve into caring, loving men.

The Golden Songbird. *New American Library, 1975.* The author's first and one of her best.

The Rose Domino. *New American Library, 1981.*

A Highly Respectable Marriage. *New American Library, 1983.*

The Incorrigible Rake. *New American Library, 1984.*

The Arrogant Lord Alistair. *Signet, 1990.*

The Perfect Bride. *Signet, 1994.*

Westhaven, Margaret (Peggy M. Hansen)

The Willful Wife. *Walker, 1986.*

Miss Dalrymple's Virtue. *Harlequin, 1988.*

Widow's Folly. *Zebra, 1990.*

Country Dance. *Signet, 1991.* Considered unacceptable because of her past, Marianne ends up capturing the attentions of a sophisticated and eligible bachelor. Country setting.

Four in Hand. *Signet, 1993.* While trying to find husbands for her teenaged daughters, Lady Jane Averham attracts the attention of a highly eligible bachelor who is much younger than she. New twist on an old plot.

Yuletide Match. *Signet, 1993.*

Chapter 9

Alternative Reality Romance

DEFINITION

One of the newest—or at least most recently recognized—of the romance subgenres, Alternative Reality, is also one of the most diverse. Actually, it is not a true subgenre at all but, rather, a collection of separate mini-subgenres linked by the common thread of fantasy or "unreality." Including everything from darkly sensual vampire tales to humorous stories of time-traveling ghosts, these romances fall roughly into four groups—Fantasy, Futuristic, Paranormal, and Time Travel. While they might be differently labeled by the publisher or broken down even further, these categories reflect the current arrangement of the subgenre and are probably sufficiently specific for most purposes.

Just as the Romantic Mystery subgenre bears a strong relationship to the larger Mystery/Suspense genre, the types included under the Alternative Reality umbrella also have direct counterparts in genres outside Romance. Compare, for example, Futuristics with Science Fiction, Romance Fantasy with Fantasy, and the Paranormal with Horror. The similarities are obvious. The element that distinguishes them, however, is the same as that which separates Romantic Mysteries from the Mystery/Suspense genre—focus. In all the Alternative Reality types, the primary focus of the story is the developing love relationship between the two main characters. In the other genres, even though there may be a strong romantic relationship, the main emphasis is on other elements of the plot. However, straightforward though this distinction sounds, in practice it is often not easy to apply. Many writers hover between types, and with the recent trend toward genreblending (the migration of elements from one genre into another, resulting in stories with characteristics of both), the lines between the genres are becoming increasingly blurred and less well defined, making it more and more difficult to decide what, exactly, the story's basic type is.

However disconcerting this genre blurring may be for those who like to have titles categorized and neatly arranged, it is not necessarily bad, and it may not be so much of a problem for readers as we think. Many readers read cross genre lines, for example, enjoying both Science Fiction and Futuristics. For them, this problem of categorization is a nonissue. In fact, some may even appreciate the closer links between genres. In other cases, it can result in readers' exposure to genres or writers they might never have tried otherwise.

APPEAL

The essential appeal of the Alternative Reality Romance is to our imagination and inborn sense of wonder. As children most of us were fascinated by stories of fairies, elves, dragons, and other tales of myth and magic. As we grew older, ghosts, witches, vampires, and creatures both macabre and gruesome joined the list. By the time we had reached our teens, stories of aliens, space travel, interplanetary exploration, and intergalactic wars had caught our interest and fired our imaginations. And although we grew up and became more practical and realistic, most of us are still fascinated with the magical, the mystical, the supernatural, and the futuristic. It is to this basic interest that both the Fantastic Fiction genres and the Alternative Reality Romance directly appeal. But the Alternative Reality Romance, much like the Romantic Mystery, provides something its counterpart Fantastic Fiction genres generally do not—a satisfactory love story. It is this double appeal that many romance readers find so attractive.

ADVISING THE READER

General readers' advisory information is provided in chapter 3; however, there are several points to keep in mind for this particular subgenre.

- Many readers of Futuristics also read Science Fiction. A fan of Justine Davis's Futuristics might also enjoy books by Lois McMaster Bujold, and Anne McCaffrey is often popular with both groups.

- Readers often enjoy both Fantasy and Romantic Fantasy and would welcome recommendations of either type. Some writers have produced Science Fiction works with such a fantasy feel (e.g., Anne McCaffrey's Dragonriders of Pern series) or Historicals that are so mystical, even magical, that they can easily be recommended to Fantasy readers.

- Readers who enjoy some of the darker Paranormals may also enjoy Horror, Mysteries with a psychic/paranormal twist, or even a Gothic. Those who like "angel" books may also enjoy Inspirationals or some light Fantasy.

- Time travels have much in common with Historicals, and readers who enjoy Time Travels may also like reading straight Historicals set during a favorite time period. Regency readers may also enjoy Regency time travels (e.g., Joan Overfield's *The Door Ajar* and *Time's Tapestry*), and readers who enjoy Scottish settings might appreciate Diana Gabaldon's time travel series or Arnette Lamb's Historicals.

- Because of the complexity and diversity of this particular subgenre, it is important to determine exactly what the reader is looking for. Length, pacing, style, tone, and sensuality levels vary widely within each group. Does the reader prefer light, humorous fantasy (e.g., Jill Barnett), fast-paced Futuristics (e.g., Jayne Castle), emotionally involving werewolf stories (e.g., Susan Krinard), or magical fairy tales (e.g., Maggie Shayne)? These books are not the same and appeal to readers for different reasons.

- For the reader who is completely new to the subgenre, recommend standard works by major authors.

- And finally, if you are unfamiliar with the Alternative Reality Romance subgenre, you might find helpful a guide such as *Enchanted Journeys Beyond the Imagination: An Annotated Bibliography of Fantasy, Futuristic, Supernatural, and Time Travel Romances.* Volumes I and II Combined, (Beavercreek, OH: Blue Diamond Publications, 1996), Volume III (Beavercreek, OH: Blue Diamond Publications, 1997) by Susan W. Bontley and Carol J. Sheridan.

BRIEF HISTORY

Although Alternative Reality is a relatively recent addition to the Romance genre, the broader fiction types from which it evolved have roots that reach far into the past. The seeds of both science fiction and fantasy were present in the myths and legends of the earliest peoples as they wove stories to explain both the world around them and universe beyond. The Middle Eastern and Classical worlds added to the traditions with tales both earthly and divine, and they even produced a second-century Greek satire that included an imaginary voyage to the moon.[1]

The Scandinavian and Germanic mythologies added a somewhat darker influence to the fantasy tradition, and the folktales, heroic epics, legends, and Christian fantasies (e.g., Dante's *Divine Comedy)* of the Middle Ages all made contributions. Through the centuries, stories of things unreal appeared from time to time, including David Russen's *Iter Lunare: or, A Voyage to the Moon* (1703) and Jonathan Swift's still popular *Gulliver's Travels* (1726). In the mid-eighteenth century, Horace Walpole wrote his classic Gothic, *The Castle of Otranto* (1764), a story whose influence is still felt within the various fantasy, horror, and paranormal genres.

Scholars are reluctant to pinpoint the exact beginnings of the fantasy genre or to name the first fantasy novel, although *The Faerie Queene* (1590-1596) by Edmund Spenser is usually considered the earliest fantasy written in English.[2] There also seems to be general agreement that Mary Shelley's *Frankenstein: or, The Modern Prometheus* (1818) was probably the first Science Fiction novel and was certainly "the prototypical work of science fiction,"[3] replacing the supernatural with the scientific and establishing the early parameters of the genre.

The latter half of the eighteenth century saw the beginnings of the Industrial Revolution, and with it, an increased interest in science and technology. By the middle of the nineteenth century, the Industrial Age was in full swing, and the overall optimism of the period, largely based on the potential of the new technologies and the limitless possibilities of the future, was beginning to be reflected in the literature. Many writers, including Nathaniel Hawthorne, Edgar Allan Poe, and Mark Twain, tried their hand at fiction incorporating these new themes; but it was Jules Verne, with his inventive adventures (e.g., *From the Earth to the Moon* 1865 and *Twenty Thousand Leagues Under the Sea* 1870) who was the genre's first major popular success and, guaranteed its survival.[4]

Although the new scientific fiction was attracting much attention, the fantasy and Gothic threads that would also eventually become part of Alternative Reality continued to appear, including the fairy tales and fantasies of George MacDonald (e.g., *Phantastes* 1858, *The Princess and the Goblin* 1872); and *Alice's Adventures in Wonderland* (1865) by Lewis Carroll; the interesting early time travel by Mark Twain, *A Connecticut Yankee in King Arthur's Court* (1889); and the various Gothickly-tinged stories of Poe (e.g., "The Fall of the House of Usher"). Of particular note is Robert Louis Stevenson's short story, "The Strange Case of Dr. Jekyll and Mr. Hyde" (1886), which contains a fair amount of the fantastic and also has links to the modern werewolf stories.

1895 was an especially symbolic year because in that year two classic, but very different, stories with definite implications for the Alternative Reality Romance were published: Bram Stoker's *Dracula* and H. G. Wells's *The Time Machine*. And as anyone reading the genre today knows, vampire and time-travel romances are two of the more popular types.

The fantastic fiction genres continued into the twentieth century with the rising popularity of series books. The Oz stories (1900–1920) of L. Frank Baum and the fantastic adventure series (including Tarzan—beginning with *Tarzan of the Apes* in 1914—and the various space series) of Edgar Rice Burroughs were particularly popular. The publication of the pulp magazine *Amazing Stories* in 1926 precipitated the rapid expansion of the Science Fiction magazine market during the next decade and set the stage for the golden age of the genre that lasted roughly from 1938 to 1950.

Although much of the attention was on Science Fiction, Fantasy was still being written, and it was during this time that theologian C. S. Lewis produced his classic space trilogy of good, evil, and redemption (*Out of the Silent Planet* 1938, *Perelandra* 1938, *That Hideous Strength* 1945) that is still read and studied. The 1950s produced several more fantasy classics, including C. S. Lewis's *The Chronicles of Narnia* (1950-1956), J. R. R. Tolkien's *The Lord of the Rings* (1954-1955), and T. H. White's *The Once and Future King* (1958). Tolkien's works are especially important because, as Ann Swinfen observes, "Tolkien made fantasy 'respectable.' "[5]

While some of these early antecedents of the Alternative Reality Romance contain love interests, few would qualify as romances by today's standards. Nevertheless, changes were happening in these genres that eventually would impact the Romance and encourage the development of the various subgenres of the Alternative Reality Romance. One of the most important changes was the growing presence of women writers. In their hands, these traditionally male-dominated stories began to develop a "feminine perspective on plot, character, theme, structure, and imagery."[6] They featured female protagonists who were both strong and aggressive, yet caring and sensitive; plots that valued relationships and feelings over conquest and dominance; and a point of view that was feminine as opposed to masculine. A few writers, such as Anne McCaffrey, wrote stories such as *Restorée* (1967) and The Dragonriders of Pern series (*Dragonflight* 1968, *Dragonquest* 1970, and *The White Dragon* 1978) with enough sensual appeal to attract both science fiction and romance readers today. Another favorite work of romance readers is *Beauty* (1978), a lyrical retelling of

Beauty and the Beast by Robin McKinley. Also worth reading, but for totally different reasons, is William Goldman's charming spoof *The Princess Bride* (1973). Also of note is historical romance writer Anya Seton's *Green Darkness* (1972), which includes elements of reincarnation. The Gothic Romances peaked in popularity during the 1960s, providing the suspense and horror elements that have become standard in darker varieties of today's Paranormals.

One of the earliest of the true Alternative Reality romances is *Journey to Yesterday* (1979), a time travel by veteran romance writer June Lund Shiplett. She followed it with *Return to Yesterday* (1983), and gradually a few more romance writers began to experiment with their own versions of the genre (e.g., Jayne Ann Krentz with *Sweet Starfire* 1986 and *Crystal Flame* 1986, Maura Seger with *Golden Chimera* 1985 and other "Atlantis" books, Lori Copeland with *Out of This World* 1986, and Constance O'Day-Flannery with *Timeswept Lovers* 1987). By the end of the decade other writers had joined in, including veterans such as Jude Deveraux (*Wishes* 1989 and *A Knight in Shining Armor* 1989), Johanna Lindsey (*Warrior's Woman* 1989), and Rebecca Brandewyne (*Passion Moon Rising* 1988). Interest skyrocketed, and with the publication of Diana Gabaldon's *The Outlander* (first of her now classic time travel series) in 1991 and the official recognition of the subgenre in 1992 when the Romance Writers of America added a separate "Futuristic/Fantasy/Paranormal" category to its annual Rita and Golden Heart Awards, the Alternative Reality Romance was firmly established. The years that followed were big ones for the subgenre with several publishers establishing dedicated lines (e.g., Leisure LoveSpell, Topaz Dreamspun, Silhouette Shadows) and unreal elements appearing regularly in romances of all types. Vampires, angels, time-traveling heroes and heroines, ghosts, fairies, werewolves, space travelers, and other fantastic characters populated an ever-growing variety of romances that included everything from New Age Paranormals, angel-filled Fantasies, and fast-paced Time Travels to the darker stories of the supernatural, mystical tales of magic and legend, and innovative Futuristic romantic adventures. The subgenre continued to be popular through the mid-1990s, and despite various fluctuations within the individual categories and the inevitable leveling out of interest, it still commands a fair amount of interest.

The Alternative Reality Romance is a fragmented subgenre, and the subtypes listed below are discretely described. As mentioned earlier, elements from one type often are found in another, resulting in stories that are not easily categorized. The same is true of some of the authors listed below. For example, Susan Krinard has written both Paranormals and Futuristics, Maggie Shayne has written both Fantasies and Paranormals, and Flora M. Speer has written both Futuristics and Time Travels. In addition, many of the authors included also regularly write in other Romance subgenres or even in some of the broader fantastic fiction genres. Works included below are merely examples of the many romances available within these subtypes.

FANTASY

Drawing heavily from myth, legend, and fairy tales, this category corresponds roughly to the larger Fantasy subgenre; however, as with all Romance types, the love story is the primary focus, not the fulfillment of a quest, the defeat of dark forces, battles, or any of the other emphases of the traditional fantasy novel. Magic plays a big part in these romances, and they are highly mystical and lyrically written. All manner of characters people these stories, and fairies, elves, leprechauns, dragons, unicorns, and other delightful creatures are commonplace. Fantasies can be both contemporary and historical, with Historical Fantasies being the more common by far. Depending upon how the magic is treated, Historicals incorporating magical elements can fall within this type.

Selected Fantasy Bibliography

Barnett, Jill
(See also Period Romance bibliography.)

Imagine. *Pocket Books, 1995.* An escaped convict, an attorney, and three children survive on a desert island—with the help of a delightful genii.

Brandewyne, Rebecca
These stories have a fantasy quality even though they are set in the future.

The Chronicles of Tintagel
Passion Moon Rising. *Pocket Books, 1988.*

Beyond the Starlit Frost. *Pocket Books, 1991.* Iskander and Rhiannon join forces in a quest to destroy the forces of Darkness and find love in the process. Continues *Passion Moon Rising.*

Bryan, Jessica
Across a Wine Dark Sea. *Bantam Books, 1991.* Abducted by the King of Atlantis, Amazon warrior Thalassa ends up falling in love with her captor in this story that weaves myth and history with romance.

Dawn on a Jade Sea. *Bantam Books, 1992.* A merwoman and a Buddhist healer become involved in a magical, unusual story of revenge set in ninth-century China.

Beneath a Sapphire Sea. *Bantam Books, 1993.* An ancient scroll proves to be key to the merpeople's fight against evil.

Davis, Kathryn Lynn
Too Deep for Tears. *Pocket Books, 1988.*

Child of Awe. *Pocket Books, 1990.* A heroine with "the sight."

All That We Hold Dear. *Pocket Books, 1995.* When fey, intuitive Eva Crawford learns of her adoption on her 18th birthday, she leaves the remote Scottish island where she was raised and heads to the mainland in search of her heritage. A mystical sequel to *Too Deep for Tears.*

Dawson, Saranne
The Enchanted Land. *Leisure, 1992.* A professor of folklore visits an enchanted valley she has been studying and learns things about herself she had never known. A magical fairy tale.

Lindsey, Betina

Swan Maidens of Myr trilogy

Swan Bride. *Pocket Books, 1990.* Compelled to leave the magical kingdom of Myr to find a human mate, Moira finds forbidden love.

Swan Witch. *Pocket Books, 1993.*

Swan Star. *Pocket Books, 1994.* When a human warrior steals Arrah's swan skin, she becomes his captive—and eventually he becomes hers. Final volume of the trilogy.

Morgan, Kathleen

Although they have a fantasy feel, several of Morgan's books are within the Futuristic category.

Demon Prince. *Love Spell, 1994.*

A Certain Magic. *St. Martin's Press, 1995.* A beautiful warrior joins forces with a dragon to convince a conflicted, exiled sorcerer to leave his island and return to the real world. Sequel to *Fire Queen.* St. Martin's Press, 1994.

Paisley, Rebecca

Paisley writes funny, fast-paced Historicals. *(See also Period Romance and Western Romance bibliographies.)*

A Basket of Wishes. *Dell, 1995.* A fairy princess has to seduce and become pregnant by a mortal prince within three months in this lively, funny, magical tale.

Seger, Maura

Atlantis trilogy

Silver Zephyr. *Silhouette, 1984.*

Golden Chimera. *Silhouette, 1985.*

Seagate. *Silhouette, 1987.*

Veil of Secrets. *Topaz, 1996.* Arthurian legends, clerical murders, and healing and witchcraft make this an intriguing, magical romance.

Shayne, Maggie

Fairytale. *Avon Books, 1996.* Half-fairy twins, separated at birth and sent from Faery into the mortal world for safety, must find each other to fulfill their destiny.

Forever Enchanted. *Avon Books, 1997.* A princess returns to Faery to save her kingdom in this sequel to *Fairytale.*

FUTURISTIC ROMANCE

This category is often considered romantic science fiction. The settings are typically in the future and often involve other planets, space travel, and alien cultures. Futuristics differ from Fantasies in much the same way as the Science Fiction and Fantasy genres differ from each other; i.e., Science Fiction extrapolates from what is logically possible in the future, whereas Fantasy allows for the creation of entire imaginary environments with no restrictions as long as the rules established by the writer are not violated. As with all romance types, the developing romantic relationship between the protagonists is the primary focus of the plot.

Selected Futuristic Romance Bibliography

Avery, Anne

A Distant Star. *Love Spell, 1993.*

All's Fair. *Love Spell, 1994.* Former lovers are forced to work together to reach their separate goals.

Far Star. *Love Spell, 1995.* Resourceful Dayra Smith and a bitter drifter join forces against her ruthless stepfather and find a new purpose—and a new love—on the rugged Far Star Colony world.

Hidden Heart. *Love Spell, 1996.* Foppish disguise and a forced "bonding" create a lively, romantic story.

Campbell, Marilyn

Innerworld Affairs series

Pyramid of Dreams. *Love Spell, 1992.*

Topaz Dreams. *Love Spell, 1992.*

Stardust Dreams. *Topaz, 1994.* An actress and a space explorer find love aboard a spaceship on a mission to save the universe. Touched with humor.

Stolen Dreams. *Topaz, 1994.* Shara Locke illegally travels back in time to try to prevent the birth of a man who will destroy the present. Characters from Classical mythology abound.

Worlds Apart. *Topaz, 1994.*

Castle, Jayne (Jayne Ann Krentz)

These Futuristic Romantic Suspense stories are set on the imaginary planet of St. Helens, a cutoff Earth colony that has developed into a unique, synergistic world populated with psychically talented people. Castle's stories are funny, sexy, and lively.

Amaryllis. *Pocket Books, 1996.* When full-scale "prism" (psychically talented) Amaryllis Lark links minds with Lucas Trent to help him focus his psychic talent, their intensely sensual reaction startles them both—and leads them into a passionate, forbidden relationship. Family feuds and a psychic vampire add to the mix.

Zinnia. *Pocket Books, 1997.* Another pair of highly talented but "psychically unsuited" people find each other in the fast-paced, sensual story of mystery and murder that features a hero who has everything but the respectability he craves and a defiant heroine who flaunts her "Scarlet Lady" reputation.

Orchid. *Pocket Books, 1998.*

Casto, Jackie

Dreams of Destiny. *Leisure, 1990.* A gifted exile is rescued by a spaceship captain who is both suspicious of and attracted to her.

Daughter of Destiny. *Leisure, 1990.* Despite mutual suspicions, telepath Esme and starship captain Raul find love as they work together to fulfill an ancient prophecy and fight an ultimate evil. Sequel to *Dreams of Destiny.*

Davis, Justine

Both of these stories make use of the captor/captive plot pattern.

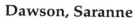 **Lord of the Storm.** *Topaz, 1994.* Spaceship Captain Shaylah Graymist and the Triotian leader, Wolf, return to his home planet to fight for freedom. A passionate, fast-paced romance with a compelling wounded hero.

The Skypirate. *Topaz, 1995.* Dax is determined to avenge the Coalition's destruction of his home planet, but when he takes the slave Califa as a captive, he has no idea that she is a former officer of the Coalition.

Dawson, Saranne

Most of Dawson's works are set in futuristic worlds; however, they have a magical, mystical, fantasy-like feel.

From the Mist. *Love Spell, 1991.* Climactic changes on Volas compel the men and women to forsake their traditional separate lifestyles and learn to live together.

Heart of the Wolf. *Love Spell, 1993.* A race of werewolves is a princess's only hope for saving her kingdom.

Awakenings. *Love Spell, 1994.* A fledgling sorceress returns to her homeland and finds herself being romantically pursued by Lord Justan, who needs her powers to save his kingdom.

Greenfire. *Love Spell, 1994.* In a sexually segregated culture, the heroine must mate and bear a child.

On Wings of Love. *Love Spell, 1994.* Vows of celibacy and passion conflict in this supernatural futuristic romance.

Glass, Amanda (Jayne Ann Krentz)

Shield's Lady. *Popular Library, 1989.* A stolen gem cutter, an accidental marriage, and a futuristic setting combine in this fast-paced romance with elements that foreshadow Krentz's later St. Helens Trilogy, written under her Jayne Castle pseudonym.

Joy, Dara

Knight of a Trillion Stars. *Love Spell, 1995.* A magician, a magical necklace, and a modern sci-fi writer travel through time and space to save his world from destruction.

Krentz, Jayne Ann

Originally published by Krentz under her Jayne Castle pseudonym, these two Futuristics were re-released under the Krentz byline in 1994.

Sweet Starfire. *Popular Library, 1986.* Galaxy-sweeping adventure.

Crystal Flame. *Popular Library, 1986.* Vengeance-driven heroine finds herself romantically drawn to a warrior in her enemy's employ.

Krinard, Susan

Star-Crossed. *Bantam Books, 1995.* Inexplicably drawn to see prisoner Rook Galloway, the man she blames for her brother's death, Lady Ariane ends up Rook's captive and eventually his partner and soulmate as they fight to set their people free.

Lindsey, Johanna

Warrior's Woman. *Avon Books, 1989.* An independent heroine is the prisoner of an insensitive hero in this captor-in-love-with-captor futuristic romance.

Keeper of the Heart. *Avon Books, 1993.* An independent heroine decides to choose her own husband and marries a warrior she both wants and fears. Pursuit, passion, and bondage are part of this sequel to *Warrior's Woman.*

Morgan, Kathleen

Morgan's Futuristics often include telepathy and other supernatural powers, giving them a fantasy-like quality.

The Knowing Crystal Trilogy

Part of the ongoing Imperium series, these three books focus on a powerful crystal and the people who use or would abuse its powers.

The Knowing Crystal. *Love Spell, 1991.* Book 2 in Imperium series.

Heart's Lair. *Love Spell, 1991.* Book 3 in Imperium series.

The Crystal Fire. *Love Spell, 1992.* Book 4 in Imperium series.

Volan series

Also part of the Imperium series.

Firestar. *Love Spell, 1993.* Book 5 in Imperium series.

Firestorm. *Love Spell, 1995.* Book 6 in Imperium series.

Heart's Surrender. *Love Spell, 1994.* First book in the Imperium series with links to *Heart's Lair* and *The Cat People.*

Robb, J. D. (Nora Roberts)

These fast-paced romantic detective stories are set in the twenty-first century and depict the adventures of police detective Eve Dallas and business tycoon Roarke.

Naked in Death. *Berkley, 1995.*

Glory in Death. *Berkley, 1995.*

Immortal in Death. *Berkley, 1996.*

Rapture in Death. *Berkley, 1996.*

Ceremony in Death. *Berkley, 1997.*

Vengeance in Death. *Berkley, 1997.*

Rock, Pam (Barbara Andrews and Pam Andrews Hanson)

Rock also writes as Jennifer Drew.

Moon of Desire. *Love Spell, 1993.*

Love's Changing Moon. *Love Spell, 1994.*

A World Away. *Love Spell, 1995.* Forbidden love blossoms between the protagonists when they are stranded on a remote planet.

Star Searcher. *Love Spell, 1996.* An antiquities expert is tricked into locating an important gem and is accused of murder.

Roenbuck, Patricia

Telepaths, both evil and benign, play important roles in these fast-paced, passionate stories that sweep their characters into interplanetary adventures.

Golden Temptress. *Love Spell, 1991.*

Golden Conquest. *Love Spell, 1992.* Follows *Golden Temptress.*

Shayne, Maggie

Out of This World Marriage. *Silhouette, 1995.* An alien from a matriarchal culture and an earthly doctor find love in this romance with a Gothic touch.

Speer, Flora M.

Dulan's Planet series

This futuristic series also includes supernatural (psychic and telepathic) elements.

Venus Rising. *Love Spell, 1989.*

Destiny's Lovers. *Love Spell, 1990.*

No Other Love. *Love Spell, 1993.* Protagonists travel back in time to save the ancient city on Dulan's Planet that they are currently excavating.

Lady Lure. *Love Spell, 1996.*

PARANORMAL ROMANCE

This category is the most eclectic of the Alternative Reality Romance subgenre, basically incorporating everything not otherwise defined. Almost anything supernatural or unexplained by natural causes is included here, and vampires, angels, psychics, ghosts, werewolves, witches, spirits, reincarnated people, and other similar characters are all at home within this grouping. Settings can be either historical or contemporary, and as with all romances, the love story drives the plot. Occasionally, aspects of the Paranormal blend with another subtype, resulting in stories, for example, about time-traveling witches or futuristic psychics.

Selected Paranormal Bibliography

Barnett, Jill

Barnett's stories are light, lively, and funny.

Bewitching. *Pocket Books, 1993.*

Dreaming. *Pocket Books, 1994.* Sequel to *Bewitching.*

Becnel, Rexanne

Where Magic Dwells. *Dell, 1994.* A twelfth-century Welsh healer finds love with an English knight despite long-held prejudices and suspicions.

Bennett, Laura Gilmour

By All That's Sacred. *Avon Books, 1991.* Published also as *A Wheel of Stars* by Viking, 1989. An heirloom chalice links present-day protagonists with the Spanish Inquisition and their tragic, romantic counterparts.

Brandon, Michelle

Touch of Heaven. *Berkley, 1992*. An interfering spirit brings a rancher and a banker together in a funny, charming, Texas-set romance.

Heaven on Earth. *Berkley, 1993*. Guardian angels have their hands full trying both to protect and unite a feminist and a fugitive nobleman stranded together on a Florida island.

Chittendon, Margaret

Forever Love. *Worldwide, 1988*.

This Time Forever. *Harlequin, 1990*.

When the Spirit Is Willing. *Harlequin, 1993*.

Claybourne, Casey

A Ghost of a Chance. *Jove, 1996*. A delightfully wicked ghost must atone for her mischief by making sure her daughter and son-in-law are happily in love—even though she had set their relationship up for failure before she died.

A Spirited Seduction. *Jove, 1997*. A ghostly madam helps a naive debutante secure the man of her dreams.

Comstock, Mary Chase

(See also Regency bibliography.)

A Sparkling Affair. *Zebra, 1993*. Regency hero and heroine find happiness with a little meddling from a ghostly ancestor.

A Midsummer's Magic. *Zebra, 1994*. Hyppolyta (Countess of Trevalyn, Mistress of Rookeshaven, and witch) is determined to continue her magical studies. Light, funny, and romantic.

Cresswell, Jasmine

To Catch the Wind. *Topaz, 1993*. A modern-day skeptic finds herself reincarnated as Catherine, wife of Charles II, but still linked to her present lover. Intrigue and passion rule.

Prince of the Night. *Topaz, 1995*. In this elegantly dark Gothic vampire romance, Cordelia arrives at her newly inherited remote Italian estate only to find it already inhabited by the enigmatic Count of Albion.

Davis, Justine

Davis also writes Futuristics and Contemporary Series Romances and has written Historicals as Justine Dare. The two stories below feature guardian angels.

R **Angel for Hire.** *Silhouette, 1991*. This contemporary romance won the first Rita Award (1992) in the Futuristic/Fantasy/Paranormal category.

Errant Angel. *Silhouette, 1995*.

Deveraux, Jude

Deveraux also writes Historicals and books with time travel elements.

Wishes. *Pocket Books, 1989*. A bit of heavenly meddling on the part of a reluctant spirit brings a sweet, poorly used young woman happiness in this romance with a Cinderella theme.

An Angel for Emily. *Pocket Books, 1998*. When Emily hits her guardian angel with her car, knocking him out and leaving him with no memory, she does what any helpful, small-town librarian would do—she takes him home with her.

Erskine, Barbara

Erskine's Gothic-like books lean toward the mainstream and often make use of reincarnation themes and other paranormal elements through which the past affects and often parallels the future. *(See also Gothic Romance bibliography.)*

Lady of Hay. *Dell, 1988.* A twelfth-century romance impacts the present in this story of dual lovers' triangles.

Kingdom of Shadows. *Dell, 1988.* A woman fights against her husband's plot to convince everyone she is mad in this atypical romance featuring heavy dollops of Scottish history, time travel/reincarnation elements, and a Gothic atmosphere.

Midnight Is a Lonely Place. *Signet, 1995.* While recovering from a romantic breakup, the protagonist is drawn into a doomed relationship from the past.

Freethy, Barbara

Freethy writes warm, compelling contemporary romances with a dash of the paranormal. She also has written for Silhouette as Kristina Logan.

Daniel's Gift. *Avon Books, 1996.* A boy hovering between life and death and his curmudgeonly guardian angel bring his long-estranged parents together. A Rita Award winner.

Ryan's Return. *Avon Books, 1996.* Teenaged sweethearts are reunited with a little ghostly help.

Ask Mariah. *Avon Books, 1997.* A "fortune teller in a crystal ball" sets six-year-old twins on a path that leads them to a new mother and changes the lives of two families in the process.

One True Love. *Avon Books, 1998.* Nick and Lisa must come to terms with the death of their child years earlier before they can find love in the present. Mystical elements.

Gordon, Deborah

Runaway Trilogy

Magic, time travel, and supernatural elements are liberally scattered through this trilogy.

Runaway Bride. *Avon Books, 1994.*

Runaway Time. *Avon Books, 1995.*

Runaway Magic. *Avon Books, 1996.*

Graham, Heather

Serena's Magic. *Dell, 1994.* Magical doings in modern-day Salem have roots in the past.

Every Time I Love You. *Dell, 1998.* Past lives once again influence the future in this story of reincarnation and betrayal.

Haley, Wendy

Danilov Chronicles

Dark vampire tales.

This Dark Paradise. *Diamond, 1994.*

These Fallen Angels. *Diamond, 1995.*

Hannah, Kristin

Many of Hannah's books have a touch of the mystical or paranormal about them.

The Enchantment. *Fawcett, 1992.* A journey to a magical kingdom brings changes to the protagonists in unexpected ways.

Once in Every Life. *Fawcett, 1993.* A loving, optimistic heroine is reincarnated as a selfish, lazy frontier wife and mother, with wonderfully warm and romantic results.

Waiting for the Moon. *Fawcett, 1995.* A telepathic doctor and a brain-damaged woman find love along the isolated Maine Coast.

Home Again. *Fawcett, 1996.* A doctor and an actor renew their life together with a little help from a ghostly priest, the actor's brother and true hero of this story, with strong mainstream appeal.

Harbaugh, Karen

The Vampire Viscount. *Signet, 1995.* A hero who is a vampire adds an interesting twist to this Regency Romance.

Cupid Trilogy

Cupid's Mistake. *Signet, 1996.* Eros has his hands full as he tries to bring a recalcitrant pair of lovers together in this light Regency Romance.

Cupid's Darts. *Signet, 1998.* A wayward arrow causes a hero to become more obsessed with the portrait of the heroine than with the lady herself.

Cupid's Kiss. *Signet, 1998.* Cupid's love life is the subject of this final volume of the series.

Heath, Sandra

(See also Regency and Time Travel Romance bibliographies.)

The Halloween Husband. *Signet, 1994.* The late Lady Margaret sets about getting her descendants' financial affairs back in order by arranging for the marriage of the innocent Rowena and a worldly lord.

Lucy's Christmas Angel. *Signet, 1995.* A young would-be angel must assure her cousin's happiness and safety before she can join the heavenly ranks.

Halloween Magic. *Signet, 1996.* A Tudor witch who was burned at the stake returns 200 years later to avenge her death on the descendants of the men who had her killed. This story is darker and more intense than some of Heath's Regencies.

Herter, Lori

Vampire series

These dark and sensual romances focus on the romantic relationships of vampire David de Morrissey and mortal Veronica Ames, and vampire Darienne Victoire and mortal Matthew McDowell.

Obsession. *Berkley, 1991.*

Possession. *Berkley, 1992.*

Confession. *Berkley, 1992.*

Eternity. *Berkley, 1993.*

Hocker, Karla

A Deceitful Heart. *Zebra, 1993.* A ghost adds to the complications in this romantic story that involves a debutante, a lawyer, and an inheritance, set in the glitter and charm of the English Regency period.

Holiday, Nikki

Funny, wacky stories that feature two Hollywood movie makers in the role of matchmaker with a little help from "on high."

Heaven Comes Home. *Avon Books, 1996.* A pair of Hollywood spirits ensure the romance of a spoiled film star and a small-town Arkansas pastor in this lively story with funny, sexy results.

Heaven Knows Best. *Avon Books, 1997.*

Heaven Loves a Hero. *Avon Books, 1997.*

Hooper, Kay

Hooper has written in several romance subgenres.

The Matchmaker. *Bantam Books, 1991.* First of a series in which a man with special powers (Fairy Godfather) brings love to various women. *The Matchmaker* sets the theme and introduces the main characters for the Once upon a Time books listed below.

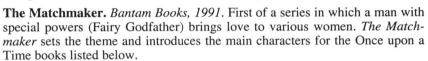

Once upon a Time: Golden Threads. *Bantam Loveswept, 1989.*

Once upon a Time: The Glass Shoe. *Bantam Loveswept, 1989.*

Once upon a Time: What Dreams May Come. *Bantam Loveswept, 1990.*

Once upon a Time: Through the Looking Glass. *Bantam Loveswept, 1990.*

Once upon a Time: The Lady and the Lion. *Bantam Loveswept, 1989.*

Once upon a Time: Star-Crossed Lovers. *Bantam Loveswept, 1991.*

The Wizard of Seattle. *Bantam Books, 1993.* Fledgling wizard Serena Smyth and master wizard Richard Merlin end up in Atlantis to save the present. Dark and unusual.

Howard, Linda

Dream Man. *Pocket Books, 1995.* A psychic and a police detective fall in love while bringing a killer to justice. Passionate and dark.

9

Son of the Morning. *Pocket Books, 1997.* Translator of ancient manuscripts is psychically linked to a warrior from the past.

Kells, Sabine

A Deeper Hunger. *Leisure, 1994.* This dark fantasy unites a vampire with a woman he is destined to love—but causes to die—time after time after time.

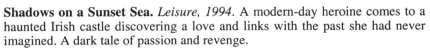

Shadows on a Sunset Sea. *Leisure, 1994.* A modern-day heroine comes to a haunted Irish castle discovering a love and links with the past she had never imagined. A dark tale of passion and revenge.

Kerstan, Lynn, and Alicia Rasley

Gwen's Christmas Ghost. *Zebra, 1995.* Faced with either eternal boredom or ensuring the happiness of his descendants, Valerian Caine reluctantly enters the world of the English Regency to set things right—and falls in love himself.

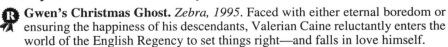

Krinard, Susan

Krinard's sensual werewolf and vampire stories provide a gentler and more lyrical interpretation of these legends than most.

Prince of Wolves. *Bantam Books, 1994.* When Joelle Randall goes to the Canadian Rockies to find the site where her parents' plane crashed 12 years earlier, she discovers answers to questions she had never even asked and finds love with a most unusual hero.

Prince of Dreams. *Bantam Books, 1995.* A psychologist and a vampire (of sorts) search for the same killer and find an attraction that could prove as dangerous as it is passionate.

Prince of Shadows. *Bantam Books, 1996.* A wolf researcher heads to the Minnesota woods for psychological healing and falls in love with a werewolf who needs healing of his own. Linked to *Prince of Wolves*.

Body and Soul. *Bantam Books, 1998.*

Kurland, Lynn

Stardust of Yesterday. *Jove, 1996.* A 700-year-old ghost meets his match in the independent, competent businesswoman who has inherited his castle in this lively, humorous story.

Lee, Rachel

Imminent Thunder. *Silhouette, 1993.* A nurse and a psychic find love in a remote, malignant, and Gothic setting.

Thunder Mountain. *Silhouette, 1994.* A wildlife biologist and a Native American shaman work together to protect a sacred, powerful mountain and its wolves from destruction.

Lowell, Elizabeth

A lyrical, mystical, highly sensual twelfth-century trilogy filled with ancient curses and Druid magic. (Note: These are quite different in overall tone and style from some of Lowell's other period romances, especially those set in the American West.)

Untamed. *Avon Books, 1993.*

Forbidden. *Avon Books, 1993.*

Enchanted. *Avon Books, 1994.*

Macomber, Debbie

These three Christmas fantasies feature the wacky doings of heavenly prayer ambassadors Shirley, Goodness, and Mercy as they try to answer the prayers of a diverse group of people.

A Season of Angels. *HarperPaperbacks, 1993.*

The Trouble with Angels. *HarperPaperbacks, 1994.*

Touched by Angels. *HarperPaperbacks, 1995.*

Miller, Linda Lael

Vampire series

Forever and the Night. *Berkley, 1993.*

For All Eternity. *Berkley, 1994.*

Time Without End. *Berkley, 1995.*

Tonight and Always. *Berkley, 1996.*

Morgan, Kathleen

Child of the Mist. *Leisure, 1993*. A witch and a laird marry to ensure peace and end up falling in love.

Fire Queen. *St. Martin's Press, 1994*. When Lady Deidra joins Hawkwind's band, she intends to become a warrior, but when it becomes apparent that her true skill is as a healer and the wielder of the ancient power of fire, her life takes on a new dimension.

Enchant the Heavens. *Zebra, 1995*. A Celtic princess struggles between her duty to her people and her love for Marcus, the governing Roman officer. Mystical and full of Celtic lore.

Enchant the Dream. *Zebra, 1996*. Sequel to *Enchant the Heavens*.

Nicholas, Deborah

Night Vision. *Dell, 1993*. When a writer begins to dream real plots, her life takes a turn for the dangerous in this story that is essentially a romantic suspense with a strong psychic twist.

O'Day-Flannery, Constance

Once in a Lifetime. *Zebra, 1992*. The ghost of an old boyfriend helps Maureen evolve into a self-confident, assertive woman after her husband of 20 years leaves her.

Second Chance. *Zebra, 1992*. A strangely matched pair of guardian angels help a dress shop owner get her life back together in a heartwarming, magical story.

The Gift. *Zebra, 1994*. Ghostly sex queen lends the heroine a helping hand.

Parker, Laura

Rose Trilogy

Three mystical stories linked by Ireland, roses, and "the sight."

Rose of the Mists. *Warner Books, 1985*.

A Rose in Splendor. *Warner Books, 1986*.

The Secret Rose. *Warner Books, 1987*.

For Love's Sake Only. *Dell, 1991*. Regina is appalled when she and her mother are literally kidnapped by Maxwell Kingsblood and forced to visit him in his country estate. However, a lively pair of ghosts see to it that things take a much more romantic turn.

Moon Shadow. *Dell, 1992*. Julianna Kingsblood is plagued by the same pair of interfering, ghostly matchmakers that united her grandparents, with the same romantic results.

Richards, Emilie

Once More with Feeling. *Avon Books, 1966*. A freak car accident transports the spirit of a society matron into the body of a sexy, flamboyant TV show hostess, allowing her the chance to experience a new life and rethink the old.

Twice upon a Time. *Avon Books, 1997*. A flashy TV show hostess is given a second chance at life in this funny, off-beat story that links an ex-reporter with a pregnant would-be nun and ties up some loose ends from *Once More with Feeling*.

Rinehold, Connie

Forever and a Day. *Dell, 1996.* Based on Alfred Noyes's poem "The Highwayman," this romantic reincarnation story unites a ghostly highwayman with his long-lost love.

Roberson, Jennifer

Lady of the Forest. *Zebra, 1992.* A beautifully crafted story that revisits the Robin Hood legend with a bit of medieval romance and magic thrown in.

Sala, Sharon

Annie and the Outlaw. *Silhouette, 1994.* Outlaw/biker Gabriel Donner has almost completed his 150-year-long penance and is headed for Heaven. Then he encounters Annie, an inner city teacher, and he wonders if he really wants to go to his "great reward" after all. Poignant, unusual, and dark—but with flashes of humor.

Saxe, Coral Smith

Enchantment. *Love Spell, 1994.* Adam Hawthorne, gentleman and investigator, sets out to prove that Bryony is not a witch and falls in love with her. Magical.

Scotch, Cheri

Werewolf Trilogy

A dark and intricate trilogy of ancient curses and modern-day werewolves.

The Werewolf's Touch. *Diamond, 1993.*

The Werewolf's Kiss. *Diamond, 1992.*

The Werewolf's Sin. *Diamond, 1994.*

Seger, Maura

Perchance to Dream. *Avon Books, 1989.* The South wins the Civil War in this romantic fantasy.

Fortune's Tide. *Avon Books, 1990.* England wins the American Revolution in this romantic fantasy with a British Isles setting.

The Lady and the Laird. *Harlequin, 1992.* A Scottish castle, a difficult laird, and a resident ghost make life difficult—and eventually romantic—for a determined heiress.

Forevermore. *Harper, 1994.* Murders, mysteries, and ancient Druid stones in a Regency setting.

Shayne, Maggie

Wings in the Night series

A series of linked books featuring vampires.

Twilight Phantasies. *Silhouette, 1993.*

Twilight Memories. *Silhouette, 1994.*

Twilight Illusions. *Silhouette, 1994.*

"Beyond Twilight" (Novella in *Strangers in the Night*. Silhouette 1995.)

Born in Twilight. *Silhouette, 1997.*

Simpson, Patricia

Ghosts and mysticism play an important part in many of Simpson's paranormal romances.

A Whisper of Midnight. *HarperPaperbacks, 1991.* Reminiscent of *The Ghost and Mrs. Muir* with a modern twist.

The Legacy. *HarperPaperbacks, 1992.* Wine, family conflicts, and ghostly monks.

Raven in Amber. *HarperPaperbacks, 1993.* Death, ghosts, and Native American lore.

Mystic Moon. *HarperPaperbacks, 1996.* A bone marrow transplant has strange and mystical results.

Just Before Midnight. *HarperPaperbacks, 1997.* Sequel to *Mystic Moon.*

Small, Bertrice

A Moment in Time. *Ballantine Books, 1991.* Protagonists fight fate, relatives, and themselves to finally make their "timeless" love a reality.

Speer, Flora M.

Heartspell series

Hearts Magic. *Love Spell, 1997.*

The Magician's Lover. *Love Spell, 1998.*

Once and Forever. *Love Spell, 1998.*

Stockenberg, Antoinette

Emily's Ghost. *Dell, 1992.* A nineteenth-century ghost convinces a modern-day investigative reporter to help clear his name in this poignant Rita Award winner

Embers. *Dell, 1994.* An old tragedy, a Victorian dollhouse, and a ghost in search of justice are part of this romantic fantasy.

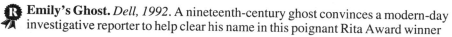

Time After Time. *Dell, 1995.* Family secrets, an old trunk, and a ghost draw a young businesswoman into an intriguing society mystery.

Beyond Midnight. *St. Martin's Press, 1996.* A persistent ghost who wants the best for her husband and daughter aids the heroine in solving a murder and avoiding her own.

Dream a Little Dream. *St. Martin's Press, 1997.* Ghosts.

Stuart, Anne

Stuart is noted for her high level of sensuality and ultra-dark heroes. Many of her stories could be categorized in the Gothic Romance subgenre. *(See also Gothic Romance bibliography.)*

Bewitching Hour. *Harlequin, 1986.* Psychics and love philters.

Special Gifts. *Silhouette, 1992.* A psychic reluctantly helps locate a missing woman.

Break the Night. *Silhouette, 1993.* The past interferes with the present in a series of murders along the California coast.

Falling Angel. *Harlequin, 1993.* An angel must redeem himself in this Rita Award winner.

Tracy, Marilyn

Memory's Lamp. *Silhouette, 1994.* A dying woman passes her memories on to the unsuspecting heroine, who then finds herself involved in a dangerous world of murder, magic, and the supernatural.

Sharing the Darkness. *Silhouette, 1994.*

Something Beautiful. *Silhouette, 1995.* An artist's paintings attract more than admiration as they become the focus of an ancient battle between good and evil.

Weyrich, Becky Lee

Weyrich's Historicals usually use paranormal or time travel elements and are often set in the South. Several of these works could also be classified within the Time Travel Romance subgenre.

Gypsy Moon. *Fawcett, 1986.* Curses, magic, and fast-paced action.

Forever, for Love. *Pocket Books, 1989.* The heroine is reincarnated as the wife of legendary pirate Jean Lafitte.

Whispers in Time. *Zebra, 1993.* 100-year-old body ends up reincarnated in nineteenth-century New Orleans.

Almost Heaven. *Zebra, 1995.* Angelic help results in a new life and love for the heroine.

Williamson, Penelope

Keeper of the Dream. *Dell, 1992.* A heroine with "the sight," a political marriage, and an unusual bard are part of this mystical twelfth-century romance.

TIME TRAVEL ROMANCE

One of the more popular of the Alternative Reality Subgenres, the Time Travel romance features protagonists who are transported from one time period to another. The exchange is usually between the present and some time in the past, but other options are acceptable. Conflicts usually result because of time-based cultural differences (e.g., when a modern heroine ends up in the male-dominated past) or the fact that the hero and heroine are from different time periods and must make sacrifices to stay together.

Selected Time Travel Bibliography

Baker, Madeline

Baker is known for her "Indian" Romances, some of which have a paranormal flavor.

A Whisper on the Wind. *Love Spell, 1991.* A 1950s Cheyenne Native American learns to appreciate his culture when he is suddenly transported to 1875.

Angel and the Outlaw. *Love Spell, 1996.* A paraplegic romance writer and a nineteenth-century Sioux shaman find love and understanding.

Feather in the Wind. *Love Spell, 1997.* Features a time-traveling romance writer.

Bennett, Janice

Bennett has written several Historicals, primarily Regencies, in the time travel mode.

Forever in Time. *Zebra, 1990.* Modern-day Erica accompanies one of Wellington's officers back to Regency England and ends up solving a mystery and falling in love.

A Timely Affair. *Zebra, 1990.* Heroine goes back in time to rectify a scandal and falls in love in the process.

A Christmas Keepsake. *Zebra, 1991.* An antique snow globe transports the heroine back to Regency England.

A Touch of Forever. *Zebra, 1992.* A jeweled dagger sends the heroine back in time, into the arms of the dashing hero and into danger as well.

Across Forever. *Zebra, 1994.* When the heroine's hot air balloon crashes into the middle of the nineteenth-century, she finds help—and love—in the surprising form of a wounded soldier.

Bretton, Barbara

Somewhere in Time. *Harlequin, 1992.* A Revolutionary War uniform and a hot air balloon trip send the protagonists into the 1770s where they find love, laughter, and a lot of adventure.

Tomorrow and Always. *Mira Books, 1994.* This time a hot air balloon trip that brings a Revolutionary spy into the present. Follows *Somewhere in Time.*

Destiny's Child. *Mira Books, 1995.* A psychic librarian finds love during the American Revolution. Follows *Tomorrow and Always.*

Cates, Kimberly

Magic. *Pocket Books, 1998.* When Fallon uses a magic brooch to summon warrior Ciaran out of the past to save Ireland from the ruthless English, she is faced with more than a legendary hero—she now has a man on her hands. Charming, sensual, and romantic.

Claybourne, Casey

Nick of Time. *Jove, 1997.* A Regency time-travel with a paranormal twist.

Copeland, Lori

Forever Ashley. *Dell, 1992.* Time travel and angels combine to bring an early-American doctor and a modern-day tour guide together during the exciting events surrounding Paul Revere's famous midnight ride. Could also be classified as a Paranormal.

Cresswell, Jasmine

Timeless. *Topaz, 1994.* A coma sends antiques expert Robyn Delany back to 1746 where she is reincarnated as the wife of Baron William Bowleigh, her current lover's ancestor.

Midnight Fantasy. *Harlequin, 1996.* Intriguing story of a futuristic L.A. cop who comes back to the present, with romantic results.

Deveraux, Jude

A Knight in Shining Armor. *Pocket Books, 1989.* An Elizabethan knight and a modern-day schoolteacher find love across time in this, one of the earliest time travel romances.

Remembrance. *Pocket Books, 1994.* A woman goes back in time to relive her past lives and unblock her ability to love and connect with her true soulmate.

Legend. *Pocket Books, 1996.*

Gabaldon, Diana

The Outlander series

This now-classic series features a twentieth-century doctor, an eighteenth-century Scotsman, and their love that defies time. A fifth volume is anticipated.

 The Outlander. *Delacorte Press, 1991.* A Rita Award winner.

Dragonfly in Amber. *Delacorte Press, 1992.*

Voyager. *Delacorte Press, 1994.*

Drums of Autumn. *Delacorte Press, 1997.*

Hannah, Kristin

When Lightning Strikes. *Fawcett, 1994.* A romance writer suddenly finds herself a character in her own story—but when she falls in love with the villain, she begins to realize the story is no longer her own.

Heath, Sandra

Heath is a well-known writer of Regency romances, some of which have paranormal elements.

Magic at Midnight. *Signet, 1995.* A trip to England lands journalist Kathryn Vansomeren back in 1815 and into the life of a handsome nobleman.

Shades of the Past. *Signet, 1996.* A modern-day actress finds love and danger in Regency England.

Summer's Secret. *Signet, 1997.* Widow finds herself in the body of a Regency woman involved in deception.

Hill, Sandra

The Reluctant Viking. *Love Spell, 1994.* A twentieth-century woman ends up in tenth-century Britain as a Viking's captive.

The Outlaw Viking. *Love Spell, 1995.* A twenty-first-century doctor is transported to tenth-century Britain where she literally meets the man of her dreams.

Frankly, My Dear. *Love Spell, 1996.* Voodoo curses, murder, and a greedy villain are part of this fast-paced romance set in steamy Louisiana.

The Last Viking. *Love Spell, 1990.*

Kurland, Lynn

The Very Thought of You. *Jove, 1998.*

Lindsey, Johanna

Until Forever. *Avon Books, 1995.* An ancient sword allows history professor Roseleen White to conjure up an eleventh-century Viking warrior as her slave. She compels him to take her back in time to see history in the making, with unexpected results.

Linz, Cathie

A Wife in Time. *Silhouette, 1995.* A pair of modern-day feuding protagonists end up in Victorian Savannah, forced to work together to solve a murder mystery. They end up actually changing the future.

Michaels, Kasey

Out of the Blue. *Dell, 1992.* A Regency romance editor visits the Tower of London, takes a wrong turn, and ends up in Regency London where she is aided by a handsome marquees.

Timely Matrimony. *Silhouette, 1994.* An Englishman from the past is washed up on Suzi Harper's beach, with romantic, funny results.

Miller, Linda Lael

Miller is a popular writer in a number of romance subgenres.

Here and Then. *Mira Books, 1992.*

There and Now. *Mira Books, 1992.*

Pirates. *Pocket Books, 1995.* Heading for the Caribbean to recover from her divorce, Phoebe Turlow ends up in the arms of an eighteenth-century pirate who thinks she is a Tory spy.

Knights. *Pocket Books, 1996.* Just as she wins the man of her dreams, the stunned heroine is wrenched back into the present and must find a way to rejoin her love. An unusual twist.

My Outlaw. *Pocket Books, 1997.* A mirror sends a contemporary artist back into an outlaw's life in nineteenth-century Nevada.

O'Brien, Judith

Ashton's Bride. *Pocket Books, 1995.* An effective Civil War time travel.

Rhapsody in Time. *Pocket Books, 1994.* A trip in time takes the heroine from a New York subway to the mob-ridden, but wonderfully musical, world of the Roaring Twenties.

Once upon a Rose. *Pocket Books, 1996.*

O'Day-Flannery, Constance

O'Day-Flannery is one of the earlier writers of time travel romances.

Timeswept Lovers. *Zebra, 1987.* Railroad intrigue in the late nineteenth-century keeps the protagonists busy, but not too busy to fall in love.

Time-Kept Promises. *Zebra, 1988.* Two time travelers return to right a few of the heroine's ancestors' wrongs.

Time-Kissed Destiny. *Zebra, 1989.*

This Time Forever. *Zebra, 1990.* Modern-day hero helps nineteenth-century heroine unmask a murderer.

Timeless Passion. *Zebra, 1991.*

A Time for Love. *Zebra, 1991.* Zapped from her dentist's chair back to nineteenth-century Texas, Elizabeth finds herself the mail-order bride of a rancher.

Bewitched. *Zebra, 1995.* Lover from the past causes interesting problems for the modern heroine.

Overfield, Joan

The Door Ajar. *Zebra, 1995*. Regency bride Miranda Winthrop flees on her wedding night and ends up in the twentieth century, leaving her perplexed husband to explain her disappearance.

Time's Tapestry. *Zebra, 1996*. A modern-day female cop ends up in Regency England and helps solve a series of murders (á la Jack the Ripper).

Riley, Eugenia

A Tryst in Time. *Love Spell, 1992*. A mansion provides a door to the past and to love.

Tempest in Time. *Love Spell, 1993*. Two women accidentally switch places (and times) on their wedding days and end up married to the men of their dreams.

Timeswept Bride. *Avon Books, 1995*.

Phantom in Time. *Avon Books, 1996*.

Wanted Across Time. *Avon Books, 1997*. A contemporary heroine is sent back in time where she is mistaken for her infamous ancestor who has a price on her head.

Waltz in Time. *Avon Books, 1997*.

Ring, Thomasina

Time-Spun Rapture. *Love Spell, 1990*. An actress wakes up in Colonial Virginia in the middle of Bacon's Rebellion and is "rescued" by a handsome colonist.

Time-Spun Treasure. *Love Spell, 1992*. The heroine ends up in pre-Revolutionary Virginia to find herself in possession of a husband and a baby. Politics, treasure, and a ghost add interest.

Saxe, Coral Smith

The Mirror and the Magic. *Love Spell, 1996*. A young woman is transported back to the fifteenth century where she is mistaken for a witch from an enemy clan.

The Shore Unknown. *Love Spell, 1997*. A fifteenth-century heroine ends up in the present with a biker mechanic hero. Interesting twist.

Simpson, Pamela

Partners in Time. *Bantam Books, 1990*. A modern-day private eye and a marshal from the Old West join forces professionally and romantically in this funny, fast-paced time travel.

Sizemore, Susan

Wings of the Storm. *HarperPaperbacks, 1992*. Scientist Jane Florian is sent from 2002 back to the thirteenth century by a coworker. She copes admirably and also finds love.

In My Dreams. *HarperPaperbacks, 1994*. A ninth-century sorceress brings a present-day biker with martial arts skills back to help her battle both the Vikings and the king.

My Own True Love. *HarperPaperbacks, 1994*. A time-traveling accountant and a nineteenth-century British spy find love, but not without a few pitfalls along the way.

After the Storm. *HarperPaperbacks, 1996*. Follows *Wings of the Storm*.

The Autumn Lord. *HarperPaperbacks, 1996*. Time travel to twelfth-century France during the reign of Louis VII.

One of These Nights. *HarperPaperbacks, 1997*.

Speer, Flora M.

These two linked stories are set in eighth-century Francia during the reign of Charlemagne and bring protagonists from the present to find love in the past.

A Time to Love Again. *Love Spell, 1993.*

A Love Beyond Time. *Love Spell, 1994.*

Christmas Carol. *Love Spell, 1994.* Spoiled woman gains happiness and love through time travel in the company of her mentor.

Love Just in Time. *Love Spell, 1995.* Despondent woman is in an accident that catapults her back to the early nineteenth century where she finds love.

Stover, Deb

Stover's romances are funny, innovative, and sexy.

A Willing Spirit. *Pinnacle, 1996.* A divorcée is swept back to late-nineteenth-century Oklahoma and ends up involved with the local marshal, who looks like her modern-day lover.

Some Like It Hotter. *Pinnacle, 1997.*

Almost an Angel. *Pinnacle, 1997.* A would-be angel haunts the Colorado town of her past, until the right person arrives for her to help so she can make up for her past mistakes.

Weyrich, Becky Lee

Sweet Forever. *Pinnacle, 1992.* An unusual time travel that sweeps the protagonists from the seventeenth to the nineteenth centuries and back, eventually allowing them to find love together.

Once upon Forever. *Pinnacle, 1994.* Separated by time as soon as they are married, Larissa and Hunter eventually solve their dilemma. A Civil War/1990s time travel.

Savannah Scarlett. *Zebra, 1996.*

Sands of Destiny. *Zebra, 1996.* Heroine travels back in time to become Cleopatra, and falls in love.

Swan's Way. *Zebra, 1997.* Civil War setting.

NOTES

1. Marshall B. Tymn, "Science Fiction," in *Handbook of American Popular Literature,* ed. M. Thomas Inge (New York: Greenwood Press, 1988), 274.

2. Charlotte Spivack, *Merlin's Daughters: Contemporary Women Writers of Fantasy* (New York: Greenwood Press, 1987), 5.

3. Karl Kroeber, *Romantic Fantasy and Science Fiction* (New Haven, CT: Yale University Press, 1988), 1.

4. Marshall B. Tymn, "Science Fiction," in *Handbook of American Popular Literature,* ed. M. Thomas Inge (New York: Greenwood Press, 1988), 275.

5. Ann Swinfen, *Defence of Fantasy: A Study of the Genre in English and American Literature Since 1945* (London: Routledge & Kegan Paul, 1984), 1.

6. Charlotte Spivack, *Merlin's Daughters: Contemporary Women Writers of Fantasy* (New York: Greenwood Press, 1987), 8–9.

Chapter 10

Sagas

"Every large family has its angel and its demon."
Joseph Roux, Meditations of a Parish Priest

"The wrongdoing of one generation lives into the successive ones"
Nathaniel Hawthorne, The House of Seven Gables

"Each family, however modest its origin, possesses its own particular tale of the past—a tale which can bewitch us with as great a sense of insistent romance as can even the traditions of kings."
Llewellyn Powys, Earth Memories

DEFINITION

The romantic Saga is a multigenerational narrative, usually centering around the activities of one, or possibly two, particular families. These stories, which appear in both single and multivolume formats, chronicle the lives and loves, successes and failures, and often the rise and fall (or sometimes just the rise) of the families involved. They deal primarily with the interpersonal relationships of the characters. Usually there is one powerful figure, often the reigning family patriarch or matriarch, around whom much of the action revolves, and if the Saga continues long enough, this role is passed on to others within the family.

The main characters in Sagas can be either male or female. In works that concentrate primarily on domestic relationships (e.g., Colleen McCullough's *The Thorn Birds*), the protagonists often are women. In Sagas with a broader historical emphasis, such as the older Wagons West series, men were often featured, although several more recent series of this latter type have placed women in the central roles. Nevertheless, because of the tendency in Sagas to rotate the point of view among several different characters, readers have sufficient opportunity to identify with both male and female characters, whatever the sex of the protagonist.

As a rule, Saga heroes and heroines tend to be stronger, more independent, and more dynamic than average, and the situations in which they find themselves have a slightly larger-than-life quality (reminiscent of the classic dragon-slaying saga). There is, however, enough everyday detail for the characters to remain believable, and they rarely degenerate into epic stereotypes.

Because sagas span many years (often several generations), they are partially historical in nature and, as a result, incorporate many characteristics of the various kinds of Historical Romance. The accuracy of historical events and the everyday realities of the settings are important to this subgenre (especially since Sagas usually deal with a number of major historical happenings within their time frames). Nevertheless, it is the characters and their interactions that sustain the reader's interest throughout the series and not simply the depiction of the period. As with most historical fiction, all periods can and have been used, but over the years several have emerged as particular favorites within the Saga subgenre. The Old American South (eighteenth and nineteenth centuries, including the Civil War and Reconstruction) and the English Victorian and Edwardian eras are especially popular. It is worth noting, however, that recently several writers have written sagas with relatively contemporary settings.

Saga plot patterns are predictable in that they deal fundamentally with the rise and decline of a particular family or group of families. However, their individual story lines vary widely, and anything from a straightforward love story or an unsolved family mystery to an ancient vendetta of hatred can be legitimately considered within the subgenre. In most cases, several diverse plotlines are included within a single Saga, giving the Saga the reputation of having something for everyone. While this is not necessarily true, the Saga subgenre does cast a broad net, often straying across other genre or Romance subgenre borders (especially those of the Historical and Soap Opera) or into the realm of mainstream fiction. As a result, Sagas often attract a more varied and larger group of readers than other types of romance fiction.

APPEAL

The Saga attracts many readers because of its wide variety and its similarity to the Historical Romance. However, the unique appeal of the Saga lies in the fact that, like the ever-popular television soap opera, it *continues*. Sagas, unlike most romance types, do not stop with the protagonists declaring their undying love for each other; rather, they allow us to see what actually happens "happily ever after" or "unhappily ever after," as the case may be. As children, we could hardly wait to find out "what happened next"; as adults, we still want to know the same thing. Did Rupert and Samantha make a success of their American plantation? Did the mischievous Algernon grow up to be staid and pompous like his father, or did he turn out more like his rakehell Uncle Thomas? And whatever happened to funny old Uncle Herbert and the scandalous memoirs he was writing? Sagas allow us to find out.

But Sagas do more than simply satisfy our curiosity; they also enable us to experience both the detail of everyday life and the broad sweep of history, a combination that is as unusual in literature as it is in life. We participate in the daily lives of the characters, yet we can also see the results of actions taken and decisions made across the years. We experience in a personal way the impact of major historical events on a particular family, yet we also see the events in the greater historical context. It is this double perspective, generally impossible to achieve in real life, that readers find so fascinating. This, combined with the serial aspect of the Saga, makes it easy to understand the appeal of this genre—even among those who would never have considered reading a romance before!

ADVISING THE READER

General readers' advisory information is provided in chapter 3; however, several additional points specifically relating to Sagas are addressed below.

- Many people who like Sagas also read Historical Romances, especially those that have complex plot patterns (particularly if they interweave several distinct plotlines and use numerous characters), that are longer than normal, or that deal with the wider historical aspects. Works such as M. M. Kaye's *The Far Pavilions*, any number of novels by Jean Plaidy (especially those of a series nature), or even Margaret Mitchell's *Gone With the Wind* might be of particular interest.

- It is important to discover why a reader likes a particular Saga. Is it the series aspect that is especially appealing? Then suggest other sagas, books with sequels, trilogies, and other "linked" books (e.g., Nora Roberts's *Born in . . .* or *. . . Dream* trilogies and Jo Beverley's "Company of Rogues" or Malloren Family books). Also suggest the currently popular continuation series (e.g., Montana Mavericks, Crystal Creek, and Fortune's Children). Is the period particularly fascinating to the reader? Then suggest Historicals—both straight fiction and romance—or even Time Travels set in the same period. Or does the reader enjoy a particular type of character? Then suggest books in other subgenres that use the same kind of character. The answers to these questions could result in entirely different recommendations and might open up a whole new genre area to the reader.

- For the reader who is new to the Saga subgenre, recommend standard works by some of the major authors (e.g., R. F. Delderfield, Roberta Gellis, Howard Fast, Taylor Caldwell, Belva Plain, Rosalind Laker, Jessica Stirling, Dorothy Dunnett) and then go on to others.

- Finally, check the "Advising the Reader" section of Historical Romances. Many Sagas are also Historicals, so most of the suggestions listed there also apply to Sagas.

BRIEF HISTORY

Although the romantic saga can theoretically trace its ancestry to the early epic Anglo-Saxon and Nordic sagas, in reality, today's generational Saga has little more than a nominal relationship to the ancient literary sagas. Today's Sagas actually bear about the same relation to the early epic sagas as Contemporary Romances have to the literary romances of the Middle Ages. Contemporary Sagas are essentially generational family chronicles rather than tales of individual heroism, and even though there are a few older examples of domestic chronicles (e.g., Tsao Hsueh-chin's *Dream of the Red Chamber* 1792), the Saga as we know it today did not gain popularity until the first half of the twentieth century.

John Galsworthy's *The Forsyte Saga* (first published as a unit in 1922, even though the initial book in the series, *A Man of Property*, was published in 1906) was one of the first contemporary Sagas and remains popular to this day. A number of other Sagas soon followed, among them Mazo De la Roche's Jalna series, the Herries Tetralogy by Hugh Walpole, and the Matriarch series by G. B. Stern. In the late 1960s there was a resurgence of interest in the Saga when *The Forsyte Saga* was made into a television series for the BBC. Shown on public television in England and the United States, it was enormously popular in both countries. Suddenly, the book was in demand, sales increased dramatically, and it was catapulted onto England's bestseller list.

During the decade that followed, authors and publishers jumped on the Saga bandwagon, rapidly producing new and resurrecting old novels written in the saga tradition. New writers (e.g., Claire Rayner and Colleen McCullough) were discovered, earlier writers (e.g., R. F. Delderfield and Mazo De la Roche) were re-discovered, and some popular writers noted for other subgenres (e.g., Rosalind Laker and Susan Howatch) began experimenting with the Saga. The 1970s also saw an interesting development—the establishment of Book Creations, Inc., a company specializing in the creation of popular Saga-type series. The firm's founder, Lyle Kenyon Engel, formulated the ideas for these paperback series and then contracted with authors who would do the actual writing. Engel then functioned as editor and agent for the series, maintaining a high degree of control over the finished work. Most of Engel's series have been published by major paperback publishers—Berkley/Jove, Playboy, Dell, to name a few. New additions to his established series routinely appeared on the paperback bestsellers lists, and The Kent Family Chronicles, the Wagons West series, and The Roselynde Chronicles were among his most popular.

Sagas of all types (domestic, political, economic, historical, business and professional, male-dominated, female-oriented, etc.) remained popular through the 1980s, and although European and exotic settings were standard fare, there was a trend toward Sagas (and other romances as well) set in America. The popularity of the traditional Saga waned during the 1990s, and currently the genre is in decline. Nevertheless, it is worth noting that while the Saga itself is languishing, the popularity of suspiciously similar books (e.g., related or linked books, trilogies, and the various continuing series) is skyrocketing. Obviously, the continuation aspect of the Saga has not lost its appeal. Readers still want to know "what happens next." All of which raises this question: Is the Saga truly declining, or it is simply reinventing itself and evolving into something that better meets the needs of readers today?

The following early sagas and prototypes helped establish the form for the subgenre and still influence the Sagas of today.

De la Roche, Mazo

Jalna series

Beginning in 1850, this Saga chronicles the events in the lives of several generations of the Canadian Whiteoak family. Note: The books are listed by publication date. The numbers in parentheses indicate their chronological order within the series.

Jalna. *Little, Brown, 1927.* (7)

Whiteoaks of Jalna. *Little, Brown, 1929.* (8)

Finch's Fortune. *Little, Brown, 1931.* (9)

The Master of Jalna. *Little, Brown, 1933.* (10)

Young Renny. *Little, Brown, 1935.* (4)

Whiteoak Harvest. *Little, Brown, 1936.* (11)

Whiteoak Heritage. *Little, Brown, 1940.* (5)

Wakefield's Course. *Little, Brown, 1941.* (12)

The Building of Jalna. *Little, Brown, 1944.* (1)

Return to Jalna. *Little, Brown, 1946.* (13)

Mary Wakefield. *Little, Brown, 1949.* (3)

Renny's Daughter. *Little, Brown, 1951.* (14)

The Whiteoak Brothers. *Little, Brown, 1953.* (6)

Variable Winds at Jalna. *Little, Brown, 1954.* (15)

Centenary at Jalna. *Little, Brown, 1958.* (16)

Morning at Jalna. *Little, Brown, 1960.* (2)

Galsworthy, John

The trials and tribulations of assorted members of the British Forsyte family. Note: The books in the first two trilogies are linked by short stories or "interludes."

The Forsyte Saga. *Scribners, 1922.*

    A Man of Property. *Heinemann, 1906.* "Indian Summer Forsyte."

    In Chancery. *Heinemann, 1920.* "Awakening."

    To Let. *Scribners, 1921.*

A Modern Comedy. *Scribners, 1929.*

    The White Monkey. *Scribners, 1924.* "A Silent Wooing."

    The Silver Spoon. *Scribners, 1926.* "Passers By."

    Swan Song. *Scribners, 1928.*

End of the Chapter. *Scribners, 1934.*

    Maid in Waiting. *Heinemann, 1931.*

    Flowering Wilderness. *Heinemann, 1932.*

    Over the River. *Heinemann, 1933.* Published as *One More River* by Scribners, 1933.

Stern, G(ladys) B(ronwyn)

Stern's work, especially the Matriarch series, influenced Mazo De la Roche.

Matriarch series

Chronicles the events in the lives of a Viennese Jewish family.

The Matriarch. *Alfred A. Knopf, 1924.*

A Deputy Was King. *Alfred A. Knopf, 1926.*

Mosaic. *Alfred A. Knopf, 1930.*

Shining and Free: A Day in the Life of the Matriarch. *Alfred A. Knopf, 1935.*

The Young Matriarch. *Macmillan, 1942.*

Walpole, Hugh

Herries Chronicles

Spanning 200 years, this sweeping saga chronicles the events in the lives of the English Herries family from the Georgian period to the 1930s. Walpole's last completed novel about the Herries family was *Bright Pavilions* (1940). Set in Elizabethan England, it was intended to be the first in a series about earlier Herries generations; however, this was precluded by the author's death in 1941.

Rogue Herries. *Doubleday, Doran, 1930.*

Judith Paris. *Doubleday, Doran, 1931.*

The Fortress. *Doubleday, Doran, 1932.*

Vanessa. *Doubleday, Doran, 1933.*

SELECTED SAGA BIBLIOGRAPHY

The following authors are known for their sagas or series, although they may also write in other subgenres. Only their sagas or series are listed below. Any of their other romance works included in this book are discussed in the appropriate chapters. This list includes both multivolume and single volume works. Most of the titles listed here are older, reflecting the lack of current interest in this subgenre.

Adamson, Yvonne

Bridey's Mountain. *Delacorte Press, 1993.* A four-generational Saga centering on a family mountain in Colorado.

Adler, Elizabeth

Fortune Is a Woman. *Delacorte Press, 1992.* Rejected by her wealthy father, Francie Harrison achieves success and survives natural disasters and family treachery. This story moves around the world and spans more than the first half of the twentieth century.

Argo, Ellen

A trilogy of one woman's love affair with the sea set during America's "Glory Age of Sail."

Jewel of the Seas. *Putnam, 1977.*

The Crystal Star. *Putnam, 1979.*

The Yankee Girl. *Putnam, 1980.*

Arlen, Leslie (Christopher Nicole)

The Borodins series

A tempestuous saga of an aristocratic family that moves from the doomed, glittering upper-class world of pre-revolutionary Russia through the revolution and beyond.

Love and Honor. *Jove, 1980.*

War and Passion. *Jove, 1981.*

Fate and Dreams. *Jove, 1981.*

Hope and Glory. *Jove, 1982.*

Rage and Desire. *Jove, 1982.*

Fortune and Fury. *Jove, 1984.*

Beauman, Sally

Destiny. *Bantam Books, 1988.* This rags-to-riches story of love and retribution spans three decades and two continents.

Birmingham, Stephen

Those Harper Women. *McGraw-Hill, 1964.*

The Auerbach Will. *Little, Brown, 1983.*

Bittner, Rosanne

Bittner is a popular writer of Western romances, some of which tend in the Saga direction.

In the Shadow of the Mountain. *Bantam Books, 1991.* A marriage of necessity results in the founding of a Colorado dynasty.

Thunder on the Plains. *Doubleday, 1992.* The building of the intercontinental railroad and the attendant turmoil is the focus of this sweeping romance.

Wildest Dreams. *Bantam Books, 1994.* A marriage of convenience endures to create a Montana empire.

The Forever Tree. *Bantam Books, 1995.* An intense, emotional story of success, tragedy, and love in a mid-nineteenth-century California setting.

Blair, Leona

A World of Difference. *Bantam Books, 1989.* Set during the first half of the twentieth century, this turbulent story matches the daughter of a wealthy industrial family with the son of a labor leader.

Bonds, Paris Afton

Dream Time. *HarperPaperbacks, 1993.* This complex story of love and revenge focuses on the lives of Nan Briscoll, her two daughters, and the men in Nan's life. Rich in nineteenth-century Australian history.

Bradford, Barbara Taylor

Woman of Substance. *Doubleday, 1979.* A powerful tale of driving ambition in which Emma Harte fights to become "a woman of substance." The books that follow continue the story through her granddaughter, Paula.

Hold the Dream. *Doubleday, 1985.*

To Be the Best. *Doubleday, 1988.*

Bregman, Sandra

Reach for the Dream. *Dell, 1990.* The multigenerational story of a Russian immigrant and her struggles, successes, and enduring love for the one man she thinks she will never have.

Briskin, Jacqueline

Although Briskin's novels are glitzy and fast paced, it is her superb handling of historical and cultural details and her ability to provide a true sense of time and place that make them a cut above the rest.

Paloverde. *McGraw-Hill, 1978.*

Rich Friends. *Delacorte Press, 1976.*

The Onyx. *Delacorte Press, 1982.*

Bristow, Gwen

Plantation Trilogy (published as a whole in 1962 by Thomas Y. Crowell)

Describes the lives of seven generations of two Louisiana families from pre-Revolutionary days through World War I.

Deep Summer. *Thomas Y. Crowell, 1937.*

The Handsome Road. *Thomas Y. Crowell, 1938.*

This Side of Glory. *Thomas Y. Crowell, 1940.*

Byrne, Beverly

Mendoza Trilogy

Spanning the nineteenth and much of the twentieth centuries and set in both Europe and America, this trilogy follows the fortunes of various women who become involved with the powerful Mendoza family.

A Lasting Fire. *Bantam Books, 1991.*

The Flames of Vengeance. *Bantam Books, 1991.*

The Firebirds. *Bantam Books, 1992.*

Carleton, Jetta

The Moonflower Vine. *Simon & Schuster, 1962.* A gentle and dramatic saga of a Missouri family spanning the first 50 years of this century.

Carr, Philippa (Eleanor Burford Hibbert, also writes as Victoria Holt and Jean Plaidy)

Philippa Carr terms her own works "Historical Gothics," and indeed many of them do exhibit Gothic characteristics. Roughly written in chronological order and using related or linked characters (many of whom are descendants of Bruno and Damask from *The Miracle at St. Bruno's*), these books have been designated as the Daughters of England series by the author and form a Saga of sorts that begins with the English Reformation and ends with World War II. Each book, however, is complete in itself and does not have to be read as part of the series.

The Miracle at St. Bruno's. *Putnam, 1972.*

The Lion Triumphant. *Putnam, 1974.*

The Witch from the Sea. *Putnam, 1975.*

Saraband for Two Sisters. *Putnam, 1976.*

Lament for a Lost Lover. *Putnam, 1977.*

The Love-Child. *Putnam, 1978.*

The Song of the Siren. *Putnam, 1980.*

Will You Love Me in September. *Putnam, 1981.* Published in England as *The Drop of the Dice* by Collins 1984.

The Adulteress. *Collins, 1982.*

Knave of Hearts. *Putnam, 1983.* Published in England as *Zipporah's Daughter* by Collins 1983.

Voices in a Haunted Room. *Putnam, 1984.*

The Return of the Gypsy. *Putman, 1985.*

Midsummer's Eve. *Putnam, 1986.*

The Pool of St. Branok. *Putnam, 1987.*

The Changeling. *Putnam, 1989.*

The Black Swan. *Putnam, 1991.*

A Time for Silence. *Putnam, 1991.*

The Gossamer Cord. *Putnam, 1992.*

We'll Meet Again. *Putnam, 1993.*

Coffman, Virginia

This book is set in the American South.

The Gaynor Women. *Arbor House, 1978.*

Coleman, Lonnie

Beulah Land series

A tale of the nineteenth-century American South as depicted by the fortunes of the Kendrick family and their Georgia plantation, Beulah Land.

Beulah Land. *Doubleday, 1973.*

Look Away, Beulah Land. *Doubleday, 1977.*

The Legacy of Beulah Land. *Doubleday, 1980.*

Cookson, Catherine

Both prolific and popular, Cookson produces compelling works filled with memorable characters, realistic settings and situations, and plots that often focus on relevant social issues, particularly class differences. Her works often span decades and can be historical, contemporary, or both.

The Mallen Trilogy

This somewhat melodramatic series spans from 1851 to World War I and chronicles the events in the lives of the notorious Mallen family.

The Mallen Streak. *E. P. Dutton, 1973.*

The Mallen Girl. *E. P. Dutton, 1973.*

The Mallen Lot. *E. P. Dutton, 1974.* Published in England as *The Mallen Litter* by Heinemann, 1974.

Tilly series

A Victorian era trilogy chronicling one woman's strength and determination.

Tilly. *William Morrow, 1980.* Published in England as *Tilly Trotter.*

Tilly Wed. *William Morrow, 1981.* Published in England as *Tilly Trotter Wed.*

Tilly Alone. *William Morrow, 1982.* Published in England as *Tilly Trotter Widowed.*

The Bannaman Legacy. *Summit, 1985.* Published in England as *A Dinner of Herbs* by Heinemann, 1985.

The Black Candle. *Bantam Books, 1989. Summit, 1990.* This saga spans 50 years and is one of the author's best.

Cradock, Fanny

An upstairs/downstairs saga of England from the Edwardian Era to modern times.

Lorme Family Saga

The Lormes of Castle Rising. *W. H. Allen, 1975.*

Shadows over Castle Rising. *W. H. Allen, 1976.*

War Comes to Castle Rising. *W. H. Allen, 1977.*

Wind of Change at Castle Rising. *W. H. Allen, 1978.*

Thunder over Castle Rising. *W. H. Allen, 1980.*

Gathering Clouds at Castle Rising. *W. H. Allen, 1981.*

Dailey, Janet

Calder series

A contemporary Western saga centering around the lives and fortunes of the Calder family. These modern-day stories have a vaguely historical quality.

This Calder Sky. *Pocket Books, 1981.*

This Calder Range. *Pocket Books, 1982.*

Stands a Calder Man. *Pocket Books, 1983.*

Calder Born, Calder Bred. *Pocket Books. 1983.*

The Great Alone. *Poseidon, 1986.* An epic tale of Alaska, spanning 200 years of love and adventure.

Davenport, Marcia

Valley of Decision. *Scribners, 1942.* A classic American saga detailing the strange and not especially happy love story of the son of a wealthy steel magnate and a young Irish servant.

De Blasis, Celeste

Most of De Blasis's books depict her affection for both the sea and animals.

Falconer saga

Beginning in 1813, this saga sweeps from England to Maryland and from California to the East Coast as it chronicles the lives of the Falconers. Horse breeding and shipbuilding are key focuses in these stories of love, ambition, and change.

Wild Swan. *Bantam Books, 1984.*

Swan's Chance. *Bantam Books, 1985.*

A Season of Swans. *Bantam Books, 1989.*

de Jourlet, Marie

Windhaven series

This 14-book series is set in the southern and western United States and focuses on the lives and loves of the Bouchard family. They are examples of the Plantation and Sweet/Savage Romance types. *Windhaven Plantation* (Pinnacle, 1977) is the first title in the series, each of which has "Windhaven" in the title. The most recent title is *Windhaven's Glory* (Pinnacle, 1985).

Delderfield, R(onald) F(rederick)

Swann Family Saga

A saga of Victorian and Edwardian England spanning the last half of the nineteenth century and the twentieth century prior to World War I.

God Is an Englishman. *Simon & Schuster, 1970.*

Theirs Was the Kingdom. *Simon & Schuster, 1971.*

Give Us This Day. *Simon & Schuster, 1973.*

Craddock Family Saga

A saga of English country life spanning the first half of the twentieth century.

A Horseman Riding By. *Hodder & Stoughton, 1966.* Simon & Schuster, 1967.

The Green Gauntlet. *Simon & Schuster, 1968.*

Dunnett, Dorothy

More adventure than romance, Dunnett's novels may appeal to readers who enjoy a little bit of romance with a lot of fast-paced, swashbuckling action.

Lymond Chronicles

The setting for this popular series is sixteenth-century Europe and Russia.

The Game of Kings. *Putnam, 1961.*

Queen's Play. *Putnam, 1964.*

Disorderly Knights. *Putnam, 1966.*

Pawn in Frankincense. *Putnam, 1969.*

The Ringed Castle. *Putnam, 1972.*

Checkmate. *Putnam, 1975.*

House of Niccoló series

This action-packed series takes its fifteenth-century hero from Bruges (Flanders) to Italy and other exotic places, many of which are located around the Mediterranean.

Niccoló Rising. *Alfred A. Knopf, 1986.*

The Spring of the Ram. *Alfred A. Knopf, 1988.* Michael Joseph, 1987.

Race of Scorpions. *Alfred A. Knopf, 1990.* Michael Joseph, 1989.

Scales of Gold. *Alfred A. Knopf, 1992.* Michael Joseph, 1991.

The Unicorn Hunt. *Michael Joseph, 1993.*

To Lie with Lions. *Alfred A. Knopf, 1996.* Michael Joseph, 1995.

Caprice and Rondo. *Alfred A. Knopf, 1998.* Michael Joseph, 1997.

Ellis, Julie

Pain, violence, and love fill this saga of one of the "first families of Atlanta." The story sweeps from the end of the nineteenth century to World War I.

The Hampton Heritage. *Simon & Schuster, 1978.*

The Hampton Women. *Simon & Schuster, 1980.*

Fast, Howard

The Immigrants (The Lavette Family Saga)

A powerful story of struggle, perseverance, and success that spans four generations of Californians from the early 1900s to the Vietnam War.

The Immigrants. *Houghton-Mifflin, 1977.*

The Second Generation. *Houghton-Mifflin, 1978.*

The Establishment. *Houghton-Mifflin, 1979.*

The Legacy. *Houghton-Mifflin, 1981.*

The Immigrant's Daughter. *Houghton-Mifflin, 1985.*

Gaan, Margaret

A fascinating saga of China, beginning with the early nineteenth century and featuring the people, Chinese and European alike, who called it home.

Red Barbarian. *Dodd, Mead, 1984.*

White Poppy. *Dodd, Mead, 1985.*

Blue Mountain. *Dodd, Mead, 1987.*

Gaskin, Catherine

Although still somewhat Gothic, Gaskin's later contemporaries are broader in scope, depicting the fortunes and foibles of assorted rich and successful families.

Family Affairs. *Doubleday, 1980.*

Promises. *Doubleday, 1982.*

The Ambassador's Women. *Charles Scribner's Sons, 1986.* Collins, 1985.

The Charmed Circle. *Charles Scribner's Sons, 1989.* Collins, 1988.

Gavin, Catherine

The Sunset Dream. *St. Martin's Press, 1984.* Hodder & Stoughton, 1983. An epic tale chronicling the lives of the powerful California Estrada family from 1846 to post-World War II.

Gedge, Pauline

The Eagle and the Raven. *Dial Press, 1978.* A three-generational saga of Celtic Britain and the family that led the struggle against the might of Rome.

Gellis, Roberta

Most of Gellis's works are well researched, highly detailed, and sensual.

The Roselynde Chronicles (Engel Creation)

These well-researched romances of Medieval England (and sometimes France), detail the lives of six women who are connected to the powerful keep Roselynde. A classic series.

Roselynde. *Playboy, 1978.*

Alinor. *Playboy, 1978.*

Joanna. *Playboy, 1978.*

Gilliane. *Playboy, 1979.*

Rhiannon. *Playboy, 1982.*

Sybelle. *Berkley/Jove, 1983.*

The Heiress series (Engel Creation)
These adventurous tales take place during the French Revolution and Napoleonic Era.

The English Heiress. *Dell, 1980.*

The Cornish Heiress. *Dell, 1981.*

The Kent Heiress. *Dell, 1981.*

Royal Dynasty series (Engel Creation)
Siren Song. *Playboy, 1981.*

Winter Song. *Playboy, 1982.*

Fire Song. *Berkley/Jove, 1984.*

Gilchrist, Rupert
Dragonard series
One of the several once-popular Plantation Romance series.

Dragonard. *Souvenir, 1975.* First of the six-volume series, each of which has "Dragonard" in the title.

Goldreich, Gloria
A story of persecution, love, and persistence that begins in Russia in 1919 and ends in America in the 1970s.

Leah's Journey. *Harcourt Brace Jovanovich, 1978.*

Leah's Children. *Macmillan, 1985.*

Gordon, Emma
Crossing Eden. *Warner Books, 1992.* In this complex, dual story, London Kirkland's exotic past affects her entire family, especially her American granddaughter, Sara Ashford.

Gower, Iris
A series of novels about six women during the first decades of the twentieth century who live in the small town of Sweyn's Eye in South Wales.

Copper Kingdom. *St. Martin's Press, 1983.*

Proud Mary. *St. Martin's Press, 1985.* Century, 1984.

Spinner's Wharf. *St. Martin's Press, 1985.*

Morgan's Woman. *Century, 1986.*

Fiddler's Ferry. *St. Martin's Press, 1987.*

Black Gold. *Century, 1988.*

Graham, Winston

Poldark Saga

Novels of the Poldark family set in the wild and beautiful Cornwall of the eighteenth and nineteenth centuries.

Ross Poldark. *Doubleday, 1951.* Original title *The Renegade.*

Demelza. *Doubleday, 1953.* Original title *Elizabeth's Story.*

Jeremy Poldark. *Doubleday, 1950.* Original title *Venture Once More.*

Warleggan. *Doubleday, 1955.* Original title *The Last Gamble.*

The Black Moon. *Doubleday, 1974.*

The Four Swans. *Doubleday, 1977.*

The Angry Tide. *Doubleday, 1978.*

The Stranger from the Sea. *Doubleday, 1982.*

The Miller's Dance. *Doubleday, 1983.*

Loving Cup. *Doubleday, 1985.*

Gregory, Phillipa

Wideacre Trilogy

A dark and passionate trilogy that focuses on the Lacey family and the estate Wideacre.

Wideacre. *Simon & Schuster, 1988.* Viking, 1987.

The Favored Child. *Simon & Schuster, 1989.*

Meridon. *Simon & Schuster, 1990.*

Hardwick, Mollie

Hardwick also writes Romantic Historicals and Period Romances. She is noted for her novelization of the television series *The Duchess of Duke Street* and for her novels based on the characters from the *Upstairs, Downstairs* television series. *(See also Romantic Historical and Period Romance bibliographies.)*

The Atkinson Heritage Saga

A well-written family saga based on real characters in the author's life.

The Atkinson Heritage. *Futura, 1978.*

Sisters in Love. *Futura, 1979.*

Dove's Nest. *Futura, 1980.* Also published as *The Atkinson Century* by Severn House, 1980.

Upstairs, Downstairs series

Sarah's Story. *Pocket Books, 1975 (1973).*

The Years of Change. *Dell, 1974.*

Mrs. Bridges' Story. *Sphere, 1975.*

The War to End Wars. *Dell, 1975.*

The Duchess of Duke Street series

The Way Up. *Futura, 1976.*

The Golden Years. *Futura, 1976.*

The World Keeps Turning. *Futura, 1977.*

Harris, Marilyn

Eden Saga

Beginning in the late Georgian period (1790s), this saga details several generations of the English Eden family.

This Other Eden. *Putnam, 1977.*

The Prince of Eden. *Putnam, 1978.*

The Eden Passion. *Putnam, 1979.*

The Women of Eden. *Putnam, 1980.*

Eden Rising. *Putnam, 1982.*

American Eden. *Doubleday, 1987.* Brings members of the family to America and sweeps from the post-Civil War South to California.

Eden and Honor. *Doubleday, 1988.* Brings the Eden story through World War I.

Harrison, Sara

Tennent Family Saga

An upstairs/downstairs type of family saga that follows the lives of three women through the devastation of both World Wars.

The Flowers of the Field. *Coward, McCann & Geoghegan, 1980.*

A Flower That's Free. *Simon & Schuster, 1984.*

Heaven, Constance

"Constance Heaven is to Moscow what Georgette Heyer is to Fulham." Heaven is the author of many period romances, including two sets of linked books.

Kuragin Trilogy

These three novels are a series of related stories set in the glitter and wealth of Tsarist Russia.

The House of Kuragin. *Coward, McCann & Geoghegan, 1972.*

The Astrov Legacy. *Coward, McCann & Geoghegan, 1973.*

Heir to Kuragin. *Coward, McCann & Geoghegan, 1979.*

Ravensley series

Set in the fens of England, this duo details the loves and lives of the Aylsham family.

Lord of Ravensley. *Coward, McCann & Geoghegan, 1978.*

The Ravensley Touch. *Coward, McCann & Geoghegan, 1982.*

Hill, Deborah

Merrick Family Trilogy

A trilogy of the New England Merrick family.

This Is the House. *Coward, McCann & Geoghegan, 1976.*

The House of Kingsley Merrick. *Coward, McCann & Geoghegan, 1978.*

Kingsland. *New American Library, 1981.*

Hill, Pamela

Daneclere. *Hale, 1978.* St. Martin's Press, 1979.

The House of Cray. *St. Martin's Press, 1982.*

Howatch, Susan

Noted for her chilling Gothics, Howatch's more recent contributions have been in the Saga subgenre, many of which are modern recreations of the stories of early English nobility. She also has recently written a series of novels that focus on the Church of England but do not fall within the Romance genre.

Penmarric. *Simon & Schuster, 1971.*

Cashelmara. *Simon & Schuster, 1974.*

The Rich Are Different. *Simon & Schuster, 1977.* This novel and its sequel, *Sins of the Fathers*, center on the lives of the Van Zales, a family of successful American bankers, and span from 1922 to 1967.

Sins of the Fathers. *Simon & Schuster, 1980.*

The Wheel of Fortune. *Simon & Schuster, 1984.* A saga of the Godwin family of Oxmoon, England.

Jakes, John

Kent Family Chronicles (Engel Creation)

This sweeping, passionate, eight-volume saga of America is also known as The American Bicentennial series. It begins with *The Bastard* (Pyramid, 1974) and concludes with *The Americans* (Jove, 1986).

The following books chronicle the lives of several families during the Civil War. *North and South* was made into a TV miniseries.

North and South. *Harcourt Brace Jovanovich, 1982.*

Love and War. *Harcourt Brace Jovanovich, 1984.*

Heaven and Hell. *Harcourt Brace Jovanovich, 1987.*

Jeckel, Pamela

Deepwater. *Kensington, 1994.* This story chronicles the building of the Deepwater Plantation in the Carolinas and four generations of its inhabitants. It begins in 1711.

Johansen, Iris

Wind Dancer Trilogy

This series follows the fortunes of the legendary Wind Dancer statue from Renaissance Italy through revolutionary France to today's international scene.

The Wind Dancer. *Bantam Books, 1991.*

Storm Winds. *Bantam Books, 1991.*

Leap the Wind. *Bantam Books, 1991.*

Johnson, Barbara Ferry

This trilogy of the American South also deals with the broader issue of what it means to be black in Confederate and post-Civil War times.

Delta Blood. *Avon Books, 1977.*

Homeward Winds the River. *Avon Books, 1979.*

The Heirs of Love. *Avon Books, 1980.*

Laker, Rosalind (Barbara Ovstedal)

The Warwycks of Easthampton Trilogy

A tale of three generations of Warwycks, set in an English seaside resort.

Warwyck's Woman. *Doubleday, 1978.* Also published as *Warwyck's Wife* by Eyre Methuen, 1979.

Claudine's Daughter. *Doubleday, 1979.*

Warwyck's Choice. *Doubleday, 1980.* Also published as *The Warwyck's of Easthampton* by Eyre Methuen, 1980.

Lofts, Norah

The Godfrey Tallboys Trilogy

A tale of knighthood, war, and everyday life in fifteenth-century England.

Knight's Acre. *Doubleday, 1975.*

The Homecoming. *Doubleday, 1976.*

The Lonely Furrow. *Doubleday, 1977.*

The Suffolk House Trilogy

This trilogy spans from 1381 to the present and is the story of a house and the people who have lived in it.

The Town House. *Doubleday, 1959.*

The House at Old Vine. *Doubleday, 1961.*

The House at Sunset. *Doubleday, 1962.*

Long, William Stewart (Vivian Stuart)

The Australians Saga (Engel Creation)

A strong, violent, multivolume saga of Australia and the people who made her great from the penal colonies of the late eighteenth century to the Boer War. Begins with *The Exiles* (Dell, 1979) and ends with *The Nationalists* (Dell, 1989).

Longstreet, Stephen

A saga of the California investment banking dynasty founded by Italian immigrant George Fiore, spanning the years from the 1850s to the Vietnam War.

All or Nothing. *Putman, 1983.*

Our Father's House. *Putnam, 1985.*

Sons and Daughters. *Putnam, 1987.*

The Pedlock series

Not actually a saga, each book in this series is complete within itself and deals with a different group of family members in the far-flung Jewish Pedlock family. However, the first book is a saga and chronicles the family's history from 1866 to the mid-twentieth century.

The Pedlocks: The Story of a Family. *Simon & Schuster, 1951.*

Pedlock and Sons. *Delacorte Press, 1966.*

Pedlock Saint, Pedlock Sinner. *Delacorte Press, 1969.*

The Pedlock Inheritance. *David McKay, 1972.*

God and Sarah Pedlock. *David McKay, 1976.*

The Pedlocks in Love. *Avon Books, 1978.*

Macdonald, Malcolm

The following books chronicle the events in the lives of the Stevenson and Thornton families. This saga of Victorian England is rife with hypocrisy, lust, intrigue, and ambition.

The World from Rough Stones. *Alfred A. Knopf, 1975.*

The Rich Are with You Always. *Alfred A. Knopf, 1976.*

Sons of Fortune. *Alfred A. Knopf, 1978.*

Abigail. *Alfred A. Knopf, 1979.*

Mackey, Mary

A Grand Passion. *Simon & Schuster, 1986.* A three-generational tale of the glittering world of the ballet set in pre-revolutionary Russia.

McCullough, Colleen

The Thorn Birds. *Harper & Row, 1977.* A story of wealth, power, and illicit passion set in the Australian outback.

Melville, Anne

Melville's sagas are filled with interesting social commentary and attitudes, some of which are ahead of their time.

Lorimer Saga

An English saga from Victorian times to post-World War II.

The Lorimer Line. *Doubleday, 1977.*

Alexa. *Doubleday, 1979.* Also published as *The Lorimer Legacy.*

Blaize. *Doubleday, 1981.* Includes *Lorimers at War* and *Lorimers at Peace.*

Family Fortunes. *Doubleday, 1984.* Includes *The Last of the Lorimers* and *Lorimer Loyalties.*

Hardies Saga

This series takes the Hardies from Edwardian times to the middle of the twentieth century.

The House of Hardie. *Grafton, 1987.*

Grace Hardie. *Grafton, 1988.*

The Hardie Inheritance. *Grafton, 1990.*

Michaels, Fern

(See Soap Opera bibliography.)

Michaels, Kasey

This series follows the fortunes of the Crown family in eighteenth-century England and the American colonies.

The Homecoming. *Pocket Books, 1996.*

The Untamed. *Pocket Books, 1996.*

The Promise. *Pocket Books, 1997.*

Montgomery, Lucy Maud

Although both of Montgomery's series listed here were originally considered within the adult fiction genre, they have long since been appropriated by the young adult readership.

Anne of Green Gables series (reprinted by Bantam Starfire)

This classic series chronicles the life of irrepressible Anne Shirley from her "adoption" by an elderly couple on Prince Edward Island to the coming of age of her youngest daughter during World War I.

Anne of Green Gables. *Page, 1908.*

Anne of Avonlea. *Page, 1909.*

Anne of the Island. *Page, 1915.*

Anne of Windy Poplars. *Fred A. Stokes, 1936.*

Anne's House of Dreams. *Fred A. Stokes, 1917.*

Anne of Ingleside. *Fred A. Stokes, 1939.*

Rainbow Valley. *Fred A. Stokes, 1919.*

Rilla of Ingleside. *Fred A. Stokes, 1921.*

The Emily series (reprinted by Bantam Starfire)

This somewhat autobiographical trilogy details the life of determined and unpredictable Emily from the time her father dies and leaves her an orphan to her marriage and successful career as a writer.

Emily of New Moon. *Fred A. Stokes, 1923.*

Emily Climbs. *Fred A. Stokes, 1925.*

Emily's Quest. *Fred A. Stokes, 1927.*

Nicolaysen, Bruce

New York series

These stories center around the de Kuyper family of New York and span more than three centuries from 1613 to the 1930s.

From Distant Shores. *Avon Books, 1983.*

On Maiden Lane. *Avon Books, 1983.*

Beekman Place. *Avon Books, 1983.*

The Pirate of Gramercy Park. *Avon Books, 1983.*

Gracie Square. *Avon Books, 1984.*

Nicole, Christopher

Caribbean Saga

A sweeping saga of life at Hilltop, a Jamaican sugar plantation, from colonization to the emancipation of the slaves.

Caribee. *St. Martin's Press, 1974.*

The Devil's Own. *St. Martin's Press, 1975.*

Mistress of Darkness. *St. Martin's Press, 1976.*

Black Dawn. *St. Martin's Press, 1977.*

Sunset. *St. Martin's Press, 1978.*

Ogilvie, Elisabeth

Jennie Trilogy

This series takes Jennie from Scotland to Maine in the early nineteenth century.

Jennie About to Be. *McGraw-Hill, 1984.*

10

The World of Jennie G. *McGraw-Hill, 1985.*

Jennie Gilroy. *Down East, 1993.*

Although not a true series, most of Ogilvie's books focus on the coastal islands of Maine and the people who lived there, in particular the Bennett family. Among others, these titles include:

High Tide at Noon. *Thomas Y. Crowell, 1944.*

Storm Tide. *Thomas Y. Crowell, 1945.*

Ebbing Tide. *Thomas Y. Crowell, 1947.*

How Wide the Heart. *McGraw-Hill, 1959.*

An Answer in the Tide. *McGraw-Hill, 1978.*

The Summer of the Osprey. *McGraw-Hill, 1987.*

Plaidy, Jean (Eleanor Burford Hibbert. Also writes as Victoria Holt and Philippa Carr)

Many of Plaidy's historical novels have been organized into trilogies or series and could fall within the saga subgenre. *(See also Historical Romances bibliography.)*

Plain, Belva

Anna Friedman Saga

This series chronicles the lives of Jewish immigrant Anna Friedman and her family from the first part of the twentieth century through the Vietnam War.

Evergreen. *Delacorte Press, 1978.*

The Golden Cup. *Delacorte Press, 1986.*

Tapestry. *Delacorte Press, 1988.*

Harvest. *Delacorte Press, 1990.*

Random Winds. *Delacorte Press, 1980.* A three-generational saga of the New York Farrell doctors spanning the years from the turn of the century to the present.

Crescent City. *Delacorte Press, 1984.* A saga of nineteenth-century New Orleans.

Porter, Donald Clayton

Colonization of America series (Engel Creation)

A continuing saga of the American wilderness and the Iroquois nation. (This series is labeled both the Colonization of America series and the White Indian series.)

White Indian. *Bantam Books, 1979.* First in this series that includes nearly 30 books.

Rayner, Claire

Rayner is a multitalented writer noted for her sharply drawn characters, intriguing plots, and accurate historical research. Rayner has also written other fiction and non-fiction titles including some early nurse romances and a wide variety of popular advice books on subjects ranging from sex and family health to housekeeping and child care.

Performers series

A 12-volume series that follows the varying fortunes of the doctors and actors of the Lackland and Lucas families in Victorian England, beginning with *Gower Street* (Simon & Schuster, 1973) and ending with *Seven Dials* (Weidenfeld, 1987).

The Poppy Chronicles

This series chronicles the lives of Poppy and her family through much of the twentieth century.

Jubilee. *Weidenfeld, 1987.*

Flanders. *Weidenfeld, 1988.*

Flapper. *Weidenfeld, 1989.*

Blitz. *Weidenfeld, 1990.*

Festival. *Weidenfeld, 1991.*

Sixties. *Weidenfeld, 1992.*

Renault, Mary

Renault's exceptionally well-researched and readable stories of the ancient world are included in the Historical Novel bibliography.

Rofheart, Martha

The Savage Brood. *Thomas Y. Crowell, 1978.* A monumental saga that spans five centuries of the theatrical Savage family's life, from Renaissance England to Hollywood's heyday.

Ross, Dana Fuller

Wagons West series. (Engel Creation)

Fast-paced, action-filled stories of the American westward movement. The main characters vary from book to book, but continuity is maintained by characters who have appeared before or are related to those in earlier books. The stories span the years between 1837 and 1876. This 24-book series begins with *Independence!* (Bantam Books, 1979) and ends with *Celebration!* (Bantam Books, 1989).

The Holts: An American Dynasty series

This ten-volume series picks up where Wagons West leaves off and follows the fortunes of the Holts, characters from the earlier series, beginning with *Oregon Legacy* (Bantam Books, 1989) and concluding with *Awakening* (Bantam Books, 1995).

Spellman, Cathy Cash

So Many Partings. *Delacorte Press, 1983.*

An Excess of Love. *Delacorte Press, 1985.*

Paint the Wind. *Delacorte Press, 1990.* A saga of the Old West during the second half of the nineteenth century.

Steel, Danielle

Thurston House. *Delacorte Press, 1982.*

Family Album. *Delacorte Press, 1985.*

Stirling, Jessica

Stirling is noted for well-written, carefully plotted books peopled with strong, memorable characters in realistic settings and situations. Most of her works are linked into series. Two of her more popular series are:

Beckman Family Saga

These books center on Holly Beckman, a young Jewish girl in London during the 1920s and 1930s, who becomes a part owner of an antique store.

The Drums of Time. *St. Martin's Press, 1980.* Published as *The Deep Well at Noon* by Hodder & Stoughton, 1979.

The Blue Evening Gone. *St. Martin's Press, 1981.*

The Gates of Midnight. *St. Martin's Press, 1983.*

Stalkers of Blacklaw series

A saga of a Scottish mining town in the nineteenth century and the struggles of the people to survive.

Strathmore. *Delacorte Press, 1975.* Published as *The Spoiled Earth* by Hodder & Stoughton, 1974.

Call Home the Heart. *St. Martin's Press, 1977.* Published as *The Hiring Fair* by Hodder & Stoughton, 1976.

The Dark Pasture. *St. Martin's Press, 1978.* Hodder & Stoughton, 1977.

Stubbs, Jean

The Howarth Chronicles

A saga that sweeps from 1760 to the present and chronicles the lives of the Howarths, iron industrial magnates of Wydendale Valley, Lancastershire.

By Our Beginnings. *St. Martin's Press, 1979.* Published as *Kit's Hill* by Macmillan, 1978.

An Imperfect Joy. *St. Martin's Press 1981.* Published as *The Ironmaster* by Macmillan, 1981.

The Vivian Inheritance. *St. Martin's Press, 1982.*

The Northern Correspondent. *St. Martin's Press, 1984.*

Swindells, Madge

Swindells's sweeping stories take strong, aggressive characters; focus them on sex and vengeance; and put them in glitzy international settings.

Summer Harvest. *Doubleday, 1984.* Macdonald, 1983.

Song of the Wind. *Doubleday, 1985.*

Shadows on the Snow. *Macdonald, 1987.*

The Corsican Woman. *Warner Books, 1988.*

Taylor, Lucy

Avenue of Dreams. *New American Libraries, 1990.* An Italian immigrant seamstress fights for the American dream in this three-generational saga that spans the tumultuous first half of the twentieth century.

Thane, Elswyth

Williamsburg series

These stories follow the lives of several families from the American Revolution to World War II.

Dawn's Early Light. *Duell, 1943.*

Yankee Stranger. *Duell, 1944.*

Ever After. *Duell, 1947.*

The Light Heart. *Duell, 1947.*

Kissing Kin. *Duell, 1948.*

This Was Tomorrow. *Duell, 1951.*

Homing. *Duell, 1957.*

Thomas, Rosie

All Sins Remembered. *Bantam Books, 1990.*

Trent, Lynda

Everlasting. *HarperPaperbacks, 1991.* Two very different sisters take steps to save the family home in this story that moves from the 1920s to the 1980s.

Ware, Ciji

Wicked Company. *Bantam Books, 1992.* A dramatic tale of a woman writer's struggles for success in the British theatre world of the eighteenth century.

Williams, Jeanne

The Valiant Women. *Pocket Books, 1980.* Romance with a Western flavor.

Winston, Daoma

Emerald Station. *Avon Books, 1974.* A three-generational saga of strong women and the men who loved them.

The Fall River Line. *St. Martin's Press, 1983.* A four-generational saga centering around the people involved with the Fall River Line of passenger ships that sailed between Boston and New York.

There were also a number of other historical series popular during the 1970s and 1980s. Although they are not necessarily sagas, and the stories are often individual and not always connected, they feature a common theme. The Making of America series (50 volumes), including the Women Who Won the West series and Americana: The Making of the Cities series, and the Women at War series are examples.

10

Chapter 11

Gay and Lesbian Romance

DEFINITION

Gay and Lesbian Romances are love stories in which the romantic interest focuses on gay or lesbian couples. Except for this basic difference, these novels are much like other romances, i.e., their plots revolve around the love relationship of the two main characters, they allow the reader to become emotionally involved in the courtship process, and they come in a variety of types (such as Gothic, Historical, Contemporary, Young Adult). As in all romances, there are problems that the main characters must work out before they can be happily united, and in the Gay or Lesbian Romance, these problems are typically related to their sexuality. For example, one of the main characters may have a difficult time accepting his or her homosexuality, or outside prejudice may threaten the relationship. Nevertheless, as long as the love relationship between the two protagonists is the focus of the story, these are generally not considered problem novels; they are romances.

Gay and Lesbian Romances aimed at the young adult market run a greater risk of being labeled problem novels than do those appealing to other readership segments. This is because the young adult novel by its nature tends to focus on the problems of growing up. Choosing values, making friends, dealing with feelings and emotions, becoming independent, and coming to terms with one's sexuality are examples of problems the young adult novel treats. During the 1970s the emphasis in these books expanded to include more serious social issues (such as drugs, pregnancy, abortion, divorce, death, suicide, mental illness) and the problem novel was born. Even though in recent years the trend has been away from the hard-core, often depressing examples of this type, much of young adult fiction still reflects the influence of the problem novel. This influence is found especially in books that deal with serious topics, such as homosexuality, and finding a true young adult romance that deals with serious issues is not easy. There are some young adult gay novels, however, such as *Annie on My Mind* (1982) by Nancy Garden, which play down the "gayness as a problem" aspect of the plot and focus on the love story line. Novels of this type are definitely within the Romance genre.

As with other romances, sexual explicitness in Gay and Lesbian Romances varies; and while sex is an important aspect in these stories, its treatment can range from relatively innocent to nearly pornographic.

The plot patterns and characters in Gay and Lesbian Romances are as varied as those in heterosexual romances. For example, a tall, arrogant, mysterious hero is tamed by an innocent, large-eyed young man in a typical gay Gothic; a pair of teenagers discover love and bring a rapist to justice in a classic young adult lesbian romance; and a divorcée comes to terms with her own sexuality and finds love with a younger woman in a contemporary lesbian romance. Plots include secrets, mysteries, betrayals, and misunderstandings on the part of the lovers—all of which, of course, are cleared up by the end of the book. In addition, certain stereotypical characters (e.g., the other man/woman, the villain, the loyal friend/servant) appear with regularity.

APPEAL

The primary appeal of the Gay or Lesbian Romance is to the homosexual reader looking for a love story with which he or she can more easily identify. Most readers enjoy a book more when they have something in common with the characters and situations it describes, when they can empathize with the characters and relate their experiences. However, until recently, the gay or lesbian reader has not been able to do this, particularly in the area of romance fiction. The Gay or Lesbian Romance offers an alternative to heterosexual status quo—a love story that assumes the validity of the gay or lesbian lifestyle and proceeds from there.

Although Gay and Lesbian Romance is a very small and highly specialized niche market, the appeal of these books is not necessarily limited to members of the gay and lesbian community. These stories may also be of interest to heterosexuals who have an interest in the gay lifestyle. The likelihood of crossover readership is especially enhanced by books that contain both gay and straight characters and portray them all with realism, openness, and warmth.

ADVISING THE READER

General readers' advisory information is provided in chapter 3; several points to consider when advising Gay and Lesbian readers are listed below.

- Readers who enjoy Gay or Lesbian Romances may also enjoy other types of gay or lesbian fiction as well—short stories, essays, poetry, biographies, mysteries, science fiction, etc.

- Readers of Gay or Lesbian Romances might also be interested in works that, while not exclusively gay, describe cultures in which the homosexual lifestyle is a valid and accepted option. Many of these are found in the science fiction or fantasy categories and are exemplified by works such as Marion Zimmer Bradley's Darkover novels. It is also interesting to note that sensitively treated gay or lesbian secondary characters are beginning to appear in romance novels. *Dearly Beloved* by Mary Jo Putney and *An Arranged Marriage* by Jo Beverley are two of the many examples.

- Sexual explicitness varies within the Gay and Lesbian Romance subgenre, just as it does in other romance subgenres, and the same caveats apply to both.

- Occasionally, a reader new to gay or lesbian fiction will ask for advice on what to read first. In general, classics or particularly well-done titles such as *Patience and Sarah*, *The Well of Loneliness*, or *Annie on My Mind* are good choices.

- Although it is important for advising readers in all romance types, the reference interview is especially important in the area of Gay and Lesbian Romance. Unless they live in an urban or university setting where bookstores likely carry a good supply of gay literature, most homosexuals are dependent upon the library.[1] A sensitive and aware librarian (in addition to a progressive collection development policy) are invaluable for putting readers in touch with relevant and appropriate books.

In the past decade the number of books addressing the topic of gay and lesbian literature, particularly in the scholarly arena, has increased dramatically. Several of the more general reference works are listed below and may be helpful to those wanting additional information.

Cruikshank, Margaret
Lesbian Studies: Present and Future. *New York: The Feminist Press, 1982.*

Gough, Cal, and Ellen Greenblatt, eds.
Gay and Lesbian Library Service. *Jefferson, NC: McFarland and Company, Inc., 1990.* Primarily of interest to librarians who serve the gay and lesbian community. Limited discussion of genre fiction.

Malinowski, Sharon, ed.
Gay and Lesbian Literature. *Detroit, MI: St. James Press, 1994.* This bio-bibliographic source covers more than 200 writers, including some who have written romance. Includes introductory essays, "Gay Male Literature" and "Lesbian Literature" by Wayne R. Dynes and Barbara G. Grier, respectively.

Summers, Claude J. , ed.

> **The Gay and Lesbian Literary Heritage: A Reader's Companion to the Writers and Their Works, from Antiquity to the Present.** *New York: Henry Holt, 1995.* Alphabetically arranged by topic, this well-done companion provides essays on a variety of topics and authors. Bibliographies are provided for most entries.

The following older works may also still be of interest.

Young, Ian

> **The Male Homosexual in Literature: A Bibliography.** 2nd ed. *Metuchen, NJ: Scarecrow, 1982.*

PUBLISHERS

Although a number of major publishers do produce an occasional gay or lesbian romance, most are published by smaller firms, often specializing in gay and lesbian titles. Names of several of these are listed below. For more complete information, refer to chapter 21, "Publishers."

Alyson Publications, Inc.

Firebrand Books

Naiad Press, Inc.

Rising Tide Publications

Seal Press

Spinster's Ink

BRIEF HISTORY

Although homosexual literature has existed since antiquity, the Gay and Lesbian Romance as we know it today is a relatively new phenomenon. Prior to the birth of the modern gay movement in 1969 (precipitated by the police raid on the Stonewall gay bar), the availability of gay and lesbian literature was limited. There were a few isolated novels, such as Radclyffe Hall's *The Well of Loneliness* (1928), which was banned on both sides of the Atlantic, or Claire Morgan's *The Price of Salt* (1952), which achieved a certain amount of acclaim and general exposure. However, except for the lesbian pulps popular during the late 1950s and early 1960s, gay and lesbian literature was more or less dormant.

The 1969 Stonewall raid changed all that. By the mid-1970s gay and lesbian publishing of all types was in full swing. Some earlier works were being republished, and new materials, such as *Rubyfruit Jungle* (1973) by Rita Mae Brown, were appearing. Late in the decade a number of major publishers tried to appeal to the gay market, contracting with writers not only for serious materials but also for light fiction, such as *Gaywick* (1980) by Vincent Virga. Unfortunately, the endeavor was not successful from the publishers' point of view, and much gay and lesbian publishing moved to the smaller, specialized publishing houses.

Although serious non-fiction gay and lesbian materials continued to be published, the first half of the 1980s saw a new trend—a growing interest in gay fiction of the genre variety. Mystery series, science fiction, and romances, all with homosexual orientations, began to appear in the market. Older works of this type that had been neglected were reprinted and marketed, and new genre authors were actively sought. In spite of society's recent conservative swing, this trend has endured; and despite the expected ups and downs, the gay genre market, particularly for Mystery, Science Fiction, and Fantasy, continues to expand and to provide crossover appeal to the reading community in general. Romance, however, has not necessarily benefited from this trend, and although improving in quality, it remains, for the present, a small niche market. Readers interested in a good, recent article on the state of the gay and lesbian publishing market may wish to read James A. Martin's "Gay and Lesbian Publishing: The Rainbow Shines Brighter." *Publishers Weekly* 244 (April 28, 1997): 32–35.

SELECTED GAY AND LESBIAN ROMANCE BIBLIOGRAPHY

The following are merely a few examples of the wide variety of materials, from classics to contemporaries, currently available. Many authors have other titles also of interest to gay and lesbian romance readers. When applicable, the year a work was originally published appears in parentheses following current publication information.

Aldridge, Sarah

The Late Comer. *Naiad Press, 1974.*

Tottie: A Tale of the Sixties. *Naiad Press, 1975.*

Cytherea's Breath. *Naiad Press, 1976.*

All True Lovers. *Naiad Press, 1978.*

The Nesting Place. *Naiad Press, 1982.*

Madame Aurora. *Naiad Press, 1983.* Politics, social upheaval, and love in late nineteenth-century America.

Magdalena. *Naiad Press, 1987.*

Keep to Me Stranger. *Naiad Press, 1989.* An upscale department store is the setting for this contemporary lesbian romance that features gentile and Jewish protagonists, with all the attendant complications.

A Flight of Angels. *Naiad Press, 1992.* Romance in McCarthy era Washington, D. C.

Michaela. *Naiad Press, 1994.* This innocent lesbian romance addresses the problems of AIDS, abuse, betrayal, and jealousy.

Bannon, Ann

Bannon is one of the classic pulp writers of the 1950s. These books are currently available under the Volute imprint (classic lesbian reprints) from Naiad Press. The following titles are all part of the Beebo Brinker series. Original publication dates are in parentheses.

Odd Girl Out. *Naiad Press, 1986. (1957)*

I Am a Woman. *Naiad Press, 1986. (1959)*

Women in Shadows. *Naiad Press, 1986. (1959)*

Journey to a Woman. *Naiad Press, 1986. (1960)*

Beebo Brinker. *Naiad Press, 1986 (1963)*

Bohan, Becky

Sinister Paradise. *Madwoman Press, 1993.* Chilling mystery and romance.

Bradley, Marion Zimmer

Although her novels cannot be labeled gay romance, some of Bradley's science fiction Darkover titles deal with gay relationships and may appeal to readers of gay romances.

Thendara House. *DAW, 1983.*

Burford, Lolah

Edward, Edward. *Macmillan, 1973.* A complex tale of love, sexuality, and self-acceptance set in Regency England.

Chambers, Jane

Burning. *JH Press, 1978.* The spirits of two women from an earlier time seek to control two modern-day women and live out their love through them. A lesbian Gothic romance of passion and possession.

Christian, Paula

Christian is a writer of pulps from the 1950s and 1960s. Many of her books have straight endings and are available as reprints from her publishing company, Timely Books, P.O. Box 267, New Milford, CT 06776.

Love's Where You Find It. *Timely, 1961.*

The Cruise. *Timely, 1982.*

This Side of Love. *Timely, 1963.*

Cohen, Celia

Smokey O: A Romance. *Naiad Press, 1994.*

Payback. *Naiad Press, 1995.*

Courted. *Naiad Press, 1997.* A policewoman and a tennis player find romance.

Davidson, Diane

Deadly Gamble. *Rising Tide, 1997.*

Dawkins, Cecil

Charleyhorse. *Viking, 1985.* A novel of love, mother/daughter relationships, acceptance, and romance set on a vast ranch on the Kansas prairie.

Ennis, Catherine

To the Lightning. *Naiad Press, 1988.* An unusual survival story.

South of the Line. *Naiad Press, 1989.*

Clear Water. *Naiad Press, 1991.* Mystery and romance in small-town Louisiana.

Up, Up and Away. *Naiad Press, 1994.* On the run from the Mob, Sarah and Margaret take to the air in a hot air balloon—and crash-land in a Louisiana swamp.

Forbes, Edith

Alma Rose. *Seal Press, 1993.* A lovely, flamboyant trucker changes the life of quiet Pat Lloyd in this well-reviewed novel.

Forrest, Katherine V.

Forrest has written romances as well as created the popular Kate Delafield Mystery series.

Curious Wine. *Naiad Press, 1983.* A classic lesbian romance.

Daughters of a Coral Dawn. *Naiad Press, 1984.* An erotic lesbian science fiction romance.

The Emergence of Green. *Naiad Press, 1986.* Carolyn Blake must choose between her husband and the woman she loves.

Kate Delafield Mystery series

Amateur City. *Naiad Press, 1984.*

Murder at the Nightwood Bar. *Naiad Press, 1987.*

Beverly Malibu. *Naiad Press, 1989.*

Murder by Tradition. *Naiad Press, 1991.*

Liberty Square. *Berkley, 1996.*

Apparition Alley: A Kate Delafield Mystery. *Berkley, 1997.*

Futcher, Jane

Crush. *Avon Press, 1981.* Jinx develops a crush on beautiful Lexis and learns a lot about love, friendship, and betrayal. Features a 1960s girls' school setting. For YAs.

Dream Lover. *Alyson, 1997.* Love blooms when two women meet again after 20 years apart. Northern California (Marin County) setting.

Garden, Nancy

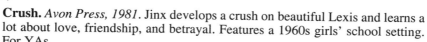

Annie on My Mind. *Farrar, Straus & Giroux, 1982.* High school seniors Eliza Winthrop and Annie Kenyon come to terms with their own homosexuality and deal with the repercussions of their actions in this classic lesbian coming-of-age love story. A classic.

Grumbach, Doris

The Ladies. *E. P. Dutton, 1984.* A classic, fictionalized account of two unconventional eighteenth-century women, Eleanor Butler and Sarah Ponsonby, who chose to live as a married couple.

Guy, Rosa

Ruby. *Bantam Books, 1976.* A classic story dealing with the lesbian relationship of two young black women.

Hall, Radclyffe

The Well of Loneliness. *(1928) Avon Books, 1981.* A classic in lesbian fiction set in Paris during the 1920s.

Hamilton, Wallace

Kevin. *St. Martin's Press, 1980.* When teenage Kevin meets older, successful Bruce, they are attracted to each other. In spite of problems of their own making and society's attempts to split them apart, their relationship survives.

Hartman, Melissa

The Sure Thing. *Naiad Press, 1994.* A geologist and a television reporter find love in earthquake-prone Southern California.

Hautzig, Deborah

Hey, Dollface! *Bantam Books, 1978.* Best friends Val and Chloe suddenly realize there may be more to their relationship than just friendship. Recommended for the young adult market.

Hayes, Penny

The Long Trail. *Naiad Press, 1986.* Blanche and Teresa discover love in the Old West while enduring Indian attacks, a covered wagon journey, and other assorted hardships.

Yellowthroat. *Naiad Press, 1988.* A pioneer romance with a New Mexico setting.

Kathleen O'Donald. *Naiad Press, 1994.* Irish immigrant Kathleen and English immigrant Rose fight for workers rights and their love in early twentieth-century America.

Kallmaker, Karin

In Every Port. *Naiad Press, 1989.* Two businesswomen find love in the 1970s.

Touchwood. *Naiad Press, 1991.*

Paperback Romance. *Naiad Press, 1992.* Masquerades, music, and romance with a Parisian flavor.

Car Pool. *Naiad Press, 1993.* A car pool friendship deepens into something more in this romance set in the San Francisco Bay area.

Painted Moon. *Naiad Press, 1994.* A Sierra snowstorm leads two women to friendship and then to love.

Wild Things. *Naiad Press, 1996.*

Embrace in Motion. *Naiad Press, 1997.*

Kennedy, Evelyn

Cherished Love. *Naiad Press, 1988.*

Of Love and Glory. *Naiad Press, 1989.* Romance in a World War II setting.

To Love Again. *Naiad Press, 1991.*

Forever. *Naiad Press, 1995.* Romance with a "clerical" touch.

Lamb, Cynthia

Brigid's Charge. *Bay Island Books, 1997.* Persecution and charges of witch-craft plague two healers in Colonial America.

Lynch, Lee

The Swashbuckler. *Naiad Press, 1985.*

Toothpick House. *Naiad Press, 1986.*

Mann, Bill

The Men from the Boys. *E. P. Dutton, 1997.*

Merrick, Gordon

All these books are mass-market and are sexually explicit.

The Lord Won't Mind. *Avon Books, 1970.* Linked by characters to the next two books.

One for the Gods. *Avon Books, 1971.*

Forth into Light. *Avon Books, 1974.*

An Idol for Others. *Avon Books, 1977.*

The Quirk. *Avon Books, 1978.*

Now Let's Talk About Music. *Avon Books, 1981.*

The Great Urge Downward. *Avon Books, 1984.*

A Measure of Madness. *Warner Books, 1986.*

Miller, Isabel (Alma Routsong)

Patience and Sarah. *McGraw-Hill, 1972.* Originally published as *A Place for Us*, 1969. This classic lesbian historical romance is based on the lives of an eighteenth-century American artist and her companion.

The Love of Good Women. *Naiad Books, 1996.* World War II setting.

Morgan, Claire

The Price of Salt. *Coward-McCann, 1952.* Classic lesbian romance, considered one of the finest examples of the genre.

Newbold, Elisabeth

The City Within. *Maurice Gerodias, 1973.*

Newman, Leslea

Good Enough to Eat. *Firebrand, 1986.* Liza comes to terms with both her buli-mia and her sexuality.

Ramstetter, Victoria

The Marquise and the Novice. *Naiad Press, 1981.* A lesbian Gothic Romance.

Renault, Mary

Many of her historical novels deal with gay relationships, although they would not be classified gay romances.

Fire from Heaven. *Pantheon, 1969.* This and the book that follows tell the story of Alexander the Great.

The Persian Boy. *Pantheon, 1972.*

Roberts, Michele

A Piece of the Night. *Women's Press, 1980.*

The Visitation. *Women's Press, 1980.* Interesting in that it describes "heterosexual sex from a female point of view with all the force and lyricism of those male authors, like D. H. Lawrence, who have so famously falsified the female experience" (*Guardian*).

Rofheart, Martha

My Name Is Sappho. *Putnam, 1974.* The story of the sixth-century B.C. poet, activist, rebel, and feminist.

Rule, Jane

Rule is an award-winning novelist who writes both fiction and non-fiction.

Desert of the Heart. *World, 1965.* c.1964, Macmillan.

Memory Board. *Naiad Books, 1987.*

After the Fire. *Naiad Books, 1989.*

Scoppetone, Sandra

Happy Endings Are All Alike. *Harper & Row, 1978.* A well-handled story of prejudice, self-acceptance, and lesbianism.

Simmonds, Diana

Heart on Fire. *Naiad Press, 1996.*

Forty Love. *Naiad Press, 1997.* A tennis pro and an Australian artist find love.

Smith, Shelley

Horizon of the Heart. *Naiad Press, 1986.* A passionate romance set along the New England coast.

The Pearls. *Naiad Press, 1987.* Mystery, impersonation, and conflict.

Stevenson, Sylvia

Surplus. *Naiad Press, 1986.* D. Appleton, 1924.

Stewart, Jean

Emerald City Blues. *Rising Tide Press, 1996.*

Sturtevant, Katherine

A Mistress Moderately Fair. *Alyson, 1988.* Romance in seventeenth-century London.

Taylor, Valerie

Love Image. *Naiad Press, 1977.*

Journey to Fulfillment. *Naiad Press, 1982. (1964)* This and the two books that follow are pulp reprints and are linked by the protagonist, Erika Frohmann, a survivor of a Nazi concentration camp.

A World Without Men. *Naiad Press, 1982. (1963)*

Return to Lesbos. *Naiad Press, 1982. (1963)*

Virga, Vincent

Gaywick. *Avon Books, 1980.* A Gothic gay classic.

A Comfortable Corner. *Avon Books, 1982.* This gay romance has a contemporary setting.

Wilson, Barbara

An award-winning author, Wilson writes in a number of forms and is noted for the political and social issues explored in her mysteries and short stories. The following novels feature Pam Nilsen, a lesbian feminist sleuth, and are more mystery and suspense than romance; nevertheless, they may appeal to some romance readers.

Murder in the Collective. *Seal Press, 1984.*

Sisters of the Road. *Seal Press, 1986.*

The Dog Collar Murders. *Seal Press, 1989.*

The Cassandra Reilly Mysteries

Gaudi Afternoon. *Seal Press, 1990.*

Trouble in Transylvania. *Seal Press, 1993.*

Zanger, Molleen

Gardenias Where There Are None. *Naiad Press, 1994.* A romantic lesbian ghost story.

NOTES

1. Sasha, Alyson, "What Librarians Should Know About Gay and Lesbian Publishing," *Collection Building* (spring 1984): 22-23.

Chapter 12

Inspirational Romance

DEFINITION

The Inspirational Romance is essentially a love story infused with religious (typically Christian) values and beliefs. These stories usually employ a basic story line of the Innocent or Sweet Romance variety, but as the love relationship progresses, the characters also grow spiritually. They come to grips with their feelings regarding some basic tenet of faith as they learn to deal with their romantic feelings. Usually, they need to resolve things with God before their love relationship can work out. This combination of romantic and spiritual growth is the distinguishing characteristic of the Inspirational Romance subgenre.

Settings for Inspirationals can be either contemporary or historical, and according to recent statistics, titles published in 1996 were evenly divided between the two types.[1] Inspirationals are as varied as other romance types and are becoming even more so. Styles range from the cheerily upbeat or sweetly nostalgic to the hard-hitting and emotionally wrenching; characters are rich and polished, poor and unsophisticated, or firmly middle-class; and settings run the gamut from modern urban America to first-century Rome. Currently, romances set in the nineteenth-century American West, especially those with small-town or rural Americana settings, are particularly popular.

Typically, the Inspirational Romance plot introduces a religiously oriented heroine to a worldly, wounded, or alienated hero (or vice versa); arranges for them to be attracted to each other; and then provides obstacles, often in the form of conflicting religious values, to their relationship. Eventually, they are allowed to live "happily ever after," but not before both characters have done much soul-searching and have reconciled most of their differences, religious and otherwise. Although the less religious member of the couple usually comes to accept the beliefs of the other, occasionally it is the "religious" one who experiences the most spiritual growth. Often this happens when the more religious individual has been especially rigid in his or her beliefs or intolerant and judgmental of nonbelievers. This plot pattern, as well as the themes of redemption and spiritual awakening, have been staples of the subgenre for years. However, variations exist, and with the growing popularity of the Inspirational Romance and the entry of mainstream publishers into the market, the variety is likely to increase.

In most cases the Inspirational Romance is nondenominational, expressing generic, rather than denomination-specific, beliefs. (Occasionally, a particular religious group publishes romances that promote its own denomination, but this is the exception rather than the rule.) However, while the views expressed in these stories are not denomination-related, as a whole, the general slant of the Inspirational Romance is toward the conservative. There are some exceptions, but in general, these romances express basic fundamentalist rather than more liberal religious views.

APPEAL

The appeal of the Inspirational Romance is primarily to those who espouse the religious views presented in the stories. Readers enjoy stories about people who share their beliefs; it lends a certain validity to their own views. In fact, reading about someone who successfully deals with problems similar to one's own and within a similar frame of reference can be helpful, sometimes even "inspirational."

Because of their selective focus, Inspirational Romances, unlike many romance subgenres, do not have a broad, general appeal. For their target audience, however, they fill a definite need, and recently, their popularity has been growing. Fueled by the generally conservative mood of the country and the increasing visibility and influence of Christian fundamentalist groups and churches, Inspirationals are being published, marketed, and read in increasing numbers. This growing popularity was recognized by the Romance Writers of America in 1995 when it reinstated both its Rita and Golden Heart Awards in the Inspirational Romance category. They had been discontinued in 1987 for lack of entries and interest.

ADVISING THE READER

General readers' advisory information is provided in chapter 3; several points to consider when advising Inspirational Romance readers are listed below.

- Religious fiction is not new. Many inspirational romance readers will also enjoy some of the older religious historical novels such as Henryk Sienkiewicz' *Quo Vadis?*, Lloyd C. Douglas's *The Robe*, or *The Silver Chalice* by Thomas Costain. Also consider recommending novels that present fictionalized accounts of Biblical characters' lives, such as *Two from Galilee* by Marjorie Holmes.

- Readers who like Inspirational Romances might also like other types of inspirational literature, for example, religious poetry, inspirational guides to daily life, testimonials, or biographies of popular religious figures.

- Readers of Inspirational Romances may also enjoy some romances of the non-Inspirational variety, especially some in the traditional sweet category lines. Traditional Regencies might also appeal, even though religion or faith are rarely mentioned. Note: Explicit sex is not part of most Inspirationals, so be sure your non-Inspirational recommendations are innocent rather than sensual.

- Although the religious emphasis in most of these romances is non-denominational, some publishing houses are church related, and their romances reflect a specific religious doctrine. It is important, therefore, to be aware of this during the reference interview and try to match the reader with the appropriate book. For example, some conservative Christians might not find Inspirationals expressing certain Mormon principles acceptable, and vice versa.

- The reference interview is particularly important in the area of Inspirational Romance. Religious beliefs are personal and deeply felt, and many people have very strong opinions concerning them. Therefore, it may be necessary to spend a bit more time than usual determining the specific type of romance the reader wants.

> Note: Those who want more information on Inspirational Romances may find helpful the periodic review columns on Inspirational Fiction in *Library Journal* or Lynda Cole's "Inspirational Romance—a Survey," *Romance Writers' Report* 17(February 1997):14-15.

PUBLISHERS

Although one major publisher currently has an Inspirational Romance line and others occasionally handle religious novels and romances, most Inspirational Romances are produced by a number of smaller religious publishing houses. The names of several of these are listed below. (For more complete information refer to chapter 21, "Publishers.")

Barbour and Company, Inc.

Beacon Hill Press (Subsidiary of Nazarene Publishing House)

Bethany Publishers

Crossway Books

Harvest House Publishers, Inc.

Multnomah Publishers (formerly Questar)

Steeple Hill (division of Harlequin/Silhouette)

Thomas Nelson Publishers

Tyndale House Publishers, Inc.

Victor Books

Zondervan Publishing House

BRIEF HISTORY

Although the Inspirational Romance in its current form is a relatively recent addition to the romance market, novels that express religious principles, promote certain religious beliefs, or depict religious events have been around for years. Some, of course, aren't even religious by design; they simply reflect the customs and widely held beliefs of the times. For example, the highly successful mid-nineteenth-century novel, *The Wide, Wide World* (1850) by Elizabeth Wetherell (Susan Warner) was not a religious book *per se*. Nevertheless, in addition to having a universally appealing plot situation—an orphaned heroine in the care of a singularly unsympathetic relative—it also managed incidentally to promote the desirability of a Christian home and lifestyle by featuring the children of a local clergyman as important characters in the story. A number of other writers during the same general period, however, intentionally used religious themes in their works. Novels of this type were extremely popular during and just after the Civil War, and many of the favorites were written by women who were part of the most active writing group of the period, the Domestic Sentimentalists. Two particularly popular works of this kind were *St. Elmo* (1867) by Augusta Jane Evans and *The Gates Ajar* (1868) by Elizabeth Stuart Phelps.

Following the 1860s, the popularity of the religious novel declined. However, it was renewed in the mid-1880s with the belated popularity of Lew Wallace's *Ben-Hur* (1880) and firmly reestablished by the next decade with a host of *Ben-Hur* imitations and other Religious Historicals, including the perennial favorite *Quo Vadis?* (1896) by Henryk Sienkiewicz. By the turn of the century interest in religious romances had waned in favor of other types, in particular the Nationalistic Historical. There were isolated exceptions, such as the extremely popular *The Rosary* (1910) by English writer Florence Barclay and the popular inspirational love stories by Grace Livingston Hill. It wasn't until the decades of the 1930s and 1940s, with the grim realities of the Great Depression and World War II, that religious novels once again began to appear on the bestseller lists. Works such as *Magnificent Obsession* (1932) and *The Robe* (1942) by Lloyd C. Douglas, *The Keys to the Kingdom* (1941) by A. J. Cronin, and Sholem Asch's *The Nazarene* (1939) were some of the more popular.

The next few decades saw a leveling off in popularity of religious materials, except for a surge of interest during the 1950s in large-scale religious motion pictures (e.g., Cecil B. DeMille's *The Ten Commandments*, *Ben-Hur*, and *Quo Vadis?*). However, from the late 1970s and into the mid-1980s, in keeping with the general feeling of the times, there was renewed interest in romantic novels with a specific religious message. The movement was strong, and both the adult and young adult markets were targeted. Earlier religious writers were reprinted, established writers experimented with the Inspirational genre, and new Inspirational Romance writers appeared in print. In the late 1980s interest slumped. Series were canceled (including Silhouette's Inspirations line) and the Romance Writers of America discontinued the Inspirational Romance category in its Rita (then the Golden Medallion) and Golden Heart Awards. Eventually, the market rebounded and now appears to be thriving. New publishers and lines have come on the scene (e.g., Questar with its Palisades and Palisades Presents lines, Barbour with its Heartsong Presents, and Harlequin/Silhouette with its Love Inspired line under the Steeple Hill imprint). In 1995 the Romance Writers of America reinstated the Inspirational Romance category of their Rita and Golden Heart Awards. Accounting for only three percent of the romances published in 1996, the Inspirational Romance is clearly a niche market, and because of its specific appeal, it is likely to remain so.[2] Nevertheless, the age-old combination of faith, hope, and love is reaching a broader audience than ever before and is currently enjoying a long-awaited revival.

SELECTED INSPIRATIONAL ROMANCE BIBLIOGRAPHY

Bacher, June Masters

A noted writer of inspirational non-fiction, Bacher also writes Inspirational Romance fiction, primarily of the pioneer or Period Americana variety. Many of her older works have been republished, and some are available on audiocassette.

Love Is a Gentle Stranger series

The following romances form a series about two women and how they and their families find new lives in the Oregon West.

Love Is a Gentle Stranger. *Harvest House, 1983.*

Love's Silent Song. *Harvest House, 1983.*

Diary of a Loving Heart. *Harvest House, 1984.*

Love Leads Home. *Harvest House, 1984.*

Love Follows the Heart. *Harvest House, 1990.*

Love's Enduring Hope. *Harvest House, 1990.*

Journey to Love series

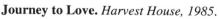

In this series of books, what begins as a "marriage of convenience" ends as a union of true love grounded in faith.

Journey to Love. *Harvest House, 1985.*

Dreams Beyond Tomorrow. *Harvest House, 1985.*

Seasons of Love. *Harvest House, 1986.*

My Heart's Desire. *Harvest House, 1986.*

The Heart Remembers. *Harvest House, 1990.*

From This Time Forth. *Harvest House, 1991.*

Love's Soft Whisper series

A series of love and faith primarily set in the American Northwest.

Love's Soft Whisper. *Harvest House, 1986.*

Love's Beautiful Dream. *Harvest House, 1987.*

When Hearts Awaken. *Harvest House, 1987.*

Another Spring. *Harvest House, 1988.*

When Morning Comes Again. *Harvest House, 1988.*

Gently Love Beckons. *Harvest House, 1989.*

Heartland Heritage series

The turbulent 1930s and 1940s serve as the time frame for this series.

No Time for Tears. *Harvest House, 1992.*

Songs in the Whirlwind. *Harvest House, 1992.*

Where Lies Our Hope. *Harvest House, 1992.*

Return to the Heartland. *Harvest House, 1993.*

Bergren, Lisa Tawn

Bergren primarily writes contemporary Christian romance.

Chosen. *Palisades, 1996.*

Firestorm. *Palisades, 1996.* A Rita Award nominee.

Treasure. *Palisades, 1995.*

Refuge. *Palisades, 1994.*

Blackstock, Terri

Blackstock often includes mystery and thriller elements in her romances and also writes non-Inspirational stories as Terri Herrington and Tracy Hughes.

The Suncoast Chronicles

A series of Christian suspense novels.

Evidence of Mercy. *Zondervan, 1995.*

Justifiable Means. *Zondervan, 1996.*

Ulterior Motives. *Zondervan, 1996.*

Presumption of Guilt. *Zondervan, 1997.*

Second Chances series

Never Again Good-Bye. *Zondervan, 1996.*

When Dreams Cross. *Zondervan, 1997.* A light, Christian romance with an unusual amusement park setting.

Blind Trust. *Zondervan, 1997.* A strained romantic relationship, attempted murder, and a fast-paced pursuit keep things moving in this light thriller.

Broken Wings. *Zondervan, 1997.*

Newpointe 911 series

Private Justice. *Zondervan, 1998.*

Blackwell, Lawana

Victorian Serenade series

This Inspirational series is set in Victorian England.

Like a River Glorious. *Tyndale House, 1995.*

Measures of Grace. *Tyndale House, 1996.*

Jewels for a Crown. *Tyndale House, 1996.*

Song of a Soul. *Tyndale House, 1997.*

Gresham Chronicles

The Widow at Larkspur Inn. *Tyndale House, 1997.*

Canfield, Muriel

I Wish I Could Say I Love You. *Bethany House, 1983.*

Anne. *Bethany House, 1984.*

A Victorian Marriage. *Bethany House, 1986.* A deeply troubled marriage, a Christian servant girl, and the disastrous Chicago fire of the 1870s combine in this story of love and faith.

Crow, Donna Fletcher

Crow is a multipublished Inspirational Romance and historical fiction writer who has won several awards, including one presented by the National Federation of Press Women in 1993 for her historical novel *Glastonbury: The Novel of Christian England.* Some of her more important series are listed here.

Daughters of Courage Trilogy

Trilogy set in nineteenth- and twentieth-century Idaho.

Kathryn: Days of Struggle and Triumph. *Moody Press, 1992.*

Elizabeth: Days of Loss and Hope. *Moody Press, 1993.*

Stephanie: Days of Turmoil and Peace. *Moody Press, 1993.*

Cambridge Chronicles series (some published as Cambridge Collection series)

Focuses on the Christian evangelical movement in eighteenth- and nineteenth-century England.

To Be Worthy. *Crossway, 1994.* Victor Books, 1986.

A Gentle Calling. *Crossway, 1995.* Victor Books, 1987.

Treasures of Her Heart. *Crossway, 1994.*

Where Love Begins. *Crossway, 1995.*

Encounter the Light. *Crossway, 1995.*

Into All the World. *Crossway, 1996.*

Virtuous Heart series

All Things New. *Beacon Hill Press, 1997.* Her father's remarriage forces a deeply Christian, marriage-oriented young woman to redirect her life in unexpected ways.

Dodson, DeAnna Julie

Dodson's medieval Historicals are more sensual than many other Inspirational Romances.

In Honor Bound. *Crossway, 1997.* Commanded by the king to marry, Lady Rosalynde ends up united with a man who can't forget his former love and has given up on God. Good historical detail.

By Love Redeemed. *Crossway, 1997.* Separated for two years by politics and war, Lady Elizabeth and Thomas of Brenden begin their marriage all over again in this tale of treachery and intrigue.

Hardy, Robin

Lystra series

These tales of love, romance, intrigue, and faith are set in a mythical kingdom during a mythical time. This trilogy contains many elements of the fantasy genre. They were re-published in 1994 as The Annals of Lystra series by NavPress.

The Chataine's Guardian. *Word Books, 1984.*

Stone of Help. *Word Books, 1985.*

High Lord of Lystra. *Word Books, 1986.* Published as *The Liberation of Lystra* by NavPress, 1994.

Hatcher, Robin Lee

Hatcher also writes Period Historical Romances.

The Forgiving Hour. *WaterBrook Press, 1998.* A woman must deal with the fact that the girl who destroyed her marriage is now the woman her son loves.

Hickman, Patricia

Land of the Far Horizon series

Voyage of the Exiles. *Bethany House, 1995.*

Angel of the Outback. *Bethany House, 1995.*

The Emerald Flame. *Bethany House, 1996.*

Beyond the Wild Shores. *Bethany House, 1997.* An independent schoolteacher finds violence and love in this story set in early nineteenth-century New South Wales (Australia).

Hill, Grace Livingston

A prolific and popular novelist for more than half a century, Hill wrote religious romances filled with adventure, conflict, and domesticity. In spite of the fact that her stories are dated (especially in regard to ethnic, racial, and gender references), evangelistic, and predictable, Hill's works strike a chord with many of today's readers, and some are still popular and in print. Many of her works can be found in their original editions in older public libraries, but several publishers have reissued some of them in series. Hill's works include:

According to the Pattern. *Griffith and Rowland, 1903.* Revell, 1982. A troubled marriage is healed when the partners find Christ.

The Story of a Whim. *Golden Rule, 1903.* Revell, 1982. When Hazel sends an organ to a "poor struggling, missionary girl, Christie," she doesn't know that Christie is a man, a citrus rancher, and not a Christian.

Matched Pearls. *J. B. Lippincott. 1933.* Considered one of the author's more important works.

Head of the House. *J. B. Lippincott, 1940.* Concerns the efforts of a family of siblings not to be separated upon the death of their parents. Not a "typical Livingston Hill."

Hill, Ruth Livingston (Ruth Hill Munce)

Ruth is the daughter of writer Grace Livingston Hill.

John Nielson Had a Daughter. *J. B. Lippincott, 1950.* Published as *The Homecoming* by Harvest House, 1985.

The South Wind Softly Blew. *J. B. Lippincott, 1959.*

This Side of Tomorrow. *Zondervan, 1962.*

Holmes, Marjorie

Although a writer of various other literature types, including some young adult romances in the late 1950s and early 1960s, *Two from Galilee* is probably the author's most popular and best-known fictional work.

Two from Galilee. *Revell, 1972.* A love story of Mary and Joseph.

Three from Galilee. *Harper & Row, 1985.* A sequel to *Two from Galilee*, this is a story of Jesus, from the time he was 12 years old to when he began his ministry at age 30. (This is not a romance, but it may be of interest to those who liked the first book.)

The Messiah. *Harper & Row, 1987.*

Hunt, Angela E.

Legacies of the Ancient River series

Ancient Egyptian setting.

Dreamers. *Bethany House, 1996.* A Rita Award nominee.

Brothers. *Bethany House, 1997.*

Journey. *Bethany House, 1997.*

Keepers of the Ring series

Colonial American Setting

Roanoke: The Lost Colony. *Tyndale House, 1996.*

Jamestown. *Tyndale House, 1996.*

Hartford. *Tyndale House, 1996.*

Rehoboth. *Tyndale House, 1997.*

Charles Towne. *Tyndale House, 1998.*

Johnson, Grace

The Rebel. *Tyndale House, 1996.*

Scottish Shores series

Tempest at Stonehaven. *Tyndale House, 1997.* The life of a lonely, widowed schoolteacher takes on new meaning and unexpected danger when a mysterious stranger comes to her small village on Scotland's wild coast. Gothic flavor.

Karr, Kathleen

Karr writes other fiction, including children's books.

Light of My Heart. *Zondervan, 1984.*

From This Day Forward. *Zondervan 1985.* A Rita Award winner.

Chessie's King. *Zondervan, 1986.*

Destiny's Dreamers series

Gone West. *Barbour & Co., 1993.*

The Promised Land. *Barbour & Co., 1993.*

Kraus, Jim, and Terri Kraus

Treasures of The Caribbean series

Christian romance in an exotic setting.

Pirate of the Heart. *Tyndale House, 1996.*

Passages of Gold. *Tyndale House, 1996.*

Journey to the Crimson Sea. *Tyndale House, 1997.* A romance between the vicar and a reformed prostitute appalls the local congregation in this tropical romance.

Laity, Sally, and Dianna Crawford

Freedom's Holy Light series

Revolutionary War Setting.

The Gathering Dawn. *Tyndale House, 1994.*

The Kindled Flame. *Tyndale House, 1994.*

The Tempering Blaze. *Tyndale House, 1995.*

Fires of Freedom. *Tyndale House, 1996.*

The Embers of Hope. *Tyndale House, 1996.*

The Torch of Triumph. *Tyndale House, 1997.*

Langsdale, R. M.

The Sixth Jar. *Vantage, 1973.* This unusual story of Jesus and Mary Magdalene (refreshing to some, heretical to others) is no longer in print and may be difficult to find.

Loring, Emilie

This early twentieth-century writer wrote more than 50 romances, most of which reflect her conservative nationalistic and moralistic views. Some of her books fall within the Inspirational Romance category. *(See also Basic Romance bibliography.)*

Swift Water. *Penn, 1929.* A worldly young woman returns to her hometown and becomes attracted to the local minister. A lively romance with strong inspirational overtones.

MacDonald, George

A nineteenth-century author, currently known for his children's stories and fantasies, MacDonald also produced a number of religious novels and romances which have been rewritten, retitled, and republished by Bethany house under the title "The George MacDonald Classics Series, Retold for Today's Readers." Victor Books has also reprinted at least one trilogy.

The Maiden's Bequest. *Bethany House, 1985.* Originally published as *Alec Forbes of Howglen*, 1865. After a bout with love, rejection, and guilt, Alec finds true love in the arms of his long-time friend, Annie.

The Marshmallows Trilogy

All three of these books have been edited (rewritten) by Dan Hamilton.

A Quiet Neighborhood. *Victor Books, 1985.* Published as *Annals of a Quiet Neighborhood*, 1867.

The Seaboard Parish. *Victor Books, 1985. (1868)*

The Vicar's Daughter. *Victor Books, 1985. (1872)*

The Thomas Wingfold Trilogy

The Curate's Awakening. *Bethany House, 1985.* Published as *Thomas Wingfold, Curate*, 1876.

The Lady's Confession. *Bethany House, 1986.* Published as *Paul Faber, Surgeon*, 1879.

The Baron's Apprenticeship. *Bethany House, 1986.* Published as *There and Back*, 1891. Richard, a skilled bookbinder, discovers the well-kept secret of his birth.

The Highlander's Last Song. *Bethany House, 1986.* Originally published as *What's Mine's Mine*, 1886. Set at the beginning of the nineteenth century, this story details the social, cultural, and spiritual changes highland chief Alister Macruadh faces, as well as the choices he must make for the good of his people.

The Shepherd's Castle. *Bethany House, 1983.* Originally published as *Donal Grant*, 1883. A Gothic story involving a young tutor, the owner of a castle, Lady Arctura, and a long-kept secret that threatens to destroy the present.

The Fisherman's Lady. *Bethany House, 1982.* Originally published as *Malcolm*, 1875. This and the following book tell of a fisherman who discovers he is really a marquis and the aristocratic woman he loves. Gothic Romances set in nineteenth-century Scotland.

The Marquis' Secret. *Bethany House, 1982.* Originally published as *Marquis of Lossie*, 1877.

MacLean, Amanda

Westward. *Questar, 1995.*

Stonehaven. *Questar, 1995.* Returning to Stonehaven, the family home she was taken from years earlier, Callie finds intrigue, deceit, a dangerous cause to work for, and love. Sequel to *Westward.*

Promise Me the Dawn. *Questar, 1996.* Historical San Francisco setting.

Kingdom Come. *Questar, 1997.*

Marshall, Catherine

A writer of inspirational literature and best known for her biography of her husband, *A Man Called Peter*, Catherine Marshall has also written two classic young adult books that can also be considered within the Inspirational Romance subgenre.

Christy. *McGraw-Hill, 1967.*

Julie. *McGraw-Hill, 1984.*

Morris, Gilbert

This multipublished, popular writer of Inspirational Romances is noted for his series, some of which are The Wakefield Dynasty, The Spirit of Appalachia, and The Far Fields. Some of his series are written with other people. A recent example is:

Chronicles of the Golden Frontier
(Written with J. Landon Ferguson)

Riches Untold. *Tyndale, 1998.*

Unseen Riches. *Tyndale, 1999.*

12

Nichols, Charlotte

 For the Love of Mike. *Silhouette Inspirational, 1984.* A Rita Award winner.

Oke, Janette

Oke is one of the most prolific and best-known writers of Inspirational Romances, especially those of the Period Americana variety. Many of her works are in series, some of which are listed here.

Love Comes Softly series

This series describes the continuing story of pioneers Marty and Clark and their descendants.

Love Comes Softly. *Bethany House, 1979.*

Love's Enduring Promise. *Bethany House, 1980.*

Love's Long Journey. *Bethany House, 1982.*

Love's Abiding Joy. *Bethany House, 1983.*

Love's Unending Legacy. *Bethany House, 1984.*

Love's Unfolding Dream. *Bethany House, 1987.*

Love Takes Wing. *Bethany House, 1988.*

Love Finds a Home. *Bethany House, 1989.*

The Canadian West series

The Story of Elizabeth and Wynn as they make a new home in the Canadian West of the nineteenth century.

When Calls the Heart. *Bethany House, 1983.*

When Comes the Spring. *Bethany House, 1985.*

When Breaks the Dawn. *Bethany House, 1986.*

When Hope Springs New. *Bethany House, 1986.*

Seasons of the Heart series

A quartet of gentle farm-life stories that follows the growth of Joshua Chadwick Jones from childhood to maturity.

Once upon a Summer. *Bethany House, 1981.*

The Winds of Autumn. *Bethany House, 1987.*

Winter Is Not Forever. *Bethany House, 1988.*

Spring's Gentle Promise. *Bethany House, 1989.*

Women of the West series

The Calling of Emily Evans. *Bethany House, 1990.*

Julia's Last Hope. *Bethany House, 1990.*

Roses for Mama. *Bethany House, 1991.*

A Woman Named Damaris. *Bethany House, 1991.*

They Called Her Mrs. Doc. *Bethany House, 1992.*

The Measure of a Heart. *Bethany House, 1992.*

A Bride for Donnigan. *Bethany House, 1993.*

Heart of the Wilderness. *Bethany House, 1993.*

Too Long a Stranger. *Bethany House, 1994.*

The Bluebird and the Sparrow. *Bethany House, 1995.*

A Gown of Spanish Lace. *Bethany House, 1995.*

Drums of Change. *Bethany House, 1996.*

A Prairie Legacy series
The Tender Years. *Bethany House, 1997.* This sequel to the Love Comes Softly series tells the story of teenage Virginia, Marty's and Clark's granddaughter.

Another Homecoming. *Bethany House, 1997.*

The Matchmakers. *Bethany House, 1997.* A pair of charming matchmakers get a taste of their own medicine.

Page, Carole Gift
In Search of Her Own. *Steeple Hill, 1997.* Originally published as *To Chase a Shadow* by Accent Books, 1985.

Heartland Memories series
The House on Honeysuckle Lane. *Thomas Nelson, 1994.*

Home to Willowbrook. *Thomas Nelson, 1995.*

The Hope of Herrick House. *Thomas Nelson, 1996.*

Page, Carole Gift, and Doris Elaine Fell
The following books are inspirational mystery romances, all dealing with the same two protagonists.

Mist over Morrow Bay. *Harvest House, 1985.*

Secret of the East Wind. *Harvest House, 1986.*

Storm Clouds over Paradise. *Harvest House, 1986.*

Palmer, Catherine

Heartquest series
The Treasure of Timbuktu. *Tyndale House, 1997.* When Tillie wishes for a bit more excitement in her life, being kidnapped by an adventurer isn't quite what she had in mind. But their escapades are lively and fun in true romance tradition.

The Treasure of Zanzibar. *Tyndale House, 1997.*

The Treasure of Kilimanjaro. *Tyndale House, 1999.*

A Town Called Hope series
Prairie Rose. *Bethany House, 1997.* Illegitimate Rosie escapes the Kansas City orphanage that has been her only home and heads west as housekeeper with Seth Hunter and his young son.

Pella, Judith

The Russians series
The continuing saga of the Fedorcenko family.

The Crown and the Crucible. *Bethany House, 1991.*

A House Divided. *Bethany House, 1992.*

Travail and Triumph. *Bethany House, 1992.*

Heirs of the Motherland. *Bethany House 1993.*

The Dawning of Deliverance. *Bethany House, 1995.*

12

White Nights, Red Mornings. *Bethany House, 1997.* The Russian Revolution disrupts the country and divides Anna Fedorcenko's children.

Phillips, Michael, and Judith Pella

The Stonewycke Trilogy

Romance and mystery in the nineteenth century. A three generational saga in the Gothic style tells about the love of Maggie and Ian for each other and for Stonewycke. Sweeps from Scotland to America and back again.

The Heather Hills of Stonewycke. *Bethany House, 1985.*

Flight from Stonewycke. *Bethany House, 1985.*

The Lady of Stonewycke. *Bethany House, 1986.*

Rivers, Francine

Winner of three Rita Awards in the inspirational category and a member of the Romance Writers of America's Hall of Fame, Rivers has also written non-inspirational romances.

 An Echo in the Darkness. *Tyndale House, 1994.*

Redeeming Love. *Tyndale House, 1994.* A young prostitute is saved by the love of a Christian man. (A version of this book, rewritten specifically for the Christian Inspirational Romance market, was published under the same title by Questar in 1997.)

As Sure as the Dawn. *Tyndale House, 1995.*

The Scarlet Thread. *Tyndale House, 1996.*

The Atonement Child. *Tyndale House, 1997.* Pregnant as a result of rape, Dynah Carey leaves college and returns home to deal with her situation. More soul-searching and social issues than romance.

Snelling, Lauraine

Dakota Dawn. *Heartsong Presents, 1993.*

Dakota Dream. *Heartsong Presents, 1993.*

Dakota Dusk. *Heartsong Presents, 1994.*

Dakota December. *Heartsong Presents, 1996.*

Thoene, Bodie, and Brock Thoene

The Thoenes are a popular team of Inspirational Romance writers and have a number of series to their credit, such as The Waywant Wind series and the Gresham Chronicles. One of their more recent series is:

The Galway Chronicles

This series focuses on nineteenth-century Ireland.

Only the River Runs Free. *Thomas Nelson, 1997.* Irish conflict during the 1830s.

Of Men and Angels. *Thomas Nelson, 1998.* Ireland of the 1840s.

Ashes of Remembrance. *Thomas Nelson, 1999.*

Turnbull, Agnes Sligh

Turnbull writes sentimental romances, many involving the clergy and containing inspirational elements.

The Golden Journey. *Houghton Mifflin, 1955.*

The Wedding Bargain. *Houghton Mifflin, 1966.*

A Victorian Christmas Tea. *Tyndale House, 1997.* An anthology of four historical Christmas novellas in the Inspirational tradition, complete with favorite recipes by the authors. Included are "Angel in the Attic" by Catherine Palmer, "A Daddy for Christmas" by Dianna Crawford, "Tea for Marie" by Peggy Stokes, and "Going Home" by Kathie Chute.

Wells, Marian

Raised in Utah, Wells often mentions Mormonism and its history in her non-Mormon romances.

When Love Is Not Enough. *Bethany House, 1979.* Published as *Karen* by Bethany House, 1983.

The Wedding Dress. *Bethany House, 1982.*

With This Ring. *Bethany House, 1984.* Sequel to *The Wedding Dress.*

The Starlight Trilogy

The story of Jenny—her love, her marriage, and her search for herself and true faith—that takes her from nineteenth-century New York to Ohio, Missouri, and Illinois.

The Wishing Star. *Bethany House, 1985.*

Morningstar. *Bethany House, 1986.*

Star Light, Star Bright. *Bethany House, 1986.*

Treasure Quest series

Nineteenth-century American settings.

Colorado Gold. *Bethany House, 1988.*

Out of the Crucible. *Bethany House, 1988.*

The Silver Highway. *Bethany House, 1989.*

Jewel of Promise. *Bethany House, 1990.*

Wick, Lori

Wick's historical series are set in Victorian England and in various locales throughout the nineteenth-century American West.

A Place Called Home series (re-released 1996-1997)

A Place Called Home. *Harvest House, 1990.*

A Song for Silas. *Harvest House, 1990.*

The Long Road Home. *Harvest House, 1990.*

A Gathering of Memories. *Harvest House, 1991.*

The Californians

Whatever Tomorrow Brings. *Harvest House, 1992.*

As Time Goes By. *Harvest House, 1992.*

Sean Donovan. *Harvest House, 1993.*

Donovan's Daughter. *Harvest House, 1994.*

Kensington Chronicles

The Hawk and the Jewel. *Harvest House, 1993.*

Wings of the Morning. *Harvest House, 1994.*

Who Brings Forth the Wind. *Harvest House, 1994.*

The Knight and the Dove. *Harvest House, 1995.*

Rocky Mountain Memories series

Where the Wild Rose Blooms. *Harvest House, 1996.*

Whispers of Moonlight. *Harvest House, 1996.*

To Know Her by Name. *Harvest House, 1997.*

Promise Me Tomorrow. *Harvest House, 1997.* A woman who adores children and a man who has a lot to learn about his own son find love and true faith in turn-of-the-century Colorado.

NOTES

1.   Shirley Hailstock, "ROMSTAT: 1996 Romance Statistics," *Romance Writers' Report* 17 (June 1997): 12–15.

2.   Ibid., 12–15.

Chapter 13

Ethnic/Multicultural Romance

DEFINITION

In its simplest form, the Ethnic, or Multicultural, Romance is a love story in which one or both of the protagonists are African American, Latino, Native American, Asian, Pacific Islander, or have a heritage other than the traditional "generic European." Additionally, in these romances, the ethnicity of the characters is both important and acknowledged, lending a culturally authentic flavor to the book and providing a realistic setting for the story. Obviously, this aspect varies in degree from story to story—in some cases the characters' ethnicity is critical to the plot; in others, it merely provides the background. But whatever the situation, these are not "plug and play" romances into which one can drop characters of any ethnic origin and have the story ring true.

Ethnic Romances employ both contemporary and historical settings, which vary according to the story and the particular ethnic group being portrayed. For example, the historical American West is the traditional setting for stories including Native American characters, while most of the recent romances featuring African American protagonists are set in contemporary urban environments. However, writers such as Kathleen Eagle are also writing about contemporary Native American concerns, and interest in African American Historicals, especially those set around the time of the Civil War or in the American West of the mid-to-late 1800s, is increasing. Obviously, nothing can be taken for granted in this rapidly developing subgenre.

The plot patterns used in Ethnic Romances are not necessarily predictable or one-dimensional either. Diverse and wide-ranging, they mirror much of what is found in the non-ethnic romance arena, and although many are straightforward man-meets-woman love stories, some are fast-paced tales of romantic suspense. And as with the settings, no doubt there is much more variety to come.

Although Ethnic Romance encompasses a wide variety of cultural groups, the current emphasis is on the African American segment, and African American romances are the easiest to find because of Pinnacle's highly successful and visible Arabesque line. However, romances featuring characters of other cultures exist, and plans for series that focus on them are being discussed. At the present they are hidden within the regular series and lines, and while they are available, it takes a little more creativity to find them.

APPEAL

The basic appeal of the Ethnic Romance is to readers who are part of the particular cultural group portrayed in the story. Readers enjoy characters and situations with which they can identify—that they can connect with. Until recently (with the exception of the often stereotypical Native American hero present in many Historicals set in the West) there have been few opportunities for romance readers from many ethnic groups to do this. The recent surge in multicultural (particularly African American) romances is providing that opportunity for a large number of long-neglected readers. This is not to say, however, that other readers will not enjoy books about ethnic groups and cultures other than their own. (It is, after all, what many African American, Latino, Asian, and Native American romance readers have been doing for years.) But, in general, the attraction is greatest for readers who see themselves and their cultures reflected in the story and can identify with characters who share a similar heritage.

ADVISING THE READER

General readers' advisory information is provided in chapter 3; however, there are a few points that might be helpful for advising Ethnic and Multicultural Romance fans.

- Readers who enjoy Ethnic/Multicultural Romance may also enjoy non-ethnically oriented romances of a similar type. A reader who enjoys some of the sexy, faster-paced stories in the Arabesque line might also be interested in a Silhouette Desire or a Bantam Loveswept. Readers who like their ethnic romances with a bit of mystery or suspense might also enjoy a Harlequin Intrigue.

- Readers who like Ethnic/Multicultural Romances may also enjoy non-fiction or fiction other than romance that focuses on a particular cultural group. Consider recommending established writers such as Amy Tan, Maya Angelou, and Alice Walker, as well as newer, up-and-coming writers.

- Don't assume that you know what readers want before they tell you. In particular, don't assume that readers will want to read African American romances simply because they are black, are interested only in books related to Asians because they are Japanese, or for that matter are not interested in Ethnic Romances because they don't look "ethnic." In other words, don't assume anything. Ask—and by asking questions, making suggestions, and evaluating readers' reactions, let them tell you what they really want.

- Be sensitive and aware. Whatever your own ethnic background, it is easy to offend without intending to; and offending readers defeats your purpose, which is to put readers in touch with good books that they will enjoy.

BRIEF HISTORY

Although the Ethnic/Multicultural Romance as we know it today is a relatively recent phenomenon, love stories that feature characters from a variety of cultural and ethnic backgrounds are not new. One has only to look at Shakespeare's *Othello* or *Anthony and Cleopatra* (albeit these are not your average uplifting romances), to see that ethnically diverse protagonists have been falling in and out of love for years. In America, stories set in the South or along the frontier were fertile ground for secondary, if not primary, romantic plotlines involving African American, Native American, or Latino (primarily Mexican) characters. While most of these are not essentially romances and were written for other purposes (e.g., Harriett Beecher Stowe's *Uncle Tom's Cabin* 1852), a few, such as *Ramona* (1884) by Helen Hunt Jackson or Edna Ferber's *Show Boat* (1926), have strong romantic themes.

By the late 1950s, ethnic characters, primarily African American or Caribbean, were playing important roles in the lusty, violent Plantation Romances. Launched in 1957 by Kyle Onstott's *Mandingo*, these steamy, often brutal tales of sex and slavery remained popular for several decades, eventually lending some of their characteristics to the Sweet/Savage Romances of the 1970s. With the advent of the 1980s came the publication of Rosalind Welles's *Entwined Destinies* (Dell Candlelight, 1980), one of the earliest category romances with African American characters, and things slowly began to change. Ethnic heroes and heroines were still few and far between, and they were never emphasized, but they were there. Native American heroes (and occasionally heroines) began to appear in Historicals set in the West (e.g., *Savage Ecstasy*, Zebra, 1981, by Janelle Taylor) and by the end of the decade, "Indian" Romances were an accepted fact. But other ethnic characters were still facing an uphill struggle. Even though a number of African American and Latino writers were producing romances, they mainly wrote about white characters. In 1990 Leticia Peoples launched Odyssey Books and began publishing romances with African American heroes and heroines. Several other small houses established their own lines, but it wasn't until Kensington Publishing decided to get involved. With the July 1994 launch of Pinnacle's Arabesque line of multicultural romances with *Serenade* by Sandra Kitt and *Forever Yours* by Francis Ray, things really took off. The line proved highly successful and in 1996 went from producing two books a month to three. Now, other major publishers are getting onboard, including Ballantine, which is collaborating with Genesis Press to reprint some of Genesis's Indigo line of African American contemporaries under Ballantine's One World/Indigo imprint. Although Kensington and Ballantine are currently the only ones with dedicated ethnic/multicultural lines, most of the major houses are systematically adding African American romances to their lists.

Currently, African American romances dominate the Ethnic/Multicultural Romance field, but their widely reported success has attracted new interest. Pinnacle has plans for a new Spanish/English bilingual romance line and has already begun soliciting manuscripts. Currently, there is less interest in the Asian Romance area, as witnessed by the relatively short list of Asian romances included in the following bibliography. This is likely to change. The Native American Romance bibliography contains an overabundance of books with "sexy noble savage"

characteristics, primarily because Native Americans were originally featured only in Western Historicals, and these books were often sexy and violent. However, books including Native American characters in contemporary settings (e.g., those by Kathleen Eagle) are appearing more often, and it is only a matter of time before the entire Multicultural Romance subgenre becomes more representative of its readership.

PUBLISHERS

The following publishers produce African American Romance. For additional information refer to chapter 21, "Publishers."

Ballantine (One World—Indigo Love Stories)

The Genesis Press, Inc.

Odyssey Books

Kensington Books (Arabesque)

SELECTED ETHNIC AND MULTICULTURAL ROMANCE BIBLIOGRAPHY

This bibliography is not comprehensive; the titles listed below are merely examples of the growing number of ethnic/multicultural romances being produced.

African American

Alers, Rochelle

Hidden Agenda. *Pinnacle, 1997.* In a desperate attempt to get her son back, Eve Blackwell agrees to marry a man she hardly knows—a man who has a deadly agenda of his own—with passionate and dangerous results. Mexican setting.

Benson, Angela

Benson's works are light, warm, and enjoyable, with a muted cultural emphasis.

Bands of Gold. *Pinnacle, 1994.*

For All Time. *Pinnacle, 1995.* A couple's relationship endures a major test when she is promoted and he loses his job.

Between the Lines. *Pinnacle, 1996.* An all-business newspaper owner struggles to keep her Alabama paper from being taken over by a suave, debonair New Yorker.

A Family Wedding. *Silhouette, 1997.* Two long-time friends marry, with a little help from the young daughter of the groom. Warm and family centered.

The Way Home. *Pinnacle, 1997.*

Second Chance Dad. *Silhouette, 1997.*

Bunkley, Anita Richmond

Bunkley's historical novels feature African American characters.

Emily, the Yellow Rose. *Rinard, 1989.* Focuses on the Battle of San Jacinto in 1836 and a popular legend.

Black Gold. *E. P. Dutton, 1994.* More Texas history. This time the focus is oil and its effects on one African American family.

Wild Embers. *E. P. Dutton, 1995.* Focuses on African American nurses during World War II.

Starlight Passage. *E. P. Dutton, 1996.* A young woman's search for her roots leads her into unexpected danger as she retraces her ancestors' journey along the Underground Railroad.

Balancing Act. *E. P. Dutton, 1997.*

Ford, Bette

For Always. *Pinnacle, 1995.* A single, too-busy attorney father; a determined high school counselor; and a troubled, teenaged runaway drive the plot in this realistic, compelling contemporary romance.

Forever After. *Pinnacle, 1995.* Secret pasts, exotic cruises, and vivid descriptions are part of this story of reunited lovers.

All the Love. *Pinnacle, 1997.*

Forster, Gwynne

Sealed with a Kill. *Pinnacle, 1995.*

Against All Odds. *Pinnacle, 1996.*

Gilmore, Monique

No Ordinary Love. *Pinnacle, 1994.*

Hearts Afire. *Pinnacle, 1995.* The past returns to cause problems for Celeste's and Dante's budding romantic relationship.

The Grass Ain't Greener. *Pinnacle, 1996.* Touches on the currently important issues of burnout and workaholism.

Soul Deep. *Pinnacle, 1997.*

Hailstock, Shirley

Whispers of Love. *Pinnacle, 1994.*

Clara's Promise. *Pinnacle, 1995.*

White Diamonds. *Pinnacle, 1996.*

Hill, Donna

Rooms of the Heart. *Odyssey Books, 1990.*

Indiscretions. *Odyssey Books, 1991.*

Temptation. *Pinnacle, 1994.*

Scandalous. *Pinnacle, 1995.* Love and politics with a dash of scandal.

Deception. *Pinnacle, 1996.*

Intimate Betrayal. *Pinnacle, 1997.*

Jenkins, Beverly

Jenkins's romances are set primarily in historical America.

Night Song. *Avon Books, 1994.* A Kansas schoolteacher finds love with a Union officer despite her dislike of all Union soldiers. Good historical detail.

Vivid. *Avon Books, 1995.* Dr. Viveca Lancaster is excited about her new practice in Michigan, but the chauvinistic mayor makes life both difficult and passionate for her in this romance that focuses on African Americans after the Civil War.

Indigo. *Avon Books, 1996.*

Kitt, Sandra

One of the best-known writers of African American romance, Kitt was the first African American writer to sign with Harlequin. She also launched Pinnacle's Arabesque line in 1994. Her recent books feature mainstream elements.

Adam and Eva. *Harlequin, 1985.* Reprinted 1997.

Love Everlasting. *Odyssey Books, 1992.*

Serenade. *Pinnacle, 1994.* A wedding reunites two lovers in a warm romance that was one of two books to launch Pinnacle's Arabesque line in 1994.

Sincerely. *Pinnacle, 1995.* A romantic glimpse into the world of television broadcasting.

The Color of Love. *Signet, 1995.* Leah's and Jason's relationship begins with a cup of coffee and ends with love in this story that sensitively examines interracial romantic relationships.

Significant Others. *Onyx, 1996.* A biracial teenager struggles to find himself with the help of his school counselor and his father, who has adjustment problems of his own.

Suddenly. *Pinnacle, 1996.*

Between Friends. *Signet, 1998.* Explores the dynamics of an interracial friendship between two women.

Mason, Felicia

Body and Soul. *Pinnacle, 1995.*

Seduction. *Pinnacle, 1996.*

Rhapsody. *Pinnacle, 1997.*

Ray, Francis

Fallen Angel. *Odyssey Books, 1992.*

Forever Yours. *Pinnacle, 1994.* Her grandmother's ultimatum forces Victoria Chandler into a marriage deal with rancher Kane Taggart. Unexpectedly, they fall in love. Funny and lively.

Undeniable. *Pinnacle, 1995.* Wealthy, successful Logan Prescott returns to his hometown determined to make his former love and her family pay for rejecting and humiliating him.

The Bargain. *Pinnacle, 1995.*

Only Hers. *Pinnacle, 1996.* Shannon Johnson inherits part-ownership in a Texas ranch and finds she has also "inherited" Matt Taggart, the very angry owner of the other part of the ranch.

Incognito. *Pinnacle, 1997.*

Snoe, Eboni

Snoe often makes use of mystery elements and exotic settings.

A Sheik's Spell. *Odyssey Books, 1992.* Love with an Egyptian flavor.

Beguiled. *Pinnacle, 1994.* Deception in Belize.

The Passion Ruby. *Pinnacle, 1995.* Jewels, journals, and Martinique.

Emerald's Fire. *Pinnacle, 1996.*

Tillis, Tracey

Flashpoint. *Onyx, 1997.* Suspense and romance combine in this fast-paced, gripping story of racial hatreds, revenge, politics, and scandal.

Vaughn, Patricia

Murmur of Rain. *Pocket Books, 1996.* A talented, biracial pianist leaves Paris with her sophisticated, but enigmatic, new husband for his family home in Haiti and ends up in a web of decadence and evil that threatens her life and her love. Gothic influences.

Walker, Margie

A Sweet Refrain. *Pinnacle, 1994.* Musical love, Texas-style.

Breathless. *Pinnacle, 1995.* Sparks fly when Solomon Thomas, the new manager of Monique Robbins's club, demands total control.

Indiscretions. *Pinnacle, 1996.*

Conspiracy. *Pinnacle, 1997.*

Welles, Rosalind (Elsie B. Washington)

Entwined Destinies. *Dell, 1980.* Reprinted by Genesis Press. One of the earliest series romances featuring African American characters, this sweet traditional takes a capable magazine reporter and an arrogant oil company executive, sets them down in England, and lets them fall in love.

Wheeler, Amanda

Arms of the Magnolia. *Fawcett Gold Medal, 1994.*

Beyond the Fire. *Fawcett Gold Medal, 1996.*

Asian

Early, Margot

Mr. Family. *Harlequin, 1996.* A family-centered romance that features Hawaiian characters and culture.

Lowell, Elizabeth

Jade Island. *Avon Books, 1998.* American Asian heroine finds love with an adventurer hero. Interesting cultural insights.

Mahon, Annette

Mahon's romances are set in the Hawaiian Islands and often feature characters with Hawaiian, Pacific Islander, and other Asian heritages.

Above the Rainbow. *Avalon, 1995.*

Lei of Love. *Avalon, 1996.*

Maui Rose. *Avalon, 1996.*

Massey, Sujata

The Salaryman's Wife. *HarperPaperbacks, 1997.* When the beautiful wife of a successful Japanese businessman is murdered at a historic Japanese resort, biracial Rei Shimura and Scottish Hugh Glendinning are caught in a web of suspicion and danger in this cross-cultural romantic suspense.

Stone, Katherine

Pearl Moon. *Fawcett Columbine, 1995.* An Amerasian architect caught between two worlds comes to terms with her heritage, meets her unknown half sister, and falls in love with a powerful developer. Emotionally involving and exotic.

Latino

Bittner, Rosanne

Shameless. *Zebra, 1993.* Horse thief Nina Juarez causes problems for Lt. Clay Youngblood of the U.S. Camel Corps—not the least of which is the fact that he loves her.

The Forever Tree. *Bantam Books, 1994.* A logging baron and a Spanish aristocrat eventually create a successful life for themselves and their family in this involving California saga.

Dailey, Janet

Touch the Wind. *Pocket Books, 1979.* A contemporary captive/captor story set in Mexico's High Sierras.

Davis, Justine

Lover Under Cover. *Silhouette, 1996.* The vicious murder of a Southern California teenager brings an activist teacher and a Latino police detective together. Good cultural detail.

De Blasis, Celeste

The Proud Breed. *Coward-McCann, 1978.* This action-filled, three-generational saga features a biracial heroine, compelling passion, palomino horses, and lots of California history.

Faith, Barbara

Dark, Dark My Lover's Eyes. *Silhouette, 1994.* Gothic overtones.

Samuel, Barbara

Dancing Moon. *HarperPaperbacks, 1996.* Features biracial Native American/Latino hero.

Shayne, Maggie

Reckless Angel. *Silhouette, 1993.*

Tracy, Marilyn

Sharing the Darkness. *Silhouette,1994.*

Wind, Ruth (Barbara Samuel)

The Last Chance Ranch. *Silhouette, 1995.* This Janet Dailey Award winner focuses on abuse issues and has a Latino hero.

Native American (sometimes called "Indian" in the trade)

Many of the writers listed below also write Western Romances that do not necessarily feature Native American characters.

Anderson, Catherine

This series also deals with physical handicaps and abuse issues.

Comanche Moon. *HarperPaperbacks, 1991.*

Comanche Heart. *HarperPaperbacks, 1992.*

Indigo Blue. *HarperPaperbacks, 1992.*

Baker, Madeline

Baker writes action-oriented, occasionally stereotypical, Western romances that feature Native American characters (often the hero) from various tribes.

Midnight Fire. *Leisure, 1992.* Adopted by a Nebraska Indian tribe, a runaway heroine and an alcoholic hero find a new life together—and then civilization interferes.

The Spirit Path. *Leisure, 1993.* A nineteenth-century Sioux shaman comes through time to bring healing and love to a modern-day handicapped writer of Indian romances.

Cheyenne Surrender. *Leisure, 1994.* A biracial bounty hunter returns to Cheyenne to claim his inheritance and discovers that he is guardian of the young daughter of his father's mistress.

Apache Runaway. *Leisure, 1995.*

Chase the Wind. *Leisure, 1996.*

Renegade Heart. *Leisure, 1996.*

Feather in the Wind. *Leisure, 1997.*

Bird, Beverly

Bird writes both contemporary and historical romances, often using Native American characters.

Comes the Rain. *Avon Books, 1990.* Healer Gray Eyes and warrior Hawk work together to help their people in a futile attempt to keep the white world from destroying them. Poignant.

Touch the Sun. *Berkley, 1994.*

A Man Without a Wife. *Silhouette, 1995.* When a Navajo nurse decides to locate the son she gave up for adoption years earlier, she finds danger as well as love in the process.

The Pony Wife. *Jove, 1995.*

Bittner, Rosanne

Bittner is a noted writer of Western romances, many of which involve Native American characters.

Arizona Ecstasy. *Zebra, 1989* (as F. Rosanne Bittner). Bittersweet story of star-crossed lovers and the final years of the free Apache nation.

Sioux Splendor. *Zebra, 1990* (as F. Rosanne Bittner). "Rescued" from Red Wolf, the Sioux warrior she loves and the father of her child, Cynthia unwillingly returns to the East. But when they meet again years later, circumstances have changed and it takes time for love to win out.

Unforgettable. *Zebra, 1994.* Love blooms between Oklahoma Land Rush settler Allyson Mills and Cheyenne army scout Ethan Temple despite separation, prejudice, and their pasts.

Tame the Wild Wind. *Bantam Books, 1996.* A biracial hero seeking revenge for the murder of his wife and child finds healing when he meets a woman with wounds of her own.

Bonander, Jane

Bonander's Historicals often focus on California Native Americans and cultures.

Secrets of a Midnight Moon. *St. Martin's Press, 1991.* Kidnapped to be a teacher for some Indian children, Anna Jensen eventually finds love with her kidnapper.

Dancing on Snowflakes. *Pocket Books, 1995.* Abuse, murder, and wounded protagonists are key to this compelling story of love and trust.

Wild Heart. *Pocket Books, 1995.*

Winter Heart. *Pocket Books, 1996.*

Warrior Heart. *Pocket Books, 1997.* An adventurer returns to claim the daughter he left 12 years ago when his Native American wife was murdered and discovers she has been legally adopted by the heroine.

Dailey, Janet

Night Way. *Pocket Books, 1981.*

The Pride of Hannah Wade. *Pocket Books, 1985.*

The Proud and the Free. *Little, Brown, 1994.* Focuses on the Cherokee Trail of Tears in 1838.

Legacies. *Little, Brown, 1995.*

Dellin, Genell

Dellin has written a number of Indian romances, many of which have been grouped into trilogies or series (e.g., Comanche Trilogy and Cherokee Nation series).

Cherokee Dawn. *Avon Books, 1990.* Orphaned and alone, Tracey Longbaugh saves Ridge Chekote's life, only to find herself falling in love with him. A story of hardship, separation, and prejudice. First in the Cherokee Trilogy.

Cherokee Nights. *Avon Books, 1991.* Attorney Celina Hawthorne wins a case for developer King Chekote, but he wins her heart. Her search for her own Cherokee heritage adds to the historical detail of this romance. Second in the Cherokee Trilogy.

Comanche Wind. *Avon Books, 1992.* Comanche Chief Windrider goes against tribal tradition to keep his captive, Jennie O'Bannion, for himself. Part of the Comanche Trilogy.

Cherokee Sundown. *Avon Books, 1992.* Tiana and Standing Deer fight to save their love as they help their people fight for their land. Third in the Cherokee Trilogy.

Comanche Flame. *Avon Books, 1994.* Lost gold, murder, a Spanish Don, and native American mysticism propel this story to its fast-paced conclusion.

Silver Moon Song. *Avon Books, 1996.* Even though Tay Nashoba knows he must marry within his tribe, he finds himself drawn to schoolteacher Emily Harrington—an attraction that leaves them with an impossible decision. Second in the Choctaw Indian Trilogy.

Eagle, Kathleen

Eagle is noted for her sensitive portrayal of Native American culture and issues.

Medicine Woman. *Harlequin, 1989.*

Heaven and Earth. *Harlequin, 1990.* Sick, widowed, and deserted by her wagon train, missionary Katherine Fairchild is healed by Native American trapper Jed West. Their growing love, however, must endure separation and a bit of soul-searching if it is to survive.

This Time Forever. *Avon Books, 1992.* A rodeo champion falsely imprisoned for murder and a nurse who served on his jury find healing and love in this sensitive and emotionally involving story.

Fire and Rain. *Avon Books, 1994.* The parallel love stories of two white women—separated by 100 years—who choose to live with the Lakota warriors they each love.

Reason to Believe. *Avon Books, 1995.* Clara and Ben Pipestone are reunited by their daughter and find love and healing during a sacred winter journey.

Sunrise Song. *Avon Books, 1996.* Parallel love stories juxtapose the 1930s and the 1970s as Michelle Benedict and Zane Lone Bull work to uncover the mystery that surrounds the old Hiawatha Asylum for Insane Indians and uncover some secrets in Zane's past as well.

The Night Remembers. *Avon Books, 1997.* Native American mysticism and lore combine with crime and gangs in an inner-city Minneapolis setting.

Edwards, Cassie

Many of Edwards's Western romances include Native American protagonists.

When Passion Calls. *Leisure, 1990.*

Savage Promise. *Leisure, 1991.*

Wild Splendor. *Topaz, 1993.*

French, Judith E.

Many of French's Colonial American historical romances focus on Native American themes.

Indian Moon Trilogy

Moonfeather. *Avon Books, 1990.*

Highland Moon. *Avon Books, 1991.*

Moon Dancer. *Avon Books, 1991.*

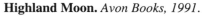

Gentry, Georgina

Gentry writes sexy, action-filled romances that can be stereotypical and use sweet/savage conventions.

Cheyenne Captive. *Zebra, 1987.*

Comanche Cowboy. *Zebra, 1988.*

Cheyenne Caress. *Zebra, 1990.*

Apache Caress. *Zebra, 1991.* Classic captive-in-love-with-captor romance.

Sioux Slave. *Zebra, 1992.* When Brand Erickson is captured in battle and then falls in love with the Sioux maiden who heals him, they face prejudice, hostility, and an angry ex-fiancée when they return to the white world.

Half-Breed's Bride. *Zebra, 1993.*

Cheyenne Splendor. *Zebra, 1994.*

Song of the Warrior. *Zebra, 1995.* When Willow returns to her people, the Nez Perce, to help them adjust to the white world's ways, she falls in love with a man who has no love for a "white Indian" or her ideas.

Timeless Warrior. *Zebra, 1996.* Time travel elements.

Warrior's Prize. *Zebra, 1997.*

Harrington, Kathleen

Cherish the Dream. *Avon Books, 1990.* A biracial Cheyenne army scout and a member of the USGS mapmaking team find love in the Old West.

Warrior Dreams. *Avon Books, 1992.*

Dreamcatcher. *Avon Books, 1996.* When fiery Rachel Robinson's proxy marriage to an abusive army officer turns out to be a disaster, she breaks his nose and flees into the wilderness, only to be rescued by Cheyenne warrior Strong Elk and his people.

Hayes, Allison (Lynn Coddington)

Hayes writes Historicals and contemporaries, both of which deal with Native American characters and cultures.

Spellbound. *Avon Books, 1990.* Although the protagonists in this historical are both white, the hero was raised among the Ogalala Sioux. Well-handled Native American issues.

Storm Dancers. *Avon Books, 1991.* Tenderfoot Genny sets up solitary housekeeping along the Oregon Trail; but she is taken by Gus Renard, a handsome, mixed-blood cardsharp, to his Lakota family for safety. Cultural differences and fear of commitment are issues.

Hudson, Janis Reams

Apache Magic. *Zebra, 1991.*

Apache Legacy. *Zebra, 1994.*

Apache Heartsong. *Zebra, 1995.*

Johnson, Susan

Johnson writes some of the most sensual romances in print. Her Braddock-Black Absarokee series features strong protagonists and is especially popular.

The Braddock-Black Absarokee series

Blaze. *Berkley, 1986.* Spoiled Boston debutante Blaze Braddock and Absarokee chief Hazard Black find passion, love, and commitment—and found a dynasty.

Silver Flame. *Berkley, 1988.* The story of Trey, Blaze's and Hazard's son.

Forbidden. *Bantam Books, 1991.* The story of Daisy, Hazard Black's natural daughter.

Pure Sin. *Bantam Books, 1994.* Lady Flora and Adam Serre find love in the wilds of Montana.

Lee, Rachel

Lee's popular Conard County books often have Native American characters.

Cherokee Thunder. *Silhouette, 1992.*

Ironheart. *Silhouette, 1993.*

Thunder Mountain. *Silhouette, 1994.*

Lindsey, Johanna

Savage Thunder. *Avon Books, 1989.* An English widow and a troubled, angry guide find love, passion, and healing in the American West.

McCall, Dinah

Dreamcatcher. *HarperPaperbacks, 1996.* Time travel and Native American mystical elements.

Tallchief. *HarperPaperbacks, 1997.* Running for her life, Kathleen Ryder takes her teenaged daughter and heads for Morgan Tallchief, the man she has never stopped loving. A sometimes violent adventure story of love, commitment, and renewal.

Smith, Deborah

Beloved Woman. *Bantam Books, 1991.* A poignant, involving story set during the time of the Cherokee Trail of Tears.

The Cherokee Trilogy (republished as a single volume in a slightly edited version as Follow the Sun by Bantam Books, 1991.)
Sundance and the Princess. *Bantam Books, 1989.*

Tempting the Wolf. *Bantam Books, 1989.*

The Cherokee Trilogy: Kat's Tale. *Bantam Books, 1989.*

Taylor, Janelle

Most of Taylor's romances feature Native American characters; she is especially known for her early Ecstasy series.

Gray Eagle/Alisha series (Ecstasy series)
Taylor's noted eight-volume series begins with *Savage Ecstasy* (Zebra, 1981) and concludes with *Forever Ecstasy* (Zebra, 1991). The word "Ecstasy" is in each title. (Like many Romance series, this series didn't start out with a name; it just evolved.)

Savage Conquest. *Zebra, 1985.* The passionate story of Blazing Star, Indian warrior, and Miranda is set in the nineteenth-century American West.

Chase the Wind. *Kensington, 1994.* A fast-paced story of gunrunning and violence that pairs undercover agents Bethany Wind and Navarro Breed in a business relationship that turns romantic.

Destiny Mine. *Kensington, 1995.* An Indian maiden who has taken on the celibate role as "the chosen one" questions her decision when she falls in love.

Webb, Peggy

Witch Dance. *Bantam Books, 1994.* Dr. Kate Malone goes to practice on the Chickasaw tribal lands in Oklahoma in this lore-laden story of the old ways versus the new.

Wind, Ruth (Barbara Samuel)

Wind's romances often deal with Native American or Latino characters and cultures.

Walk in Beauty. *Silhouette, 1994.*

Rainsinger. *Silhouette, 1996.*

Part 3

Research Aids

Chapter 14

History
and Criticism

    At long last there is some indication that scholars are finally beginning to realize what popular fiction readers have known all along—that romance fiction, like mystery, science fiction, fantasy, and all the other genres before it, bears serious consideration. Although few will argue its merits as Great Literature—indeed, most genre fiction rarely aspires to such a designation—the appeal of romance fiction is well documented. A genre that has achieved and retained such long-term popularity can no longer be ignored, and researchers in the fields of literature, women's studies, and popular culture have begun to show an interest. *Begun*, of course, is the operative word. Although the scholarly material available for romance fiction is still merely a trickle compared to that for the other genres,* the situation has improved during the past decade. More books and articles are being published, more graduate theses and dissertations are appearing, and the scholarship that is being presented is, in general, more thoughtful, insightful, and evenhanded than in the past. We don't have the whole library yet, but at least we have a healthy start toward building a body of critical, historical, and reference literature in this long-neglected area of study.

    *The mystery/detective, science fiction, and fantasy genres, in particular, boast numerous reference sources and critical and historical materials. Although many individual guides exist for these genres, *Genreflecting: A Guide to Reading Interests in Genre Fiction*, 4th ed., by Diana Tixier Herald (Englewood, CO: Libraries Unlimited, 1995) covers many of the basic sources in a single volume.

Though many of the sources listed below are books, much critical and historical information available on the romance genre is in the form of magazine or journal articles. Certain publications, such as *Publishers Weekly*, *The Writer*, *Journal of Popular Culture*, *RWR: Romance Writers' Report*, and *Library Journal*, carry the bulk of such information, but consulting the major indexes is also recommended. *Readers' Guide to Periodical Literature*, *Expanded Academic ASAP* (InfoTrac Searchbank), and LEXIS/NEXIS are useful in locating materials that appear in popular magazines and newspapers, while *Library Literature*, *Humanities Index*, and the *MLA Bibliography* are helpful for locating materials in professional or scholarly journals. The Internet is also an invaluable source of scholarly and popular material on a number of topics, including romance fiction. Note: In any sources that use Library of Congress subject headings (including library catalogs), the primary heading "love stories" is useful in retrieving materials on romantic fiction. For computerized sources try using a keyword approach. "Romance novels," "romance fiction," "popular romance," "romances" or "love stories" are only a few of the many possibilities.

GENERAL

Although as of this writing a definitive Critical History of the Development and Appeal of the Genre Romance Novel has yet to be produced, a potential candidate will probably be released in 1999. Currently under contract to the University of Pennsylvania Press to write a history of the romance novel from *Pamela* to the present, Pamela Regis will look at "the formal features of the romance, seeking there a more full, less politically weighted answer to why readers like these books." Edited by Pat Smith, the same editor who worked with Jayne Ann Krentz on *Dangerous Men and Adventurous Women*, this forthcoming addition to the growing body of romance scholarship will be one to look for. In the interim, critical and historical information on the genre can be gleaned from several of the excellent general surveys and studies that currently exist. The following sources are classics and especially helpful.

Cawelti, John G. *Adventure, Mystery, and Romance: Formula Stories As Art and Popular Culture*. Chicago: University of Chicago Press, 1976.

An excellent older study of the literary and aesthetic aspects of contemporary genre fiction. Provides a careful and thoughtful analysis of the various forms and discusses their broad and continuing appeal. Unfortunately, the romance genre receives minimal treatment.

Hart, James D. *The Popular Book: A History of America's Literary Taste*. New York: Oxford University Press, 1950. Westport, CT: Greenwood Press, 1976.

This classic is an excellent historical account of popular fiction and reading preferences in America from the religious writings of the early settlers to the highly secular works of the twentieth century. Information on romance fiction is scattered throughout the book, but a comprehensive index provides easy access. The style is readable and the chapter headings (taken from titles of relevant popular books) are delightful.

Nye, Russel B. *The Unembarrassed Muse: The Popular Arts in America.* New York: Dial Press, 1970.

> This encompassing historical study of the popular arts in America is classic in the field and a necessity for anyone studying American popular culture. Topics range from popular fiction and comics to vaudeville and the Wild West Show. Romance readers may find the following chapters of particular interest: "Stories for the People," "Novels in the Marketplace," and "The Dime Novel Tradition." An index and an excellent bibliography are included.

GUIDES TO THE LITERATURE

In recent years, as interest in the romance genre has grown, guides to the literature have slowly begun to appear. Several examples are listed here:

Baym, Nina. *Women's Fiction: A Guide to Novels By and About Women in America, 1820-1870.* Ithaca, NY: Cornell University Press, 1978.

> More a thorough critical study than a true bibliographic guide, this source analyzes the works of a number of authors of the nineteenth century, provides numerous plot descriptions, and lists relevant bibliographic references. Narrower in scope, this book supplements Herbert Ross Brown's classic (see below) but does not replace it. Readers particularly interested in history may find of interest Baym's *American Women Writers and the Work of History, 1790-1860* (New Brunswick, NJ: Rutgers University Press, 1995).

Falk, Kathryn, Melinda Helfer, and Kathe Robin, eds. *Romance Reader's Handbook.* New York: Romantic Times, 1989.

> Authored by the publisher of *Romantic Times* (see "Periodicals") and two of its primary reviewers, this source provides a variety of information, including lists of recommended romances, authors' pseudonyms, authors' addresses, publishers and agents, and bookstores. No inclusion criteria are given.

Fallon, Eileen. *Words of Love: A Complete Guide to Romance Fiction.* New York: Garland Publishing, 1984.

> This eclectic work contains a little bit of everything, including several historical essays; a number of lists; a brief bibliography of romance criticism; and two large, alphabetically arranged sections on historical and current romance writers. Now dated, this work is primarily of historical interest.

Herald, Diana Tixier. "Romance." In *Genreflecting: A Guide to Reading Interests in Genre Fiction*, 4th ed., 162–206. Englewood, CO: Libraries Unlimited, 1995.

> Originally written by Betty Rosenberg and now in its fifth edition, this delightfully written guide to romance fiction discusses the enduring appeal of the romance; describes the various romance subgenres

(complete with author lists); and provides information on reference sources, publishers, book clubs, periodicals, and authors' associations. Although not comprehensive, it provides a good place to start for those unfamiliar with the romance genre. Since the romance genre is continually changing, readers may also find the earlier editions of *Genreflecting* of interest.

Hoffman, Frank W. "Romance." In *American Popular Culture: A Guide to the Reference Literature*. 73–74. Englewood, CO: Libraries Unlimited, 1995, 73-74.

This brief, but competently done, section on romance reference sources includes six annotated entries divided into the following categories: Bibliographies, Biographies, Guides to the Literature, and Handbooks.

Mussell, Kay. "Gothic Novels." In *Handbook of American Popular Literature*, edited by M. Thomas Inge, 157–73. New York: Greenwood Press, 1988.

Similar in format to "Romantic Fiction" (described below), this is a concise guide to Gothic fiction. Much of the material is found in Mussell's *Women's Gothic and Romantic Fiction: A Reference Guide,* but because of its clarity and brevity, researchers may find this a useful beginning guide to the Gothic.

———. "Romantic Fiction." In *Handbook of American Popular Literature*, edited by M. Thomas Inge, 251–72. New York: Greenwood Press, 1988.

Much of the material in this essay is included in Mussell's *Women's Gothic and Romantic Fiction: A Reference Guide*. However, this is a good, brief introduction to the multifaceted world of romantic fiction.

———. *Women's Gothic and Romantic Fiction: A Reference Guide*. Westport, CT: Greenwood Press, 1981.

Concentrating primarily on scholarly literature of interest to researchers, this is the first (now classic) guide to organize the widely scattered material on romance fiction. The material is presented in the form of bibliographic and critical essays that address a number of topics (e.g., "History of Women's Gothic and Romantic Fiction," "Sociological and Psychological Approaches to Gothic and Romantic Fiction: Studies of Reading and Audience," "Popular Commentary on Gothic and Romantic Fiction: Journalism, Reviews, and How-To Advice"). The work concludes with two appendices, "Collections and Research Facilities" and "Selected Chronology," and an index. Although the general emphasis of this work is on scholarly sources, the chapter on popular commentary may be of particular interest to those researching the traditionally hard-to-find material on modern romance fiction.

———. *Women's Romance Fiction: A Reference Guide*. Westport, CT: Greenwood Press, 1998.

Using a format similar to her guide discussed above, Mussell continues her coverage of the scholarly literature on romance fiction, focusing primarily on works that have been generated since the beginning of the 1980s. The increase in romance scholarship during the past decade is reflected in her detailed coverage. There is also a large section on the romance industry (including publishers, Romance Writers of America, etc.), a bit less on related genres, and an appendix on cyberspace. A welcome and much-needed supplement to a classic source in the field.

HISTORY, SURVEYS, AND CRITICISM

Of all the areas of interest within the romance fiction genre, the works of the original Gothic novelists and the American Domestic Sentimentalists have received the most attention and are, therefore, the best documented. Although much of this research appears in articles that pepper the literature, a number of relevant books also exist. In addition to Baym's book (discussed above), two other important ones are listed below. Both are considered classics in the field and have been reprinted.

Brown, Herbert Ross. *The Sentimental Novel in America, 1789-1860*. Durham, NC: Duke University Press, 1940.

> A standard in the field for more than 50 years, this work (especially when used in conjunction with Baym's book) is a must for anyone seriously interested in early American romance fiction. It is particularly useful as a bibliographic reference source.

Papashvily, Helen Waite. *All the Happy Endings: A Study of the Domestic Novel in America, the Women Who Wrote It, the Women Who Read It, in the Nineteenth Century*. New York: Harper, 1956.

> Interesting discussion of the domestic novels of the nineteenth century. Although still considered a standard work in the field, the references are now dated, and the reader must keep in mind that the "present" to which the book refers is more than 40 years in the past. Contains a bibliography and an index.

Those especially interested in the early Gothics might wish to consult the following:

Frank, Frederick S. *Guide to the Gothic: An Annotated Bibliography of Criticism*. Metuchen, NJ: Scarecrow Press, 1984.

> Concerned primarily with the original literary Gothics (e.g., Horace Walpole's *Castle of Otranto*) and their subsequent influences, this comprehensive bibliography does an excellent job of covering the scholarly literature of the field. Updated by *Guide to the Gothic II: An Annotated Bibliography of Criticism, 1983-1993*. Lanham, MD: Scarecrow Press, 1995.

———. *Through the Pale Door: A Guide to and Through the American Gothic*. New York: Greenwood Press, 1990.

> A scholarly look at the Gothic on the American side of the Atlantic.

Those interested in the British point of view might enjoy the following surveys. Both are popular, rather than scholarly, in style and are highly readable.

Anderson, Rachel. *The Purple Heart Throbs: The Sub-Literature of Love*. London: Hodder & Stoughton, 1974.

> Although most of the authors included in this entertaining survey of nineteenth- and twentieth-century romantic fiction are British, many are available and widely read by American readers. The general arrangement of the work is chronological, with each chapter covering a different type

of romance popular at the time. The chapter headings are wonderfully descriptive and include such offerings as "High Passions in Big Houses," "Aseptic Love," and "Ah! Love, My Hope Is Swooning in My Heart or the Death of the Three-Decker Novel." Anderson provides lengthy plot summaries and discusses the plots and themes in relation to current social attitudes. Currently out of print, this book is available in larger libraries or through interlibrary loan.

Cadogan, Mary. *And Then Their Hearts Stood Still: An Exuberant Look at Romantic Fiction Past and Present.* London: Macmillan, 1994.

    Similar in tone and style to *The Purple Heart Throbs*, this lively survey is "an appreciative assessment of twentieth-century romance fiction" and covers everything from Gothics to glitz, with the notable exception of the newest of the romance subgenres, Alternative Reality. The arrangement is primarily by theme or type, resulting in a vaguely chronological sequence, and the chapter titles (e.g., "Piety and Passion," "Taming the Beast," "From Sahara Sands to Shangri-La," and "Sex, Shopping, and Social Responsibility") are as intriguing as their content. No index or bibliography are provided.

In addition to the more general and comprehensive studies listed above, many books and articles have been written about specific aspects of romantic fiction. These can be found by consulting the guides and bibliographies listed above or the various bibliographies and reading lists included in the selected works listed below. For a more comprehensive listing, consult Johanna Tuñon's bibliography included in *North American Romance Writers, 1985–1995*. Note: While not all authors dealt with in the following studies fall strictly within the romance genre, many of them produced prototypes of romance forms that are used today.

Abartis, Caesarea. "The Ugly-Pretty, Dull-Bright, Weak-Strong Girl in the Gothic Mansion." *Journal of Popular Culture* 13 (fall 1979): 257–63.

    This brief, older article compares the heroines in *Jane Eyre* (Brontë), *Rebecca* (du Maurier), *Kirkland Revels* (Holt), and *House at Hawk's End* (Burroughs) and determines that the modern Gothic teaches the reader "to be passive and to hanker after mansions."

Alberts, J. K. "The Role of Couples' Conversations in Relational Development: A Content Analysis of Courtship Talk in Harlequin Romance Novels." *Communication Quarterly* 34 (spring 1986): 127–42.

    Alberts uses M. Knapp's stage model of relational development (*Social Intercourse: From Greeting to Goodbye*. Boston: Allyn & Bacon, 1978.) to analyze the courtship conversations in ten Harlequin romances.

Aronowitz, Beverly-Lynne. "Women's Fiction and Popular Romance: Student Audience and Teaching Dilemma." ERIC Document ED298525.

    In this paper, originally presented at the third annual National Literature Conference in Chicago in 1988, Aronowitz discusses the problems arising from the differing expectations of students and instructors when critically evaluating women's fiction. She contends that students' expectations are derived from the popular romance fiction genre. Part of her solution involves a comparative text analysis of similar portions in both types of works, using traditional critical methods to help students learn to critically evaluate literature of all types.

Brownstein, Rachel M. *Becoming a Heroine: Reading About Women in Novels*. New York: Viking, 1982.

An interesting study demonstrating how women over the years have defined and molded themselves in accordance with literary heroines. Among the authors included are Jane Austen, Charlotte Brontë, George Eliot, Henry James, and Virginia Woolf.

Brunt, Rosalind. "A Career in Love: The Romantic World of Barbara Cartland." In *Popular Fiction and Social Change*, edited by Christopher Pawling, 127–56. New York: St. Martin's Press, 1984.

Using Cartland as an extreme example, Brunt considers both the values of romance and what Cartland typifies about the contemporary romance genre and concludes that "through her fiction Cartland offers a stranger truth: the romantic writer as inadvertent feminist." Since Cartland is British, this book emphasizes the British point of view.

Christian-Smith, Linda K. *Becoming a Woman Through Romance*. New York: Routledge, 1990.

In this study of the young adult romance novel, Christian-Smith provides an analysis of 34 YA romances from 1942 to 1982, as well as the results of her field work with teenage girls in several middle and junior high schools. She discusses the role romances play in adolescent development. Includes notes, a bibliography, an index, and five useful appendices.

Cohn, Jan. *Romance and the Erotics of Property: Mass-Market Fiction for Women*. Durham, NC: Duke University Press, 1988.

Working from her thesis that "power, not love, lies at the heart of the fictions of popular romance," Cohn examines both contemporary (chiefly Harlequins) and Victorian romance to show that while the surface story is always about love, marriage, and sex, the underlying text is the battle for economic power. Includes footnotes and an index.

Coles, Claire D., and M. Johnna Shamp. "Some Sexual, Personality, and Demographic Characteristics of Women Readers of Erotic Romances." *Archives of Sexual Behavior* 13 (1984): 187–209.

The researchers administered questionnaires to 72 women (college students, housewives, and businesswomen) in two separate studies designed to discover what function erotic romances serve for their readers. An older, but often referenced, study detailing various characteristics of women romance readers.

Crane, Lynda L. "Romance Novel Readers: In Search of Feminist Change?" *Women's Studies* 23 (1994): 257–69.

Working with two women writers, Crane administered questionnaires to 80 women and interviewed 24 of them by telephone to discover what aspects of romances most appeal to them, how the relationships portrayed in the novels relate to desires for their own lives, and what their attitudes concerning feminism are.

Dubino, Jeanne. "The Cinderella Complex: Romance Fiction, Patriarchy and Capital-ism." *Journal of Popular Culture* 27 (winter 1993): 103–18.

> Based on a sample of six (four are Harlequins) romance novels from the 1980s, two mainstream women's novels, and Fay Weldon's satiric anti-romance *The Live and Loves of a She-Devil*, Dubino determines that romances relegate women to the home, destroy female independence, glamorize sexual harassment, "condition women for subservience," and "combine the desire for a man with the inscription of the reader into patriarchal heterosexual ideology."

Ebert, Teresa L. "The Romance of Patriarchy: Ideology, Subjectivity, and Postmodern Feminist Cultural Theory." *Cultural Critique* 10 (fall 1988): 19–57.

> In a highly theoretical discussion, Ebert uses Harlequin romances to exam-ine "the way patriarchy acts on individuals to reproduce gendered subjectivities through the consumption of commodities, notably texts" and answer the question "How does patriarchy successfully maintain and reproduce the domination of one gender over the other" despite the currently changing social and economic roles of men and women? Novels analyzed are primarily from the 1970s and early 1980s.

Fleenor, Juliann E. *The Female Gothic*. Montreal: Eden Press, 1983.

> A collection of essays by noted feminist scholars on the popular "female Gothic" genre.

Fowler, Bridget. *The Alienated Reader: Women and Romantic Literature in the Twen-tieth Century*. New York: Harvester Wheatsheaf, 1991.

> This controversial discussion begins with the assumption that "throughout its long history, the romance has both legitimated female subordination and spo-ken of the needs of women—hence its lack of appeal for men and, to a lesser ex-tent for 'emancipated' women" and concludes that "the romance represents a schizophrenic oscillation between realism and fantasy." It features a historical overview of the genre, a dissection of current popular texts (primarily of Cather-ine Cookson), and an analysis (in light of the works of Pierre Bourdieu and Ernst Bloch) of a series of interviews with 115 Scottish women. The sample interviews provided in the appendix are especially interesting. But the strong elitist emphasis on social class, culture, and taste may alienate readers in general and American readers in particular.

Frenier, Mariam Darce. *Goodbye Heathcliffe: Changing Heroes, Heroines, Roles, and Values in Women's Category Romances*. Contributions in Women's Studies, no. 94. New York: Greenwood Press, 1988.

> A concise (122 pages, including bibliography), informative look at romance fiction from the 1970s through the mid-1980s. Of particular interest—primarily because it is often ignored—is the chapter detailing the differences between American and British romances, "Silhouettes aren't Harlequins."

———. "The Booming Popularity of Romance Fiction." *USA Today* 111 (September 1982): 60–63.

> A brief article defining romances as "books in which heroines do not have to take responsibility for their lives (what is never likely to happen to real women)

because heroes come along (courtship) and take care of the heroines' lives for them. In exchange for this security, heroines will provide heroes with moral guidance because women are morally superior to men." This definition sets the article's tone.

Hazen, Helen. *Endless Rapture: Rape, Romance, and the Female Imagination.* New York: Charles Scribner's Sons, 1983.

An interesting, controversial study that discusses various aspects of romance and feminism and asserts, among other things, that romances often use rape or some version of it as a plot convention and that the "rape fantasy is quite healthy . . . and need[s] no grounding in masochism—that is to say, masochism as a disease." The title of the final chapter, "The Errors Within Feminism," indicates the slant of the book. Includes notes and an index.

Hubbard, Rita C. "The Changing-Unchanging Heroines and Heroes of Harlequin Romances 1950–1979." In *The Hero in Transition*, edited by Ray B. Browne and Marshall W. Fishwick, 171–79. Bowling Green, OH: Bowling Green State University Popular Press, 1983.

Using data from her original doctoral research, Hubbard briefly assesses the heroes and heroines of the Harlequin Romance lines of the 1950s, 1960s, and 1970s. Although not a substitute for her dissertation, the article is short and easy to read and the book is available in most academic libraries. (Updated by the following article.)

———. Magic and Transformation: Relationships in Popular Romance Novels, 1950 to the 1980s." In *Popular Culture: An Introductory Text*, edited by Jack Nachbar and Kevin Lause, 476–88. Bowling Green, OH: Bowling Green State University Popular Press, 1992. [Similar version first published in *Communication Quarterly* 33 (spring 1985): 113–25.]

Updating her original research, Hubbard analyzes several contemporary category romances published in 1983 by various publishing houses (not just Harlequin) and concludes that romances underwent a major change in the 1980s. Reflecting more feminist views, the heroine now is truly liberated; she holds at least equal power with the hero in the romantic relationship; and love "enriches her life, but it does not change its other dimensions." Her original findings are also discussed. A short, interesting assessment.

Hughes, Helen. *The Historical Romance.* London: Routledge, 1993.

Essentially a revamping of her doctoral dissertation, Hughes surveys historical novels published between 1890 and 1990 to study "the ways in which an artificial 'past' can gain 'mythical' significance, confirming attitudes or highlighting fears and hopes which arise from the nature of contemporary society." Although primarily British in focus, many of the authors discussed (e.g., Sabatini, Heyer, Farnol, Orczy, Conan Doyle, Cartland, Dunnett) are familiar to most American readers. Includes notes, a bibliography, and an index.

Jensen, Margaret Ann. *Love's Sweet Return: The Harlequin Story*. Bowling Green, OH: Bowling Green State University Popular Press, 1984.

The outgrowth of a doctoral dissertation, this interesting study details the structure and rise of the Harlequin romance and discusses the appeal, social significance, and impact of this pervasively popular genre.

Juhasz, Suzanne. *Reading from the Heart: Women, Literature, and the Search for True Love*. New York: Viking, 1994.

Written by an academic for "real people" (as opposed to scholars) this study proposes the reason women read romance fiction is to "replicate the facilitating environment of the mother-infant bond." Although the author's selections are often literary classics (e.g., Austen, the Brontës, Alcott) and not popular romance, her ideas and observations may interest some readers. Includes notes, a bibliography, an index, and an appendix detailing the psychoanalytic theories used or mentioned.

Kahler, Anne K., ed. *Romantic Conventions*. Bowling Green, OH: Bowling Green State University Popular Press, 1998.

This recent, important collection of essays focuses on the various literary conventions common to the romance genre. Contributing scholars include several who are also romance writers (e.g., Jennifer Crusie Smith and Julie Tetel Andresen), and the essays are divided among three sections, "Archetypes and Stereotypes," "Conventions of Time and Place," and "Language and Love," and discuss a wide variety of topics that range from the Jungian shadow archetype, captivity, and the Cinderella myth through Fabio, time travel, and witchcraft.

Kray, Susan. "Deconstructive Laughter: Romance Author as Subject—The Pleasure of Writing the Text." *Journal of Communication Inquiry* 11 (summer 1987): 26–46.

Kray takes an interesting look at what women may gain from writing romance novels. One of the few articles that discusses the authors, rather than the readers or the texts.

Krentz, Jayne Ann, ed. *Dangerous Men and Adventurous Women: Romance Writers on the Appeal of the Romance*. Philadelphia: University of Pennsylvania Press, 1992.

This groundbreaking collection of essays provides insights from published romance writers on the appeal of and the rationale behind the romance genre. This diverse collection included articles both long and short and popular and scholarly in tone. All are well written and provocative. Includes a brief bibliography and an index. Note: This was a best-selling book for the University of Pennsylvania Press and was reissued in mass-market format in 1996. It also received the American Popular Culture Association's Susan Brownmiller Award.

Kundin, Susan G. "Romance versus Reality: A Look at YA Romantic Fiction." *Top of the News* 41(summer 1985): 361–68.

An interesting study that compares the "treatment of adolescent 'problem-concerns' in formula romance fiction to the treatment of these problems in contemporary realistic fiction." The results may surprise detractors of young adult romances.

Lewallen, Avis. "*Lace*: Pornography for Women?" In *The Female Gaze: Women as Viewers of Popular Culture*, edited by Lorraine Gamman and Margaret Marshment, 86-101. Seattle, WA: The Real Comet Press, 1989.

    Lewallen uses *Lace* by Shirley Conran to discuss the use of explicit sex in romance and its implications for feminism and "the female gaze."

Mann, Peter H. *The Romantic Novel: A Survey of Reading Habits*. London: Mills & Boon, 1969.

    One of the earliest romance reader surveys, this one was commissioned by Mills and Boon and conducted in 1968. The results indicate that romance readers are a less homogeneous and more literate group of women than previously supposed.

———. "The Romantic Novel and Its Readers." *Journal of Popular Culture* 15 (Summer 1981): 9–18.

    Based on a speech given at the Popular Culture Association Conference in England in 1980, this article clearly defines "literary" as opposed to "popular" fiction, discusses the merits of the two, examines romance fiction and its readers in slightly greater detail, and posits the idea that what people really want to read is a good story with a positive solution to any problems. British emphasis.

Margolis, David. "Mills & Boon: Guilt Without Sex." *Red Letters* 14 (winter 1982-1983): 5–13.

    An interesting discussion of Mills & Boon romances, including comments on the commercial success, the mass production, cookie-cutter aspects, the marketing, characteristics of the romances themselves, and social implications of their success and content. British emphasis.

McCafferty, Kate. "Palimpsest of Desire: The Re-Emergence of the American Captivity Narrative as Pulp Romance." *Journal of Popular Culture* 27 (spring 1994): 43–56.

    McCafferty uses several of Zebra's captivity narrative romances from the 1980s to show how the captivity narrative, dating from the 1680s but losing popularity in the 1930s, has changed and resurfaced as mass-market romance. She also discusses the reasons for the recent popularity and what it means for the genre.

Miner, Madonne M. "Guaranteed to Please: Twentieth-Century American Women's Bestsellers." In *Gender and Reading: Essays on Readers, Texts, and Contexts*, edited by Elizabeth A. Flynn and Patrocinio P. Schweickart, 187-211. Baltimore, MD: Johns Hopkins University Press, 1986.

    Grounding her discussion on the theory that because men and women are raised differently, they choose to read different things, and if they do read the same text, will perceive it differently. Miner examines and discusses three popular novels, *Gone With the Wind*, *Forever Amber*, and *Valley of the Dolls*.

————. *Insatiable Appetites: Twentieth-Century American Women's Bestsellers.* Westport, CT: Greenwood Press, 1984.

> A serious, in-depth study of five women's bestsellers—*Gone With the Wind* by Margaret Mitchell, *Forever Amber* by Kathleen Winsor, *Peyton Place* by Grace Metalious, *Valley of the Dolls* by Jacqueline Susann, and *Scruples* by Judith Krantz. An interesting analysis of the stories and heroines and what they have in common.

Modleski, Tania. *Loving with a Vengeance: Mass-Produced Fantasies for Women.* Hamden, CT: Shoe String Press, 1982. (Archon Books)

> Serious study of Harlequin romances, female Gothics, and soap operas and their appeal for today's women.

Mussell, Kay J. "Beautiful and Damned: The Sexual Woman in Gothic Fiction." *Journal of Popular Culture* 9 (summer 1975): 84–89.

> A short, well-written essay that examines the women in the popular Gothics (and some romantic suspense) of Victoria Holt, Mary Stewart, Phyllis Whitney, and Dorothy Eden. Concludes that feminine sexual passion and beauty often lead to corruption, and sometimes villainy, while the more preferable traditional domestic qualities (usually found in the heroine) result in love and marriage. One of the earlier works on the subject and something of a classic.

————. *Fantasy and Reconciliation: Contemporary Formulas of Women's Romance Fiction.* Westport, CT: Greenwood Press, 1984.

> Critical study and analysis of contemporary romance fiction to demonstrate the role these novels play in the lives of today's readers in affirming both traditional domestic values and women's feelings of self-worth. Chapter notes, a bibliography of both romances and secondary sources, and an index are included.

Mussell, Kay, ed. "Where's Love Gone? Transformations in the Romance Genre." *PARA*DOXA: Studies in World Literary Genres* 3 (1-2) 1997.

> Coordinated and edited by Kay Mussell, this groundbreaking issue of PARA*DOXA examines important changes within the popular romance genre. It contains 20 relevant research articles, a bibliography of romance reference sources, a discussion of online resources, a book review essay, and interviews with four romance writers (Jayne Ann Krentz, Nora Roberts, Barbara G. Mertz, and Janet Dailey). This publication adds immeasurably to the research in the field, and although it may be difficult to locate, it is definitely worth the effort. Contributors include: Kay Mussell, Tania Modleski, Beth Rapp Young, Lynn Coddington, Barbara Samuel, Jennifer Crusie Smith, Sandra Marie Booth, Deborah K. Chappel, Harriet Margolis, Pamela Regis, Sylvia Kelso, Julia Bettinotti, Marie-Francoise Truel, Gabriele Linke, Patricia Koski, Lori Holyfield, Marcella Thompson, Sara Webster Goodwin, Victoria Badik, Kathleen Giles Seidel, Norbert Spehner, Robert Ellrich, and Darby Lewes. A provocative, well-crafted collection of scholarly criticism by researchers who understand the genre.

Nyquist, Mary. "Romance in the Forbidden Zone." In *Reimagining Women: Representations of Women in Culture*, edited by Shirley Neuman and Glennis Stephenson, 160–81. Toronto: University of Toronto Press, 1993.

Using Peter Rutter's *Sex in the Forbidden Zone: When Men in Power—Therapists, Doctors, Clergy, Teachers, and Others—Betray Women's Trust*, as well as well-known romance studies, Nyquist discusses the traditional role of male mentorship of women and how it is perpetuated in modern romance fiction. She incorporates relevant racial, sexual, and gender orientation topics.

Pearce, Lynne, and Jackie Stacey, eds. *Romance Revisited*. New York: New York University Press, 1995.

Originating from a conference hosted by the Centre for Women's Studies at Lancaster University in March 1993, this collection of essays by various scholars and feminists takes a new look at the romance novel. Heterosexual, homosexual, and interracial romances are all discussed. Contributors are primarily British.

Rabine, Leslie W. *Reading the Romantic Heroine: Text, History, Ideology*. Ann Arbor, MI: University of Michigan Press, 1985.

A critical study of selected romantic narratives that have "since the twelfth century, made romantic love a cultural model which continues to dominate women's imaginations even today . . . [to] build a theory that finds connections between an unconscious feminine personality structure, the culture that shapes women's consciousness, and women's social situation." (Preface) Of particular interest to contemporary romance readers is the chapter "Sex and the Working Woman in the Age of Electronics: Harlequin Romances." Chapter notes, a selected bibliography, and an index are included.

———. "Romance in the Age of Electronics: Harlequin Enterprises." In *Feminist Criticism and Social Change: Sex, Class and Race in Literature and Culture*, edited by Judith Newton and Deborah Rosenfelt, 249-67. New York: Methuen, 1985.

In a discussion of Harlequin Enterprises and its phenomenal success within the romance publishing world, Rabine contends that current romances, with their dual themes of revolt and fantasy escape, appeal directly to the needs of working women and the powerlessness they feel within the increasingly impersonal technological culture.

Radford, Jean, ed. *The Progress of Romance: The Politics of Popular Fiction*. London: Routledge & Kegan Paul, 1986.

A diverse collection of essays (most of which were originally presented at the first History Workshop Conference on Popular Literature, in England in 1984), each of which "refuses the notion of popular writing as the contaminated spawn of industrialism, in favour of a historically specific understanding of popular forms and their uses." Although all are useful and worth reading, the final essay by novelist Michele Roberts, "Write, She Said," is unique. Includes a brief index.

Radstone, Susannah, ed. *Sweet Dreams: Sexuality, Gender, and Popular Fiction*. London: Lawrence & Wishart, 1988.

This diverse collection of essays focuses on the various issues concerning gender and identity raised by feminist, gay, and lesbian popular novels. "What Is Life Without My Love: Desire and Romantic Fiction" by Amal Treacher and "Robots and Romance: The Science Fiction and Fantasy of Tanith Lee" by Sarah Lefanu may be of particular interest to romance readers.

Radway, Janice. "Interpretive Communities and Variable Literacies: The Functions of Romance Reading." *Daedalus* 113 (summer 1984): 49–73.

Using research from her study of the "Smithton" romance readers discussed in her book listed below, Radway discusses the nature of romance reading and the "nature and function of literacy" in these readers' lives.

———. *Reading the Romance: Women, Patriarchy, and Popular Literature*. Chapel Hill, NC.: University of North Carolina Press, 1984.

In this fascinating survey, Radway details the romance reading preferences of 42 diverse women (all, however, from one Midwestern town), describes her methodology (including providing sample questionnaires), analyzes the results (largely in terms of the theories advanced in Nancy Chodorow's *The Reproduction of Mothering: Psychoanalysis and the Sociology of Gender*. Berkeley, CA: University of California Press, 1978), and draws a number of both expected and unexpected conclusions.

Raub, Patricia. "Issues of Passion and Power in E. M. Hull's *The Sheik*." *Women's Studies* 21 (1992): 119–28.

Noting that Carol Thurston considers *The Sheik* to be "the first romance of the twentieth century," Raub takes a fresh look at this infamous book and concludes that it is "a significant work in the development of popular women's fiction."

Reep, Diana. *The Rescue and Romance: Popular Novels Before World War I*. Bowling Green, OH: Bowling Green State University Popular Press, 1982.

A brief, focused study detailing the use and importance of "the rescue" in American popular novels written between 1800 and 1914. Bibliographic information and plot synopses of more than 50 novels used in the study are included, as well as a brief critical bibliography and an index.

Rose, Suzanna. "Is Romance Dysfunctional?" *International Journal of Women's Studies* 8 (May-June 1985): 250–65.

Rose analyzes both romance and adventure scripts in various popular literatures and fairy tales to "examine how social constructions of sexuality shape desire in women and men and the consequences of sexual scripting for relationships." She determines that they have profound, and not necessarily positive, implications for relationships.

Ruggiero, Josephine A., and Louise C. Weston. "Conflicting Images of Women in Romance Novels." *International Journal of Women's Studies* 6 (January/February 1983): 18–25.

This concise, clearly presented study contrasts the heroines of the modern Gothic and the historical romance, observing that Gothic heroines have more options but historical heroines are more sexual. The authors suggest that the historical romance will eventually become more popular and more relevant, but they raise a concern about the danger of the possible stereotyping of women.

Snitow, Ann Barr. "Mass Market Romance: Pornography for Women Is Different." *Radical History Review* 20 (spring/summer 1979): 141–61.

This older and now dated, but much quoted, article uses several Harlequin titles to analyze the appeal of the romance and concludes that though Harlequins may be considered pornographic for a number of sexual and exploitive reasons, it is pornography of a different, more complex variety.

Taylor, Helen. "Romantic Readers." In *From My Guy to Sci-Fi: Genre and Women's Writing in the Postmodern World*, edited by Helen Carr, 58–77. London: Pandora, 1989.

A short, interesting article that concludes romance readers are a diverse group, reading romance for different reasons and responding in a variety of ways. She warns that it "is politically crucial that feminist critics become aware of those varied responses" and take care in making generalizations of any kind about readers. Includes notes and a bibliography.

Thomas, Audrey. "A Fine Romance, My Dear, This Is." *Canadian Literature* 108 (spring 1986): 5–12.

A brief, personal article that not only ridicules the romance genre but presents it as dangerous and frightening.

Thurston, Carol. "The Liberation of Pulp Romances." *Psychology Today* 17 (April 1983): 14–15.

Brief commentary on the recent trends toward more sensuous romances and feisty, independent heroines.

———. "Popular Historical Romances: Agent for Social Change?—An Exploration of Methodologies." *Journal of Popular Culture* 19 (summer 1985): 35–45.

Thurston uses both qualitative and quantitative methodologies in examining erotic historical romances first "to explore the value of two social science research tools—content analysis and the semantic differential—in analyzing popular literature," and second "to assess the potential of these books as agents of social change." She concludes that the combined methodological approach is more rewarding than using a single approach and contends that the data show that erotic Historicals are both reflections and agents of social change.

———. *The Romance Revolution: Erotic Novels for Women and the Quest for a New Sexual Identity*. Urbana, IL: University of Illinois Press, 1987.

> In examining romances, their publishers, writers, and consumers, Thurston shows how the romance has changed, discusses its evolution and its impact, and contends that a new form, erotica for women, has emerged. Several useful appendices, a fiction bibliography, a reference list, and an index are included.

Thurston, Carol, and Barbara Doscher. "Supermarket Erotica: Bodice-Busters Put Romantic Myths to Bed." *The Progressive* (April 1982): 49–51.

> Counters the contention that all romantic heroines are weak, dependent, and submissive with the assertion that heroines of the new erotic historical subgenre are aggressive, self-sufficient, and in some cases militantly feminist in their stances.

Tsagaris, Ellen M. *The Subversion of Romance in the Novels of Barbara Pym*. Bowling Green, OH: Bowling Green State University Popular Press, 1998.

> This recent study explores the relationship between Barbara Pym's novels and the popular romance and concludes that in subverting a number of classic elements of romance, Pym shows that the true "happy ending" for her heroines is living and enjoying "life on their own terms, without looking over their shoulder to see if society approves." An interesting, thought-provoking study.

Wardrop, Stephanie. "The Heroine Is Being Beaten: Freud, Sadomasochism, and Reading the Romance." *Style* 29 (fall 1995): 459–73.

> Using the sadomasochism dynamic as a strategy for reading popular romance fiction, Wardrop examines Linda Howard's *McKenzie's Mission* (Silhouette Intimate Moments, 1992) and shows that women see these texts as empowering rather than subjugating and concludes that "by emphasizing power as a dialectic and acknowledging the strength of the masochist [heroine], the paradigm of sadomasochism presents a strategy for reading and identification that does not position the reader regressively." Makes use of Lynn S. Chancer's theories as presented in *Sadomasochism in Every-Day Life: The Dynamics of Power and Powerlessness*. (New Brunswick, NJ: Rutgers University Press, 1992).

Wilcox, Clyde. "The Not-So-Failed Feminism of Jean Auel." *Journal of Popular Culture* 28 (winter 1994): 63–69.

> Although not a discussion of romance, as such, this brief article counters the argument of Bernard Gallagher that *The Clan of the Cave Bear* is a failed feminist novel and may be of interest to readers who enjoy Auel's books.

Woodruff, Juliette. "A Spate of Words, Full of Sound & Fury, Signifying Nothing: Or, How to Read a Harlequin." *Journal of Popular Culture* 19 (fall 1995): 25–32.

> A short, somewhat personalized descriptive article that divides the world of romance fiction into Gothics, Harlequins, and romantic sagas (Woodruff's term for historical romance) and discusses various attributes of each. Also comments on the appeal of the romance and its value.

As any reader of historical romances knows, household employees (particularly the governess, the companion, or the abigail/lady's maid) often play a prominent part—either as the heroine (a particularly popular convention in Gothics) or as a supporting character. The following studies provide a serious, yet entertaining, look at the English governess and abigail of fact and fiction. Unfortunately, the Stuart and the West books are now out of print; however, they should be available in larger libraries.

Hughes, Kathryn. *The Victorian Governess*. London: Hambledon Press, 1993.
> Meticulously documented and nicely illustrated, this study uses both primary and secondary sources to examine the role of the governess in Victorian society. Serious, well researched, and readable.

Stuart, Dorothy Margaret. *The English Abigail*. London: Macmillan, 1946.

Thomson, Patricia. *The Victorian Heroine: A Changing Ideal, 1837-1873.* New York: Greenwood Press, c. 1956, 1978 (reprint).

West, Katharine. *Chapter of Governesses: A Study of the Governess in English Fiction, 1800-1949.* London: Cohen and West, 1949.

DISSERTATIONS AND THESES

One indication of a subject's legitimacy, at least within the academic community, is the number of doctoral dissertations and masters theses it generates. Although romance fiction has been minimally represented in this literature, the last decade has seen an exponential increase in scholarly studies of this type. A selection of examples is listed below.

Allan, Janice Morag. "The Romantic Reading Process: Towards a New Definition." University of Alberta, Edmonton, Canada, 1990. Abstract in *Masters Abstracts International* 30 (summer 1992): 216.
> Addresses the perception of romance fiction by critics and revisits material from Janice Radway's earlier study, *Reading the Romance: Women, Patriarchy, and Popular Literature.*

Bereska, Tami M. "Adolescent Romance Novels: Changes over Time." Master's thesis. University of Alberta, Edmonton, Canada. 1992. Abstract in *Masters Abstracts International* 31 (fall 1993): 1099.
> Discusses the decline in popularity of the adolescent series romance from its introduction in 1980 to the end of the decade.

Brown, Lisa L. "Recovering the Reader: Literary Theory, Mass Culture, and the Modern Romance." Master's thesis, University of Calgary, Calgary, Canada, 1990. Abstract in *Masters Abstracts International* 30 (winter 1992): 1026.
> A comparative analysis of Tania Modleski's *Loving with a Vengeance: Mass-Produced Fantasies for Women* and Janice Radway's *Reading the Romance: Women, Patriarchy and Popular Literature.*

Bywaters, Barbara Lee. " 'Re-reading Jane': Jane Austen's Legacy to Twentieth Century Women Writers (Pym, Heyer, Gibbons, Brookner)." Ph.D. diss., Bowling Green State University, Bowling Green, Ohio, 1989. Abstract in *Dissertation Abstracts International* 50 (May 1990): 3577A.
    Includes a discussion of Austen's impact on the development of Georgette Heyer's Regencies.

Cannatella, Bonnie M. "The 'Demon Lover': Female Psychology and the Alter Ego in the Romance and Gothic Novel of the Nineteenth and Twentieth Centuries." Master's thesis. University of New Orleans, Louisiana, 1988.
    Chapter 4, "The Demon Lover Today: Mass Produced Gothic Novels and the Female Audience," and its discussion of *Gone With the Wind* and Victoria Holt's *The Demon Lover* may be of particular interest.

Chappel, Deborah Kaye. "American Romances: Narratives of Culture and Identity." Ph.D. diss., Duke University, Durham, North Carolina, 1991.
    This wide-ranging study examines the relationship between the American popular romance and American feminism. An important dissertation.

Coddington, Lynn. "Romance and Power: Writing Romance Novels As a Women's Writing Practice." Ph.D. diss., University of California, Berkeley, 1997.
    Analyzes "the ways in which a small group of professional and aspiring romance writers create and negotiate identity and community through their writing practices." Recent and informative.

Hubbard, Rita Cooper. "Relationship Styles in Popular Romance Fiction: A Fantasy Theme Analysis of Harlequin Romances, 1950–1979. Ph.D. diss., Temple University, Philadelphia, Pennsylvania, 1981.
    One of the earlier dissertations on the romance genre.

Jocks, Yvonne Annette. "Adventure and Virtue: Alternating Emphasis in the Popular Romance Tradition." Master's thesis, University of Texas at Arlington, 1988.
    Traces the origins of romance not only from Richardson's *Pamela* but also from the more adventurous and erotic romances of ancient Greece and twelfth- and seventeenth-century France.

Kolko, Beth E. "Writing the Romance: Cultural Studies, Community, and the Teaching of Writing." Ph.D. diss., University of Texas at Austin, 1994. Abstract in *Dissertation Abstracts International* 55 (December 1994): 1561A.
    One of the more recent dissertations in the field, this study focuses on the writers, the act of writing, and the resulting community.

———. "Writers Revisioning Romance: Towards a Feminist Restructuring of the Genre." Master's report, University of Texas at Arlington, 1991.
    Focuses on the writers, largely in the context of the Romance Writers of America, and their role in effecting change within the genre. Insightful.

Lin, Fang-Mei. "Social Change and Romantic Ideology: The Impact of the Publishing Industry, Family Organization, and Gender Roles on the Reception and Interpretation of Romance Fiction in Taiwan, 1960-1990." Ph.D. diss., University of Pennsylvania, Philadelphia, Pennsylvania, 1992. Abstract in *Dissertation Abstracts International* 53 (November 1992): 1675A.

> An interesting look at the tensions between high and popular culture.

Moffitt, Mary Anne Smeltzer. "Understanding Middle-Class Adolescent Leisure: A Cultural Studies Approach to Romance Novel Reading." Ph.D. diss., University of Illinois at Urbana-Champaign, 1990.

> A series of three studies that examine the popularity of adolescent leisure reading, the romance reading habits of teenaged girls, and the differences and similarities between adult and adolescent readers.

Mussell, Kay Johnson. "The World of Modern Gothic Fiction: American Women and Their Social Myths." Ph.D. diss., University of Iowa, Iowa City, Iowa, 1973.

> One of the earliest dissertations to treat modern romance fiction seriously.

Owen, Mairead. "Women's Reading of Popular Romantic Fiction: A Case Study in the Mass Media: A Key to the Ideology of Women." Ph.D. diss., University of Liverpool, 1992. Abstract in *Dissertation Abstracts International* 52 (February 1992).

Radcliffe, Polly. "Accounting for Romance: Women's Explanations for Reading Romance Fiction." Master's thesis, University of Toronto, Canada. 1991.

Starr, Marian. "Sweet Savage Book: The Romance in America, 1855-1980. Paper, n.p., 1981.

> Focuses on the rape fantasy aspects of Historical Romances à la Rosemary Rogers and deduces that romances are insidious. An interesting example of the scholarship of the period.

Zachik-Smith, Susie. "Romance by the Book: A Morphological Analysis of the Popular Romance." Master's thesis, California State University, San Bernardino, 1993.

> Flawed by dated statistics, inaccuracies, a highly limited sample (13 romances, almost exclusively Harlequin Presents), and the author's apparent unfamiliarity with the current genre as a whole.

TRADE AND LIBRARY PUBLICATION ARTICLES

The primary source of articles on the topic of the romance, particularly for writers, is *RWR: Romance Writers' Report* (see chapter 16, "Periodicals and Review Sources"), but articles on romance do appear in more general publications. A selection of these articles, both older and more recent, is listed here.

Charles, John, Shelley Mosley, and Ann Bouricus. "Romancing the YA Reader." *VOYA 21* (February 1999): 414–19.

    Providing a brief overview and discussion of the adult romance genre and its relevance to teenage readers, this well-crafted article includes lists of selected reference resources and recommended romances, and is essential reading for teachers and librarians who work with YAs.

Chelton, Mary K. "Unrestricted Body Parts and Predictable Bliss: The Audience Appeal of Formula Romances." *Library Journal* (July 1991): 44–49.

    A lively, groundbreaking article on the appeal of the popular romance, its conventions, its place in libraries, and how to select and handle materials and advise readers. Includes a useful grid analysis of various romance lines.

Danford, Natalie. "Seducing the Reader." *Publishers Weekly* (May 30, 1994): 28–30.

    Overview of romance promotion, including covers, contests, and TV campaigns.

Dyer, Lucinda. "Love, Thy Magic Spell Is Everywhere." *Publishers Weekly* (May 13, 1996): 41–48.

    Readable discussion of current and forthcoming trends in romance fiction.

Krentz, Jayne Ann. "The Alpha Male." *Romance Writers' Report* (January/February 1990): 26–28.

    This seminal article defines and discusses one of the basic romance hero types.

Linz, Cathie, Ann Bouricius, and Carole Byrnes. "Exploring the World of Romance Novels." *Public Libraries* (May/June 1995): 144–51.

    An informative and practical article that not only "explor[es] the world of romance novels" but also tells librarians what to do with the "results." Should be required reading for any librarian who works with the genre.

Maxwell, Ann, and Jayne Ann Krentz. "The Wellsprings of Romance." *Romance Writers' Report* (September 1989): 21–22.

    Excellent discussion of basic myths and archetypes on which romance is based.

Mosley, Shelley, John Charles, and Julie Havir. "The Librarian As Effete Snob: Why Romance?" *Wilson Library Bulletin* (May 1995): 24–25+.

    A hard-hitting, articulate article that takes librarians to task for the profession's traditional superior attitude toward the romance genre. Destroys the time-honored excuses librarians use for keeping romances out of their collections and then provides credible reasons for collecting them. Winner of RWA's 1995 Veritas Award, given for the publication that best represents the romance genre in a positive way. Another required read.

Schulhafer, Joan. "Embracing the Niche." *Publishers Weekly* (June 14, 1993): 43–49.

    One of PW's regular "Category Closeup" features on Romance. Discusses the niche markets that are developing in romance and publishers' responses.

———. "Wooing the Buyers." *Publishers Weekly* (January 24, 1994): 29–33.
> Another of PW's regular "Category Closeup" features on Romance that takes an interesting and informative look at marketing the romance genre.

Spano, Susan. "Flower Power." *Publishers Weekly* (December 14, 1992): 31–35.
> This "Category Closeup" presents a discussion of the trends in romance novel covers and what they say about the writer's career.

Thurston, Carol. "Romance Readers—A 'Moving Target.' " *Romance Writers' Report* (February 1987): 20–22.

———. "Romance Readers—The 'Moving Target' Moves On (Part 2)." *Romance Writers' Report* (April 1987): 12–14.

Tuñon, Johanna. "A Fine Romance: How to Select Romances for Your Collection." *Wilson Library Bulletin* (May 1995): 31–34.
> A concise, well-focused article that gives librarians sufficient information to begin the process of building a good romance collection.

POPULAR PRESS ARTICLES

Over the years, the popular romance has garnered a bit of coverage in the popular press—most often negative. Recently, however, the coverage has been less condescending and more evenhanded; and although there is still a fair amount of romance bashing around, the debate is not nearly as one-sided as in the past.

Brown, Elizabeth A. "Paperback Plots: Happily Ever After." *The Christian Science Monitor* (June 9, 1989): 13.
> Based on interviews with readers, publishers, psychologists, scholars, and booksellers, this overview article packs a lot into a single page.

"Criticism a Disservice; Romance Novels Help Strengthen Women." *USA Today*, January 26 1995, Final Edition, News section, 12A.
> Responses by three romance writers, an editor, and RWA's president to article by Judith Sherven (see below).

Fredman, Catherine. "A Man's Guide to Heaving-Bosom Women's Fiction." *Playboy* (May 1990): 72–75.
> An article that lumps Krantz, Steel, Woodiwiss, Lindsey, Spencer, and Collins together under the heading of romance and terms them "trashy."

Graham, Ellen. "Romances, Long Denied Reviews, Get Some Respect." *Wall Street Journal* (June 28, 1995): B1.
> Short, evenhanded commentary on the romance genre and the reviews (and new respect) the books are now receiving in mainstream publications.

Linden, Dana Wechsler, and Matt Rees. "I'm Hungry. But Not for Food." *Forbes* (July 6, 1992): 70–74.
> The business world looks at the romance publishing industry in a statistics-laden article that discusses, among other things, the proposed purchase of Zebra by Harlequin.

"Living the Fantasy: Romance Writers Get Some Respect, Scholarly Interest and Tons of Readers," edited by Betsy Carpenter. *U.S. News & World Report* (November 6, 1995): 78–81.
> A well-done, evenhanded article on the current situation in romance fiction. Winner of the 1996 Romance Writers of America Veritas Award.

"Mills and Boon: Heartthrobs Unlimited." *The Economist* (July 20, 1985): 88.
> Brief history and current (1985) status of M & B romances, plus commentary.

Robinson, Jo. "The Seduction of the Romance Novel: 'Not Tonight, Honey, I'm Reading a Book.' " *New Woman* (November 1994): 106–7+.
> A short, readable "testimonial" article by a freelance writer on the sensual appeal of the romance.

Sherven, Judith, and James Sniechowksi. "Why Women Stay with Abusers." *USA Today* (January 24, 1995) Final edition, News Section, p. 11A.
> Controversial article that refers to the O. J. Simpson trial and contends that romance novels encourage domestic violence. Sherven is a popular psychologist who was interviewed for the CBS *48 Hours* segment "America's Love Affair With Romance Novels," which aired in the fall of 1995. (See above citation for responses from authors, an editor, and RWA's president.)

Stanley, Alessandra. "Romance Novels Discover a Baby Boom." *New York Times* (April 3, 1991) National Edition, A1.
> Although the writer's understanding of the genre is somewhat confused, her article does quote some knowledgeable publishers and writers who help provide balance in this discussion of the then-current direction of romance plotlines.

Wynde, Augusta. "Love's Quivering Rose: In Defense of Romance Novels." *Whole Earth Review* 78 (winter 1993). Also available at gopher.well.sf.ca.us:70/0/wer/romance (accessed December 11, 1998).
> A spirited, readable defense of the genre. The author is a published romance writer and lives in Berkeley, CA.

Yagoda, Ben. "Steamy Nights. Lusty Loins. Burning Passions. Brainy Romance." *Los Angeles Times Magazine* (May 14, 1995): 14–17.
> Commentary on the romance genre, including mention of the Sherven article listed above and an interview with Jayne Ann Krentz.

Chapter 15

Author Biography and Bibliography

Biographical and bibliographical information for writers whose romantic novels have been deemed worthy of the appellation "literature" is abundant and readily available. This is particularly true for authors of historical importance, such as Jane Austen and the Brontës. However, although the situation is improving, this same kind of information for less well-known historical and current writers of romance is not so easily located. Often this information is scattered, and when it does appear, it is often in sources that are not indexed in standard reference tools, making access difficult.

Publications that include biographical articles on current romance writers are among those listed in the "Periodicals" section that follows. In addition, particularly popular current authors may be profiled in certain general interest magazines, many of which are indexed in tools such as *Readers' Guide to Periodical Literature* and *Expanded Academic ASAP* and other InfoTrac databases. Standard author biography sources, such as *Contemporary Authors*, list brief biographical and bibliographical information for a number of authors, including some relatively well-established romance writers. In addition, a number of sources that provide information on specific types of non-romance authors may also include writers of romantic fiction. For example, *American Women Writers: A Critical Reference Guide from Colonial Times to the Present* (New York: Frederick Ungar, 1979) includes among its entries a number of not-quite-so-well-known early romance writers in addition to more recent ones. The *St. James Guide to Crime and Mystery Writers* (Detroit: Gale, 1996), fourth edition, (previous editions were titled *Twentieth Century Crime and Mystery Writers*), a source similar in format and coverage to *Twentieth-Century Romance and Historical Writers* listed below, contains entries for several writers in the romantic suspense genre. The other "siblings," *Twentieth-Century Western Writers* (Chicago: St. James,

1991), third edition; *St. James Guide to Science Fiction Writers* (Detroit: St. James, 1995), fourth edition; and *St. James Guide to Fantasy Writers* (New York: St. James, 1996), may also yield information on romance writers whose works cross over into these other genres. A basic general author biography index that covers a wide variety of sources and might be worth consulting is the *Author Biographies Master Index* (Detroit: Gale, 1994), fourth edition, which contains references to sources for biographical information on more than one million authors, including a number of past and present romance writers. The "mother" index for this source, *Biography and Genealogy Master Index*, is also useful, particularly in its CD-ROM or online version. (Incidentally, a number of the works mentioned in this section are indexed by these tools.)

Over the past two decades, works that specifically target romance authors have appeared. Several are listed below.

Falk, Kathryn. *Love's Leading Ladies*. New York: Pinnacle Books, 1982.

> This fascinating source provides biographical information, bibliographies of in-print titles, photographs, and other information (including favorite recipes) for 65 primarily American romance authors. Like *Words of Love*, this source is more than 15 years old and suffers many of the same deficiencies. Nevertheless, it contains unique information and may be useful to some readers.

Fallon, Eileen. *Words of Love: A Complete Guide to Romance Fiction*. New York: Garland, 1984.

> Although mentioned in the section on "History and Criticism," this work is primarily a biographical source, and when published 15 years ago, it provided information not readily available elsewhere on more than 200 romance authors. Since then, however, it has been superceded by new sources or recent editions of earlier works (e.g., *Twentieth-Century Romance and Historical Writers* and *North American Romance Writers* listed below). Nevertheless, this is one of the first biographical guides to the genre and, despite its flaws, is something of a classic.

Mussell, Kay, and Johanna Tuñon, eds. *North American Romance Writers: 1985 to 1995*. Metuchen, NJ: Scarecrow, 1999.

> Focusing on North American romance authors and how they have shaped the genre during the last 20 years, this source features essays by 50 influential writers and provides biographical and bibliographical information for each. This work is introduced by an informative and readable essay on the development of the romance genre since 1950 by Kay Mussell and concludes with a comprehensive bibliography of materials on the subject of the popular romance by Johanna Tuñon.

Vasudevan, Aruna, and Lesley Henderson, eds. *Twentieth-Century Romance and Historical Writers*. 3rd ed. London: St. James, 1994.

> Introduced by prefaces by Kay Mussell and Alison Light, this source provides brief biographical sketches, complete chronological bibliographies of published works, and signed critical essays for more than 500 authors. Both British and American authors are included, although the emphasis is toward the British. (A source that focuses on North American romance writers is *North American Romance Writers: 1985 to 1995*, listed above.) A valuable, easy-to-use source of hard-to-find information. Note: Although this source is relatively cumulative, a number of authors included in previous editions have been dropped; however, references to the appropriate editions are provided.

Although volumes of bio-bibliographical materials are readily available for "historically classic" romance writers, whole books devoted to one current popular romance author are fairly rare. Articles, of course, exist in abundance and can be located by searching the appropriate indexes. Below are examples of the few books that do exist:

Cartland, Barbara. *I Reach for the Stars: An Autobiography*. London: Robson, 1994.

> The autobiography of one of the legends in the romance field, complete with pictures and portraits.

Chris, Teresa. *Georgette Heyer's Regency England*. London: Sidgwick & Jackson, 1989.

> Discussed in the section on Regency Romance, this book links British sites with Heyer's Regencies and provides an interesting "tour" for her fans.

Cloud, Henry. *Barbara Cartland: Crusader in Pink*. London: Weidenfeld and Nicolson, 1979.

> An admiring, noncritical biography of Cartland's rise to fame, her personal and family life, and her various social crusades. Many photographs.

Dailey, Janet, Martin Harry Greenberg, and Sonja Massie. *The Janet Dailey Companion: A Comprehensive Guide to Her Life and Her Novels*. New York: HarperCollins, 1996.

> A recent guide to Dailey's life and works, featuring interviews and other commentary.

Hodge, Jane Aiken. *The Private World of Georgette Heyer*. London: Bodley Head, 1984.

> A delightful, beautifully illustrated journey into the "private world" of the very private First Lady of the Regency.

Munce, Robert. *Grace Livingston Hill*. Wheaton, IL: Tyndale, 1986.

Robyns, Gwen. *Barbara Cartland: An Authorized Biography*. Doubleday, 1985.

> A spirited account by the biographer of Princess Grace and Agatha Christie.

From time to time various serial publications appear devoted to one particular writer. Most of these are short lived and have limited circulation. The *Dailey Report* (Janet Dailey) and *The Friends of Elizabeth Peters Newsletter* (Elizabeth Peters) are two examples.

The works listed above include both biographical and bibliographical information in varying degrees; those that follow are strictly bibliographical. Books devoted solely to the Romance genre and its divisions and books that target other genres but include various romance subgenres are included. Note: An obvious, but often incomplete and sometimes messy, source of author bibliographies is one of the large online databases, such as OCLC World Cat or RLIN.

Bontly, Susan W., and Carol J. Sheridan. *Enchanted Journeys Beyond the Imagination: An Annotated Bibliography of Fantasy, Futuristic, Supernatural, and Time Travel Romances.* 3 vols. Beavercreek, OH: Blue Diamond Publications, 1996-1997. Index.

> Providing access to information on more than 1,100 alternative reality romances, this handy bibliography (in two volumes—1 and 2 are combined) is arranged by type of romance and further divided by subtype, if necessary; works are listed alphabetically within each section by author. Each entry includes bibliographic information, a brief annotation, and the author's pseudonym(s), if applicable. Various appendices and separate author and title indexes complete the volumes, and a separate master index for authors and titles aids access. This easy-to-use resource is useful for both readers' advisory and collection development (even though many of the titles are already out of print). Includes works from the middle of this century, although most titles are from the 1980s and 1990s.

Hubin, Allen J. *Crime Fiction II: A Comprehensive Bibliography, 1749–1990.* New York: Garland, 1994.

> This well-organized and indexed tool updates Hubin's earlier works and includes listings for various important romantic suspense and gothic writers.

Husband, Janet, and Jonathan F. Husband. *Sequels: An Annotated Guide to Novels in Series.* 3rd ed. Chicago: American Library Association, 1997.

> A number of the items included in this useful source are in the romance or saga genres and should be of interest to romance readers.

Jaegly, Peggy J., ed. *Romantic Hearts: A Personal Reference for Romance Readers.* Third Edition. Lanham, MD: Scarecrow, 1997.

> This hefty book (928 pages) is essentially a resource for readers to use in locating works by specific romance writers. Jaegly provides a comprehensive listing of romances (author and title) arranged by publisher, series, and date or number (whichever is more appropriate), a number of author commentaries, and a remarkable pseudonym list, complete with cross-listings. Even though this source is not a true bibliography and omits essential bibliographic data, it provides useful listings and may be of interest to romance readers. Note: Earlier editions functioned as "logbooks" and provided similar, but not identical, information, some of which has been omitted from this version.

Kay, Mary June. *The Romantic Spirit: A Romance Bibliography of Authors and Titles.* San Antonio, TX: MJK Enterprises, 1982. (1983-1984 Update, 1984; 1985-1986 Update, 1986; 1987-1988 Update, 1988).

> This computer-produced source is a concise listing of approximately 5,000 romance authors and the titles of their books. Entries are not annotated, and publication and copyright information is not given. However, this source is useful because it lists so many romance writers. Authors are cross-indexed by pseudonym, and publishers' series are listed at the end. Although care is advised when using this tool and further information may need to be obtained from other sources, it can be very helpful in locating an elusive author or title.

McGarry, Daniel D., and Sarah Harriman White. *World Historical Fiction Guide: An Annotated, Chronological, Geographical and Topical List of Selected Historical Novels*, 2nd ed. Metuchen, NJ: Scarecrow Press, 1973.

> Although the focus of this briefly annotated bibliography is the historical novel in general, enough historical romances are included to make this a useful reference source for older works. Considering its publication date, a third edition would be welcome.

Radcliffe, Elsa J. *Gothic Novels of the Twentieth Century: An Annotated Bibliography*. Metuchen, NJ: Scarecrow Press, 1979.

> Containing just under 2,000 entries, this eclectic bibliography includes not only Gothic romances, but also mysteries and romances of the historical, sentimental, and suspense varieties and a number of books that do not actually fall into any category within the romance genre. Annotations of varying quality are provided for approximately half the entries.

THE INTERNET

The Internet is also a source of biographical and bibliographical information on Romance authors. In addition to the various sites mentioned in chapter 18, "Societies and Organizations," that often discuss authors and have a number of writers as participants, there are several Web sites that focus on romance authors and their works. One that is particularly useful as of this writing is The Write Page's Romance Novels and Women's Fiction (www.writepage.com/romance.htm, accessed December 10, 1998). It provides information of various sorts, including links to a number of authors' home pages, which often include bibliograpies of their works, mentions of their forthcoming romances, occasional snippets of biographical information, and often the author's e-mail address. Author homepages can also be searched for directly on the Internet. Simply access the Web (via Netscape or something similar), use a good search engine (e.g., Alta Vista or Yahoo), and search by author name. However, keep in mind that while some Web sites are stable, others come and go quickly, and addresses change. What is there today may not be there tomorrow—but there might be something even better!

Chapter 16

Periodicals and Review Sources

PERIODICALS

Although romance fiction is discussed, analyzed, or reviewed in a number of general periodicals such as *Publishers Weekly*, *The Writer*, *The Writer's Digest*, *Booklist*, *Public Libraries*, *Library Journal*, and *Wilson Library Bulletin* (ceased publication in 1995), the publications listed below are exclusively devoted to romance genre fiction.

Affaire de Coeur
Louise Sneed, Publisher/Editor
3976 Oak Hill Road
Oakland, CA 94605-4931
Phone: (510) 569-5675
FAX: (510) 632-8868
E-mail address: Sseven@MCN.com
Published monthly

This publication provides ranked "Reviews and Previews for the Romantic Reader and Writer," articles, short stories in the "Affaire D'Amour" section, author interviews, agent profiles, author pseudonyms, information on publishing trends, and other items of interest to romance readers and writers.

> *The Gothic Journal*
> P. O. Box 6340
> Elko, NV 89802-6340
> Phone: (702) 738-3520
> Web site: GothicJournal.com/romance (accessed December 10, 1998)
> E-mail address: Kglass@GothicJournal.com
> Published bimonthly

Features reviews and information about the Gothic romance subgenre. Note: Ceased publication with the September/October 1998 issue.

> *Heartland Critiques* (formerly *Barbra Critiques)*
> Julie Meisinger, Editor
> 125 E. Linden
> Independence, MO 64050-4407
> Published monthly

Provides ranked reviews for most romances published each year. Also provides an annual "Best of the Year" list.

> *PANdora's Box*
> Romance Writers of America
> 13700 Veterans Memorial, Suite 315
> Houston, TX 77014
> Phone: (713) 440-6885
> Published bimonthly

Published by the Published Authors Network (PAN) of RWA, this newsletter features articles, columns, and other information primarily of interest to published romance writers. Note: Although *PANdora's Box* has now been incorporated into RWA's primary publication, *RWR: Romance Writers' Report*, older issues still exist.

> *The Quizzing Glass*

The official newsletter of the Beau Monde, the Regency Special Interest Chapter of RWA, contains articles and other information of interest to chapter members. It is free to all members of the Beau Monde, who must also be members of RWA. For current information, contact the RWA national headquarters in Houston (address above).

Rawhide and Lace
P. O. Box 11593
Bainbridge Island, WA 98110
Published quarterly

Aimed at readers and writers of western fiction, this "newsletter for, by, and about the women in the west" features reviews, author profiles and interviews, articles on various Western topics, questions and answers, and other items of interest to the target audience. This is one example of the various subgenre-related publications available.

The Regency Reader Newsletter
P. O. Box 8216
Federal Way, WA 98003-0216
Published quarterly

Published by the Beau Monde, the Regency Special Interest Chapter of RWA, this newsletter is aimed at alerting librarians and booksellers to upcoming Regency Romances being published. Books are summarized rather than critically reviewed, and Regency type (e.g., traditional, romp, sensual, paranormal) is indicated. Some articles are included.

Rendezvous: A Monthly Review of Contemporary and Historical Romances, Mysteries, and Women's Fiction

Love Designers Writers' Club, Inc.
1507 Burnham Avenue
Calumet City, IL 60409
Phone: (708) 862-9797
Published monthly

This simply presented source includes reviews for most romances published each month. No advertising is accepted, and books do not receive ratings. Overall, a credible review source.

Romance Forever Magazine
Michael J. Powazinik, Editor
FOROM Publishing, Inc.
P. O. Box 297158
Brooklyn, NY 11229-9840
Published quarterly

This new, nicely done periodical features articles, interviews, columns, reviews, and other information of interest to romance readers.

RWR: Romance Writers Report
Romance Writers of America
13700 Veterans Memorial, Suite 315
Houston, TX 77014
Phone: (713) 440-6885
FAX: (713) 440-7510
Published monthly (free to RWA members)

This monthly (bimonthly prior to March 1996) publication provides readers information on market trends; surveys; interviews with writers, agents, editors, and publishers; how-to articles by practicing writers; organizational news; contest and conference announcements; and a wealth of other features of interest to romance writers and readers.

Romantic Times
Romantic Times Publishing Group
55 Bergen Street
Brooklyn, NY 11201
Phone: (718) 237-1097
FAX: (718) 624-4231
Web site: www.romantictimes.com (accessed December 10, 1998)
Published monthly

The best-known and most comprehensive periodical in the field, *RT* includes ranked reviews of most romances published each month, publishing news, author sketches, interviews, articles, and other items of interest to romance fans and professionals. Even though the reviews tend to be overly positive, the amount of advertising occasionally overwhelming, and the style flamboyant, RT currently provides the best overall coverage of the genre. And if you could subscribe to one romance periodical, this would be it.

Romantics at Heart
Romance Readers Association
P. O. Box 24584
San Jose, CA 95154
Phone: (408) 978-3416
FAX: (408) 978-9363
Published bimonthly (free to RRA members)

As the official newsletter of the Romance Readers Association, this publication features columns, reviews, author appearance/signing listings, contests, interviews, and other information of interest to romance readers.

The SFR Newsletter (Science Fiction Romance)
P. O. Box 496
Endicott, NJ 13761-0496
E-mail: yeep@aol.com
Published monthly

This newsletter focuses on "speculative fiction that puts an emphasis on romance and characterization" and is available in both print and online versions (from "Sapphire Award, 1997," www.sff.net/people/asaro/sappire.htp, accessed September 9, 1998).

BOOK REVIEW SOURCES

When looking for romance reviews, in addition to consulting the periodicals listed above that include reviews, readers may find the following sources helpful. Note: These indexes are most useful for locating reviews of specific romances by major, established romance authors.

Indexes

Book Review Digest

Arranged by author and indexed by title, this annually compiled source provides a brief synopsis of the book, excerpts from various reviews, and bibliographic citations for those and others not quoted. Only the most widely read and reviewed romance authors are found in this tool, because a book must have received at least four reviews to be included.

Book Review Index

More comprehensive than *Book Review Digest*, this annually compiled source provides brief citations of book reviews in various journals. Romance novels reviewed in the periodicals indexed by this source are included.

Expanded Academic ASAP (on InfoTrac Searchbank)

This computerized database is available online and lists citations to articles in a variety of popular and scholarly magazines and journals published during the most recent three years. Romance novels reviewed in the periodicals indexed in this source are included. Some articles indexed by Expanded Academic ASAP are reproduced in full.

Lexis/Nexis

Although this is a full-text online database rather than an index, it is included here because the Nexis portion is an excellent source of reviews of books too recent to be included in other indexes. Nexis includes a wide variety of newspapers and popular magazines, many of which are updated daily. Unfortunately, because of its extremely high cost, this source is inaccessible to many readers.

National Newspaper Index (on InfoTrac Searchbank)

This computerized database is available online and lists citations to articles in five major newspapers published during the most recent three years. Romance novels reviewed in the newspapers indexed in this source are included.

Readers' Guide to Periodical Literature ("Book Review" section)
   The "Book Review" section at the back of each volume contains an alphabetical listing by author of the book reviews included in the magazines and journals indexed in *Readers' Guide*.

Review Columns and Other Sources

In addition to the review columns in the romance periodicals discussed above, romance reviews and review columns are beginning to appear in more general and mainstream sources. Newspaper review columns are popping up throughout the country, e.g., *Star-Tribune* (Minneapolis)/Kathleen Eagle, *Contra Costa Valley Times* (California)/Lynn Coddington, and *Atlanta Journal-Constitution*/Helen Holzer. *Publishers Weekly*, *USA Today*, and *Booklist* are reviewing romances more often, and *Library Journal* has a quarterly romance review column (see below).

"Romance Reviews" in *Library Journal*
   In the May 15, 1995, issue, *LJ* inaugurated the first romance review column to appear regularly in a major publishing trade or library publication. It was published three times a year until 1996, when it became a quarterly column. It appears in the February 15, May 15, August 15, and November 15 issues. Although reviews of all types of romances may be found in any one column, most columns focus on a particular type of romance or theme and include a definition and discussion of the theme.

The Internet
   Not surprisingly, the Internet is also a source of romance reviews and commentary. The various lists mentioned in chapter 18, "Societies and Organizations," often discuss specific romances, sometimes on a scheduled basis, and there are a number of Web sites that publish formal reviews, e.g., The Romance Reader (www.theromancereader.com, accessed December 10, 1998) and *The Literary Times* (www.tlt.com/revws/revwsl.htm, accessed December 10, 1998). In addition, several commercial bookstore Web sites, e.g., Amazon, and Barnes and Noble, also list some reviews. However, the Internet is fluid in the extreme, and because home pages and addresses change so rapidly, the best approach to finding reviews is simply to use a good search engine and a few well-chosen keywords, and see what you find.

Chapter 17

Miscellaneous Romance Reference Sources

ROMANCE AUTHORSHIP AIDS

For anyone contemplating a career as a romance writer, the obvious and best first resource is the Romance Writers of America (see chapter 18, "Societies and Organizations"). With its broad network of local chapters, wide array of professional services, and "prime directive" to help romances writers succeed, RWA can provide much of what the beginning writer needs, and it is definitely a good place to start. However, abundant help also exists in print. From the classic how-tos of basic fiction writing to handbooks specifically tailored to the romance genre, literature that guides the writer from "plot to print" abounds and is easily found in libraries and bookstores. The list that follows is a sampling of the many works that exist.

Barnhart, Helene Schellenberg. *Writing Romance Fiction for Love and Money.* Cincinnati, OH: Writer's Digest Books, 1983. (Republished in 1987 by TorStar.)

  A comprehensive, well-written book that advises romance writers on how to plot stories; develop characters; write convincing dialogue, description, and sex scenes; prepare manuscripts for submission; deal with editors and publishers; and maintain a writing schedule. Out of print, but should be available in local libraries.

Borcherding, David H., ed. *Romance Writer's Sourcebook: Where to Sell Your Manuscripts.* Cincinnati, OH: Writer's Digest Books, 1996.

  A first for Writer's Digest Books, this readable guide includes a little bit of everything and features essays on trends and techniques by successful romance writers (e.g., Nora Roberts, Kristin Hannah, and Jennifer Crusie); chapters on agents, markets, successes; and resources by appropriate experts. Also includes lists of contests, journals, online resources, organizations, conferences, workshops, markets, agents, and RWA chapters. Several indexes provide easy access to this useful, comprehensive resource that is scheduled for periodic updates.

Falk, Kathryn, ed. *How to Write a Romance and Get It Published: With Intimate Advice from the World's Most Popular Romantic Writers.* rev. ed. New York: Signet, 1990. (1989 edition published by NAL-Dutton.)

  An updated version of Falk's original 1983 guide, this is an interesting and helpful collection of essays by writers and other professionals in the romance field.

Lowery, Marilyn M. *How to Write Romance Novels That Sell.* New York: Rawson Associates, 1983.

  This entertaining and well-organized book discusses various romance writing techniques. Although it is no longer in print, it does discuss the often-ignored areas of young adult and gay romantic fiction.

MacManus, Yvonne. *You Can Write a Romance and Get It Published.* rev. ed. Laceyville, MD: Toad Hall Press, 1996.

  A revised, updated, and expanded edition of her 1983 guide, filled with practical, step-by-step information for getting published.

Paludan, Eve. *The Romance Writer's Pink Pages: The Insider's Guide to Getting Your Romance Novel Published.* Rocklin, CA: Prima Pub., 1996.

  First published in 1993, this source is updated periodically (usually on an annual basis) and contains an abundance of information, including various lists (e.g., agents and publishers) that may be useful to romance writers.

Pianka, Phyllis Taylor. *How to Write Romances.* New York: Writer's Digest Books, 1988.

  A well-written basic text by a popular romance writer who also teaches workshops and courses on writing.

Swain, Dwight V. *Techniques of the Selling Writer.* Norman, OK: University of Oklahoma Press, 1965.

  Practical, no-nonsense advice on writing fiction that sells. Reprinted at least five times, this book is considered one of the best by many fiction writers, including those who write romance.

Although most historical romance writers logically head for the special collections or history sections of their libraries when they need to do serious research for their books, a number of handbooks out there simplify the process. A few of them are listed below. Nothing, of course, can take the place of doing thorough, primary-source research, and the books that follow must be used with care. Nevertheless, they may prove useful, and they are definitely fun to read.

Laudermilk, Sharon H. *The Regency Companion.* New York: Garland, 1989.
   This handy volume provides detailed information about the English Regency period (1811–1820) and is useful to readers and writers alike. Includes an extensive bibliography.

McCutcheon, Marc. *The Writer's Guide to Everyday Life in the 1800s.* Cincinnati, OH: Writer's Digest Books, 1993.
   Focusing on nineteenth-century America, this guide is essentially an alphabetical listing to terms arranged in broad chapters (e.g., "Out on the Range," "Courtship and Marriage," "Getting Around"). Concludes with five useful chronologies and a list of reference sources, arranged by chapter. Includes some illustrations.

Pool, Daniel. *What Jane Austen Ate and Charles Dickens Knew: From Fox Hunting to Whist—the Facts of Daily Life in 19th-Century England.* New York: Simon & Schuster, 1993.
   Similar in purpose to the McCutcheon guide, this source focuses on nineteenth-century England. Some illustrations.

WORD BOOKS, RECIPE BOOKS, AND OTHER MISCELLANY

The following items do not fall into any of the more serious research aid categories included in this guide. They are, however, potentially useful and fun to read.

Biederman, Jerry, and Tom Silberkleit, eds. *My First Real Romance: Twenty Bestselling Romance Novelists Reveal the Stories of Their Own First Real Romances.* New York: Stein and Day, 1985.
   Although technically an author biographical source, the highly specific focus of this book (the authors' first real-life, personal romances) limits its usefulness as a general biographical reference. Fascinating reading.

Cartland, Barbara. *Barbara Cartland's Book of Love and Lovers.* New York: Ballantine, 1978.
   A well-illustrated, readable coffee-table book that takes an artistic look at love.

————. *Recipes for Lovers*. New York: Bantam, 1978.

This unique recipe book describes romantic dinners and provides do-it-yourself information for creating them (e.g., the "pink dinner" for celebrating the first time you met, fell in love, made love, etc. Most of the foods and decorations are pink). Recipes are provided, and settings and arrangements are described in detail.

Friedman, Gil, comp. *A Dictionary of Love*. Arcata, CA: Yara Press, 1990

Accessible through a detailed table of contents that functions more like a subject index, this collection of more than 600 quotes (grouped into 191 categories) on the topic of love runs the gamut from Shaw to Socrates and includes verbal gems from people as diverse as Phyllis Diller, Napoleon Hill, and Mother Teresa.

Guiley, Rosemary. *LoveLines: A Romance Reader's Guide to Printed Pleasures*. New York: Facts on File, 1983.

A delightful collection of anecdotes, interviews, and fascinating tidbits, both historical and contemporary, of the wonderful world of romance.

Kent, Jean, and Candace Shelton. *The Romance Writer's Phrase Book*. New York: Putnam, 1984.

Still in print, this source contains lists of descriptive phrases for romance writers. Its purpose is actually to stimulate the writer's imagination rather than to provide a definitive listing of all "appropriate" romance phrases. Outdated and irrelevant to today's romances, these suggestions, nevertheless, make for interesting reading.

Kipfer, Barbara Ann, comp. *Bartlett's Book of Love Quotations*. Boston: Little, Brown, 1994.

Containing almost 1,000 quotations on love and romance gleaned from the venerable *Bartlett's Familiar Quotations*, this source is divided into five broad sections ("Romance," "Passion," "Marriage," "Family and Friendship," and "God, Country, the World"). Quotes are arranged alphabetically by author within each section. Interesting, but the larger *Bartlett's Familiar Quotations* is more useful.

Reed, Tina, ed. *Words of Love II . . . The Romance Continues*. New York: Perigee, 1994.

This pocket-sized book of love quotations follows Reed's earlier *Words of Love* and provides an eclectic collection of serious and humorous quotes from a diverse group of people that includes, among others, Bette Midler, Edgar Allan Poe, and Napoleon Bonaparte. No index or table of contents.

INTERNET SITES

The Internet is a great source of general information, and many writers have discovered that whether their story requires photographs of Jupiter's moons, the text of the president's latest speech, or a recipe for tabouli, they probably can find it somewhere on the Net. For the savvy searcher, the Internet is also a gold mine of romance-specific resources, including chapters of books in progress, publishers' home pages, and detailed lists of reference resources. Naturally, the usual caveats apply to all information found on the Net (e.g., Is it accurate? Is it current? What is the source? Is there a bias?) and sites and addresses can change without notice. Nevertheless, it can provide useful information and is well worth a try. Simply use a good search engine, a few appropriate terms (e.g., romance fiction or romance writers resources), and see where you end up. In many cases, the sites you find will provide links to other pages of interest. The sites listed below are simply a few examples of what was available at the time of this writing. See other sites listed in chapter 16, "Periodicals and Review Resources"; chapter 15, "Author Biography and Bibliography"; and chapter 18, "Societies and Organizations."

Resources for Romance Writers (www/inkspot.com/genres/romance.html, accessed December 10, 1998)

> A good place to get started with a number of links to other useful sites.

Romance Writers of America (RWA) (www.rwanational.com, accessed December 10, 1998)

> An excellent source of information for aspiring and published romance writers. Provides membership information, industry statistics, lists of award winners, and much more.

The Write Page (www.writepage.com/index.html, accessed December 10, 1998)

> Basically a newsletter for readers and writers of genre fiction. Includes a page for romance ("Romance Novels and Women's Fiction") that contains a number of good links.

Publishers' Pages

These are only a few of the publishers of romance fiction who currently have Web sites. Others can be located simply by searching for them by name. Note: In most cases the parent company (e.g., Penguin, Kensington) has the main home page with links to other sites.

Avon Books—www.AvonBooks.com (accessed December 10, 1998)

Harlequin Enterprises—www.romance.net/harlequin_books.html (accessed December 10, 1998)

Kensington Publishing—www.pinnaclebooks.com (accessed December 10, 1998)

Penguin Putnam, Inc.—www.penguinputnam.com (accessed December 10, 1998)

Random House—www.randomhouse.com (accessed December 10, 1998)

Chapter 18

Societies and Organizations

A number of organizations for readers and writers of romance fiction currently exist. Some of them are formally organized, with constitutions, by-laws, and all the accoutrements of serious enterprise; others are less rigidly structured; and others exist primarily in the "virtual" world of the Internet. Note: Although organizations for readers and writers are listed separately, in many cases the distinction between the two is fluid, and many of the groups would be of equal interest to both readers and writers.

WRITERS' ORGANIZATIONS

Writing is a solitary occupation, but writers are not necessarily solitary people. Most find it important, if not absolutely essential, to communicate with the world in general and fellow writers in particular—especially those who write within the same genre. While this communication is often done on an informal basis, several official organizations have been established to meet this need. These organizations offer a variety of services for their constituencies; however, it is the network of shared interests, information, and personal contact they provide that is one of their primary membership benefits. Those listed here are ones that romance writers might want to consider joining. Several also welcome readers of genre fiction in addition to writers.

Romance Writers of America (RWA) Established 1980
13700 Veterans Memorial, Suite 315
Houston, TX 77014
Phone: (713) 440-6885
FAX: (713) 440-7510
E-mail: www.rwanational.com

Founded to provide support for writers of romance fiction and to encourage the recognition of the romance genre as a valid literary form, RWA sponsors competitions, workshops, and conferences; maintains a telephone hotline, (713) 440-8081; and publishes the monthly *RWR: Romance Writer's Report*, *PANdora's Box* (a bimonthly newsletter), and the *Chapter Presidents Bulletin* (a monthly newsletter). Note: *PANdora's Box* has now been incorporated into RWR. RWA also presents a number of annual awards, including the Rita and Golden Heart Awards, at its conference each July. RWA has a number of subgenre-specific interest groups as well as the Published Authors Network (PAN). Unpublished as well as published writers are welcome, as are agents, publishers, librarians, and others interested in the genre. Dues are $70 initially, $60 annually thereafter.

Mystery Writers of America (MWA) Established 1945
17 E. 47th Street, 6th Floor
New York, NY 10017
Phone: (212) 888-8171
FAX: (212) 888-8107

Aimed at fostering and promoting the causes and interests of writers of mystery fiction, MWA supports various legislation, provides contract advice, sponsors an annual mystery writing workshop, and publishes an annual anthology (*Mystery Writers Annual*) and a monthly periodical (*The Third Degree*). MWA also sponsors the Edgar Allan Poe Awards which are presented at an annual awards banquet in New York City each spring. Several classes of membership are offered, including: Active, for published writers in the mystery field, and Associate, for professionals in related fields (e.g., publishers, agents, librarians, and writers of other genres). Annual dues are $65. Although the focus of this organization is on the mystery genre, it may be of interest to writers of the Romantic-Suspense and Gothic genres.

Novelists, Inc. Established 1989
P. O. Box 1166
Mission, KS 66222-0166

Open to any writer who has published two or more novels, one within the last five years, Novelists, Inc. publishes a newsletter and provides a variety of useful information for writers in all genres. Dues are $50 a year.

Science Fiction and Fantasy Workshop (SF&FW) Established 1980
1193 S. 1900 E.
Salt Lake City, UT 84108-1855
Phone: (801) 582-2090
E-mail: k.woodbury@genie.geis.com

Established to encourage and support writers of Science Fiction and Fantasy, this organization provides a variety of useful services and special interest groups for both neophyte and experienced writers. Dues are $15 for the first year, $10 annually thereafter. In addition to the monthly *Science Fiction and Fantasy Workshop Newsletter*, the workshop also publishes several other practical items, including the biennial *Basic Market List* and the quarterly *Outlines, Synopses, Proposals That Sold*. Writers of Alternative Reality Romances might find this organization or some of its publications of interest.

Science-Fiction and Fantasy Writers of America (SFWA)
Established 1965
c/o Michael Capoblanco, Pres.
532 La Guardia Pl., Apt. 632
New York, NY 10012-1428

Formerly known as Science Fiction Writers of America, this organization of professional science fiction and fantasy writers promotes public interest in the genre, maintains a speakers bureau, conducts seminars and lectures, and encourages the production of high-quality science fiction and fantasy literature. SFWA sponsors the Nebula Awards, which are presented at an annual awards banquet each April. It also publishes the annual *Nebula Awards Anthology*, the quarterly *Bulletin*, and the bimonthly *Forum*.

Sisters in Crime (SinC) Established 1987
P. O. Box 442124
Lawrence, KS 66044-8933

Similar to RWA in purpose (but focusing on mystery rather than romance), this worldwide organization of those "who have a special interest in mystery writing," deals with discrimination against women mystery writers, educates publishers and the public at large on the topic, and serves as a support for new writers. Dues are $25 a year.

Western Writers of America Established 1952
Jim Crutchfield, Secretary-Treasurer
1012 Fair Street
Franklin, TN 37064-2718
Phone: (615) 791-1444

This organization welcomes freelance writers of many types of Western fiction and non-fiction, including romance. Membership levels and requirements vary; dues are $60 a year. WWA sponsors various competitions, issues the bimonthly periodical *Roundup* , and presents the Spur Awards in three fiction categories: Best Western Novel, Best Novel of the West, and Best Paperback Original. Spurs are also given for various non-fiction works. In addition, WWA presents the Medicine Pipe Bearer Award for the best first Western novel each year. Although the focus of this organization is primarily on "all things Western," writers of romances set in the American West may find this group helpful.

Of interest to some may be the following British counterpart to the Romance Writers of America:

Romantic Novelists Association Established 1960
5, St. Agnes Gate
Wendover
Bucks, HP22 6DP
Web site: freespace.virgin.net/marina/oliver/rna.htm
(accessed December 10, 1998)

Similar in purpose and intent to the RWA, RNA offers various services to its membership, holds several meetings and seminars each year, and publishes the *RNS News*, a quarterly newsletter. RNA presents the New Writers' Award (Netta Muskett Award) for unpublished romance authors and the RNA Major Award for published writers. The RNA Historical Award was presented until 1974 and has since been subsumed by the RNA Major Award.

Romance Writers Listserv (RW-L) Established 1994
E-mail: RW-L@SJUVM.stjohns.edu

A spin-off of RRA-L (see below), this active list serves as a forum for romance writers to exchange ideas, critique each other's work, and discuss other issues of interest to romance writers.

READERS' ORGANIZATIONS

A number of societies and organizations for writers have been in existence for some time, but it has been only recently that groups focusing on readers have begun to form. Two that might be of interest to romance readers are listed below.

Romance Readers Association Established 1995
Terri Farrell, Founder
Debbie Mekler, Newsletter Editor
P. O. Box 24584
San Jose, CA 95154
Phone: (408) 978-3416
E-mail: LYZU16A@prodigy.com
E-mail: mekler@best.com

Founded to "effectively bridge the gap between readers, authors, and booksellers," RRA publishes a bimonthly newsletter (*Romantics at Heart*), provides a variety of author promotional material to its members, and actively works to promote the romance genre. Dues are $25 a year and include a subscription to the newsletter.

Romance Readers Anonymous Listserv (RRA-L)
E-mail: RRA-L@kentvm.kent.edu

Established in 1992 by Leslie Haas and Kara Robinson, this list is one of the most active and discusses romance novels, authors, publishers, and a wide variety of romance-related topics. Welcomes readers and writers alike.

COMMERCIAL ONLINE SOURCES

In addition to the two Internet listservs mentioned above, which are available to anyone with access to the Net, there are a number of romance-centered groups for those who subscribe to the various commercial online services. Most of these are more than listservs, and they offer much information to romance writers and readers. Several groups and their parent service providers are listed below. For more detailed, and current, information, contact the service provider. Note: in most cases, these service providers allow access to the Internet, and from there you can get to the listservs mentioned above.

Literary Forum—CompuServe. Of particular interest are Section 23, RWA Online, and Section 17, Romance

Romance and Women's Fiction Exchange (RomEx)—GEnie

Romance Novels—Prodigy

Romance Writers Group (RWG)—American Online (AOL)

Chapter 19

Awards

Awards for American romance fiction have existed since the early 1980s, but compared with awards for the other literary genres, they are a relatively recent phenomenon and, as such, are still evolving. In the past few years numerous new awards have been established. Some of these are offered by new groups, but many are presented by the individual chapters within RWA, often in conjunction with a contest (e.g., Maggie and Silver Heart). Within the ranks of the existing awards, names have changed and categories have been added, dropped, reinstated, and redefined—all reflecting the dynamic nature of the genre. Most of these awards are for individual novels and are based on the style and quality of writing, however, some publishers' awards are given on the basis of sales. In addition, a few awards are given in recognition of an outstanding career or for other contributions to romance fiction. Many of these awards are presented by RWA; however, several publications, including the *Romantic Times* and *Affaire de Coeur,* also recognize romance writers through "best" lists, certificates, or by other means. The list that follows includes only a portion of the major national awards given. [Note: Lists of many of the individual award winners can be found in the publications of the organizations presenting the awards, in the annual volumes of *What Do I Read Next?* (Gale, 1980), the spin-off *What Romance Do I Read Next?* (Gale, 1997), and in a forthcoming book on romance awards edited by Leslie Haas and tentatively titled *Award-Winning Romances.*

AFFAIRE DE COEUR READER-WRITER POLL AWARDS

Selected by popular vote of the *Affaire de Coeur* magazine readership and presented at the Affaire de Coeur Annual Conference, these awards are given in a wide variety of categories which vary from year to year and may include: Best Contemporary Novel, Contemporary Ethnic, Overall Historical, Foreign Historical, American Historical, Regency, Futuristic, Time Travel, Sci-Fi, Supernatural, and Inspirational. Awards can also include Outstanding Achiever, Best Up and Coming Author, Top Ten Favorite Romance Authors, Best Cover, Outstanding Heroine, Outstanding Hero, Romance of the Year, and the Affaire de Coeur Hall of Fame.

ROMANCE WRITERS OF AMERICA AWARDS

Each year Romance Writers of America (RWA) presents a number of awards, honoring romance writers for their works and others for significant contributions to the genre. Considered by many to be the most prestigious in the genre, most of these awards are based on excellence in writing rather than popularity or sales. The names of some awards have changed over the years. All awards are presented at the annual RWA Conference in July.

Golden Heart Awards

These awards are presented annually at the RWA Conference to unpublished writers of book-length fiction of any type. Golden Hearts are awarded in a number of categories that have varied over the years and currently include the following: Traditional, Short Contemporary, Long Contemporary, Contemporary Single Title, Romantic Suspense/Gothic, Paranormal, Regency, Short Historical, Long Historical, Inspirational, and Young Adult. All entrants must be members of RWA.

Rita Awards

Formerly known as the Golden Medallion Awards, these awards are named for RWA's first president, Rita Clay Estrada, and are presented to published writers of romance fiction. Ritas are awarded in a number of categories that have varied over the years and currently include the following: Traditional, Short Contemporary, Long Contemporary, Contemporary Single Title, Romantic Suspense/Gothic, Paranormal, Regency, Short Historical, Long Historical, Inspirational, Young Adult, and Best First Book. All entrants must be members of RWA.

Regional Service Awards

These awards are given to the RWA members in each of the six regions who have made major contributions to the organization. Nominations are made by the membership at large; the final decisions are the responsibility of the national RWA board.

Emma Merritt National Service Award

Also named for a past president of RWA, this award is presented to the RWA member who has made the most significant contribution to the organization at the national level. Nominations are made by the membership at large; the final decision is the responsibility of the national RWA board.

Lifetime Achievement Award

Formerly known as the Golden Treasure Award, this award is presented "to a living writer whose career in romantic fiction dates back at least 15 years." This award of excellence recognizes long-term contributions to the romance genre.

Hall of Fame Award

This honor is given to writers who have won at least three Ritas in the same romance category. Nora Roberts was the first member, inducted in 1986.

Favorite Book of the Year Award

The winner of this award is selected by a popular vote of the RWA membership at large.

Janet Dailey Award

This award is presented for the romance novel that best raises public consciousness about an important social issue and includes a $10,000 prize. Note: This award was not offered in 1998 and has been discontinued.

Veritas Award

This award is presented for the "best article in print that approaches the romance industry in the most positive way."

Librarian of the Year Award

This award is presented to the librarian who has best supported, promoted, and generally advanced the cause of romance fiction within the library community.

Bookseller of the Year Award

This award recognizes the bookseller who has "approached the romance industry in the most positive way."

Industry Award

This award is presented for outstanding contributions to the romance industry and genre as a whole. Recipients have included publishers, agents, editors, and writers.

ARTemis Awards

Chosen by popular vote at the annual RWA Conference, these awards are presented for excellence in romance cover art in various categories.

ROMANTIC TIMES AWARDS

Sponsored by *Romantic Times Magazine*, these awards are presented at the annual Romantic Times Booklovers' Convention.

Reviewers' Choice Awards

Presented for outstanding romances, these awards are made in a wide variety of categories that may vary from year to year. Selection is made by the appropriate RT romance reviewer and a committee.

Career Achievement Awards

These awards are presented to romance writers in recognition of outstanding career achievement in the various categories of romance fiction.

ROM-CON AWARDS

Presented at the annual ROM-CON, a romance lover's conference sponsored by Barbara Keenan of East Bay Books (San Leandro, CA), these awards are given in a wide variety of romance-related categories.

SAPPHIRE AWARD

Presented by *The SFR Newsletter*, this "Best Science Fiction Romance of the Year" award acknowledges outstanding novel-length books, either genre or mainstream, of "speculative fiction where both interpersonal relationships and science fiction or fantasy are intrinsic to the plot" (from "Sapphire Award, 1997" www.sff.net/people/asaro/ sapphire.htp, accessed September 9, 1998). The award is administered by *The SFR Newsletter* editor.

WALDENBOOKS BESTSELLING ROMANCE AWARDS

These awards are based on sales and are presented in categories that vary annually and may include: Long Contemporary Romance, Original Series Romance, Series Romance by a New Author, Long Historical Romance, Short Historical or Regency Romance, Multicultural Romance, Hardcover Debut Romance, Sales Growth, Special Achievement Award, and Lifetime Achievement Award.

ROMANCE READERS ANONYMOUS LISTSERV (RRA-L) AWARDS

These awards are selected annually by the members of the RRA-L electronic mailing list and are presented in a wide variety of categories.

Because there is so much crossover between the American and British romance market, readers may find the following British awards of interest.

ROMANTIC NOVELISTS' ASSOCIATION AWARDS

Romantic Novelists' Association Major Award

Established in 1960 and presented by the Romantic Novelists Association, this award for the best romantic novel of the year is open to all writers who reside in the UK. To be eligible, works must have been published between December 1 of the previous year and November 30 of the year under consideration. This award consists of a cash prize of £5000 and is presented at an annual luncheon held in the spring. Note: The RNA Historical Award was discontinued in 1974 and has been combined with this award.

New Writer (Netta Muskett) Award

Established in 1960 and presented by the Romantic Novelists Association, this award is open to writers who are probationary members of RNA and are unpublished in the romance novel genre. Manuscripts for consideration are submitted in September for critique. Manuscripts which then are accepted by a publisher for publication are eligible for this award. Note: This award is not necessarily given every year.

GEORGETTE HEYER PRIZE

Established in 1977 by Bodley Head and Corgi Books but now discontinued, this award was presented for an outstanding full-length historical novel and commemorated Heyer's contribution to the serious historical novel genre. Although this award is no longer given, readers may find references to it in the literature, and it is listed here for that reason.

THE BETTY TRASK PRIZE AND AWARDS

Presented by The Society of Authors, these awards are given to authors under age 35 for a published or unpublished first novel of "a romantic or traditional nature." Applicants must be Commonwealth citizens. The monies for the Betty Trask Prize and up to five additional Betty Trask Awards vary from year to year (at least £25,000 in 1998) and must be used for foreign travel related to future writing plans. For further information, contact The Society of Authors, 84 Drayton Gardens, London SW10 9SB, or e-mail: authors@writers.org.uk.

Chapter 20

Collections

Romance fiction can be found in two basic types of library collections: the general or recreational reading collection and the research collection. While both may contain items of interest to readers and researchers alike, in general, researchers will want to explore the research collections, and romance readers will want to use the recreational reading collections corresponding to their reading interests.

READING COLLECTIONS

Most often located in public libraries, general or recreational reading collections do an excellent job of providing access to current romance novels. Although fiction in public libraries, especially those using the Dewey Decimal Classification System, is usually arranged in a single alphabet by author's last name, many libraries have established separate genre collections in which books of certain types (e.g., mysteries, Westerns, and fantasies) are grouped together. Romances are often shelved in this fashion. While such an arrangement is helpful, it is important to remember that novels of the Romantic Suspense and Gothic genres often find their way into the mystery section, and romances of other varieties are occasionally found among the general fiction. Check to be sure.

Most public libraries have some romances in their collections; however, the number and the type generally depend upon the demands of the local clientele (unless the library maintains a retrospective romance collection for archival purposes, either as a part of a large library system or for other reasons). In many large metropolitan library systems, the largest fiction collection is often kept in the main branch; however, this might be the best source for romances. For example, if a branch library has a greater demand for romances or a librarian particularly interested in the genre, it may have a larger, more diverse, and more current collection than the main library. To find out, either ask the local library staff or, if there is a system-wide online catalog, check that resource to see which branch has the largest holdings.

Perhaps the best way to find out where the prime romance collections are in your area is simply to ask other people interested in the genre. As with other types of fiction, some of the best sources of information about books, authors, and collections are often satisfied, interested fans and readers. A few minutes of discussion with a knowledgeable reader often provides the best and most practical answers in the shortest amount of time. Note: This includes online discussion, too. Listservs and chat groups often have participants living in your local area who would be more than happy to help.

Finally, although library collections are by far the most common way for most readers to access romance fiction, some readers are busy building their own collections. Some do this by intent; others do so simply because they prefer to buy books rather than borrow them. Either way, there are some extensive private romance collections in existence. Access to these, of course, is strictly by invitation, but just knowing of their existence and learning something of their strengths and weaknesses can be valuable information in its own right.

RESEARCH COLLECTIONS

Anyone interested in researching romance fiction should consult Lee Ash's standard reference work, *Subject Collections: A Guide to Special Book Collections and Emphases as Reported by University, College, Public, and Special Libraries and Museums in the United States and Canada*, 7th ed. (New Providence, NJ: Bowker, 1993). Also, sections of several works by Kay Mussell are helpful. See her discussion of "Collections and Research Facilities" in *Women's Gothic and Romantic Fiction: A Reference Guide* (Westport, CT: Greenwood Press, 1981) and the sections on research collections in her essays titled "Gothic Novels" and "Romantic Fiction" in *Handbook of American Popular Literature,* edited by M. Thomas Inge (New York: Greenwood Press, 1988).

Ash's guide is current and provides comprehensive listings for a large number of specialized collections. It is arranged by subject; however, because there is no one subject heading that covers all American romance fiction and authors, several headings should be consulted to find all relevant sources. Mussell's works are less current—although a supplement to her 1981 guide is forthcoming—but more to the point. Her brief bibliographic essays provide a good overview of research collections in the United States that contain examples of romantic and Gothic fiction, and they are an excellent starting point for those interested in research in this area. Both sources, however, should be consulted—Mussell's for specific coverage, Ash's for currency. Librarians and researchers might also find this older, but still relevant, article interesting: Sewell, Robert G. "Trash or Treasure? Pop Fiction in Academic and Research Libraries." *College and Research Libraries* 45 (November 1984): 450–61.

Several of the major collections are listed below. This list is not comprehensive and does not include the many manuscript collections that exist hidden in the archives of smaller academic and public libraries, local historical societies and museums, and private collections. It merely serves as an example of the resources available to the researcher in the romance fiction field.

Boston University

Collects papers, manuscripts, and works by and about twentieth-century authors, including writers of popular fiction. Among the romance authors represented are Norah Lofts, Catherine Cookson, Dorothy Eden, Faith Baldwin, Barbara Cartland, Margaret Mitchell, Anya Seton, and Phyllis Whitney.

Bowling Green State University

The Popular Culture Library at Bowling Green actively collects and maintains a large, cataloged collection of popular fiction, much of which is romance. In addition to more than 8,300 series romance titles (including many from now-defunct lines) and a large collection of single title mass-market romances, the Library also collects relevant supporting materials, reference works, and periodicals. Since January 1996, the library has been the official archive for the Romance Writers of America and the romance genre. As such, it collects papers and manuscripts of current romance writers, reviewers, and scholars; book covers; and other materials of interest to romance scholars. Materials do not circulate. One of the largest and best collections available. The University Library Catalog, BGLINK provides online access. See PCL's Romance Collection Web site at www.bgsu.edu/colleges/library/pcl/pcl13.html (accessed December 10, 1998) for further information.

Michigan State University

A number of romances are included in the Russel B. Nye Popular Culture Collection, but the Library is no longer actively acquiring in this area.

University of Virginia

This university boasts a 300,000-volume collection of American fiction published between 1775 and 1980. The collection purports to be complete for the period 1775-1875. For the years 1975–1980, the collection contains all major and some minor authors. Because of its comprehensiveness, this collection is of particular interest to researchers of the women writers of the nineteenth century. The papers of various authors are also available, including those of Frances Parkinson Keyes, Mary Johnston, and early writer Susanna Rowson. The 2,000-volume Sadleir-Black Gothic Collection, a major source of Gothic novels, is also located here.

Library of Congress

Because it is the copyright depository, LC is one of the primary sources of hardcover romance novels published in the United States during the twentieth century. Because romance novels are usually not cataloged by subject, primary access is by author. Of particular interest to researchers of earlier women's fiction is LC's 20,000-volume collection of dime novels. Many of the important mid-nineteenth-century writers of women's fiction are included, although access is not easy as this collection is indexed only by series title.

New York Public Library

Included within the various collections of this vast resource are materials on a number of American romance authors such as Susanna Rowson, Catharine Maria Sedgwick, Jean Webster, Elizabeth Oakes Smith, E.D.E.N. Southworth, and Mary Roberts Rinehart. Early romance fiction can also be found in the Beadle Collection of Dime Novels and the Arents Collections of Books in Parts.

The majority of romance writers included in research collections are of early or historical importance. However, materials on an increasing number of popular contemporary authors are appearing; and with the continuing growth in women's studies and literatures, along with a growing interest in the area of women's romantic fiction, the number of current romance writers represented will likely increase. The 1996 establishment of the archive for the romance genre and the Romance Writers of America at the Popular Culture Library at Bowling Green State University was a milestone for the romance genre. Not only does it validate the genre from both a popular culture and a literary point of view, but it also ensures that this often ephemeral material now will be collected and preserved as it is being generated and will be available for future researchers and historians.

Chapter 21

Publishers

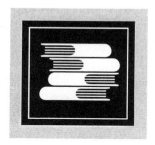

Romances are published in paperback; hardcover; large-print hardcover; and, to a lesser degree, in a number of experimental, non-print formats (e.g., audio, video, computerized, and online). Traditionally, most romance fiction has been published in paperback — and more than 97 percent still is; however, in recent years an increasing number of houses have begun to publish new romances in hardcover, with excellent results. In addition, a number of original paperback romances are currently being reprinted in hardcover, and many romances (both paperback and hardcover originals) are routinely reprinted in large-print hardcover editions. A number of houses publish romance fiction; however, two large conglomerates, Harlequin/Silhouette/Mira and Kensington/Pinnacle/Zebra, account for well over half of all the romance releases each year (57 percent in 1996 according to RWA statistics), with the difference being made up by the 20 or so remaining houses. Note: As noted in a previous chapter, megers and buyouts have been commonplace in the publishing industry during the past two decades. As a result, many smaller houses, along with their imprints, have either disappeared or been renamed in the process of being acquired by larger publishers. This trend does not seem to be over.

The following list of publishers also includes some line or series listings. Most of these are still being published; however, because many now-defunct series are still available in libraries some may be included here.

Alyson Publications, Inc.
40 Plympton Street
Boston, MA 022118

Founded in 1977, this house produces both gay/lesbian fiction and non-fiction. Lace MA (**Lace Publications**) is among Alyson's imprints.

Amereon Ltd.
Box 1200
Mattituck, NY 11952

Hardcover reprints of older best-selling works, including some romance authors.

Avalon Books
401 Lafayette Street
New York, NY 10003

Hardcover, single title Contemporary Romance, Career Romance, Mysteries, and Westerns. Short (40-50,000 words), sweet, and innocent books. Focus is library market.

Avon Books
1350 Avenue of the Americas
New York, NY 10019
Historical and Contemporary Romance.

Ballantine Books/Fawcett Books
(Division of Random House)
201 East 50th Street
New York, NY 10022

Publishes Historicals, Contemporaries, Regencies and Multicultural romances under its **Ballantine**, **Fawcett**, and **One World** imprints.

Indigo Love Stories (One World)
This line debuted in February 1998 and will initially feature reprints of titles originally published by Genesis Press.

Bantam Books
1540 Broadway
New York, NY 10036
Historical and Contemporary Romances.

Loveswept

This long-standing, popular line of short, sensual romances was discontinued at the end of 1998.

Barbour and Company, Inc.
P. O. Box 719
Uhrichsville, OH 44683

Heartsong Presents

Historical and Contemporary Inspirational Romances. Settings are varied and characters may be ethnic.

Beacon Hill Press (subsidiary of Nazarene Publishing House)
P. O. Box 419527
Kansas City, MO 64141

Christian Inspirational Fiction.

The Berkley Publishing Group
200 Madison Avenue
New York, NY 10016

Historical, Contemporary, and some Alternative Reality Romances under both **Jove** and **Berkley** imprints.

Jove

Haunting Hearts
Historical and contemporary ghost romances

Time Passages
Time Travel Romances.

Our Town
Period Americana with a small-town setting.

Homespun
"Romance from the Heart of America." Period Americana.

Bethany Publishers
6820 Auto Club Road
Minneapolis MN 55438

21

Publishes a wide variety of Christian inspirational material, including Historical and Contemporary romances for both the YA and adult markets.

Crossway Books
1300 Crescent Street
Wheaton, IL 60187

Publishes a variety of Christian fiction, including some romance.

Dell Publishing Company
1540 Broadway
New York, NY 10036

Several Historical and an occasional Contemporary Romance each month.

Delacorte

Occasional romances.

Dorchester Publishing
276 Fifth Avenue, Room 1008
New York, NY 10001

Primarily Historical and Alternative Reality Romance.

Leisure Books

Historical Romance.

Love Spell

Futuristic, Time-Travel, Paranormal, Fantasy, and Fairy Tale Romance.

Legendary Lovers
Proposed series featuring classic romantic characters from popular culture.

Perfect Hero
Proposed series featuring very sexy, romantic heroes.

Dutton/Signet
375 Hudson Street
New York, NY 10016

Publishes Historical, Contemporary, Romantic Suspense, Regency, and Alternative Reality Romance under its various imprints.

Signet Regencies

Light, short, sweet Regency Romance.

Topaz Romance

Historical and some Alternative Reality Romance.

Signet

Contemporary Romance.

Onyx

Contemporary Romance.

Firebrand Books
141 The Commons
Ithaca, NY 14850

Gay and lesbian materials.

The Genesis Press, Inc.
406 A 3rd Avenue North
Columbus, MS 39701-0101

Indigo

Featuring "Sensuous Love Stories for Today's Black Woman." Stories may include cross-cultural or interracial relationships. (See also Ballantine.)

Note: Genesis has plans for future Latino American and Asian American Romance lines.

Robert Hale, Ltd.

Clerkenwell House
45/47 Clerkenwell Green
London EC1R 0HT

Light, short, British contemporary and historical romance in hardcover format.

G. K. Hall

70 Lincoln Street
Boston, MA 02111

Large-print and hardcover reprints of original paperbacks. Includes most popular Romance subgenres.

Harlequin Enterprises, Ltd.
225 Duncan Mill Road
Don Mills
Ontario, Canada M3B 3K9

Harlequin Books

Primarily contemporary romances, some with elements of intrigue, adventure, or suspense.

Harlequin Romance series

"The series that started it all." This short, innocent contemporary line features warm, appealing love stories often set in exotic places.

Harlequin Presents series

These short, realistic contemporaries are more sensual than those in the original Harlequin Romance line.

Superromance series

These longer, sophisticated, contemporary romances feature multidimensional characters, fairly complex story lines, and a high degree of sensuality.

American Romance series (handled through Harlequin/Silhouette New York office)

These mid-length, sensual, contemporary romances use American settings, heroes and heroines typifying the middle class, and the problems of everyday life to provide a flavor that is uniquely American.

Harlequin Historical series (handled through Harlequin/Silhouette New York office)

Longer-length historical romances. Currently, Harlequin's only historical series.

Love & Laughter series

Short, funny romantic comedies. One of the newest of Harlequin's lines.

Harlequin Intrigue series (handled through Harlequin/Silhouette New York office)

This series of mid-length, sensual contemporary romances combines a strong love story with elements of intrigue, suspense, and the unexpected.

Harlequin Temptation series

These fast-paced sensual contemporary romances feature challenges, choices, dilemmas, and resolutions of modern-day problems — all surrounded by a vague aura of romantic fantasy.

> **Harlequin Mills & Boon, Ltd.** (Division of Harlequin)
> Eton House, 18-24 Paradise Road
> Richmond, Surrey TW9 1SR

Generally sweet, contemporary, and medical romances that are more British than American in tone.

Note: This London firm was purchased by Harlequin in 1972. Harlequin actually established its romance reputation in North America during the 1950s and early 1960s by reprinting Mills & Boon's hardcover romances.

Mira Books (Division of Harlequin)
225 Duncan Mill Road
Don Mills
Ontario, Canada M3B 3K9

Original and some reprinted Contemporary and Historical Mainstream Women's Romantic Fiction. Includes Romantic Suspense, Sagas, and most kinds of longer Contemporary Romance.

Silhouette Books (Division of Harlequin)
300 E. 42nd Street, 6th Floor
New York, NY 10017

Contemporary paperback romances, some with elements of suspense and adventure.

Silhouette Romance series

Similar to the original line of Harlequin Romances, these innocent contemporaries are gentle romances "depicting all the wonder of falling in love."

Silhouette Special Edition series

These longer, more sensual contemporary romances feature well-developed characters, believable situations, high emotional tension, and exotic settings.

Silhouette Desire series

This sophisticated, provocative line features short, "highly charged stories of sensual romance."

Silhouette Intimate Moments series

These longer, more sensual contemporary romances combine a strong love story line with melodrama, adventure, suspense, glamour, or Gothic intrigue to provide "the perfect combination of love and excitement."

Silhouette Yours Truly series

Contemporary romances that use "the written word" as a plot device.

Steeple Hill (Division of Harlequin)
300 E. 42nd Street, 6th Floor
New York, NY 10017

Love Inspired

Sweet, contemporary Inspirational Romance.

Harper Paperbacks
10 E. 53rd Street
New York, NY 10022

Contemporary and Historical Romances, and Women's Romantic Fiction.

Harvest House Publishers
1075 Arrowsmith
Eugene, OR 97402

Evangelical Christian materials and some Inspirational Romance.

Kensington Publishing Corporation
850 Third Avenue
New York, NY 10022

Publishes Contemporary, Historical, and Regency Romances and Women's Romantic Fiction under its Zebra, Pinnacle, and Kensington imprints.

Arabesque
Multicultural (primarily African American) historical and contemporary romances. Note: A bilingual Spanish/English series is reportedly in the development stages at Kensington.

Precious Gems
Novella-length romances.

Regencies
Light romances set during the British Regency period, 1811–1820.

William Morrow and Company, Inc.
105 Madison Avenue
New York, NY 10016

Occasional romance fiction. Very selective.

Multnomah Publishers (Formerly Questar)
204 W. Adams Avenue
P. O. Box 1720
Sisters, OR 97759

Palisades Romances
Christian Inspirational Romances.

Naiad Press, Inc.
Box 10543
Tallahassee, FL 32302

Publishes lesbian fiction and non-fiction, including a good selection of romance. A major source for lesbian romance and some classic reprints.

Thomas Nelson Publishers
Box 141000
Nashville, TN 37214

Christian Inspirational materials.

Penguin Books
27 Wrights Lane
London, England W8 5TZ

Signet

Women's Romantic Fiction, post-World War II Sagas, and Romantic Suspense.

Pocket Books (Division of Simon & Schuster)
1230 Avenue of the Americas
New York, NY 10020

Contemporary and Historical Romances.

Red Sage Publishing
P. O. Box 4844
Seminole, FL 33775

Secrets

Sexy and erotic romance, primarily novellas in an anthology format.

Rising Tide Publications
5440 SW Westgate Drive, No. 340
Portland, OR 97221

Gay and lesbian materials.

Robinson Publishing
7 Kensington Church Court
London, England W8 4SP

Scarlet

Contemporary, Regency, and Medical Romances.

St. Martin's Press
175 Fifth Avenue
New York, NY 10010

Contemporary, Historical, Romantic Suspense, and some Alternative Reality Romances.

Seal Press
3131 Western Avenue, Suite 410
Seattle, WA 98121-1028

Gay and lesbian materials.

Spinster's Ink
32 E. First Street, Suite 330
Duluth, MN 55802

Lesbian and women's literature.

Thorndike Press
One Mile Road
Thorndike, ME 04986

Large-print editions of most romance subgenres.

Tyndale House Publishers, Inc.
P. O. Box 80
Wheaton, IL 60189

Contemporary and Historical Inspirational Romances.

Victor Books
Wheaton, IL 60187

Christian materials.

Warner Books
1271 Avenue of the Americas
New York, NY 10020

Historical and Contemporary Romances.

Zondervan Publishing House
5300 Patterson Avenue S.E.
Grand Rapids, MIchigan 49530

Wide variety of Christian fiction, including romance, much of which is part of various series.

Appendix 1

Sample Core Collection

Despite the fact that each romance collection must be developed with its unique target audience in mind, there are, nevertheless, some works that are appropriate for most collections. The list that follows contains a number of such works and provides recommendations for a basic romance collection. However, it should be used only as a guide to the possibilities that exist and should be adapted and expanded to fit the needs of each situation. Note: For reasons of age or current publishing practices, some of these works may be out of print temporarily and, therefore, difficult to add.

LITERARY AND EARLY ROMANCE CLASSICS

Several of the works that follow are not strictly romances, but they had an impact on the development of the genre and therefore deserve a place in any collection that takes a serious approach to romance fiction. Note: This list does not include anything earlier than *Pamela*; however, some libraries may wish to include relevant earlier materials such as the Greek sensual romances, medieval romances, or works by some of the late seventeenth-century and early eighteenth-century women writers.

Richardson, Samuel. *Pamela: or Virtue Rewarded* (1740)

Richardson, Samuel. *Clarissa Harlowe* (1747)

Walpole, Horace. *The Castle of Otranto* (1764)

Burney, Fanny. *Evelina: Or, The History of a Young Lady's Entrance into the World* (1778)

Rowson, Susanna Haswell. *Charlotte Temple: A Tale of Truth* (1791, England; 1794, United States)

Foster, Hannah. *The Coquette* (1797)

Radcliffe, Ann. *The Mysteries of Udolpho* (1794)

Austen, Jane. *Sense and Sensibility* (1811), *Pride and Prejudice* (1813), *Mansfield Park* (1814), *Emma* (1814), *Northanger Abbey* (1818), *Persuasion* (1818)

Scott, Sir Walter. *Waverly* (1814), *Rob Roy* (1818), *Ivanhoe* (1819)

Shelley, Mary. *Frankenstein* (1817 or 1818)

Cooper, James Fenimore. *The Spy* (1821) and "The Leatherstocking Tales," especially *The Pathfinder* (1840)

Sedgwick, Catharine Maria. *Hope Leslie* (1827)

Dumas, Alexandre. *The Three Musketeers* (1844), *The Count of Monte Cristo* (1845), *Man in the Iron Mask* [1850, third section of *Le Vicomte de Bragelonne*, usually published in English in three separate volumes—*Le Vicomte de Bragelonne, Louise de la Vallière, The Man in the Iron Mask*]

Brontë, Charlotte. *Jane Eyre* (1847)

Brontë, Emily. *Wuthering Heights* (1847)

Wetherell, Elizabeth (Susan Warner). *The Wide, Wide World* (1850)

Hentz, Caroline Lee. *Linda; or The Young Pilot of the Belle Creole* (1850), *The Planter's Northern Bride* (1854)

Yonge, Charlotte M. *The Heir of Redclyffe* (1853)
Some trace the roots of romance from this book because of its emotional intensity, the author's own emotional involvement with the characters and readers, and its premise that love solves all the problems.

Cummins, Maria Susanna. *The Lamplighter* (1854)

Fern, Fanny (Sara Payson Willis). *Ruth Hall: A Domestic Tale of the Present Time* (1855)

Holmes, Mary Jane. *Tempest and Sunshine* (1854), *Lena Rivers* (1856)

Dickens, Charles. *A Tale of Two Cities* (1859), *David Copperfield* (May 1849 to November 1850, 20-part serial)

Southworth, E.D.E.N. *The Hidden Hand* (1859)

Evans, Augusta Jane. *St. Elmo* (1867)

Phelps, Elizabeth Stuart. *The Gates Ajar* (1868)

Libby, Laura Jean. Any of her story papers—mid 1810s to 1920s

Clay, Bertha M. (Pseudonym for group of dime novel Gothic writers) Any works available

Jackson, Helen Hunt. *Ramona* (1884)

Stevenson, Robert Louis. "The Strange Case of Dr. Jekyll and Mr. Hyde" (1886, short story)

Hope, Anthony. *The Prisoner of Zenda* (1894)

Stoker, Bram. *Dracula* (1895)

Johnston, Mary. *To Have and To Hold* (1900)

McCutcheon, George Barr. *Graustark* (1901)

Galsworthy, John. Forsyte Saga (First volume: *A Man of Property*—1906)

Glyn, Elinor. *Three Weeks* (1907)

Montgomery, Lucy Maud. Anne of Green Gables series (First volume: *Anne of Green Gables*—1908)

Webster, Jean. *Daddy-Long-Legs* (1912)

Hull, Edith M. *The Sheik* (1919)

Sabatini, Rafael. *Scaramouche: A Romance of the French Revolution* (1921)

Norris, Kathleen. *Certain People of Importance* (1922) and *The American Flaggs* (1936)

Prouty, Olive Higgins. *Stella Dallas* (1923) and *Now, Voyager* (1941)

De la Roche, Mazo. Jalna series (First volume: *Jalna*—1927)

Douglas, Lloyd C. *Magnificent Obsession* (1932) and *The Robe* (1942)

Allen, Hervey. *Anthony Adverse* (1933)

Hill, Grace Livingston. *Matched Pearls* (1933)

Seton, Anya. All works, especially *Katherine* (1954) and *Dragonwyck* (1944)

Shellabarger, Samuel. *Prince of Foxes* (1947)

Baldwin, Faith. All works, especially *Blaze of Sunlight* (1959) and *The High Road* (1939)

Golon, Sergeanne. *Angelique* (1958), plus others in series

Cadell, Elizabeth. *Honey for Tea* (1962, 1961 in England), *Canary Yellow* (1965), plus others

White, T. H. *The Once and Future King* (1958, parts published earlier)

MODERN ROMANCE CLASSICS

The works and writers listed below have either provided innovation, set a standard, defined a prototype, or have otherwise significantly influenced the development of the modern romance genre. While some of these are recent titles, many are older but are still widely read. A number of these classics have managed to hold up quite well, but because the genre has changed with the times, others have not and should definitely be read with their historical context in mind.

Anderson, Katherine. *Coming Up Roses* (1993), *Cheyenne Amber* (1994), and others

Auel, Jean. *The Clan of the Cave Bear* (1980)

Bannon, Ann. Beebo Brinker series (*Odd Girl Out* 1957, *I Am a Woman* 1959, *Women in Shadows* 1959, *Journey to a Woman* 1960, and *Beebo Brinker* 1963)

Brandewyne, Rebecca. *No Gentle Love* (1980)

Cartland, Barbara. *Jig-Saw* (1925) and *The Black Panther* (1939) reissued as *Lost Love* (1970)

Castle, Jayne. *Gentle Pirate* (1980)

Dailey, Janet. *No Quarter Asked* (1976, 1974 England), *Ivory Cane* (1978, 1977 England), the Calder series (*This Calder Sky* 1981, *This Calder Range* 1982, *Stands a Calder Man* 1982, *Calder Born, Calder Bred* 1983) and *The Pride of Hannah Wade* (1985)

Deveraux, Jude. *The Black Lyon* (1980), the Velvet series (*The Velvet Promise* 1981, *Highland Velvet* 1982, *Velvet Angel* 1983, and *Velvet Song* 1983), and *A Knight in Shining Armor* (1989)

Du Maurier, Daphne. *Rebecca* (1938)

Forrest, Katherine V. *Curious Wine* (1983)

Gabaldon, Diana. The Outlander series (*The Outlander* 1991, *Dragonfly in Amber* 1992, *Voyager* 1994, and *Drums of Autumn* 1997)

Garwood, Julie. *The Bride* (1989)

Gellis, Roberta. *Bond of Blood* (1965), the Roselynde Chronicles (*Roselynde* 1978, *Alinor* 1978, *Joanna* 1978, *Gilliane* 1979, *Rhiannon* 1982, and *Sybelle* 1983), and others.

Heyer, Georgette. All works, but especially *These Old Shades* (1926), *An Infamous Army* (1937), *Frederica* (1965), and *Sylvester, or the Wicked Uncle* (1957)

Holt, Victoria. Most early works, but especially *Mistress of Mellyn* (1960)

Johnson, Susan. *Love Storm* (1981), *Golden Paradise* (1990), and others

Kinsale, Laura. *Prince of Midnight* (1990), *Flowers from the Storm* (1992), *For My Lady's Heart* (1993), *Uncertain Magic* (1987), and others

Kitt, Sandra. *Serenade* (1994), *The Color of Love* (1995), and others

Korbel, Kathleen. *A Rose for Maggie* (1991), *A Soldier's Heart* (1994), and others

Krentz, Jayne Ann. *Gift of Gold* (1988), *Gift of Fire* (1989), *Sweet Starfire* (1986), and others

Lindsey, Johanna. *Captive Bride* (1977) and others

McCaffrey, Anne. The Dragonriders of Pern series (*Dragonflight* 1968, *Dragonquest* 1970, and *The White Dragon* 1978), *Restorée* (1967), and others

Metalious, Grace. *Peyton Place* (1956)

Michaels, Barbara. All works, but especially *Ammie, Come Home* (1968)

Miller, Isabel. *Patience and Sarah* (1972)

Mitchell, Margaret. *Gone With the Wind* (1936)

Morgan, Claire. *The Price of Salt* (1952)

Orczy, Baroness. *The Scarlet Pimpernel* (1905)

Plaidy, Jean. Any works.

Peters, Elizabeth. All works, but especially *Crocodile on the Sandbank* (1975)

Putney, Mary Jo. *The Rake and the Reformer* (1989)

Ray, Francis. *Forever Yours* (1994)

Rogers, Rosemary. *Sweet Savage Love* (1974)

Shiplett, June Lund. *Journey to Yesterday* (1979), *Return to Yesterday* (1983)

Small, Bertrice. *Skye O'Malley* (1980)

Spencer, LaVyrle. *The Fulfillment* (1979), *The Endearment* (1982), *Hummingbird* (1983), *Loved* (1984), *Sweet Memories* (1984), *Years* (1986), *The Gamble* (1987), *Vows* (1988), *Morning Glory* (1989)

Stewart, Mary. All works, but especially *Nine Coaches Waiting* (1958) and *My Brother Michael* (1960)

Taylor, Janelle. Ecstasy series (*Savage Ecstasy* 1981, *Defiant Ecstasy* 1982, *Forbidden Ecstasy* 1982, and *Brazen Ecstasy* 1983)

Virga, Vincent. *Gaywick* (1980)

Welles, Rosalind. *Entwined Destinies* (1980)

Whitney, Phyllis A. All works, but especially *Window on the Square* (1962) and *Spindrift* (1975)

Winsor, Kathleen. *Forever Amber* (1944)

Woodiwiss, Kathleen. *The Flame and the Flower* (1972)

CURRENT ROMANCES

The following list includes a selection of currently popular romance writers and, in a few cases, some of their more important or more popular titles. It is intended to serve only as a sampling of the writers and titles available and to suggest several representative authors for each of the various romance subgenres. The switch was made from titles (as in the first two sections) to authors at this point because, although there are a number of excellent titles that could be singled out for special mention, in many cases it is still too early to tell which ones will become classics. Those titles that have already achieved that status are listed in the previous section. In addition, since most readers make selections by author rather than specific title, a recommended list of current writers who consistently produce well-written romances would seem to be the better, and more logical, choice. Note: Many authors write and have written in a number of subgenres. Many who are currently writing single titles releases began by writing category (series) romances, and some writers continue to do both.

Contemporary

Series

Accounting for the largest number of titles in any of the romance subgenres, the contemporary series are popular with readers and should be represented in any core romance collection. The selection of specific series will vary from library to library, but several different types (e.g., a sweet, innocent line; a short, sexy line; a longer, more complex line; and a specialty line) should be included. Each series has several authors, some of whom write for more than one line. A few popular writers in each series are included here as examples. Series and authors are listed in alphabetical order.

Bantam Loveswept—Jennifer Crusie, Debra Dixon, Marcia Evanick, Judy Gill, Faye Hughes, Fayrene Preston

Harlequin American—Barbara Bretton, Cassie Miles, Victoria Pade, Anne Stuart

Harlequin Intrigue—Tess Gerritsen, Laura Gordon, Cassie Miles, Amanda Stevens, Rebecca York

Harlequin Love and Laughter—Lori Copeland, Jennifer Crusie, Kasey Michaels, JoAnn Ross

Harlequin Presents—Emma Darcy, Robyn Donald, Charlotte Lamb, Penny Jordan

Harlequin Romance—Bethany Campbell, Ruth Jean Dale, Debbie Macomber, Barbara McMahon, Betty Neels, Catherine Spencer, Rebecca Winters

Harlequin Superromance—Pamela Bauer, Sharon Brandos, Sandra Canfield, Evelyn A. Crowe, Margot Dalton, Madeline Harper

Harlequin Temptation—Lynn Michaels, Elda Minger, Carla Neggers, Tiffany White, Roseanne Williams

Silhouette Desire—Dixie Browning, Carole Buck, Jennifer Greene, Naomi Horton, Kathleen Korbel, Cathie Linz, Ann Major

Silhouette Intimate Moments—Beverly Bird, Justine Davis, Judith Duncan, Kathleen Eagle, Marie Ferrarella, Linda Howard, Karen Leabo, Rachel Lee, Merline Lovelace, Laura Parker, Emilie Richards, Paula Detmer Riggs, Nora Roberts, Dallas Schulze, Sharon Sala, Maggie Shayne

Silhouette Romance—Lindsay Longford, Helen R. Myers, Diana Palmer, Rita Rainville, Karen Rose Smith

Silhouette Special Edition—Ginna Gray, Christine Flynn, Allison Hayes, Cheryl Reavis, Christine Rimmer, Diana Whitney, Ruth Wind

Silhouette Yours Truly—Jennifer Drew, Hayley Gardner, Lori Herter, Laurie Paige, Lass Small, Tiffany White

Single Title

Jennifer Blake, Barbara Bretton, Sandra Brown, Lori Copeland, Catherine Coulter, Janet Dailey, Barbara Delinsky, Kathleen Eagle, Barbara Freethy, Kay Hooper, Linda Howard, Jayne Ann Krentz, Cait Logan, Debbie Macomber, Judith McNaught, Kasey Michaels, Rosamunde Pilcher, Heather Graham Pozzessere, JoAnn Ross, Susan Elizabeth Phillips, Paula Detmer Riggs, Nora Roberts, Kathleen Gilles Seidel, LaVyrle Spencer, Katherine Stone, Anne Stuart

Women's Romantic Fiction

Sandra Bregman, Catherine Coulter, Barbara Delinsky, Meryl Sawyer, Erica Spindler, Penelope Williamson

Historical

Catherine Anderson, Jill Barnett, Victoria Barrett, Rexanne Becnel, Rosanne Bittner, Rebecca Brandewyne, Marsha Canham, Loretta Chase, Catherine Coulter, Jasmine Cresswell, Judy Cuevas, Jude Deveraux, Christina Dodd, Denise Domning, Elizabeth Elliott, Julie Garwood, Jane Feather, Gail Feyrer, Dorothy Garlock, Heather Graham, Kristin Hannah, Robin Lee Hatcher, Lorraine Heath, Jane Aiken Hodge, Iris Johansen, Susan Johnson, Joan Johnston, Brenda Joyce, Betina Krahn, Arnette Lamb, Jill Marie Landis, Johanna Lindsey, Elizabeth Lowell, Judith McNaught, Teresa Medeiros, Kasey Michaels, Linda Lael Miller, Pamela Morsi, Rebecca Paisley, Patricia Potter, Maggie Osborne, Amanda Quick, Karen Robards, Nan Ryan, Bertrice Small, LaVyrle Spencer, Anne Stuart, Elizabeth Stuart, Jodi Thomas, Patricia Veryan, Susan Wiggs, Penelope Williamson

Romantic Mysteries

Romantic Suspense

Sandra Brown, Eileen Dreyer, Barbara Erskine, Patricia Gardner Evans, Tami Hoag, Kay Hooper, Iris Johansen, Ann Maxwell, Marilyn Pappano, Joanne Pence, Elizabeth Peters, Karen Robards, J. D. Robb, Nora Roberts, Alicia Scott, Mary Stewart, Elise Title, Sherryl Woods

Gothic

Dorothy Eden, Victoria Holt, Kay Hooper, Barbara Michaels, Mary Stewart, Phyllis Whitney

Alternative Reality

Futuristic

Anne Avery, Marilyn Campbell, Jayne Castle, Justine Davis, Kathleen Morgan, J. D. Robb

Fantasy

Jill Barnett, Barbara Freethy, Debbie Macomber, Maura Seger, Maggie Shayne

Paranormal

Lori Copeland, Barbara Erskine, Kristin Hannah, Lori Herter, Susan Krinard, Linda Lael Miller, Modean Moon, Cheri Scotch, Antoinette Stockenberg

Time Travel

Janice Bennett, Jude Deveraux, Diana Gabaldon, Lynn Kurland, Kasey Michaels, Linda Lael Miller, Constance O'Day-Flannery, Joan Overfield, Eugenia Riley, Thomasina Ring, Patricia Simpson, Susan Sizemore, Flora M. Speer, Deb Stover

Regencies

Mary Balogh, Anne Barbour, Jo Beverley, Loretta Chase, Jean R. Ewing, Marion Chesney, Mary Chase Comstock, Clare Darcy, Carola Dunn, Sarah Eagle, Gail Eastwood, Elisabeth Fairchild, Karen Harbaugh, Sandra Heath, Emily Hendrickson, Georgette Heyer, Carla Kelly, Lynn Kerstan, Mary Kingsley, Edith Layton, Barbara Metzger, Kate Moore, Patricia Oliver, Joan Overfield, Phyllis Taylor Pianka, Mary Jo Putney, Alicia Rasley, Evelyn Richardson, Jeanne Savery, Joan Smith, Patricia Veryan

Inspirational

June Masters Bacher, Terri Blackstock, Donna Fletcher Crow, Susan Kirby, Janette Oke, Carole Gift Page, Judith Pella, Francine Rivers, Marian Wells, Lori Wick

Ethnic/Multicultural

African American

Angela Benson, Anita Richmond Bunkley, Donna Hill, Beverly Jenkins, Sandra Kitt, Francis Ray, Eboni Snoe, Tracey Tillis, Margie Walker, Amanda Wheeler

Asian

Margot Early (*Mr. Family*, 1996), Annette Mahon, Sujata Massey, Katherine Stone (*Pearl Moon*, 1995)

Latino

Barbara Faith (*Dark, Dark My Lover's Eyes*, 1994), Barbara Samuel, Maggie Shayne (*Reckless Angel*, 1993), Marilyn Tracy (*Sharing the Darkness*, 1994)

Native American (sometimes called "Indian" in the trade)

Madeline Baker, Beverly Bird, Rosanne Bittner, Genell Dellin, Kathleen Eagle, Georgina Gentry, Allison Hayes, Susan Johnson, Rachel Lee, Johanna Lindsey, Deborah Smith, Janelle Taylor, Peggy Webb

Saga

Belva Plain, Janet Dailey (the Calder series), Marie de Jourlet (Windhaven series), Roberta Gellis (the Roselynde Chronicles), Marilyn Harris (the Eden Family Saga), Susan Howatch, Iris Johansen (Wind Dancer Trilogy), Rosalind Laker, (the Warwyck's of East Hampton Trilogy), Jean Plaidy, Alexandra Ripley, Elswyth Thane, Daoma Winston

Gay/Lesbian

Sarah Aldridge, Catherine Ennis, Katherine V. Forrest, Nancy Garden (*Annie on My Mind,* 1982, YA), Penny Hayes, Karin Kallmaker, Michelle Martin, Victoria Ramstetter, Jane Rule, Sandra Scoppetone (YA), Molleen Zanger

Appendix 2

Selected Romance Writers by Style, Plot Pattern, or Theme

Note: This selective list is intended merely as a starting point. In addition, it is important to be aware that many of the writers included also write books that do not fall into the categories listed below.

Dark (plots deal with the "darker side of human nature"; can be Gothic or evil in mood)

Mary Balogh	Linda Howard
Connie Brockway	Brenda Joyce
Stella Cameron	Dinah McCall
Raine Cantrell	Mary Jo Putney
Catherine Coulter	Anne Stuart
Geralyn Dawson	Katherine Sutcliffe

Erotic (very sensual, explicit sex)

Lolah Burford	Brenda Joyce
Thea Devine	Mallory Rush
Virginia Henley	Nan Ryan
Jennifer Horsman	Bertrice Small
Susan Johnson	

Innocent/Sweet (little or no explicit sex)

Susan Aylworth	Debbie Macomber
Bethany Campbell	Alice Sharpe
Georgette Heyer	Mary Stewart
Victoria Holt	Phyllis Whitney

The Innocent/Sweet Catagory also includes most traditional Regency romances, romances published by Avalon Books, romances published by any of the Christian publishing houses, and most romances in the Harlequin Romance or Silhouette Romance lines.

Humorous (light, funny, can range from witty to slapstick)

Anne Barbour	Cathie Linz
Jill Barnett	Teresa Medeiros
Lori Copeland	Barbara Metzger
Jennifer Crusie	Pamela Morsi
Debra Dixon	Rebecca Paisley
Eileen Dreyer	Susan Elizabeth Phillips
Julie Garwood	Amanda Quick
Hannah Howell	Rita Rainville
Joan Johnston	Lass Small
Betina Krahn	
Jayne Ann Krentz	

Lyrical (gracefully, musically written with attention paid to language and mood; can be mystical)

Kathryn Lynn Davis	Elizabeth Lowell (medieval romances)
Rosemary Edghill	
Elisabeth Fairchild	Penny Williamson (*Keeper of the Dream*, 1992)
Mary Lide	

Sweet/Savage (sexy, often containing rape or other hero-to-heroine violence, usually fast paced, and adventurous)

Lolah Burford	Bertrice Small
Brenda Joyce	Kathleen Woodiwiss
Rosemary Rogers	
Nan Ryan	

Beauty and the Beast (plot pattern)

Susan Carroll (*The Bride Finder*, 1998)	Robin McKinley (*Beauty*, 1978)
Geralyn Dawson (*Capture the Night*, 1993)	Mary Jo Putney (*Thunder and Roses*, 1993)
Elisabeth Fairchild (*The Silent Suitor*, 1994)	Amanda Quick (*Ravished*, 1992)
Hannah Howell (*Beauty and the Beast*, 1992)	Anne Stuart (*The Night of the Phantom*, 1991)
Judith Ivory (*Beast*, 1997)	

Cinderella (plot pattern)

Nancy Berland (*Glass Slippers*, 1996)

Jude Deveraux (*Wishes*, 1989)

Jill Gregory (*Forever After*, 1993)

Barbara Dawson Smith (*A Glimpse of Heaven*, 1995)

Sleeping Beauty (fairy tale plot pattern)

Judith Ivory (*Sleeping Beauty*, 1998)

Pygmalion/My Fair Lady (mythological plot pattern)

Virginia Brown (*Hidden Touch*, 1992)

Emily Hendrickson (*The Scoundrel's Bride*, 1994)

Kathryn Kramer (*Lady Rogue*, 1991)

Burgess Mallory (*Ballenrose*, 1991)

Kasey Michaels (*Bride of the Unicorn*, 1993)

Louisa Rawlings (*Promise of Summer*, 1989)

Ugly Duckling/Swan (fairy tale plot pattern)

Catherine Coulter (*Beyond Eden*, 1991)

Iris Johansen (*The Ugly Duckling*, 1996)

Virginia Lynn (*River's Dream*, 1991)

Captor/Captive (plots where captives come to love their captors)

Elaine Barbieri (*Midnight Rogue*, 1995)

Charlene Cross (*Splendor*, 1995)

Victoria Holt (*The Captive*, 1989)

Jill Marie Landis (*Come Spring*, 1992)

Mary Lide (*Isobelle*, 1988)

Johanna Lindsey (*Captive Bride*, 1977, *A Pirate's Love*, 1978, *Fires of Winter*, 1980)

Kathleen Woodiwiss (*The Wolf and the Dove*, 1974, *Shanna*, 1977)

Non-Traditional Matches

Jennifer Crusie (*Anyone but You*, 1996, older heroine/younger hero)

Judith Ivory (*Sleeping Beauty*, 1998, older, scandalous heroine/younger, respected hero)

Carla Kelly (*The Lady's Companion*, 1996, Social differences)

Pamela Morsi (*Courting Miss Hattie*, 1991, older heroine/younger hero)

Social Issues (plot includes serious issues such as abuse, alchoholism, illness, insanity, etc.)

Catherine Anderson	Betina Krahn
Dinah McCall	Melinda McRae
Kathleen Eagle	Emilie Richards
Laura Kinsale	Barbara Samuel
Kathleen Korbel	Ruth Wind

Wounded Heroes (heroes/heroines who have been seriously hurt in the past)

Kimberly Cates	Laura Kinsale
Patricia Coughlin	Ruth Langan
Justine Davis	Mary McBride
Judith Duncan	Patricia Potter
Lorraine Heath	

Appendix 3

Selected Young Adult Romance Bibliography

The following is representative of the many romance materials available specifically for young adults. Note also that many YAs who like romance also read adult romances.

SELECTED SERIES

Many paperback series target the young adult market. Although some focus primarily on dating and friendship, a number combine mystery/suspense/horror elements with some love interest. The following two bibliographies may be of interest to selectors of young adult materials.

Anderson, Vicki. *Fiction: Sequels for Readers 10 to 16: An Annotated Bibliography of Books in Succession*. Jefferson, NC: McFarland, 1990.

Roman, Susan. *Sequences: An Annotated Guide to Children's Fiction Series*. Chicago: American Library Association, 1985.

Love Stories (Bantam Books)

Nancy Drew Files (Archway Paperbacks)

Nancy Drew and the Hardy Boys (Archway Paperbacks)

Sweet Dreams (Bantam Books)

Sweet Valley High (Bantam Books)

Sweet Valley University (Bantam Books)

White Dove Romances (Bethany House) Inspirational/Christian

Adler, C.S.

Binding Ties. *Delacorte Press, 1985.* Classic family loyalty versus love conflict.

Anderson, Mary

Catch Me, I'm Falling in Love. *Delacorte Press, 1985.* A broken ankle, an injured father, and the man of her dreams manage to make this a summer that sensible, practical Amelia will never forget.

Angell, Judie

Many of Angell's works are "first love" stories for younger YAs.

Ronnie and Rosey. *Bradbury Press, 1983.*

Suds: A New Daytime Drama. *Bradbury Press, 1983.* A spoof.

Applegate, Katherine

Popular writer in many YA romance series.

Beaches, Boys, and Betrayal. *Archway Paperbacks, 1996.* (Summer series)

Boardwalk. *HarperPaperbacks, 1993.* (Ocean City series)

Sharing Sam. *Bantam Books, 1995.* (Love Stories series)

Swept Away. *HarperPaperbacks, 1995.* (Ocean City series)

Beckman, Delores

Who Loves Sam Grant? *E. P. Dutton, 1983.* Heroine's quest to win back her old boyfriend is a journey of self-discovery.

Berg, Elizabeth

Joy School. *Random House, 1997.* A new town and a first crush are highlights of this story for younger YAs.

Blume, Judy

Forever. *Bradbury Press, 1975.* This controversial, now classic, story of two teenagers' first sexual relationship reads more like a how-to manual than a real romance.

Brooks, Martha

Bone Dance. *Orchard, 1997.* A cabin on the Manitoba prairie, a common Native American heritage, and a quest for self-discovery link the two teenaged protagonists.

Clapp, Patricia

Constance: A Story of Early Plymouth. *Lothrop, Lee & Shepard, 1968.* Coming-of-age story in seventeenth-century Colonial America.

Cleary, Beverly

Fifteen. *William Morrow, 1956.* A classic story of first romance.

Jean and Johnny. *William Morrow, 1959.* Well-handled story of the first crush and all its attendant joy and misery.

The Luckiest Girl. *William Morrow, 1958.*

Sister of the Bride. *William Morrow, 1963.*

Clements, Bruce

Tom Loves Anna Loves Tom. *Farrar, Straus, & Giroux, 1990*. Poignant story of love and death.

Colman, Hila

Don't Tell Me That You Love Me. *Archway Paperbacks, 1983*. A story of friendship, first love, and trust.

A Fragile Love. *Archway Paperbacks, 1980*. Originally published as *Accident* by William Morrow, 1980. A tragic accident sets the scene for this novel of love, jealousy, and growing up.

Conford, Ellen

Strictly for Laughs. *Pacer, 1985*. A funny, lighthearted "first love" story aimed at younger YAs.

Crush: Stories. *HarperCollins, 1998*. Linked stories.

Cooney, Caroline B.

I'm Not Your Other Half. *Putnam, 1984*. Explores the theme of boy-girl relationships and how they can change the patterns of existing friendships.

Both Sides of Time. *Delacorte Press, 1995*. Time Travel romance.

Cormier, Robert

Tenderness. *Delacorte Press, 1997*. Heroine loves a teenaged serial killer. Dark and unusual.

Crook, Beverly C.

Fair Annie of Old Mule Hollow. *McGraw-Hill, 1978*. A long-standing family feud causes obvious problems for the hero and heroine.

Daly, Maureen

Seventeenth Summer. *Dodd, Mead, 1942*. Still a classic.

Act of Love. *Scholastic, 1986*. A warm, moving story of love, family, and adolescent romance. Daly's first YA novel since her classic *Seventeenth Summer*.

Felsen, Henry Gregor

Two and the Town. *Charles Scribner's Sons, 1952*. Classic story about teen pregnancy.

Foley, June

Falling in Love Is No Snap. *Delacorte Press, 1986*. Love, photography, and a communication-challenged heroine.

It's No Crush, I'm in Love. *Delacorte Press, 1982*. Heroine has a crush on her ninth-grade English teacher. Light and funny.

Love by Any Other Name. *Delacorte Press, 1982*. Heroine learns lessons about love, popularity, and being part of the "in" crowd.

Franco, Marjorie

Love in a Different Key. *Houghton Mifflin, 1983.* First love, commitment, and the fascinating world of music.

Futcher, Jane

Crush. *Avon Books, 1981.* Lesbian issues.

Garden, Nancy

Annie on My Mind. *Farrar, Straus, Giroux, 1982.* A YA lesbian classic.

Gauch, Patricia Lee

The Green of Me. *Putnam, 1978.*

Girion, Barbara

In the Middle of a Rainbow. *Charles Scribner's Sons, 1983.* High school sweethearts face the "college" dilemma.

Guy, Rosa

Ruby. *Bantam Books, 1976.* A classic.

Hart, Bruce, and Carole Hart

Sooner or Later. *Avon Books, 1978.* Young love's traditional choices and decisions.
Waiting Games. *Avon Books, 1981.* Follows *Sooner or Later.*

Head, Ann

Mr. and Mrs. Bo Jo Jones. *Putnam, 1967.* A classic story of teenage love, pregnancy, and commitment.

Holmes, Marjorie

Cherry Blossom Princess. *Dell, 1982.* Originally published by Westminster, 1960. Love and beauty contests.
Saturday Night. *Dell, 1982.* Originally published by Westminster, 1959. Carly must reconcile conflicting emotions about charming, irresponsible Danny.
Sunday Morning. *Dell, 1982.* Carly must decide between her current love, Chuck, and a still charming, but possibly more mature, Danny. Follows *Saturday Night.*

Hunter, Mollie

Hold on to Love. *Harper & Row, 1983.* Bridie confronts the classic conflict between love and ambition in this novel set in pre-World War II Scotland. Follows *Sound of Chariots.*

Irwin, Hadley

Abby, My Love. *Atheneum, 1985.* A compassionate story of love, sexual child abuse, and hope—told from the boy's point of view.

Johnston, Norma

The Watcher in the Mist. *Bantam Books, 1986.* Cindy finds danger and summer romance in this mysterious, suspenseful tale.

Jones, Adrienne

Another Place, Another Spring. *Houghton Mifflin, 1971.* Historical.

Kerner, Elizabeth

Song in the Silence. *Tor, 1997.* A well-crafted fantasy filled with dragons, adventure, and romance.

Kerr, M. E.

If I Love You, Am I Trapped Forever? *Harper & Row, 1973.*

Him She Loves? *Harper & Row, 1984.* A funny, well-written story of young love across ethnic and religious lines.

I Stay Near You: 1 Story in 3. *Harper & Row, 1985.* Ill-fated love and an ancient gold ring in a three-part family saga.

Deliver Us from Evie. *HarperCollins, 1994.* Lesbian issues.

Klause, Annette Curtis

Well-crafted books for mature teens.

The Silver Kiss. *Delacorte Press, 1990.* Vampires.

Blood and Chocolate. *Bantam Books, 1997.* Werewolves.

Knudson, R. R.

Just Another Love Story. *Farrar, Straus, & Giroux, 1983.* Attempted suicide.

LeGuin, Ursula

The Beginning Place. *HarperCollins, 1980.* Good combination of fantasy and romance.

Very Far Away from Anywhere Else. *Macmillan, 1976.* Love, friendship, and LeGuin's excellent language.

L'Engle, Madeleine

And Both Were Young. *Dell, 1986.* Originally published by Lothrop, Lee & Shepard, 1949. A caring girl helps her boyfriend deal with his painful past and look to the future.

Camilla. *Dell, 1986.* Originally published as *Camilla Dickinson* by Simon & Schuster, 1951. Perceptive story of first love and family issues.

A House Like a Lotus. *Farrar, Straus & Giroux, 1984.* Confusion, betrayal, and love in Greece and Cyprus.

Levine, Gail

Ella Enchanted. *HarperCollins, 1997.* An unusual version of Cinderella for younger YAs.

Levitin, Sonia

Escape from Egypt. *Puffin Books, 1996.* Historical Exodus story.

Littke, Lael

Shanny on Her Own. *Harcourt Brace Jovanovich, 1985.* Los Angeles teenager spends summer in Idaho with her eccentric aunt.

Mazer, Norma Fox

Someone to Love. *Delacorte Press, 1983.* A bittersweet, realistic story in which Nina learns that moving in with Mitch doesn't solve all her problems. For mature YAs.

Up in Seth's Room. *Delacorte Press, 1979.* A classic story of young love, the conflict between parental approval and physical and emotional desire, and the difficult decisions involved. For mature YAs.

McKinley, Robin

Beauty: A Retelling of the Story of Beauty and the Beast. *Harper & Row, 1978.* A classic.

Rose Daughter. *Greenwillow Books, 1997.* Another retelling of the Beauty and the Beast tale by McKinley.

Miklowitz, Gloria D.

The Day the Senior Class Got Married. *Delacorte Press, 1983.* A class "marriage experiment" has interesting results.

Love Story, Take Three. *Delacorte Press, 1986.* Teenaged TV actress wants to have a normal life.

Murphy, Barbara Beasley

One Another. *Dell, 1986.* A relationship with a French exchange student helps a teenager mature.

O'Connor, Jane

Just Good Friends. *Harper & Row, 1983.* A lively story of the dilemmas of first love. For younger YAs.

Offit, Sidney

What Kind of Guy Do You Think I Am? *Dell, 1986.* Princeton student Hilary and non-college educated Ted defy expectations and decide to make it on their own. For mature YAs.

Pascal, Francine

Light, lively, humorous romances.

My First Love and Other Disasters. *Viking, 1979.*

Love and Betrayal and Hold the Mayo. *Viking, 1985.* Follows *My First Love and Other Disasters.*

Patterson, Sarah

The Distant Summer. *Simon & Schuster, 1976.* British World War II coming-of-age story.

Peck, Richard

Amanda/Miranda. *Avon Books, 1981.* A tale of deceit, impersonation, love, and evil that reaches from England to America by way of the *Titanic.*

Close Enough to Touch. *Delacorte Press, 1981.* Grief recovery story.

Pevsner, Stella

Cute Is a Four Letter Word. *Houghton Mifflin, 1980.* Life is wonderful for popular Clara. Could anything possibly go wrong?

Peyton, K. M.

Flambards Trilogy

Christina grows to womanhood in England during the early twentieth century.

Flambards. *Oxford University Press, 1967.*

The Edge of the Cloud. *Oxford University Press, 1969.*

Flambards in Summer. *Oxford University Press, 1969.*

Quin-Harkin, Janet

Love Match. *Bantam Books, 1982.* Tennis whiz Joanna must choose between winning and love.

Sachs, Marilyn

Thunderbird. *E. P. Dutton, 1985.* A conservationist and a girl who is crazy about cars clash in this funny story.

Sallis, Susan

Only Love. *Harper & Row, 1980.* The poignant, bittersweet story of a young girl's desire to experience all she can of life and love before she dies.

Scoppetone, Sandra

Happy Endings Are All Alike. *Harper & Row, 1978.* A well-handled story of prejudice, self-acceptance, rape, and lesbianism.

Shannon, Jacqueline

Too Much T. J. *Delacorte Press, 1986.* Complications arise when hero's father plans to marry heroine's mother.

Sharmat, Marjorie

He Noticed I'm Alive . . . and Other Hopeful Signs. *Delacorte Press, 1984.* Jody's father is dating Matt's mother and Jody likes Matt—a first-class dilemma.

How to Meet a Gorgeous Girl. *Delacorte Press, 1984.* Hero tries "romance by the book" with interesting results. Funny and fast paced.

How to Meet a Gorgeous Guy. *Delacorte Press, 1983.*

Two Guys Noticed Me . . . and Other Miracles. *Delacorte Press, 1985.* Jody's mother returns in this sequel to *He Noticed I'm Alive . . . and Other Miracles.*

Snyder, Zilpha Keatley

A Fabulous Creature. *Atheneum, 1981.*

Stirling, Nora

You Would If You Loved Me. *Avon Books, 1982.* Published by M. Evans, 1969. A classic story of young love, conflict, and decision.

Stolz, Mary

A Love, or a Season. *Harper & Row, 1964.* Revised version of *Two By Two*, Houghton Mifflin, 1954.

Strasser, Todd

A Very Touchy Subject. *Delacorte Press, 1985.* Scott struggles to be the friend Paula needs instead of the lover she wants.

Workin' for Peanuts. *Delacorte Press, 1983.* Love and social class differences.

Taylor, Theodore

Walking Up a Rainbow. *Delacorte Press, 1986.* To meet a debt and save her house, orphaned Susan Carlisle heads west with her sheep to sell them at a high profit in the gold fields of California.

Towne, Mary

Supercouple. *Delacorte Press, 1985.* Pushed into becoming "supercouple" by their friends, Binky and Piers spend more time keeping up appearances than getting to know each other.

Ure, Jean

See You Thursday. *Delacorte Press, 1983.* A moving story of a girl's love for a handsome blind musician and the ultimate choice she is forced to make.

After Thursday. *Delacorte Press, 1987.* A sequel to *See You Thursday*, this is a story of love, change, and letting go.

You Win Some, You Lose Some. *Delacorte Press, 1986.* Jamie goes to London to dance and find a girlfriend. But can he do both?

Voight, Cynthia

Glass Mountain. *Harcourt Brace Jovanovich, 1991.* Hidden identity causes problems for hero when he falls in love.

Weinberg, Larry

The Cry of the Seals. *Bantam Books, 1984.* Seventeen-year-old Cory tries to stop the annual slaughter of baby seals.

Wersba, Barbara

Whistle Me Home. *Henry Holt and Co., 1997.* Gay issues from a different perspective.

West, Callie

My First Love. *Bantam Books, 1995.* Love Stories series.

Wilkinson, Brenda

Ludell and Willie. *Harper & Row, 1977.* A well-written, touching story of first love involving two black teenagers.

Winslow, Joan

Romance Is a Riot. *J. B. Lippincott, 1983.* Lighthearted.

Wittlinger, Ellen

Lombardo's Law. *Houghton Mifflin, 1993.* Fifteen-year-old girl is attracted to a 13-year-old boy.

Wolff, Virginia Ewer

Rated PG. *St. Martin's Press, 1981.* A kind of feminine version of *Catcher in the Rye.*

Zindel, Paul

The Girl Who Wanted a Boy. *Harper, 1981.* Funny, moving story about a brainy girl trying to find a boyfriend.

Author/Title Index

Subject Index